YOUR BRAIN ON TRAUMA

Your Brain on Trauma

A Practical Map for Understanding Trauma Patterns and Recovery

by Andrew Hill, PhD

Peak Brain Press LLC
Los Angeles, California

2026

Copyright

Your Brain on Trauma

A Practical Map for Understanding Trauma Patterns and Recovery

Published by Peak Brain Press LLC Los Angeles, California peakbraininstitute.com

ISBN (print): 978-1-971402-10-9 ISBN (ebook): 978-1-971402-11-6

Clinical Disclaimer

This book is intended for educational purposes. It does not constitute medical or psychological advice and is not a substitute for professional diagnosis, treatment, or clinical consultation. The information in this book describes general principles of brain function, trauma neuroscience, and recovery approaches and should not be applied to any individual situation without the guidance of a qualified clinician. The phenotype framework is an author-developed heuristic drawn from clinical observation; it is not a validated diagnostic system or treatment-matching method and has not been tested in randomized controlled trials for those purposes. Do not discontinue, adjust, or decline prescribed medication or ongoing clinical treatment based on phenotype self-assessment alone; bring phenotype observations to your clinical team for collaborative consideration. If you are in distress or crisis, please contact the 988 Suicide and Crisis Lifeline (call or text 988), an emergency department, or a licensed mental health professional.

Case Studies: Case studies in this book are composite narratives drawn from the author's neurofeedback practice. Names, identifying details, and specific circumstances have been changed to protect client confidentiality. QEEG descriptions illustrate the author's interpretive framework; they do not establish a diagnosis, a validated phenotype, or a treatment recommendation.

Disclosure: The author founded and has a financial interest in Peak Brain Institute, which provides QEEG and neurofeedback services. Some composite examples draw on observations from that practice. Mention of the institute is not independent evidence for the book's framework or an endorsement over other qualified providers.

First Edition Printed in the United States of America
10 9 8 7 6 5 4 3 2 1

Dedication

For every nervous system still running a protection program that worked once and won't turn off.

You are not broken. Your nervous system adapted. This book is a guide to what may help next.

Acknowledgments

This book exists because thousands of clients trusted me with their questions and care over two decades.

To every client who trusted me with their brain map, their story, and their honest account of what helped and what did not: thank you. Names and details have been changed beyond recognition, but the questions you brought and the care you required shaped how I think about this work.

To the Peak Brain Institute team: two and a half decades of clinical infrastructure, built carefully and still running. The observations in this book came from thousands of hours of collaborative clinical work, and none of it would exist without you.

To the researchers whose published work grounds the book's claims: Bessel van der Kolk, for making trauma embodied; Ruth Lanius, for making dissociation visible in the scanner; Martin Teicher, for mapping what developmental stress does to the developing brain; Stephen Porges, for giving clinicians a language that works even when the biology needs updating; Janina Fisher, for bridging structural dissociation and parts work; and the many others whose findings fill these pages. Any errors in interpretation are mine.

To the neurofeedback and QEEG community, and especially to Jay Gunkelman, Robert Thatcher, Juri Kropotov, and Joel Lubar: your research made the modern brain-map literature possible. Your debates, your rigor, and your willingness to follow the data made this a more careful book.

To the sensitivity readers and clinical reviewers who read early drafts and pushed back where the book needed it: the book is better for your honesty.

To my family, for giving me room. Then, and now.

And to the readers who picked this up because some part of them already knows: you are not the trauma that happened to you. You are the nervous system that survived it, and that system can change.

Contents

Copyright iii

Dedication v

Acknowledgments vi

Author's Note xi

Introduction xiii

I The Brain Trauma Changes xvii

1 The Trauma Map Is Not the Territory 1

2 The Seven Resources Trauma Recruits 10

3 What the Body Keeps and What It Can Update 24

4 Developmental Trauma Is Different 34

5 The Trauma the Brain Builds Around Conditions It Cannot Change 45

II Trauma Phenotypes 59

6 The Lifeguard 61

7 The CEO Under Threat 75

8 The Princess and the Pea 85

9 The Fog & the Tide 98

10 The Language Axis, Bard and Interpreter 113

11 The Approach/Avoid Brain 132

12 The Problem Child 146

III Parts, States, and the Autonomic System 159

13 Your Parts Have Brain Patterns 161

14 Polyvagal: Useful Language, Imperfect Biology 177

15 Why Some Trauma Work Makes People Worse 190

IV Neurofeedback and State Repair 205

16 What Neurofeedback Can Do That Talk Cannot, and How Modalities Converge on the Same Brain 207

17 Reading the Trauma Brain Map and Sequencing the Work 223

18 (Alpha-Theta) The Door That Opens Later 239

V Recovery 249

19 The Phenotype-Matched Recovery Plan 251

20 When Medical Conditions Are Driving the Map 267

21 Building What Trauma Borrowed 279

22 The Life After Survival 288

Before You Go: Your Reader Bonus 298

Appendix A: Trauma Red Flags and When to Get Clinical Help 300

Appendix B, Questions to Ask a Neurofeedback Provider 310

Appendix C: Terms Worth Keeping, Terms to Handle Carefully 317

Resources 324

References 328

About the Author 374

One Last Thing 375

Author's Note

I have recorded roughly 25,000 brain maps over two decades of clinical practice. The single most consequential lesson I have drawn from that work is that trauma does not do the same thing to every brain.

You already know which one you are. Your body knew before you had language for it.

Two people can walk through the same catastrophe and come out with different nervous systems. One scans every room for threat. The other goes numb. One cannot stop talking about what happened. The other cannot find the words. One sleeps too little. The other sleeps twelve hours and wakes up exhausted. Standard trauma frameworks treat these as variations on a theme. They are not. They are different brain patterns, with different circuit signatures, requiring different interventions.

This book is my attempt to make trauma specific: not to the event, which is what most trauma books organize around, but to what the brain did with the event. The eight phenotypes that fill Part II's seven chapters (the Lifeguard, the CEO, the Princess and the Pea, the Fog & the Tide, the Bard and the Interpreter, the Approach/Avoid Brain, the Problem Child) are not personality types. They are configurations of the seven neural resources that trauma recruits. They emerged from watching the same patterns recur across thousands of brain maps, and from listening to the people behind those maps describe what their nervous systems actually feel like from the inside.

Van der Kolk made trauma embodied. This book tries to make it readable at the level of the individual brain.

A few conventions: clinical examples are composites drawn from patterns across many clients; "you" addresses the reader and "I" marks observations from my practice; where the evidence comes from randomized trials I say so, and where it rests on clinical pattern I say that too.

A disclosure: I founded and continue to operate Peak Brain Institute, a neurofeedback clinic. I have a financial interest in neurofeedback being understood as a legitimate treatment for trauma-related patterns. I have tried to present its evidence base honestly, including where the sham-controlled literature is unsettled, but I cannot fully step outside my own position. Weigh that when you evaluate the neurofeedback chapters.

If you are a trauma survivor, a clinician, or someone who has tried the standard treatments and found them partially helpful but incomplete, this book is for you. The framework does not replace therapy. It tells you which door to walk through first.

If you are in crisis, the Introduction has the resources. Start there.

Let's look at your brain.

Introduction

You carry a nervous system that was shaped by what you experienced and by the temperament you arrived with. Your trauma is real without being the whole of you. The rest of this book is the longer version of that working thesis. The shaping was real. The patterns it produced are real. The patterns can be mapped, understood, and changed. What looks like character is often configuration. What looks like personality is often phenotype. What looks like a permanent feature of who you are is often a system doing its job under conditions that no longer require it.

You probably know the pattern from the inside: shoulders climbing before you register the stress, a room that reads wrong before you can say why, the argument you replay at 3am with no off switch. That is the territory.

The book exists because the trauma conversation has reached a particular moment. The first wave of trauma writing, which legitimized the embodied reality of trauma and gave a generation of survivors language for what they had been experiencing, did important cultural work, and parts of it are due for refinement. Trauma is real, and it is not one thing. The same childhood does not produce the same adult; the same combat does not produce the same veteran; the same accident does not produce the same survivor. The variation tracks the brain pattern underneath.

What this book offers is the framework for seeing the variation, recognizing your particular pattern, and matching the work to what your particular brain is actually doing: a more precise map with multiple paths through it, rather than a single intervention or a single diagnosis.

Before You Begin: Crisis Routing

This book is not a substitute for professional help, and it is not the right entry point for everyone at every moment. Some situations require immediate clinical care, not reading. Read this short section first.

If you are having active thoughts of suicide with a plan or means, or thoughts of harming someone else, or are experiencing psychotic symptoms you cannot distinguish from external reality, the next step is crisis support, not this book:

- **Suicide and Crisis Lifeline (US):** 988, call or text, available around the clock
- **Crisis Text Line:** text HOME to 741741
- **SAMHSA National Helpline:** 1-800-662-4357 (treatment referral and information, 24/7)
- **National Domestic Violence Hotline:** 1-800-799-7233

A note on 988: in some cases, 988 centers may dispatch police or emergency services without caller consent, which has disproportionately affected Black, trans, and disabled callers. If you prefer a peer-led alternative, Trans Lifeline (1-877-565-8860) serves trans and questioning callers and states a policy against nonconsensual active rescue, with exceptions for credible threats to others and mandated abuse or neglect reporting. BlackLine (1-800-604-5841) offers peer support centered on Black, Brown, Native, Muslim, and LGBTQ+ callers. Outside the United States, your country has equivalent resources. A web search for *crisis line* with your country name will usually identify them quickly.

If you are in active crisis, use these first. The book will still be here when the acute piece has stabilized.

If you are currently in trauma treatment that is making you worse (new symptoms, or old ones intensifying), start with Chapter 15. The harms of poorly-sequenced trauma work are real, and the chapter is for you.

If neither of those applies, welcome. The book is for you.

What the Book Is

The organizing concept is the **phenotype**: a recognizable pattern of how a particular brain has been shaped by particular experiences. This book maps eight phenotypes across seven chapters (the Bard and the Interpreter share one because the circuits overlap), each anchored to specific brain systems and the cortical resources those systems recruit. Most survivors will recognize themselves in more than one. That is expected; real nervous systems usually run several phenotypes at once, in clusters shaped by particular developmental and life conditions.

One frame the book returns to throughout: **the front of your brain handles the inside-self; the back of your brain handles the outside world**. Trauma hits the back-of-brain circuits first, which is why the work there is different in character from the work up front.

How to Read This Book

The book has five parts and three appendices. The arc is: framework, phenotypes, bridges, neurofeedback and modalities, recovery.

Part I (Chapters 1–5) sets up the framework: the map metaphor, the seven resources, the state-ledger reframe of *the body keeps the score*, the developmental-trauma distinction, and Chapter 5 on the trauma that builds around conditions that do not change.

Part II (Chapters 6–12) is the practical heart: eight phenotypes across seven chapters. Read the ones you recognize, in any order; skipping Part I and starting here is a legitimate path.

Part III (Chapters 13–15) bridges the phenotype framework to parts work, polyvagal vocabulary with honest treatment of what is settled and what is contested, and safety. Chapter 15 (on sequencing the work) is one of the most important in the book.

Part IV (Chapters 16–18) covers neurofeedback, QEEG, alpha-theta, and how the trauma modalities relate to each other.

Part V (Chapters 19–22) is the longer arc: phenotype-matched recovery plans, medical conditions that mimic trauma patterns, the bridge to *Borrowed Peace*, and the life that becomes available after the work has done its work.

Appendices give you reference: red flags for when self-help is not enough, questions to ask a neurofeedback provider, and a glossary of trauma terms.

You do not have to read in order. If you are looking for your phenotype, start with Part II and read until you recognize yourself. If your current trauma treatment is not working, read Chapter 15 first. If you are a clinician, the recommended order is phenotype chapters first, then bridges, then foundations, then interventions. If you have read *Gifted & Tortured*, the phenotype framework will be familiar; this book extends it into the trauma-overlay territory. If you are reading with a complex trauma history, read in pieces, with breaks, with support. The book will be here.

The book is a framework, not a treatment. It can help you see what is happening, what kind of work fits, and what to look for in clinical care. The work itself happens in daily practice, in clinical relationships, in regulation tools used over months and years. The phenotype framework is not a diagnosis; clinical care still requires actual clinicians.

What can be mapped can usually be changed. The next chapter starts the mapping.

Welcome to it.

Part I

The Brain Trauma Changes

Ch 1: The Trauma Map Is Not the Territory

Two clients walked into my clinic last month, three days apart. Both have a PTSD diagnosis. Both have been in therapy for years. Both have read every popular trauma book that has come out in the last decade.

The first one cannot stop scanning rooms. She is a high school teacher who sits in my office and tracks the door, the window, the slight movement of the plant in the corner. She sleeps four hours a night, jumps at the dog two apartments over, and feels like a poorly-tuned receiver picking up every signal the world puts out. When she tried meditation, she had a panic attack on the cushion. When she tried EMDR, she dissociated for a week.

The second one cannot remember her week. She arrives at appointments and cannot tell me what happened on Tuesday. She has stopped trying to keep a journal because the pages stay blank. She told me, in our third session, that the last two years felt like something she watched from behind glass. She has tried medication, body work, two trauma intensives, and a meditation retreat. The retreat helped a little. The body work made her dissociate harder.

They have the same diagnosis. They are not carrying the same problem, and what helps them does not overlap much. Several of the approaches I would reach for first with one of them are already on the other's list of what went badly. If they shared a therapist who ran one protocol for both, that therapist would be working against at least one of them, without intending to and without much clinical signal that anything was wrong.

That is what this book is about. The same diagnosis, different brains, different work, and a map I have been refining for twenty-five years that helps me figure out which is which.

1.1 Before going further: what the framework is and is not

The phenotype framework in this book is a clinical model. It is grounded in twenty-five years of neurofeedback practice and around 25,000 QEEG brain maps I have personally read or supervised, in conversation with the neuroscience literature on PTSD, the salience network, the posterior cingulate cortex, the locus coeruleus, and the half-dozen other circuits I will be naming in the chapters ahead. The anatomy is solid. The mapping from clinical pattern to anatomy is well-grounded clinical judgment supported by the studies cited throughout the book.

The matching of patterns to interventions has not been tested in randomized trials. It is what I do in my clinic with results I have watched for years, and it is what trained colleagues do, and it is consistent with a body of converging research. It is not the same thing as a treatment manual with a randomized evidence base. Treat this book as a starting point for your own work, your own self-experiment if you are reading as a trauma survivor, your own clinical experiment if you are reading as a clinician, not as a diagnostic tool that decides anything on its own.

I prefer to tell you this in chapter one rather than in an appendix. The honest version of what I know is more useful than a confident version that overclaims.

1.2 The story the field has been telling

For most of the last decade, the trauma conversation has run on a single dominant story, and that story has a primary author. Bessel van der Kolk started treating Vietnam veterans at the Boston VA in the 1970s, founded the Trauma Center in Brookline, and over four decades built a research program that did more than any other to bring trauma into clinical and public attention. His 2014 book *The Body Keeps the Score* became the best-selling psychiatry title in the world, was translated into more than 36 languages, and has been steadily on the New York Times nonfiction list since 2020.

The story that book tells goes roughly like this. Trauma is real. It changes the brain and the body. The body keeps the score. You are not crazy; you are responding to what happened to you. There are interventions that can help.

That story is mostly correct. The evidence behind it is real. Van der Kolk's 1994 fluoxetine trial was among the first randomized data showing medication could move the needle on PTSD. His group's 2014 yoga RCT showed a body-based practice could reduce PTSD symptoms in a controlled design. A 2016 neurofeedback pilot from the same lab showed EEG-based brain training could reduce chronic PTSD severity.[1] The story has done a great deal of good. It gave language to people who needed language, legitimacy to experiences that had been dismissed, and a path toward help where before there had been only bewilderment.

The story is also incomplete in a way that has begun to matter. I see the incompleteness most weeks in my clinic, when a client arrives having done good body-based work that helped her until the moment it stopped helping, or worse, started hurting. The polyvagal theory underneath much of the body-based framework has drawn serious challenge from physiologists who argue its core premises do not survive comparative anatomy. Bayesian critics have made the case that a body "keeping the score" oversimplifies what may actually be a problem of stuck prior beliefs the brain cannot update. The field's own history is more complicated than any single narrative can hold.[2]

None of that undoes the central contribution. It does mean the original story needs a second draft.

Trauma is real, and trauma is not one thing.

Trauma changes the brain, and it does not change every brain the same way.

The body keeps a score, and the score reads differently in different nervous systems.

---

[1] van der Kolk (1994); van der Kolk, Stone, West, et al. (2014); van der Kolk, Hodgdon, Gapen, et al. (2016).

[2] Grossman (2023) on polyvagal physiology; Alexander (2021) on prior-belief models.

The interventions that help one trauma survivor sometimes hurt another, and the difference tracks the brain pattern underneath. That pattern is what this book teaches you to read.

This is not a case against what worked. The field's existing tools (somatic approaches, EMDR, parts work, polyvagal-informed practice) have helped real people. The phenotype framework explains why they worked for some nervous systems, failed for others, and caused harm when the sequencing was wrong. The tools are not the problem. The absence of a decision layer above them is.

1.3 Why the phenotype matters

Diagnostic categories have their place. They let research happen, they let treatment be reimbursed, they let clinicians talk to each other. They also have a particular cost when they are applied to trauma: they collapse a great deal of variation into a single label. Van der Kolk recognized this. His Developmental Trauma Disorder proposal was an attempt to create a better category for children whose trauma did not fit standard PTSD. But DTD is still a category, and a category captures a population. It does not tell you what is happening in the particular brain in front of you.

In my clinic I see the two PTSD presentations from the opening of this chapter all the time. They look so different that, were they not both meeting the same criteria, no one would think to put them in the same diagnostic box. Sometimes I see them at opposite ends of the same week. Sometimes I see them in the same person at different points in her treatment. The label PTSD covers both, and what the label tells you is that they have both crossed a threshold of distress and impairment severe enough to warrant clinical attention. What the label does not tell you is which of them needs a quieter room and which of them needs a body in motion. The label is the bottom rung of useful information. There are several rungs above it.

The phenotype framework is the rung above. It says: trauma recruits some of your brain's resources for survival, and the particular resources it recruits depend on which systems were most available in your brain to begin with. Most people exposed to potentially traumatic events do not develop chronic posttraumatic responses; trajectory studies consistently find that roughly two-thirds follow a resilience path of stable, low symptom levels.[3] The ones who do develop lasting patterns are not weaker or more damaged. They arrived with a different configuration, temperament, prior history, autonomic baseline, genetic loading, and the interaction between that configuration and the exposure produced a phenotype. The hypervigilant survivor and the dissociated survivor are having different trauma responses, anchored in different brain patterns, sharing a common origin in *this nervous system was overwhelmed and adapted.*

This matters because the right intervention is different for each. The hypervigilant survivor needs work that brings the alarm down. Stabilization tools. Autonomic regulation. Careful titrated exposure to the present-day safety of her actual environment. The dissociated survivor needs work that brings her gently back into her body and her present, with entirely different tools. Giving them the same protocol because they share a diagnosis is category-level care applied where circuit-level care is needed.

The phenotype framework does not replace diagnosis. It is a more granular layer underneath it. You can have a PTSD diagnosis and a particular phenotype, and both pieces of information are useful. The diagnosis tells you a threshold has been crossed. The phenotype tells you what kind of brain pattern is producing the symptoms, which tells you what kind of work is most likely to help.

1.4 The seven resources, briefly

Chapter 2 owns the deep version. The short list: safety detection, sensory gating, self-location, contextual memory, inhibition, social meaning, and state integration. Each is a real cortical system with a real anatomical anchor, not a metaphor hung on a neuroscience name.

---

[3]Bonanno, Chen, & Galatzer-Levy (2024) report a 66% average resilience trajectory across diverse populations and event types in a meta-analytic review of latent trajectory studies; see also Bonanno (2004) and Bonanno & Diminich (2013) for the foundational trajectory work.

Trauma does not eliminate these resources. It changes how you have access to them. Some get over-recruited and run too loud. Some get under-recruited and run too quiet. Some lose flexibility and get stuck. The specific configuration is what produces the phenotype variation I have been describing. I will say it again because it is the central claim of the book and easy to miss: the same trauma does not produce the same trauma brain, and the difference is what determines the work.

The phenotype chapters in Part 2 are organized around these resources. The lifeguard is mostly safety detection. The princess and the pea is sensory gating and social meaning. The fog and the tide is self-location and state integration. The bard and the interpreter share a chapter on the language axis (prosody and verbal narration respectively). The CEO is inhibition and conflict monitoring. The approach/avoid brain is the motivational balance that determines what action becomes available. The problem child is the brake itself.

1.5 The front and the back

One frame to carry through the book. The front of your brain is mostly the inside of you: your appraisal, your plans, the running commentary, the *I want to* and the *I don't want to*. The frontal lobes are the most recently evolved part of the brain and the part that makes you most uniquely human. The back is mostly the outside world: what you see and hear, who is near you, what is happening in the room. Vision projects all the way to the back, to the occipital cortex, because the world arrives in your skull and gets processed at the rear. Many circuits at the back are tuned to threat by default, because threat shows up in the world before it shows up in your appraisal of it.

A trauma-shaped brain is one in which the relationship between front and back has been bent. Some people end up with too much back, threat scanning that floods the front. Some end up with too much front, chronic appraisal that prevents the back from coming down. Some end up with both. When you read the Lifeguard chapter you are reading about a back-of-brain system. When you read the

CEO chapter you are reading about a front-of-brain system. On the QEEGs I read every week, the front-back imbalance is one of the first things I check, because it tells me where the system is overworking and where it has gone quiet. The phenotypes are configurations of that relationship.

1.6 What this book is and is not

This book is a clinical-pattern reader for your own nervous system. It teaches you to recognize what your brain has been doing in response to what happened to you. It does this so you can match the right kind of work to the right kind of pattern.

Trauma explains some of what has gone wrong in your life, alongside temperament, environment, luck, and choices that, in hindsight, would have gone differently. Using trauma as the only frame narrows the picture in a way that does not help.

Different phenotypes need different interventions, and this book does not pretend there is one answer for all of them. The recommendation that helps a cramped Lifeguard differs from the one that helps a stuck CEO, a dissociative Fog, or a brake-failed Problem Child. Matching is the work.

This book does not treat you as broken. Your nervous system did what nervous systems do under the conditions you were given. The patterns that resulted are a system working. Give it different conditions and different tools and the patterns can come down to a working volume in the world you actually live in now. The patterns are durable. The patterns are also workable. Both of those are true.

1.7 Safety and pacing as you read

The chapters ahead describe phenotype patterns you may recognize in yourself, and the recognition can be powerful in both useful and uncomfortable ways. The later chapters discuss specific interventions (alpha-theta neurofeedback, exposure therapy, body work) that have caused harm when poorly sequenced.

If you are currently in a destabilized state, in active crisis, in acute dissociation, or in the middle of an unresolved trauma response, this book is probably not the right entry point at this exact moment. The work begins with regulation. Crisis support comes first [see Introduction crisis sidebar]. The deeper work has somewhere to land only after the acute pieces are addressed.

If you are not in acute crisis but you carry a complex trauma history, you may want to read in pieces, with breaks, and with support. The chapters can be read in order or out of order. The phenotype chapters in Part 2 can stand alone if you want to find your pattern first. Chapter 15 is one of the most important chapters in the book and worth reading early if you are considering or currently in any of the modalities it discusses.

1.8 What comes next

The Introduction has the full reading guide (survivor, clinician, destabilized, cross-book). Chapter 2 includes a master crosswalk table that maps every phenotype across *Your Brain on Trauma, Half a Second More,* and *Gifted & Tortured.*

The short version of what is ahead: Chapter 2 introduces the seven cortical resources in detail. Chapter 3 takes on the *body keeps the score* idea and offers a more precise version of it, what I call the state ledger. Chapter 4 takes on developmental trauma, which differs in important ways from adult-onset trauma and deserves its own treatment. Part 2 runs the eight phenotypes across seven chapters, with the Bard and the Interpreter sharing a chapter on the language axis. Parts 3 through 5 cover bridges (parts work, polyvagal, safety), interventions (neurofeedback, QEEG, alpha-theta), and recovery.

Read in order if you want the framework first, or jump to whichever phenotype chapter catches your attention if you want to find your pattern first.

The two clients from the opening of this chapter are composites of clients I have worked with. Both are still in treatment. The first one can sit at a restaurant table without tracking the door, most evenings. The second is starting to remember her Tuesdays. Their work continues, and they are recognizable, to themselves and to me, as the people they were before they had to become whatever the trauma turned them into.

That is the work this book is about. Let's start.

Ch 2: The Seven Resources Trauma Recruits

You are at a dinner party. The host is telling a story and people are laughing. You should be laughing too. You heard the words and understood the joke, but you are not in the joke. You are in the sound of a chair scraping in the next room, tracking the exit, reading the face of the person across from you who just shifted her posture, and your chest has tightened in a way that has nothing to do with anything anyone said. Someone asks you a question and the words arrive a half-second late. You answer something. You do not remember what. By the time you get home you are exhausted in a way the evening does not justify, and the thought that forms is the one that always forms: *What is wrong with me?*

Nothing is destroyed. Everything is recruited. Your safety-detection system was scanning the room at full volume. Your social-meaning system was reading micro-cues at threat intensity. Your inhibition was holding you in a pleasant mask while the rest of you worked overtime. Your capacity to simply *be there* was offline because every resource you owned was pointed at something else.

That is what this chapter maps: the seven systems your brain uses to run an ordinary life, and what happens when trauma pulls all of them toward threat at once.

I see this picture in the clinic every week. A client describes her dinner party, or her Sunday at the grocery store, or the meeting where she watched herself answer the question and could not feel the answer leaving her mouth. The QEEG map under that description usually shows the same kinds of disturbance across the same posterior midline structures. Different events, different stories, the same configuration. The configuration is the level this book works at.

2.1 What the recruitment looks like

Trauma happens when the danger does not pass, or when a nervous system is asked to handle more than it has resources for, or when the danger occurs in a context with no escape. In those conditions, the allocation changes shape. Baseline stops being a place the brain returns to. Resources stay pulled toward the danger even after the danger is gone. What was supposed to be a temporary reallocation becomes a structural one.

The lifeguard who is currently cramped is the same Lifeguard who, regulated, would give you accurate environmental orientation. The capacity is intact. It has been pulled into a configuration that no longer serves.

That changes what recovery looks like. Recovery is updating the allocation, given the right conditions and the right time. The pattern needs to change. The capacity does not.

The seven resources below are the systems trauma most often recruits. Each one has a brain system it draws on, a job it does at baseline, and a set of failure modes that show up under chronic load. Each one anchors at least one of the phenotype chapters in Part Two.

2.2 The front and the back, again

The orienting frame from Chapter 1: front-of-brain handles the inside self, back handles the outside world. I will tag each resource below so you can see at a glance which half you are reading about.

The back is tuned to threat by default, because threat shows up in the world before it shows up in your appraisal of it. Under extreme stress the fast back-anchored system dominates and the slower front-anchored system degrades. That is by design. The problem is when fast keeps winning long after the danger has passed.

The lifeguard, the Princess, the Bard, the Interpreter sit mostly at the back. The CEO, the Approach / Avoid Brain, and the Problem Child sit mostly at the front. State integration runs across the whole thing.

Hold that frame as we go.

2.3 Resource One: Safety Detection *(Back-of-brain)*

You walk into a room. You have not been in this room before. Before you have any conscious thought about the room, your safety-detection system has read it. The exits. The number of people. The angles. The acoustics. The faces. The probability that someone in here means harm. Most people never notice this happening, because the answer is usually *fine* and the system goes quiet within a few seconds.

In a trauma-recruited brain the answer never quite arrives at *fine*. The scan keeps running. The room keeps feeling provisional.

The safety-detection system is anchored in the salience network (the anterior insula and the dorsal anterior cingulate), the amygdala, and the posterior midline systems that handle environmental scanning. In Vinod Menon's triple-network model, the salience network operates a switch, toggling the brain between internal self-referential processing and external task-focused processing. Trauma can lock that switch. When I see a client with this switch stuck in the threat position, the story she tells matches the map: she cannot find rest even in rooms she has been safe in for years, because the scan is reading the room as provisional regardless of what the room actually contains. Etkin and Wager's meta-analysis across anxiety disorders found PTSD producing exaggerated amygdala and insula activation paired with quieter ventromedial prefrontal and rostral anterior cingulate engagement: salience hot, regulation soft.[1] Newer connectivity work has confirmed the anterior insula running hyperconnected to the rest of the threat-detection system, with the normal toggle stuck in the threat position.[2]

I see this on QEEG most often as elevated mid-frequency beta over the dorsal anterior cingulate and posterior midline sites, with degraded posterior alpha. The signature of safety-detection recruitment is hypervigilance, sleep disturbance, exaggerated startle, the inability to relax in environments that are objectively safe, and the dissociative

[1]Etkin & Wager (2007), meta-analysis of 88 neuroimaging studies across anxiety disorders.

[2]Abdallah et al. (2019).

shutdown that happens when the scan has been running too hot for too long.

Chapter 6 (the Lifeguard) is the main treatment of what this looks like and what helps.

2.4 Resource Two: Sensory Gating *(Back-of-brain)*

You are at a cafe. The espresso machine fires. The bus brakes outside. A toddler shrieks two tables over. The fluorescent overhead has a faint flicker you can feel in your teeth. For most people the sounds settle into a textured background. For some people the sounds compete for the foreground all at once, and the only relief is to leave.

That is sensory gating either working or not working. Gating filters incoming sensation. It decides what to attend to and what to let fade. It is anchored primarily in the posterior sensory cortices (visual, auditory, somatosensory) with regulatory input from the thalamus and from the frontal-posterior alpha-band networks that do the gating itself.

In a trauma-recruited brain the gating runs at reduced efficiency. Sounds that should fade do not fade. Lights that should not bother you bother you. Background sensations come forward as if they were threats. Some of the most reliable EEG findings in PTSD involve disrupted posterior alpha, the rhythm that does much of the gating work.[3]

I notice it first in the intake itself. A client jumps slightly at the hum of the QEEG amplifiers, then asks if I can dim the overhead light. The same client tells me she has stopped going to the grocery store on weekends.

The signature of sensory-gating recruitment is sensory overwhelm, intolerance for noisy or bright environments, exhaustion from ordinary stimulation, misophonia in some cases, and the body-level sense of being chronically over-stimulated. Chapter 8 (the Princess and the Pea) takes this up.

[3]Posterior alpha disruption is one of the most replicated EEG findings in PTSD; see Clancy et al. (2017).

2.5 Resource Three: Self-Location *(Both, mostly midline)*

You are driving home from work. You arrive in your driveway. You realize you cannot remember the last ten minutes. The car got you here. The route ran on rails. *Where were you?*

For most people this is a benign autopilot moment and they reset within seconds. For a person whose self-location resource is recruited, the question stays open longer. The week feels narrated rather than lived. The morning version and the evening version do not quite line up. There is a faint quality of watching the day instead of being inside it.

Self-location is the resource that knows where you are in your own life, in time, in your own story. It runs through the posterior cingulate cortex and precuneus (the same midline structures the Lifeguard uses, in a different functional configuration), together with the hippocampal formation and the medial prefrontal regions that handle the *me* function of the brain.

In a trauma-recruited configuration, self-location fragments. Memories of the trauma intrude into present time. Depersonalization shows up, where the self feels distant. Derealization shows up, where the world feels distant. The dissociative-subtype-of-PTSD literature, mostly developed by Ruth Lanius's group, has demonstrated that this disruption has a recognizable neural signature, distinct from the hyperaroused PTSD presentation.[4]

In the clinic the conversation that distinguishes this from ordinary forgetfulness is usually short. *Do you remember last Tuesday? Tell me anything about it.* If the answer is a long pause and then the description of a feeling rather than an event, I start thinking about self-location.

Chapter 9 (the Fog and the Tide) is the main treatment of what this looks like in practice, with specific tools for both the stuck-fog and the cycling-tide presentations.

[4] Lanius et al., extensive program of work on the dissociative subtype of PTSD.

2.6 Resource Four: Contextual Memory *(Mostly back-of-brain)*

A sentence in a song lyric, or a smell on a stranger's coat, or a particular slant of late-afternoon light pulls you back into a year you have not thought about in a long time. For most people this is a small autobiographical event, faintly nostalgic, easily set down. For a trauma survivor, the same kind of cue can drop you into the body and the autonomic state of an event from twenty years ago as if it were happening now.

Contextual memory places experiences in time and place. It is the time-stamping system, anchored in the hippocampus and the medial temporal lobe, with critical contributions from the medial prefrontal cortex and the temporal cortices that handle verbal and social meaning. When it works, you can remember a difficult event without reliving it, because the memory carries the markers that say *this is past*.

In a trauma-recruited configuration, the time-stamping fails. Memories arrive without the *past* tag. They land with present-day intensity. That is what a flashback is: contextual memory failing to stamp.

Contextual memory is also tightly coupled to the language axis. Verbal narrative is part of how the brain time-stamps. When language was offline during the trauma, the memory is usually missing the verbal scaffolding too, and the absence of scaffolding is part of why the memory does not file cleanly.

The signature of contextual-memory recruitment is intrusive memory, flashbacks, fragmented narrative of the trauma history, the difficulty of telling the story coherently even to people you trust, and gaps in autobiographical memory around traumatic periods. Chapter 10 (the language axis) takes up the verbal-scaffolding piece in detail.

2.7 Resource Five: Inhibition *(Front-of-brain)*

You are in a meeting. Someone says something that lands wrong. The sentence forms in your head before you have decided whether to say it. You feel it sitting just behind your teeth. You do not say it. The meeting continues. Twenty seconds later you have already moved on.

Most people do not notice the impulse-to-action gap because, most of the time, the gap holds.

Inhibition is the resource that holds the gap. It puts the brake on impulses so you can choose your actions rather than have actions happen to you. It is anchored in the right inferior frontal cortex (the Problem Child's territory), with critical contributions from the prefrontal cortex more broadly and from the anterior cingulate (the CEO's territory).

In a trauma-recruited configuration, inhibition either over-runs (the chronic-overcontrol pattern that Chapter 7 will cover) or fails (the brake-failure pattern that Chapter 12 will cover). Often both show up in the same person at different times. Years of overcontrol exhaust the inhibitory circuit; eventually it collapses into disinhibition.

In the clinic this often arrives as a single dramatic episode after a long stretch of seemingly held-together functioning. The client says, *I have always been the controlled one. I don't know what happened.* What happened is that the circuit that was holding the gap ran out of room.

The signature of inhibition recruitment is impulsive behavior at one extreme and rigid overcontrol at the other, with the rigid version often preceding the impulsive collapse in the same person across time.

2.8 Resource Six: Social Meaning *(Mostly back-of-brain, language-axis specific)*

Your partner says *I'm fine* and you know within a half-second that she is not fine. The information was in the tone, the timing, the slight tightness around the eyes, the way she put the glass down on the counter a fraction harder than usual. You read all of it without thinking. For most people this is an ordinary social moment. For a trauma-recruited social-meaning system, the same reading is happening constantly, on every face in every room, at threat intensity.

Social meaning is the resource that reads other people, the boundaries between you and them, the information in tone and expression and context. It is anchored in the right temporoparietal junction (the Princess), the right posterior superior temporal regions (the Bard), and the left posterior temporal regions (the Interpreter), with contributions from the medial prefrontal cortex that handles theory of mind.

In a trauma-recruited configuration, social meaning runs at high gain with a threat-biased prior. Every micro-cue gets read as potentially threatening. The boundary between self and other becomes thin, and you absorb other people's emotional states as if they were your own.

The signature of social-meaning recruitment is the rejection-sensitivity pattern, the social paranoia, the emotional contagion that flattens you, the chronic exhaustion from social interaction, and in severe cases the temporal-lobe symptoms including pseudo-hallucinations. Chapter 8 (the Princess), Chapter 10 (the language axis) cover the failure modes.

2.9 Resource Seven: State Integration *(Front- and back-of-brain in coordination)*

It is Sunday afternoon. You make a plan with a friend for Wednesday evening. You are sure of the plan when you make it. By Tuesday night you cannot understand why Sunday-you agreed to it. You text and cancel. Wednesday-you is a different person than Sunday-you was, and the two do not have a clean line of communication.

That is state integration either working or not. The resource coordinates the previous six into a coherent ongoing experience of being a person. It is the most diffuse of the seven: it does not live in any single region. It is what happens when the default-mode network, the salience network, and the central executive network hand off to each other cleanly.

State integration is what the switching looks like when it works. Nicholson and colleagues showed that different PTSD presentations can be classified by their disruption patterns across these three networks: hyperaroused-dominant has one signature, dissociative-dominant has another.[5] The networks are all present in each case. The coordination between them is what trauma has disrupted.

In a trauma-recruited configuration, integration fragments. Different states feel like different selves. The Sunday version of you and the Wednesday version of you do not quite recognize each other. The morning version cannot understand the choices the midnight version is making. The Self that the parts-work tradition describes (Chapter 13) is what well-coordinated state integration looks like from the inside.

The signature of state-integration recruitment is the parts-feeling-like-separate-selves quality, the difficulty of feeling like one person across contexts, and the inability to access certain states or memories from other states.

2.10 The trauma pattern map

The seven resources and the eight phenotypes are not independent lists. Each phenotype carries a particular signature of resource recruitment: which systems get pulled toward survival, and how hard. In each entry below, primary recruitment is the system the phenotype is built on; secondary recruitment is a system it commonly pulls along. Most trauma survivors carry a cluster, so several of these will apply at once.

The Lifeguard is built on safety detection. Sensory gating and state integration get pulled in secondarily.

The CEO recruits inhibition first, with state integration pulled in behind it.

The Princess and the Pea recruits two primary systems at once: sensory gating and social meaning. Safety detection runs secondarily underneath.

The Fog and the Tide sits on self-location and state integration, both primary. Contextual memory gets pulled along secondarily.

[5] Nicholson et al. (2020), machine-learning classification of PTSD presentations across default-mode, salience, and central-executive networks.

The Bard and the Interpreter (language axis) recruit contextual memory and social meaning as their primary systems. Safety detection runs underneath.

Approach/Avoid runs on state integration, with inhibition pulled along secondarily.

The Problem Child recruits inhibition first, with state integration pulled in behind it.

2.11 How the seven travel together

The seven resources do not run in isolation. The trauma-recruited configuration of one usually involves recruited configurations of others.

A cramped lifeguard almost always pairs with disrupted sensory gating (the system is over-attending) and some disruption of state integration (chronic alarm prevents the relaxed-baseline integration that normally happens). The princess pattern stacks safety detection, sensory gating, and social meaning. The fog pattern involves self-location and state integration primarily, with downstream effects on contextual memory and inhibition.

The Lifeguard in particular is closer to a substrate the other phenotypes sit on top of than a parallel category. Safety detection is almost always involved. The anatomy explains why. The posterior cingulate (the Lifeguard's territory) and the anterior cingulate (the CEO's territory) are directly coupled. When the environment is stressful enough to pinch the system, a loop starts: the Lifeguard flags something, the CEO worries about it, the worry raises the flag, and the two of them talk back and forth. *Did you see this?* Yeah, I'm worrying. *Did you see this?* Yeah, I'm worrying. That loop is self-reinforcing. When the CEO end runs too loud you get stuck in your head: the stream of thought, the appraisal, the value-judgment that will not settle. When the Lifeguard end runs too loud you get stuck in your gut: the body-level scan, the dread that has no sentence attached to it. Most people can tell you which end they live in on a bad day, and that answer maps them onto the framework. The loop is why a Lifeguard presentation so often arrives with a CEO presentation attached. A second route runs from the mid-right temporal cortex (the Princess's territory, where auditory and social-meaning tissue lives) forward to the anterior cingulate: intrusive material, sometimes auditory in quality, propagates into the CEO's monitoring channel and keeps it running loud. The problems travel together because the anatomy connects them. One system recruits the next.

The right-frontal quadrant does the same thing. When the avoidance system and the inhibition circuits both activate, it stops being a mood problem and becomes dread. The whole region is spasming constantly, a strong muscle under load, and without the approach system on the front left to balance it, to go outside and play, you end up with a driven avoidant negativity bias. Chapter 11 develops this in detail.

On the QEEG these patterns are often visible. You will see activation, often high beta or low alpha, in the regions involved. You will see high connectivity between the posterior and anterior cingulate, the back-and-forth showing up as regions talking to each other more than they should at rest. Or you will see a flooding of multiple brain-wave bands in one region, like tissue that is cramping up. The patterns help you understand how your brain is working. They are not diagnostically precise at the individual level and they do not hand anyone a label.

This is clinical observation, and it has not been tested as a causal chain. But it explains why I expect most trauma presentations to involve the Lifeguard somewhere in the cluster, and why reading Part Two as eight parallel boxes would be the wrong picture. All of these systems tune toward activation because the cost asymmetry demands it. Missing danger is catastrophic. Missing pleasure is a bad afternoon. You only spot that tiger once, perhaps.

This is why the phenotype framework treats the chapters as patterns rather than discrete diagnoses. When you read your way through Part Two and recognize yourself in two or three chapters, you are likely correctly identifying that your trauma recruited multiple resources together. Recovery involves attending to the resources that have been most affected, in the order your nervous system can tolerate.

2.12 What this means for recovery

The interventions across this book share a common shape. Autonomic regulation (breath, HRV, sleep, body-based co-regulation) lowers the chronic load that keeps resources recruited. The vagus nerve, named for wandering, turns out to be mostly listening; roughly 80 percent of its fibers run upward from body to brain. Chapter 14 develops this in detail. Targeted neurofeedback addresses specific brain systems stuck in particular configurations. Trauma processing addresses the unintegrated material the nervous system was holding offline because it lacked the resources to integrate it. Relational and family-systems work addresses the conditions that originally produced the recruitment.

James Gross mapped the regulation problem in a different way. He described five stages at which you can intervene in an emotional response: choosing what situations you enter, where you direct your attention within them, how you interpret what is happening, how you modulate the response after it has fired.[6] Trauma disrupts regulation at every one of those stages. No single intervention reaches all of them, which is why recovery involves more than one approach.

Different combinations help different phenotypes. The cramped Lifeguard responds best to one combination. The stuck CEO responds best to a different one. The dissociative Fog responds to another. Part Five tells you, for each pattern, what the priority interventions are.

2.13 Over-deployed resources

One last thing about the framing. Clinical descriptions of trauma usually run in deficit language: what people cannot do, the impairments, the limitations. The descriptions are often accurate at the symptom level. They miss what is true about the underlying capacity.

[6] Gross (1998), process model of emotion regulation.

A cramped lifeguard cannot relax in social environments. The deficit framing calls that a deficit in social relaxation. The resource framing calls it a high-gain safety-detection system that has been chronically recruited for environmental scanning. The deficit framing implies something is missing. The resource framing names the capacity that is present and over-deployed.

You are over-deployed. The systems currently recruited for survival can be released. The capacities that have been chronically dedicated to threat detection can return to their baseline functions, and the capacities themselves were never the problem. They were doing exactly what your brain asked them to do under conditions that asked too much.

2.14 Master phenotype crosswalk

This book is part of a four-book series using the same phenotype framework. *Half a Second More* maps the circuits in meditation-practice form. *Gifted & Tortured* maps them in their baseline-temperament form. *Borrowed Peace* maps them when dysregulation has been managed with substances or behaviors. Same circuits, different jobs.

Phenotype	This book	*Mindfulness*	*Gifted & Tortured*	Anatomical anchor
Lifeguard	Ch.6	Ch.7	n/a	PCC (Pz; CPz/POz in expanded montage)
CEO	Ch.7	Ch.7	Ch.5	ACC (Fz, FCz)
Princess (and the Pea)	Ch.8	Ch.8	Ch.8	rTPJ + insula
Fog & Tide	Ch.9	Ch.5	Ch.12	Posterior midline / alpha

Phenotype	This book	*Mindfulness*	*Gifted & Tortured*	Anatomical anchor
Bard + Interpreter (language axis)	Ch.10	Ch.8/9	Ch.9/10	Right + left temporal
Approach/Avoid	Ch.11	n/a	Ch.1+2	Frontal asymmetry
Problem Child	Ch.12	Ch.6	Ch.7	Right IFG

If you are coming from a sister book, use this table to find the trauma version of a phenotype you already know. If you want the matched meditation practice, use the Mindfulness column. If you want the baseline-temperament version, Gifted and Tortured.

The next chapter takes the *body keeps the score* idea and offers a more precise version of it. Chapter 4 takes on developmental trauma. Then Part Two: seven chapters, eight phenotypes.

Before we go on, one question to sit with. Which of the seven resources is loudest in your week?

Ch 3: What the Body Keeps and What It Can Update

You know the experience. A smell arrives on the street and you are not remembering the past, you are in it. Shoulders at your ears. Breath shallow. Thirty seconds later you are fine. The clock didn't move; your nervous system did. It made a forecast about the present moment that came from somewhere old, and it issued that forecast as a state in your body before any deliberate thinking arrived.

That is the thing this chapter is about. Not what the body stores, but what it predicts.

The version most readers know goes like this. Trauma is stored in the body. The tissues hold it. The work of recovery is to find the stored material and release it. That framing has done good in the world. It gave a generation of survivors a language for experiences that had been dismissed, and it legitimized somatic interventions that were doing real work without a clean account of why. I am not arguing with the practitioners. I am arguing with the metaphor.

In my clinic I see clients who have read every popular trauma book and have come to believe their bodies are filing cabinets full of locked drawers. They arrive looking for the right key. What I see on the brain maps is something different, and the difference matters because it changes what helps.

3.1 What is actually happening when the smell hits

That forecast from the opening is what I am calling a state ledger entry: a prediction your nervous system makes about what kind of situation this is and what kind of state is appropriate, drawn from what it has survived. The autonomic shift hits first; the cognitive labeling, if it comes at all, arrives later.

In a non-traumatized nervous system, ledger entries update fluidly. New experiences write new lines. Old predictions get revised when the world delivers something that doesn't match them. The brain holds a working model of which situations call for which states, and it keeps that model current.

In a trauma-shaped nervous system, certain entries lock in with unusually high confidence. The prediction *this kind of situation calls for high alarm* gets weighted so heavily that incoming evidence to the contrary does not register. I see this on the brain maps as elevated posterior midline activity, alpha suppression where alpha should be steady, autonomic readings that do not come back down between sessions. The state keeps arriving, faster than thought, regardless of what the present moment actually contains.

The formal version of this argument has been called a "precision pathology" of threat prediction: prior beliefs about danger are held with such certainty that the brain treats them as near-certain, overriding the evidence coming from present-day circumstances. Alexander (2021) lays this out cleanly as a prior-belief model of trauma; the broader active-inference treatment comes from Linson, Parr, and Friston.[1] The lab name for the phenomenon and the clinical name match. What I see in the room is what the predictive-coding literature describes from the outside.

3.2 Why the metaphor matters

Both framings agree that trauma produces lasting somatic change. The autonomic baseline shifts. The stress hormones cycle differently. Sleep architecture changes. Pain processing changes. Inflammation runs higher. The literature documenting those changes is real, and I see those signatures in the resting-state maps continuously.

The disagreement is about what the changes *are*. The storage metaphor says the changes are the trauma, sitting in the tissue. The state-ledger view says the changes are downstream consequences of a

[1] Linson, Parr, and Friston (2020) on PTSD as a precision pathology in active inference; Alexander (2021) on prior-belief models in trauma. See also Friston (2009) on the free-energy principle and Barrett (2017) on constructed emotion.

nervous system that has been operating in a particular allocation for a long time. The autonomic baseline shifted because the system kept running hot. The hormones cycle differently because the regulatory feedback got tuned to chronic alarm. The body adapted to the conditions the trauma created. It didn't file the trauma itself.

If you believe the body filed the trauma, recovery looks like retrieval and discharge. You go looking for what is stored, and you try to get it out. If you believe the body adapted to the conditions, recovery looks like changing the conditions and giving the system time to re-adapt. Those produce different interventions and different expectations.

The body adapted; it didn't archive. Everything in Parts 4 and 5 follows from that.

3.3 How predictions update

The neuroscience on prediction-update got a major reset in 2000, when Karim Nader and Joseph LeDoux showed that consolidated fear memories in rats became unstable again when reactivated.[2] Retrieving a memory doesn't just play it back. Retrieving a memory reopens it for editing.

The technical name is memory reconsolidation. When a prediction is activated, it enters a window of malleability. If the activation is followed by the same kind of experience that originally produced the prediction, the prediction is strengthened. If the activation is followed by a meaningful mismatch, experience that contradicts the prediction in a way that has to register, the prediction can update. The mismatch is the gatekeeper. Without it, retrieval alone changes nothing.[3]

Bruce Ecker, whose Coherence Therapy is built explicitly around this mechanism, calls the live moment of update the *juxtaposition experience*: the old prediction and the contradicting present-moment real-

[2]Nader, Schafe, and LeDoux (2000), *Nature*.

[3]Sevenster, Beckers, and Kindt (2014) on prediction error as the gatekeeper of the reconsolidation window.

ity held in awareness at once.[4] The prediction cannot be argued away. It has to be directly contradicted by lived experience while it is active.

The conditions for that update are specific, and I watch for them in every session. The activation cannot be so intense that the autonomic system floods, because flooding reactivates the prediction without updating it. The activation cannot be so brief that the malleability window never opens. The mismatch has to be a real present-moment encounter. Talking the client out of the prediction does not change the prediction. Giving the prediction a moment of contact with a present moment that doesn't match it does.

When the conditions are met, the predictions update. Sometimes a single session of properly conducted trauma processing produces a measurable shift in a long-held prediction. More often the shift accumulates gradually, across many sessions and many present-moment encounters with experience that contradicts the prediction. I have watched both versions, and the slower version is more common.

3.4 What this means for what helps

The state-ledger view gives a clean account of what the various trauma interventions are doing, and it explains why some of them sometimes do nothing.

Talk therapy that stays cognitive often fails to update predictions because it never activates them at the autonomic level. You can know intellectually that the bad thing was a long time ago. The prediction can hold its weight anyway, because intellectual knowing is a different currency from the autonomic-level forecast running underneath.

Body-based work in present-day safety, with adequate regulation, often updates predictions because it activates them and supplies the needed mismatch. The breath work, the slow movement, the orienting practices give the body new data in real time while the prediction-generating machinery is online.

[4] Ecker, Ticic, and Hulley (2012); Lane, Ryan, Nadel, and Greenberg (2015) on the requirements for memory reconsolidation in therapy.

Memory work, sequenced well, updates predictions by activating the trauma memory and supplying the mismatch of being in present-day safety while the memory is active. The right kind of memory work is reconsolidation, with careful attention to the conditions that allow updating rather than just repetition.

Neurofeedback is what I do for a living. The protocols that move trauma symptoms address the brain patterns that maintain the predictions directly. When the autonomic baseline shifts, the prediction-generating machinery has different inputs to work with, and the predictions can update without explicit cognitive engagement. Twenty years of clinic work has shown me changes that other modalities had not reached, in clients whose maps shifted measurably before their narratives did.

Relational repair updates the relational predictions by giving the relational systems new data in present-day relationships. The lifeguard who learned to scan unsafe environments updates partly through repeated experience of relational safety. The princess who learned that close contact was costly updates partly through repeated experience of close contact that does not have the cost.

The mechanism underneath every one of these is the same. Activate the prediction, supply the mismatch, let the autonomic adaptations follow. The body's slower record gets rewritten on the longer timeline.

3.5 What the body does not file

Some of the more enthusiastic versions of body-based work over-promise on this.

The body does not file specific verbal memory. Verbal narrative is encoded in cortical language and memory systems. When a client tells me they have *body memory* of a specific verbal event, what they have is implicit affective and somatic memory plus reconstructed verbal content. The reconstruction can be accurate, partly accurate, or partly constructed. The body itself does not store the words.

The body does not file events the conscious mind has no access to, with rare exceptions. The recovered-memory tradition's claim that bodies hold detailed traumatic memories retrievable through somatic intervention has not held up under careful examination. Implicit memory and state-dependent memory are well documented. The dramatic version, where forgotten detailed events live in tissue and can be recovered through bodywork, is not.

The body does not file a specific quantum of trauma material that can be discharged. The discharge metaphor, popular in some traditions, is imprecise. There is nothing to discharge. There are predictions to update, autonomic patterns to retrain, and somatic adaptations to allow to shift.

The body does not file the trauma as a permanent feature. The adaptive changes are reversible, given enough time and the right conditions. I have watched nervous systems that had been chronically activated for decades return to a more regulated baseline. The timeline is sometimes long. The changes are not, in principle, permanent.

3.6 What the body actually keeps

What the body keeps is a working record of what it has had to manage. The record shows up in places I can see and places I can measure.

It shows up in the autonomic baseline. A chronically alarmed nervous system has a different resting heart rate, a different heart rate variability, a different cortisol pattern. The baseline is the body's running estimate of how alert it needs to be by default. In my clinic this is the first thing the maps usually show, and the first thing that moves when recovery is happening.

It shows up in somatic patterns of guard. Particular postures, particular muscle tensions, particular breathing patterns settled into as low-grade defensive readiness. These are the body holding itself in configurations that were useful at some point and that have become habitual.

It shows up in interoceptive predictions. Anil Seth has described the brain as a beast machine, an organ whose primary business is predicting and regulating the internal state of its own body.[5] A body

[5]Seth (2021); Seth and Critchley (2013) on interoceptive predictive processing.

that has learned to associate certain sensations with threat will read those sensations as threatening even when the present context does not warrant the reading. I see this clinically as clients who panic when their heart rate rises for any reason, even exercise.

It shows up in the immune and inflammatory baseline, in sleep architecture, in pain processing. Chronic stress sensitizes pain systems and shifts immune signaling in particular ways. The shifts are real and measurable. The literature on trauma's downstream health consequences is one of the better-documented bodies of evidence in the field.

These are real, and they are also subject to update through the same mechanism that updates the predictions: changing the conditions the nervous system is operating under and giving it time to re-adapt.

3.7 What update looks like, on the timeline

Update is not visible session by session. It accumulates over months and years as the conditions change.

The autonomic baseline shifts. Heart rate variability that has been chronically low rises as regulation work takes hold. A resting heart rate that has been elevated drops. Sleep deepens. The body's working estimate of how alert it needs to be revises as new evidence accumulates that the present is safer than the past.

Somatic patterns soften. Held tensions release gradually as the body stops needing to maintain them. Breathing deepens. Posture loosens. Interoceptive predictions revise; sensations that used to be read as threatening get read as neutral. The chronic body-level alarm comes down.

The immune and inflammatory patterns can normalize. This takes longer than the autonomic shifts, but the chronic-stress immune signature does respond to sustained changes in conditions. Sleep architecture moves back toward baseline, and the restoration of sleep itself accelerates the rest of the recovery. Pain processing recalibrates as the chronic-stress signaling comes down.

These changes do not happen in a week. They happen over months and years, in response to changes in the underlying conditions. The ledger is being rewritten the whole time. It rewrites slowly, in the background, while the predictions update and the adaptive responses follow.

3.8 Pacing and the timeline

Many of the trauma-recovery disappointments I see come from expecting the rewriting to be faster than it is. Six weeks of regulation work that produces no visible change is the early phase of writing entries that have not yet accumulated enough weight to outvote the older ones. Six months of work that produces visible change in some areas and not others is normal too: the ledger updates where it has the most evidence and lags where it has less.

A nervous system that has been operating in a particular configuration for thirty years does not configure differently in six weeks. It begins to configure differently. The early changes accumulate. Over months and years, the cumulative effect becomes substantial.

Some interventions accelerate the timeline.[6] The more powerful tools (effective neurofeedback, well-conducted trauma processing, MDMA-assisted therapy in the right context, currently investigational; see Chapter 20 for the regulatory picture) can produce updating that would have taken much longer through gentler approaches. They activate the predictions strongly under conditions that allow integration. They are accelerations of the same underlying mechanism, and they are not appropriate for every system. The same intensity that accelerates updating in a regulated system can produce flooding in an unregulated one.

[6]On pharmacological acceleration: Brunet, Saumier, et al. (2018) tested propranolol before reactivation sessions with striking initial results; Roullet et al. (2021) found no significant advantage over placebo, likely because reliable clinic reconsolidation windows are harder to open than lab ones. MDMA-assisted therapy has shown large effect sizes in trials; the mechanism (reconsolidation, enhanced extinction, therapeutic alliance, or combination) remains open (Feduccia and Mithoefer, 2018).

The pacing question is part of what Chapter 15 (safety) addresses. The right pacing allows updating without flooding, which depends on the regulatory capacity available at any given moment. A regulated system can move faster. A dysregulated system needs to slow down. Matching pacing to capacity is much of what I do clinically with the first weeks of treatment.

3.9 Why this framing produces more useful hope

The storage metaphor implies a fixed quantity to retrieve. The state-ledger view implies a continuously revised record. Both acknowledge that trauma is real and that its somatic consequences are real. They diverge on whether the consequences are a permanent file or a working forecast.

When I sit with a client who has been told their body is keeping the score, I often hear a particular kind of resignation in how they describe themselves. They are waiting for the right intervention to unlock what is stored. They have a relationship with their trauma that treats it as an object inside them. When I show them their brain map and walk through what the elevations actually represent, the conversation shifts. The elevations are the nervous system's current best guess about what kind of situation this is. The guess came from real experience. The guess can be updated. The hope this opens is the ordinary hope that a nervous system that adapted in one direction can, given different inputs, adapt back.

This framing does not minimize what trauma did. The chronic adaptations are real, the autonomic patterns are real, the predictions are real, and updating them takes time and care. What the framing offers is a more accurate account of what recovery actually is, and more places to work.

Last Tuesday a client named Mara sat down in my office. She has carried complex trauma since childhood and has done a decade of careful regulation work. She showed me her sleep tracker from the weekend, the way someone might show a photograph: forty-one minutes of deep sleep on Saturday, fifty-three on Sunday. Five years ago her deep sleep was running under fifteen minutes a night. She wasn't celebrating it. She was just noting it, the way you note that a tree on your block has gotten taller.

Ch 4: Developmental Trauma Is Different

You never had a before. You cannot point to the thing that happened, because the thing that happened was the whole context you grew up in. You describe your childhood to a therapist and watch her face do the thing faces do, and you say, "But it was normal. That was just how it was." It was normal the way a fish doesn't know water. The brain built itself around it.

The trauma framework most people know comes from the adult-onset side: combat veterans, assault survivors, accident survivors. People who had a roughly typical life until something happened, and the something produced symptoms that fit the PTSD diagnosis. The framework grew up around that picture, and it is still mostly built for it.

A different picture has been getting clearer over the last twenty years. Not adult-onset trauma after a relatively typical developmental period, but trauma that started in childhood, often before any of it could be remembered explicitly, and that shaped the developing brain into the configuration the adult now lives in. This includes childhood sexual abuse, physical violence, emotional neglect, chronic relational disruption, and the ambient unsafety of households organized around addiction, volatility, or ongoing threat. This is developmental trauma, and the picture it produces is different from the adult-onset one in ways that matter.

A brain that experiences trauma as an adult is a brain that had years of typical development and then had to adapt to overwhelming experience. A brain that experiences trauma during its developmental window is a brain that built itself around the trauma. That difference shapes everything that follows.

In my clinic, when I look at the QEEG maps of clients with developmental-trauma histories, what I see is rarely the focal pattern an adult-onset PTSD map shows. The developmental maps look more like a *style* of brain than an injury to one. The lifeguard is loud, the Princess is overlaid on her, the Fog rolls in around month three of treatment when stabilization finally gets traction, and somewhere underneath, a Performer-Manager has been holding the whole thing together for forty years. Adult-onset PTSD usually points to a single circuit. Developmental trauma points to a configuration.

4.1 What Developmental Trauma Is

The clinical working definition of developmental trauma is roughly: trauma that occurs during the developmental period (from prenatal life through adolescence), often involving disruption of the attachment system, often chronic rather than acute, and often involving the people who were supposed to provide safety as the source of the harm rather than as protection from it.

Adult-onset trauma is usually acute, usually external, and lands against a background of completed neurodevelopment. Developmental trauma is usually chronic, often relational, and lands while the brain is still being built.

The Developmental Trauma Disorder proposal, advanced by Bessel van der Kolk and colleagues in 2005 and submitted to the DSM-5 task force in 2009, tried to name this clinical reality with a discrete diagnostic category organized around affect dysregulation, identity disruption, and relational failures. DTD was not included in DSM-5; the consensus was that existing trauma diagnoses with appropriate modifiers could capture the territory, and that DTD overlapped too much with PTSD and borderline personality disorder. The decision remains controversial among clinicians who actually work with these populations.[1]

The ICD-11, on the international side, did include a Complex PTSD category that captures a part of the developmental-trauma territory. cPTSD includes the standard PTSD criteria plus a *disturbances in self-organization* cluster: affect dysregulation, negative self-concept, and

[1]Sar (2011) on the DTD decision and its aftermath; van der Kolk, Pynoos, et al. (2009) for the original DTD proposal text.

disturbances in relationships. In my view, the ICD-11 framework fits the developmental population better than the DSM-5 framework, and many trauma-informed clinicians have begun working from the cPTSD framing even inside DSM-using systems. I do.

What you call it matters less than recognizing it. In developmental trauma, the brain's developmental trajectory itself was shaped, and that shaped pattern is the architecture.

4.2 The Brain That Built Itself Around the Trauma

Brain development is not finished at birth, or at age five, or even at twenty. The brain continues to mature into the mid-twenties, with different systems coming online at different points. The earliest postnatal years build the sensory cortices, the basic regulatory systems, and the attachment-related circuits. Later childhood builds out the social-cognitive systems and the executive-function systems. Adolescence reorganizes the prefrontal cortex and its connections to subcortical reward and threat circuits. Each window has its own work.

What development is doing, at every stage, is taking the inputs the brain is receiving and using them to build the appropriate circuits. The visual system requires visual input to develop normally. The attachment system requires interactive care. The social-cognitive systems require social experience. The executive systems require challenges that practice the relevant skills.

When the inputs are within the species-typical range, the brain develops within the species-typical range. When the inputs are outside that range, chronic threat, neglect, abandonment, abuse, severe deprivation, the brain develops in a different shape. The developmental machinery is doing what it does: building the brain for the conditions the inputs suggest the world will look like.

A child who received consistent attuned care builds attachment circuits that expect availability. A child who received chronic inconsistency builds circuits that expect unavailability, with the vigilance and wariness that come with that expectation. Both children built attachment circuits that match their inputs. The match is also modulated by temperament and genetic background, which is why the same household can produce different patterns in different children. The inputs matter; the system receiving the inputs is not a blank slate.

The result, in the second case, is an adult whose attachment system was built for an environment that is no longer present. The vigilance and the wariness were the appropriate adaptations to the original conditions. They are also, in present-day adult life, often costly. The brain that was built for chronic instability is operating in a context that may not be chronically unstable, and the built-in expectations produce responses that do not match the current environment.

Adult-onset trauma is an overlay on a typical brain. Developmental trauma is the brain's architecture. That difference shapes recovery.

4.3 What Gets Built Differently

Developmental conditions reshape several systems in particular. The four I see most often in the maps:

The attachment system. Earliest postnatal years build the basic circuits for relating. Chaotic, hostile, or absent care produces attachment circuits that expect interaction to be dangerous, depleting, or unreliable. These patterns persist into adulthood and shape relational functioning across the lifespan.

The autonomic baseline. Chronic early threat shifts the resting state toward higher activation, and the shift becomes the baseline. The adult coming out of this often has different resting HRV, tends to show different cortisol patterns (though the direction and magnitude vary by measure and population), and different sleep architecture than peers who developed under safer conditions. These are the system's adaptation to its inputs, and they are harder to shift than the autonomic patterns of someone whose baseline was different and briefly moved away from it.

The sensory-gating systems. A child who needed to attend to constant environmental threat builds sensory gating that operates at higher gain. The princess phenotype often has developmental roots; the high-resolution sensory processing that becomes the cramped

Princess in adulthood is downstream of childhood conditions that required exactly that processing as an ongoing task.

The prefrontal control systems. Chronic monitoring, chronic over-control, and chronic vigilance in childhood often produce prefrontal patterns that look adult-developed in some ways and adolescent-undeveloped in others. The CEO who learned to monitor everything because mistakes had consequences is functioning at an unusual level of control for her age, often at cost to her ability to relax. The problem child whose brake never fully developed, because the chaotic environment did not provide the conditions for typical inhibitory development, arrives at adulthood with inhibitory capacity below where it could have been.

State integration and social cognition are also commonly affected. They show up as cluster features rather than headline phenotypes; the dissociative-disorder spectrum is the severe end of the state-integration variability, and subtler versions of it are extremely common in developmental-trauma populations. Hypervigilant social reading (the Bard who hears threat in neutral tones, the Princess who reads every micro-expression) and social-cognitive flatness (the Bard who has shut down the receiving channel) are both downstream of relational developmental conditions that did not support typical social-cognitive maturation.

What ties these together is that the developmental machinery was responding correctly to its inputs. The cost shows up later, when the inputs have changed and the circuits haven't.

4.4 How This Changes the Work

A handful of practical implications follow from "the architecture itself was shaped":

The timeline is longer. Adult-onset trauma after typical development can sometimes move in a reasonable number of sessions of the right kind of treatment. Developmental trauma usually takes longer, because recovery involves building capacities that did not develop fully the first time, in addition to integrating the trauma material. Years, sometimes decades. That isn't a failure. It is the scope.

Standard PTSD protocols often fit poorly. Exposure-based protocols that work well for single-incident PTSD often do not fit developmental trauma cleanly. There may be no single discrete event to expose to. Phase-oriented models, with stabilization as a distinct first phase, are usually a better fit. The Cloitre STAIR model and the Van der Hart structural-dissociation model are both examples.

Relational repair is part of the work. These populations were shaped by relational conditions, and the therapeutic relationship itself is part of the intervention. Couples and family work can be part of the intervention. The relational architecture of the brain is part of what was shaped by the early conditions, and it cannot be entirely bypassed by symptom-focused individual work.

The phenotypes come in clusters. A developmental-trauma history rarely produces a single phenotype. It usually produces a cluster: a cramped Lifeguard with a Princess overlay, with some Fog episodes, with a Performer-Manager carrying it all. Readers with this history will often see themselves in several phenotype chapters. Working the cluster matters more than picking one circuit to address in isolation.

Body work and cognitive work both need different sequencing. Chronic dissociation common in these populations means body-based work needs careful titration; the body has been a difficult place to be for a long time, and returning to it can't happen abruptly. Cognitive-behavioral approaches that work well in some adult-onset cases usually need to wait for autonomic stabilization to settle enough to support cognitive engagement.

4.5 The Diagnostic Picture

The diagnostic situation for developmental trauma is messy.

DSM-5 and DSM-5-TR include a PTSD diagnosis with a dissociative subtype, which captures some of the territory but does not fully name it. Borderline personality disorder, applied to developmental-trauma populations, overlaps with what cPTSD would capture; clinicians have argued for years about whether these are the same thing, related things, or distinct. Other personality-disorder diagnoses also catch some developmental-trauma presentations, and the personality-disorder framing tends to be heavier in stigma than the trauma framing for similar pictures.

The ICD-11 cPTSD framework explicitly recognizes the disturbances-in-self-organization cluster these populations carry, and it does not require the single-incident framing that PTSD criteria sometimes seem to imply. Many trauma-informed clinicians use cPTSD framing in their working assessment even when the formal DSM diagnosis is something else.

For practical purposes, the diagnostic label matters less than the clinical recognition. If your history involved chronic developmental conditions that were not safe, neglect, abuse, severe instability, attachment disruption, you have a developmental-trauma history regardless of what is in your chart. The framework in this book applies whether you have PTSD, cPTSD, a personality-disorder diagnosis, no diagnosis at all, or some combination.

The pattern I see most often in clients arriving with a long psychiatric history is that the diagnostic story they have been told is a partial picture, accurate at the symptom layer and silent about the developmental layer. Someone who has been told for fifteen years that she has treatment-resistant depression and generalized anxiety has often, on closer history, also got the full developmental cluster underneath, which nobody asked about because nothing in the standard intake forces the question. The developmental-trauma frame adds the layer that the diagnoses are sitting on top of, so recovery work can address that layer too.

4.6 Adverse Childhood Experiences

The Adverse Childhood Experiences (ACE) literature has produced one of the more replicated findings in trauma science: childhood adversity has dose-response relationships with adult health outcomes across cardiovascular, autoimmune, mental health, substance use, and mortality categories.[2] Roughly forty-five percent of U.S. children experience at least one ACE; about twenty percent experience two or more.[3]

The ACE score has real limits as a clinical tool. It collapses qualitatively different adversities into a single count, and it largely misses emotional neglect and emotional abuse, the relational adversities that show up at very high rates in clinical populations and may be the most formative. McLaughlin and colleagues have shown that the threat-versus-deprivation dimension carries more predictive weight than the count alone. Treat the ACE score as a population-level epidemiological tool. A high score is associated with elevated risk; it is not a verdict. A low score does not mean someone did not have a hard childhood.

4.7 Use-Dependent Brain Development

Brain circuits develop in response to the inputs they receive during sensitive periods. When those inputs involve chronic threat, neglect, or relational failure, the circuits that handle threat detection, social processing, inhibitory control, and memory integration develop differently than they would have under safer conditions.[4] As Teicher and Samson (2016) documented, the sensory modalities most activated during sensitive windows show the most structural change in adulthood. Hippocampal effects show up decades later in episodic memory performance. The Romanian-orphans adoption studies give the cleanest evidence on what recovers and what doesn't: recovery is possible, recovery is incomplete in specific ways, and earlier deprivation ends the better. The brain has real plasticity. The plasticity is not unlimited.

A necessary caveat: prospective studies that measure brain function before trauma exposure consistently find that preexisting differences

[2]Felitti et al. (1998); CDC BRFSS prevalence data; McLaughlin & Sheridan (2014) on the threat/deprivation dimensional model.

[3]Bethell et al. (2014) using 2011-12 NSCH data; Crouch et al. (2019) using 2016 NSCH data. Both report approximately 45% of U.S. children ages 0-17 with at least one parent-reported ACE and roughly 21% with two or more.

[4]Teicher & Samson (2016) and Teicher et al. (2012) on structural findings; Nelson et al. (2007) and the English Romanian Adoptees follow-up reports; Perry (2006) neurosequential framework as a clinical organizing model consistent with these findings.

in neural reactivity predict who develops posttraumatic symptoms and who does not.[5] The developing brain is shaped by its inputs, and the brain receiving those inputs already has its own configuration. Both matter.

Hold the deterministic version of all this carefully. The popular framing (*your childhood programmed your brain*) is partly right and mostly an oversimplification. The developing brain is shaped by experience; the shaping is also subject to substantial later modification. Individual variation is enormous. What I tell clients who arrive with the deterministic version is that the brain map on their screen will not show an injury frozen in 1987. It will show a configuration that can, with the right inputs over enough time, configure differently.

4.8 The Recovery Picture

The recovery picture for developmental trauma is harder in scope and longer in timeline than adult-onset trauma. But it is more hopeful than the deterministic framing sometimes implies.

The brain that built itself around the trauma is the same brain that developed unusual capacities because of those conditions. A princess developed high-resolution social processing because she had to read her parent's mood to predict the next several hours. A Lifeguard developed sustained vigilance because the environment required close tracking. A CEO built strong executive function because mistakes had consequences. Those capacities are hers. Recovery means getting them back to the person in regulated form, freed from the chronic threat allocation that originally shaped them. The capacities were built. The conditions that required them can change.

The clients I see who do the best in long-arc developmental-trauma work tend to share two things. They get the autonomic floor stable enough to support everything else, and they stop trying to make

[5]DiGangi et al. (2013) systematic review of 54 prospective studies; Scheeringa (2021) qualitative review of 25 pre-trauma prospective neurobiological studies, 19 of which supported preexisting vulnerability; see also the 2025 prospective police-recruit study (Biological Psychiatry) on pretrauma amygdala reactivity predicting PTSD symptom increases.

the work fit a single-incident shape it was never going to take. The ones who struggle most are usually the ones whose previous clinicians ran them through exposure protocols before regulation was in place, or who were told their cluster of symptoms meant they were a personality-disorder presentation rather than a developmental one. The diagnostic and sequencing errors are correctable. The clients can usually find the work again, even after a decade of mismatched treatment, because the underlying plasticity is still there.

Not always. Recovery is hard, not everyone gets the full upside, and some of what was lost cannot be recovered. The picture is more hopeful than the deterministic version of the developmental-trauma story sometimes implies, but it is not unconditional. What I can say from twenty years of watching this work is that the brain shaped by developmental conditions is not finished shaping itself. The shaping continues through adulthood, and what you put around the system now matters for what it becomes next.

4.9 What This Chapter Makes Possible

The phenotype chapters that come next will read differently for adult-onset and developmental-trauma readers. The developmental readers will often see themselves in multiple chapters and need to think in terms of the cluster rather than picking a single phenotype.

The interventions in the later parts of the book apply to both populations, with modification. Stabilization applies to both; in developmental populations it often takes longer to build the regulatory capacity that supports deeper work. Phenotype-matched interventions apply to both, but the developmental population usually needs to address multiple phenotypes in parallel rather than in sequence. Relational work applies to both, but is more central in the developmental case.

The seven resources, the front-back framing, the phenotype patterns, the sequencing principle, all hold across developmental and adult-onset cases. The differences are in scope and pacing.

If you suspect developmental trauma in your own history, get clear on what stabilization looks like for you before you jump to the activating phenotype chapters. Read Chapter 15 first (the safety chapter; it is one of the most important in the book). Identify two or three regulation practices you can sustain daily for the next eight weeks before adding anything new. Find a clinician who is comfortable with phase-oriented work; if your current one wants to start with exposure or with deep processing before stabilization is in place, ask whether phase-oriented approaches are in their training. Then, when the autonomic floor is steady enough, work the cluster. The phenotype chapters in Part 2 are designed to be read in any order; pick the one whose opening scene lands hardest and start there.

Ch 5: The Trauma the Brain Builds Around Conditions It Cannot Change

If some of what follows describes a depletion you know from the inside, this chapter is partly for you. If it describes experiences you witness in clients or people you care for but do not personally carry, that is useful information too. I am writing it from the second position. I am a white man with a PhD in cognitive neuroscience, a clinical practice in Los Angeles, and economic security. My 25,000 brain maps include some of the patterns this chapter describes, but my experience of moving through systems that are designed to exclude people who look like me is nil. What I can contribute is the QEEG and phenotype-framework perspective on what these patterns look like and why the framework's default framing misses them. The researchers and clinicians who have done the foundational work here, Resmaa Menakem, Joy DeGruy, Thema Bryant, Kenneth Hardy, Robert Carter, Arline Geronimus, and their colleagues, have earned authority this chapter can reference but cannot replicate. I am citing them as the sources.

You are in a meeting at work. It is a routine meeting about budget projections. The room is not hostile and nobody is targeting you, but your body did the math before you walked in, and it is running at eight out of ten. You are tracking the room the way you always track it: who is looking at whom, what the two most powerful people in the room are signaling, whether the small shift in your colleague's tone means what you thought it means. You have done the work. You have been in therapy. You know your nervous system. You know the Lifeguard's scanning pattern. What you also know, and what the last four chapters have not fully named, is that the scan is not wrong. Some of what your nervous system is reading is accurate. The room is not fully safe. Not in the specific way it is safe for some of your colleagues.

You leave the meeting more depleted than the agenda warranted, and you have been explaining that depletion as a trauma response for three years. That explanation is partly right. What it misses is that the event the brain is scanning for has not ended.

The first four chapters of this book frame trauma as a past event that recruited the nervous system and left behind a configuration the brain still runs even when the environment has changed. That framing is accurate for a significant portion of trauma, the combat veteran whose war is over, the child-abuse survivor who now lives in a safe home, the accident survivor three years out. It is not accurate for everyone. For a meaningful population of trauma survivors, the threat-producing conditions are structural, ongoing, and not addressable by nervous-system regulation alone.

This chapter is about that population, and about what the phenotype framework looks like when applied to brains building themselves around conditions that do not change.

5.1 The framework's current silence

Every example in the previous four chapters treats the threat-producing event as discrete and past. That assumption does not hold for everyone who picks up this book.

A Black person in America who experiences routine encounters with law enforcement is not running a mistuned prior. The lifeguard's scan is calibrated correctly. The princess who reads threat in institutional spaces is often reading real signals. The approach/avoid brain of a trans person walking into a bathroom with hostile signage is responding to a present-tense threat. The fog of a person with a contested chronic illness who has been gaslit by medical providers is partly a response to the real ongoing cost of not being believed.

The phenotype framework, as built, has no vocabulary for this. It will tell you your Lifeguard is cramped when your Lifeguard is working. That is a failure in the framework, and it needs to be named before the phenotype chapters start.

5.2 The neurobiology of ongoing threat

When threat is a condition rather than an event, the nervous system does something different than when it adapts to a discrete past event and then gets stuck. The distinction matters for treatment, for the recovery picture, and for what the phenotype framework can and cannot offer.

Arlie Hochschild's work on emotional labor named what service workers perform for pay: managing one's emotional displays as part of doing the job. The autonomic equivalent, managing physiological state so that the body reads as non-threatening, compliant, or otherwise safe for dominant contexts, is a more metabolically expensive version of the same labor. This is what the occupational-health researchers started calling code-switching costs: the energetic toll of modulating how one presents in environments that read particular bodies as threatening. The research establishing this in Black Americans is now substantial. [12]

The allostatic-load model, developed by Bruce McEwen and colleagues across three decades of research, describes this at the neuroendocrine level. [3] Allostatic load is the cumulative physiological cost of adapting to chronic stressors, elevated cortisol, flattened diurnal cortisol rhythm, elevated inflammatory markers, autonomic dysregulation that does not return to baseline. A body under chronic threat is a body

[1]Carter, R. T. (2007). Racism and psychological and emotional injury: Recognizing and assessing race-based traumatic stress. *The Counseling Psychologist*, 35(1), 13–105. https://doi.org/10.1177/0011000006292033 Carter, R. T., & Pieterse, A. L. (Eds.). (2020). *Measuring the effects of racism: Guidelines for the assessment and treatment of race-based traumatic stress injury*. Columbia University Press. Hardy, K. V. (2013). Healing the hidden wounds of racial trauma. *Reclaiming Children and Youth*, 22(1), 24–28.

[2]Williams, D. R., & Mohammed, S. A. (2009). Discrimination and racial disparities in health: Evidence and needed research. *Journal of Behavioral Medicine*, 32(1), 20–47. https://doi.org/10.1007/s10865-008-9185-0

[3]McEwen, B. S. (1998). Stress, adaptation, and disease: Allostasis and allostatic load. *Annals of the New York Academy of Sciences*, 840(1), 33–44. https://doi.org/10.1111/j.1749-6632.1998.tb09546.x McEwen, B. S., & Stellar, E. (1993). Stress and the individual: Mechanisms leading to disease. *Archives of Internal Medicine*, 153(18), 2093–2101. https://doi.org/10.1001/archinte.1993.00410180039004

with elevated allostatic load. The allostatic load accumulates whether the threat is discrete and past or structural and ongoing; what differs is whether you can interrupt the stressor by updating your nervous system or whether the stressor will still be there tomorrow.

Arline Geronimus and colleagues developed the weathering hypothesis specifically to describe what chronic exposure to structural racism does to Black bodies over time. [4] The hypothesis, that premature biological aging results from the chronic effort of adapting to structural disadvantage, has accrued evidence across cellular aging markers, cardiovascular measures, and birth outcomes. The finding is not that Black Americans have worse health outcomes because of genetic differences. Geronimus and her colleagues document instead that the chronic labor of moving through structurally hostile environments produces a measurable physiological toll across a lifespan. Weathering is allostatic load made specific to race and structural harm.

Ilan Meyer's minority stress model provides the psychological architecture. [5] Chronic stressors specific to stigmatized minority status, discrimination, anticipation of discrimination, internalized stigma, concealment, produce excess stress load above and beyond general life stress. The model has been applied across sexual-minority, gender-minority, and racial-minority populations with convergent findings. The psychological and physiological costs of minority status are a response to ongoing environmental conditions.

Mark Hatzenbuehler and colleagues extended this to structural stigma, the community-level, institutional, and policy conditions that produce stigma and its health effects above and beyond

[4]Geronimus, A. T. (1992). The weathering hypothesis and the health of African-American women and infants: Evidence and speculations. *Ethnicity & Disease*, 2(3), 207–221. Geronimus, A. T., Hicken, M., Keene, D., & Bound, J. (2006). "Weathering" and age patterns of allostatic load scores among Blacks and Whites in the United States. *American Journal of Public Health*, 96(5), 826–833. https://doi.org/10.2105/AJPH.2004.060749 Geronimus, A. T. (2023). *Weathering: The extraordinary stress of ordinary life in an unjust society*. Little, Brown Spark.

[5]Meyer, I. H. (2003). Prejudice, social stress, and mental health in lesbian, gay, and bisexual populations: Conceptual issues and research evidence. *Psychological Bulletin*, 129(5), 674–697. https://doi.org/10.1037/0033-2909.129.5.674

individual-level discrimination experiences. [6] The distinction matters: individual-level discrimination is an event or series of events; structural stigma is the context in which those events occur and continue to occur regardless of whether any specific discriminatory event happens on a given day.

What does this look like in the brain? The neuroimaging research is younger than the epidemiological literature but is converging. Early neuroimaging evidence suggests that discrimination experiences activate amygdala and anterior insula patterns consistent with threat response during discrimination recall and anticipatory discrimination contexts. Chronic activation of these circuits, over years and decades, produces the same posterior-midline beta patterns, the same alpha suppression, the same autonomic markers that the phenotype framework describes in trauma populations, because it is the same mechanism. Chronic threat recruitment looks like chronic threat recruitment on a brain map, regardless of whether the recruiter is a past event or an ongoing condition.

The relevant distinction for the phenotype framework is this: in past-event trauma, the nervous system adapted to something, and the adaptation outlasted its usefulness. In ongoing-condition trauma, the nervous system is still adapting to something that has not ended. The phenotype pattern is the same. The recovery picture is different.

5.3 The trauma of not having enough

Resource scarcity is one of the most prevalent forms of ongoing-condition threat, and the least often named in trauma frameworks.

It is 11pm. You have been awake since 5:30am. You have a spreadsheet open on the kitchen table that you have been looking at for three hours. The numbers are not wrong. The numbers are the problem. The rent is due in nine days. The prescription runs out in six. The electric bill is overdue from last month. You can pay two of the three. You have run the math sixteen times. The math does not change. Your

[6] Hatzenbuehler, M. L. (2016). Structural stigma: Research evidence and implications for psychological science. *American Psychologist*, 71(8), 742–751. https://doi.org/10.1037/amp0000068

Lifeguard is running at full scan, but there is no threat to locate and escape from. The threat is the absence of options. Your nervous system is working correctly, solving an unsolvable problem, and it will keep solving it until you fall asleep at the table or the sun comes up.

Resource scarcity produces ongoing-condition threat, identical in its neurobiological signature to the structural threats the previous sections described, and it affects more people who will read this book than any of the clinical populations named so far.

Sendhil Mullainathan and Eldar Shafir documented what scarcity does to cognitive capacity in a series of studies summarized in *Scarcity: Why Having Too Little Means So Much.* [7] People experiencing poverty are not less capable. The cognitive load of managing genuine resource scarcity measurably reduces the bandwidth available for everything else. In a direct test, participants made worse decisions on unrelated cognitive tasks when financial scarcity was made salient than when it was not. [8] The effect size was comparable to a full night of sleep deprivation. A brain solving a resource-allocation problem with no good solution has fewer cycles for anything outside that problem. The front-midline monitoring loop that won't release (you'll meet it as the CEO in Chapter 7) is running in a person living paycheck-to-paycheck for a reason that is fully rational.

The developmental literature shows the cost accumulates over time. Gary Evans and Michelle Schamberg found that childhood poverty, operating through allostatic load, is associated with measurably reduced working memory in young adults, and the effect is mediated by chronic stress markers rather than by poverty directly. [9] Dana

[7]Mullainathan, S., & Shafir, E. (2013). *Scarcity: Why having too little means so much.* Times Books.

[8]Mani, A., Mullainathan, S., Shafir, E., & Zhao, J. (2013). Poverty impedes cognitive function. *Science, 341*(6149), 976–980. https://doi.org/10.1126/science.1238041

[9]Evans, G. W., & Schamberg, M. A. (2009). Childhood poverty, chronic stress, and adult working memory. *Proceedings of the National Academy of Sciences, 106*(16), 6545–6549. https://doi.org/10.1073/pnas.0811910106 The allostatic-load mechanism in adults is further documented in Seeman, T. E., Singer, B. H., Rowe, J. W., Horwitz, R. I., & McEwen, B. S. (1997). Price of adaptation, allostatic load and its health consequences: MacArthur studies of successful aging. *Archives of Internal Medicine, 157*(19), 2259–2268. https://doi.org/10.1001/archinte.1997.00440400111013

Hackman, Martha Farah, and Michael Meaney documented the brain-structure correlates: socioeconomic status predicts differences in prefrontal cortex volume, hippocampal volume, and amygdala reactivity, all circuits this book has been describing throughout. [10] These are the same plasticity the rest of this book relies on, shaped by conditions that were maintained over time.

Food insecurity, housing instability, and eviction risk produce the same Lifeguard, CEO, and Fog signatures described in the phenotype chapters, with the added cost that the scan is correctly calibrated to threats that arrive without warning. Children with food insecurity show elevated behavioral and emotional difficulties at rates that compound with duration and severity of insecurity. [11] Housing instability in renter families is associated with caregiver depressive symptoms and worse child health outcomes independent of income level. [12] Matthew Desmond's documentation of eviction showed what the quantitative data captures only partially: forced removal disrupts housing, employment, social networks, and every regulatory anchor a person has built. [13] For a meaningful portion of readers, the threat producing their Fog or their Lifeguard is the bank balance, the lease renewal, the question of whether there will be enough food next week. That scan reads an ongoing condition accurately.

The recovery chapters later in this book recommend building the conditions for regulation. Chapter 20 recommends a full medical

[10]Hackman, D. A., Farah, M. J., & Meaney, M. J. (2010). Socioeconomic status and the brain: Mechanistic insights from human and animal research. *Nature Reviews Neuroscience, 11*(9), 651–659. https://doi.org/10.1038/nrn2897 See also Noble, K. G., Houston, S. M., Brito, N. H., et al. (2015). Family income, parental education and brain structure in children and adolescents. *Nature Neuroscience, 18*(5), 773–778. https://doi.org/10.1038/nn.3983

[11]Shankar, P., Chung, R., & Frank, D. A. (2017). Association of food insecurity with children's behavioral, emotional, and academic outcomes: A systematic review. *Journal of Developmental & Behavioral Pediatrics, 38*(2), 135–150. https://doi.org/10.1097/DBP.0000000000000383

[12]Sandel, M., Sheward, R., Ettinger de Cuba, S., Coleman, S. M., Frank, D. A., Chilton, M., Black, M. M., Heeren, T., Pasquariello, J., Casey, P., Ochoa, E., & Cutts, D. (2018). Unstable housing and caregiver and child health in renter families. *Pediatrics, 141*(2), e20172199. https://doi.org/10.1542/peds.2017-2199

[13]Desmond, M. (2016). *Evicted: Poverty and profit in the American city*. Crown.

workup: sleep study, thyroid panel, comprehensive metabolic. Chapter 19 describes a phenotype-matched care plan. These are the right recommendations. They also carry price tags. Trauma-informed therapy, neurofeedback, somatic practitioners, adequate sleep, and proper nutrition are all gated by the same resource conditions that are maintaining the nervous-system pattern in the first place. The honest version of the framework acknowledges this: the chapters name the work; the conditions name what is and is not available. That gap belongs on the map as part of the clinical picture.

5.4 How the phenotypes extend

The seven phenotype chapters that follow this one describe what happens to seven circuits when trauma recruits them. Here is what that description needs to add when the recruiting condition is structural and ongoing.

The cramped lifeguard whose scan is accurate. The lifeguard chapter describes a safety-detection circuit running at high gain in environments that are objectively safe. For many readers, this description will fit: the threat is past, the gain is miscalibrated, and the clinical task is to help her update the prior. For other readers, the gain is correctly calibrated, and the environment is not objectively safe. The race-based traumatic stress literature, developed by researchers including Robert Carter and colleagues, documents consistently that the ongoing experience of racial discrimination and threat activates the same threat-detection circuits the Lifeguard chapter describes, and does so as an accurate read of a real environment. [14] Regulation work that tells this reader her Lifeguard is cramped can read as gaslighting. The distinction changes everything about treatment. The clinical question is not "how do we quiet this scan" but "what does this person need to

[14]Carter, R. T. (2007). Racism and psychological and emotional injury: Recognizing and assessing race-based traumatic stress. *The Counseling Psychologist*, 35(1), 13–105. https://doi.org/10.1177/0011000006292033 Carter, R. T., & Pieterse, A. L. (Eds.). (2020). *Measuring the effects of racism: Guidelines for the assessment and treatment of race-based traumatic stress injury*. Columbia University Press. Hardy, K. V. (2013). Healing the hidden wounds of racial trauma. *Reclaiming Children and Youth*, 22(1), 24–28.

sustain the scan without burning out, and where does advocacy work enter the recovery picture alongside nervous-system work."

The princess whose high gain is reading real signals. Chapter 8 describes high-gain social-meaning processing, the rTPJ running at 1.5x, reading micro-expressions and tonal shifts with unusual precision, often producing misreads driven by threat-biased priors. The same high-gain system, in a person who has been racialized as not-belonging, or whose gender expression is routinely read as threatening by institutions, is doing accurate reading of real micro-aggressions. The problem is not the gain. The problem is that the gain is never allowed to come down because the signals the person is reading do not stop. Recovery work that targets the Princess pattern without acknowledging what she is reading can inadvertently pathologize accurately-perceived racism or transphobia. The frame needs to include: her gain is producing accurate reads. The burnout comes from the volume and the persistence of the input, not from a mistuned prior.

The fog that does not lift because the load does not lift. Chapter 9 describes the Fog as a Tide that broke, cycling collapsed by chronic load, the system stuck at low tide. Weathering is this mechanism made specific to structural harm. The chronically elevated allostatic load of moving through structural racism, disability discrimination, or economic precarity produces the same stuck-cycling pattern that post-viral states and sleep apnea produce: a system that cannot rest because the conditions do not give it room to rest. Chapter 20 covers medical conditions driving the map; the structural allostatic-load pattern belongs in that same tier of "address the upstream driver before assuming the brain map is neurologically stuck." For many readers, the Fog is the weathering, and no amount of alpha-frequency neurofeedback will fix it while the structural stressor is ongoing and unaddressed.

The CEO Performer whose monitoring is accurate. Chapter 7 describes the CEO running survival-grade monitoring loops in environments that no longer require it. For many Performers from marginalized backgrounds, the monitoring is not miscalibrated. The cost of missing a signal in an institutional environment that will punish errors disproportionately is real. The eldest daughter of immigrants who learned that her family's stability was contingent on her performance is not running a stuck loop, she is running an accurate calculation. The loop does not need to be retrained so much as the conditions need to be acknowledged. Recovery in these cases involves working the CEO pattern and naming, honestly, what the monitoring was and is for, and what it would mean to trust that the cost-structure has changed when the evidence for that is incomplete.

The approach/avoid brain facing structural barriers to action. The trans person who spoke up and lost their job. The disabled person who advocated and was labeled "difficult." The community that learned through repeated experience that action has unpredictable costs. For them, the push-pull freeze described in Chapter 11 is an accurate calculation, not a stuck pattern from the past. Behavioral activation that says "the freeze is mistuned" misses that the freeze may be the most rational response to an environment that punished exactly the actions the protocol prescribes.

The problem child in context. When brake failures are happening inside this picture, what the substance use is standing in for matters. If it is standing in for an off-switch that the chronic structural load does not allow the nervous system to generate, addressing the brake circuit without addressing the stressor will produce the same relapse dynamics that integrated dual-diagnosis treatment sees in chronic-trauma populations. The circuit breaks in context.

The phenotype framework still applies to ongoing-threat populations. The recovery picture is different, and treatment work that does not engage the structural dimension risks either gaslighting the reader about what her nervous system is reading or leaving the upstream driver unaddressed while trying to retrain the downstream pattern.

5.5 What recovery means when the threat does not stop

The research on code-switching costs is concrete. Multiple studies show measurable cardiovascular and cortisol consequences of the emotional and behavioral suppression required to move through majority-culture environments as a minoritized person. [15] The act of presenting oneself as non-threatening when one has been coded as threatening, calibrating facial expression, vocal register, word choice, and physical bearing to preempt the threat-response of others, is physiologically expensive. It is labor that accumulates on every brain map without appearing on any job description. When I see a client whose allostatic markers are elevated and who presents as highly regulated in session, one of the questions I now ask is: what does it cost to be in this room in this body. That is a clinical question with a structural answer.

The nervous-system regulation work in this book is real and valuable. HRV biofeedback, targeted neurofeedback, somatic work, parts work, paced breathing, all of these build regulatory capacity, and regulatory capacity matters for people under ongoing structural threat. A more regulated nervous system is a more resilient nervous system. That is not nothing. For many people in the populations described above, the regulation work is the difference between surviving and not surviving.

And: regulation work done without acknowledgment of ongoing structural harm can land as "your nervous system is the problem" when the nervous system is correctly adapted to ongoing conditions. The implicit message of a regulation-only approach is that the solution is inside the person. That message can function as another layer of the gaslighting that medical trauma, racial trauma, and other structural harms often already include.

Resmaa Menakem's *My Grandmother's Hands* offers a different frame, in his words and from his standpoint. [16] Menakem argues that nervous systems carry the history of structural violence in their

---

[15] Trawalter, S., Richeson, J. A., & Shelton, J. N. (2009). Predicting behavior during interracial interactions: A stress and coping approach. *Personality and Social Psychology Review*, 13(4), 243–268. https://doi.org/10.1177/1088868309345850

[16] Menakem, R. (2017). *My grandmother's hands: Racialized trauma and the pathway to mending our hearts and bodies*. Central Recovery Press. DeGruy, J. (2017). *Post traumatic slave syndrome: America's legacy of enduring injury and healing* (Rev. ed.). Joy DeGruy Publications Inc. Bryant, T. (2022). *Homecoming: Overcome fear and trauma to reclaim your whole, authentic self.* TarcherPerigee.

physiology across generations, and that somatic practices for Black Americans are not aimed at quieting the body's response to racism but at building the capacity to feel its full weight without fragmenting. He draws the distinction this way: the difference between "regulate yourself so the racism bothers you less" and "regulate yourself so you can tolerate the full reality of what you are dealing with" is the difference between a coping frame and a dignity frame. That distinction is the one that matters clinically, and it belongs to him.

The research on community as regulation is relevant here. Parent-infant synchrony data show that nervous systems regulate through other nervous systems. The research on social buffering, the physiological settling that happens in the presence of safe others, extends across species and across the lifespan. [17] For people under ongoing structural threat, the co-regulation available through community, affinity groups, and solidarity relationships is one of the primary mechanisms by which the nervous system survives chronic allostatic load. Two hours with people who don't require code-switching lowers the allostatic markers. That is the mechanism. Chosen family, activist networks, and faith community (where it is not itself a site of harm) function, in neurobiological terms, as autonomic-regulation infrastructure alongside clinical work.

The clinical implications are concrete. Standard case formulation for a Lifeguard client would begin: stabilize the baseline, then process the trauma material. For a client whose Lifeguard is tracking real ongoing conditions, the formulation looks different: identify which environments allow the scan to come down, and build access to those environments as a clinical priority. The QEEG-measured Lifeguard signature in a client who leaves regulated spaces and enters hostile ones will re-elevate regardless of the regulation work, because the input is still there. The clinical goal is not to train the Lifeguard to ignore accurate data; it is to ensure that the client has enough regulated time

[17] Coan, J. A., & Sbarra, D. A. (2015). Social baseline theory: The social regulation of risk and effort. *Current Opinion in Psychology*, 1, 87–91. https://doi.org/10.1016/j.copsyc.2014.12.021

and regulated relationships that the allostatic load does not compound to the breaking point.

For princess clients moving through environments where their high-gain reading is picking up real signals, boundary-setting and social pacing look different. Organize her social life so the high-gain system gets periods of genuine rest, environments where the signals are benign and the reading is rewarded, alongside the required navigation of environments where it is not.

Structural advocacy and collective action are also, in this framing, nervous-system regulation tools. There is research on the health benefits of social connection and collective efficacy. The sense of agency that comes from acting on the conditions that are producing the harm, as one more input to the allostatic-load calculation, is part of the recovery picture for people whose threat condition is structural.

At the same time, this chapter cannot promise what it cannot deliver. The nervous-system work in this book will not end racism. It will not end transphobia, ableism, or structural economic precarity. Some of what maintains these readers' nervous-system patterns will only change through social and political transformation that is outside the scope of any individual's recovery work. Naming that honest limit is more respectful than pretending the framework can do what it cannot. The framework has an edge, and the edge deserves to be named.

The clinical goal for this population is not elimination of the Lifeguard's scan or the Princess's gain or the CEO's monitoring. The clinical goal is building enough regulatory capacity that these systems can do their work without burning out the body that carries them, and building enough ground that collective action and structural advocacy are possible rather than precluded by the chronic depletion.

5.6 Bridge to Part II

Part II runs the phenotype chapters in order. Every description there applies here, with one addition: when the ongoing condition is structural, the circuit map stays the same and the recovery picture changes. The lifeguard chapter will describe a circuit running at high gain in an environment the framework assumes is safe. Some readers will recognize a mistuned prior. Some will recognize an accurate read. Both require the framework. Neither resolves without it.

The phenotype is the fingerprint. The conditions that shaped it are part of the clinical picture. Both matter.

Part II

Trauma Phenotypes

Ch 6: The Lifeguard

You walk into a party and your eyes do a thing you didn't ask them to do. They scan the room before you've said hello to anyone. They clock the exits, the loud guy by the bar, the woman whose laugh comes a beat too sharp, the guy in the corner who hasn't moved since you walked in. You weren't trying to do this. You were already doing it.

You don't enjoy it. You wish you were the person who walks in and finds whoever's nearest and says hi. Instead you're running a low-grade evaluation on every person in the room and you don't quite know why.

You pour a drink so your hand has somewhere to be. You pick a corner that lets you see the door. Someone says your name twice before you turn. A friend asks if you're okay and you say yes and you don't know if that was true. You have been here for four minutes.

A lot of people are walking around with very loud Lifeguards and don't know they have one. They think they're paranoid. They think they're "an introvert" because parties leave them flattened. They think they need a glass of wine to relax, then two, then three. They think they're broken in some way nobody has named, and that everyone else somehow figured out how to be at ease.

Your brain has a circuit whose job is to evaluate the room, and right now that circuit is cramped: stuck, revving even when nothing is happening, looking for sharks in the indoor pool. You are not the broken or paranoid person the labels suggest but someone with a loud Lifeguard.

The lifeguard learned, somewhere along the way, that the world was not especially safe and not especially predictable. It buys insurance with attention, and you pay the premium every time you walk into a room.

6.1 Where the Lifeguard Lives

The lifeguard lives at the back midline of your brain. The anatomy most closely associated with her post is the posterior cingulate cortex. On a brain map I read her pattern at the posterior midline electrode sites: Pz in a standard nineteen-channel recording, CPz and POz in an expanded one. The PCC and the precuneus beside it are large cortical sheets whose fields project clearly to the scalp, so a posterior-midline pattern supports a coarse medial-parietal hypothesis involving both structures. The electrode does not separate them cleanly. The hypothesis is better grounded than it would be for a smaller or deeper source. She sits behind the parietal lobes and just above the visual cortex, in close coordination with the systems around her. The parietal lobes handle spatial attention. The visual cortex processes what you see. The temporal cortex handles sound and meaning. The deeper limbic systems process threat. The PCC is the meeting place of these systems. She takes their inputs and asks one question, very fast, almost continuously: *what is going on out there, and does any of it require me?*

The CEO at the front of your brain is asking a different question. He is asking *what am I doing, and is it the right thing.* His circuit runs through the anterior cingulate cortex, at the front midline. He monitors your goals, your plans, your conflicts. He is the inside-self counterpart to the Lifeguard's outside-world post. When the two of them are coordinated, your attention moves smoothly between the world and your goals, and you do not think about either system. You just feel functional.

She has a partner called the salience network, a pair of structures (the anterior insula and the dorsal anterior cingulate cortex) whose job is to decide what matters right now. In a healthy brain, the salience network flips attention between your internal world and the external task at hand. In a trauma-recruited brain, that switch sticks. Meta-analytic evidence from Etkin and Wager showed that PTSD produces exaggerated activation of the amygdala and anterior insula in response to negative stimuli, paired with reduced activation of the regions that should be calming the alarm.[1] The salience network stays locked in detection mode. The lifeguard keeps getting fed signal that says *this matters, check it now*, even when nothing in the room has changed.

A healthy Lifeguard runs her sweep at low volume. She is on duty all the time, but the duty is light. She gives your nervous system a quiet rough map of who is here and what is happening, and unless something off shows up, she does not interrupt your thinking. You can be at the same party reading a person's face and tracking the conversation and noting the time without effort. She is doing her job in the background and not asking you for anything.

A cramped lifeguard runs her sweep at high volume. Every micro-cue gets a check. The friend who shifted his weight. The shadow at the doorway. The car that slowed down outside. The change in the music. None of these is a tiger. Each of them gets evaluated as if it might be.

6.2 The Gift

It would be easy, in a chapter on a cramped circuit, to forget that the cramp is on top of a real capacity. The same circuit that over-evaluates now is the circuit that, in better calibration, gives you something most people do not have.

I see this in the clinic almost as often as I see the cost. The lifeguards in my practice are the people who walk into a meeting and read the room before anyone has spoken. They notice the friend whose face has subtly changed and ask the question that opens up the real conversation. They sense the babysitter is wrong before anyone else does, and their nervous system insists on a different sitter, and they only later find out they were right. What gets called paranoia in these people is high-resolution outside-world processing, doing what evolution built it to do.

They notice change. The room looked one way ten minutes ago and a different way now, and they catch the shift. They read environments

[1] Etkin & Wager (2007). PTSD-specific salience-network and prefrontal findings; Abdallah et al. (2019) on treatment-related normalization of salience-network connectivity in soldiers with PTSD.

accurately and learn from what they read. They remember the room. They remember the seating arrangement at a dinner two years ago and what the light was like. They remember conversations with strange precision, because the circuit that scans the present also binds the present to the past in a way that gives the past texture.

The lifeguards are the people who notice when I have changed something small in the office. They are the ones who track the appointment time to the minute, who remember what we talked about three sessions ago when I have lost track, who clock the new sound from the HVAC the morning I have not noticed it yet. The contextual awareness is real and worth keeping.

The gift and the cost are produced by the same circuit. A cramped lifeguard is a circuit that did her job in a context that demanded it. The chapter does not end with her gone. It ends with her at a working volume, in a world that no longer demands her at twelve out of ten.

6.3 Three Faces

The same circuit doing the same job in different states. You may recognize one of them more than the others.

The first face is **hypervigilance**. The lifeguard is on. All the time. You walk into rooms and you do not get the quiet rough map; you get the loud detailed audit. You sleep light and wake at every sound. Your body has a low background hum of readiness that you cannot turn off, and after a while you do not notice the hum because it has become the texture of being awake. You are the person at dinner whose head turns every time the door opens.

Startle research maps this state precisely. In Christian Grillon's neutral-predictable-unpredictable startle task, subjects face three conditions: no threat, a threat that is signaled and predictable, and a threat that could arrive at any moment without warning. People with PTSD show selectively amplified startle in the unpredictable condition, as though the uncertainty itself has become the danger.[2] the lifeguard

[2]Grillon (2008); Kreutzer & Gorka (2021). NPU task and amplified unpredictable-threat startle in PTSD.

lives in that unpredictable block. The party is unpredictable. The dinner is unpredictable. Every room you enter is the unpredictable condition, because nobody has given her the all-clear signal.

People around you may call this anxiety. Some of it is. Anxiety is the felt experience. Hypervigilance is the circuit underneath.

The second face is **rumination**. The same circuit, with the eyes turned around. The lifeguard evaluates the rooms you used to be in. She replays. She runs the threat audit on conversations from yesterday, on relationships from years ago, on the comment your boss made in the meeting that you cannot stop thinking about. People often experience rumination as a thinking problem, as if the thoughts are running away. The underlying mechanism is the same Lifeguard circuit checking the past for tigers it might have missed.

This face is harder to recognize because it does not look like watching. It looks like worrying. It looks like overthinking. It looks like lying in bed at three in the morning playing a sentence on a loop. The reason it is so hard to interrupt is that it is a circuit doing its job, not a cognitive habit you can decide your way out of.

The third face is the one most people do not connect to the Lifeguard at all. It is **dissociation**. When the circuit works at high volume for too long, it goes offline. The brain has a self-protection mechanism that throws a switch when the nervous system has been running too hot for too long. You go foggy. You feel far away from yourself. You watch your own life as if from across a glass wall. You notice you have driven home but cannot remember the drive.

This is the same circuit having quit. The lifeguard who has been evaluating at twelve out of ten for too many days in a row drops to zero. The next day she comes back at twelve. The cycle has its own particular flavor: you do not know if you are too on or too off, and you flip between them without warning.

On a brain map, the three faces are recognizable. A hypervigilant Lifeguard usually shows elevated high-frequency activity over the back midline, with the posterior alpha rhythms that normally let the sensory cortex rest suppressed or unstable. Clancy and colleagues, in a study that distinguished PTSD from generalized anxiety disorder, found that PTSD was specifically associated with reduced intrinsic posterior alpha power, source-localized to the cuneus, precuneus, and superior occipital gyrus. Using Granger causality analysis they showed the breakdown ran in both directions: the bottom-up inhibitory signal from visual cortex to prefrontal cortex was weakened, and the top-down signal from prefrontal cortex back to visual cortex was weakened too. The lifeguard was sending unfiltered sensory data forward, and the CEO was failing to tell her to quiet down. Both deficits correlated with hypervigilance severity. The more the gating had broken down, the louder the scanning.[3] A dissociated Lifeguard often looks the opposite on a brain map: low arousal, reduced posterior engagement. Same circuit. Two failure modes.

Rumination has its own flavor: sustained activity in the same posterior midline systems, but with patterns suggesting an internal-checking loop rather than an external-scanning one. The lifeguard is auditing memory instead of the room.

If you read the three faces above and one of them is your daily life, what you have is one circuit, doing its job at the wrong volume, in the wrong direction, or running so hard it tripped its own switch. Three faces, one circuit.

6.4 What This Misreads As

A cramped lifeguard gets called many things before anyone names her. Most of those names are not wrong, exactly. They describe the surface and miss the circuit underneath.

She gets called **anxiety**. Sometimes generalized anxiety. Sometimes panic. Sometimes social anxiety. The descriptions fit. She produces the racing thoughts, the chest tightness, the avoidance of crowds, the dread before phone calls. Anxiety treatments will sometimes help, especially the ones that target the autonomic nervous system rather than the cognition. But if no one looks at the trauma layer underneath,

[3]Clancy et al. (2017). PTSD-specific alpha suppression source-localized to cuneus, precuneus, and superior occipital gyrus; bidirectional alpha-band Granger causality deficits; correlation with hypervigilance severity.

anxiety becomes a permanent diagnosis instead of a circuit that can be retrained.

She gets called **PTSD**. If your trauma history is acknowledged and the symptoms are severe enough to meet criteria, this label is more accurate. It can also be heavy in a way that is not always useful. PTSD as a diagnosis often suggests one big event and a narrow set of symptoms organized around it. A cramped lifeguard is more often a developmental story, built up over years, with no single event you can point at and call the cause.

She gets called **insomnia**. The lifeguard does not sleep well, because the circuit whose job is to evaluate the room cannot let the room go unevaluated long enough for the brain to settle. People go to sleep doctors and get sleep hygiene advice and try melatonin and wonder why nothing works. The reason nothing works is that the sleep problem is not really a sleep problem.

She gets called **ADHD**. Whether the attention difficulty reflects a primary attention deficit or a scanning system running at high volume is a diagnostic question worth sorting out before treatment decisions are made. The distinction is covered in Chapter 9.

She gets called things by the people around her too. *She's so sensitive. He's a worrier. She overthinks everything. He's just high-strung.* Folk descriptions of a real circuit sit somewhere between insult and observation. What is actually happening is more useful to name. There is a circuit at the back of your brain whose job is to evaluate the world for threat, and your circuit is cramped. The labels above describe parts of what a cramped circuit produces. None of them describes the circuit.

6.5 What Helps

The first rule for a cramped Lifeguard is the one most often skipped: stabilize first.

Start by getting the alarm down: not by digging into the past, not on a meditation retreat, not by writing a trauma narrative, and not by lying on a table while someone presses on your psoas. You give the circuit some experience of safety so that she has somewhere to come down to.

If the alarm is at nine, you do not work on what set the alarm. You bring it to a four or a five. Then the rest is possible.

This is the rule most trauma treatment gets wrong, and it is one of the reasons the next chapter on safety exists. The lifeguard has to come down to a working volume before any of the deeper work has anywhere safe to land. Trauma processing on top of an alarm at nine usually sends the alarm to ten and keeps it there for weeks. The processing was not wrong; the circuit was not ready for it.

Here is what helps a cramped Lifeguard come down.

Resonance-frequency breathing. Pace your breath at about six breaths a minute, with the exhale slightly longer than the inhale. Five to ten minutes. The effect is on the autonomic nervous system, through the baroreflex and cardiac-vagal axis, and it shifts the balance toward parasympathetic tone in a way that is measurable on heart rate variability. You do not need a device. You can do it in your car. The effect is usually felt within the session and accumulates with daily practice.

Heart rate variability biofeedback. A more structured version of the same idea, with a sensor and a screen that shows you the rhythm in real time. Daily ten-minute sessions, sustained for several weeks, raise resting HRV, which is one of the most reliable autonomic markers of regulatory capacity. The lifeguard begins to operate from a less aroused baseline. You do not consciously decide this. The circuit settles.

Grounding practices. The simplest interventions, and they work surprisingly well when applied at the right moments. Orient your senses to the actual room you are in. Name five things you see, four you hear, three you can touch. Feel your feet on the floor. Feel the temperature of the air on your skin. These work because they speak the Lifeguard's own language. She is an outside-world processor. Direct her sensory channels at neutral data and you give her something to do that is not alarming. She does not have to fight you. She has to evaluate the chair, and the chair is not a tiger.

Body-based co-regulation. Slow walking with another nervous system. Sitting next to someone whose system is calmer than yours and letting your physiology entrain. Working with an animal. Nervous systems regulate through other nervous systems. The implementation matters: not every nervous system co-regulates well with yours. The right person, the right pet, the right pace.

Targeted neurofeedback. When the Lifeguard is the dominant pattern, the neurofeedback move is to train alpha rhythms over the posterior midline electrode sites and to support the brain's ability to modulate the default-mode network. Nicholson and colleagues ran a double-blind randomized controlled trial with forty PTSD patients and found that alpha-desynchronization neurofeedback produced a counterintuitive but important effect: after training, participants showed alpha resynchronization in exactly the regions that had been abnormally low at baseline. Sixty percent of the experimental group no longer met PTSD criteria at three-month follow-up, compared with thirty-three percent of the sham group; the between-group difference on the primary outcome did not reach statistical significance. The alpha rebound appears to reflect homeostatic plasticity, the brain's own capacity to recalibrate its gating rhythms when given the right feedback signal.[4] Your Lifeguard can learn to close the gate again. This is a clinical intervention and benefits from a provider who understands trauma populations and can explain why they are starting where they are starting. Not every neurofeedback provider does this well. Appendix B has the questions to ask.

EMDR, when the Lifeguard is regulated enough to use it. EMDR is one of the better-studied trauma processing modalities and is a first-line PTSD treatment in the VA/DoD clinical practice guidelines. EEG-during-EMDR work and neuroimaging comparisons converge on a

[4]Nicholson et al. (2023). Double-blind sham-controlled RCT (N=40); alpha-desynchronization neurofeedback in PTSD; alpha resynchronization at follow-up in experimental group; 60% experimental vs 33% sham no longer meeting PTSD criteria at three months; between-group CAPS difference not statistically significant.

picture of temporal-lobe engagement during processing, with activation shifts consistent with memory consolidation. The brain regions EMDR appears to engage are also accessible to certain neurofeedback protocols, sub-Hz training over temporal sites. The mechanistic overlap is not yet well-studied in controlled trials, but clinically the two modalities often do related work. Either can help a Lifeguard who has stabilized enough to use them. Neither is appropriate as a starting move for a Lifeguard at nine.

Somatic experiencing, with titration. Slow, careful work with body sensation, in very small doses, with a clinician trained in handling activation. The keyword is *titration*. You do not flood. You touch sensation, return to neutral, touch again, return again. A cramped lifeguard tolerates body work in this dose; she does not tolerate it in larger ones.

Now the negative list. What does not help, and often makes a cramped Lifeguard worse.

Long meditation retreats for someone who is not stabilized. Silent days are not safe for a Lifeguard at high volume. The circuit has nothing to do during the silence and turns inward, where it finds the rumination material, and the retreat becomes a multi-day flooding event. The literature on adverse effects of intensive meditation supports this, and Lifeguard presentations are among the more commonly reported populations in the adverse-effects case literature.

Body scans in dysregulated nervous systems. The instruction to attend to body sensation in detail can produce flooding for someone whose body is full of trauma cues. Body scans are dangerous in the wrong sequence. After stabilization is in place, they are useful. Before, they often are not.

Memory excavation. Asking a cramped Lifeguard to retrieve more trauma memory is asking the circuit to feed itself the data that cramped her in the first place. There are clinical situations where memory work matters, and in those situations it should be done with appropriate sequencing and clinician support. On your own, or in a setting that does not include the stabilization frame, it is one of the most reliable ways to make a Lifeguard worse.

Alpha-theta neurofeedback before stabilization. Alpha-theta is a deep-state protocol that, in the right sequence, can support memory integration and trauma resolution. In the wrong sequence, it can flood an unstable nervous system with material the system was protectively suppressing. Alpha-theta belongs later in the arc. Chapter 18 covers the sequencing in detail.

Prazosin for nightmares, with a caveat. Prazosin blocks norepinephrine receptors and seemed, for a time, like the answer to trauma-driven nightmares. Early trials were striking: combat veterans sleeping through the night for the first time in years. Then the VA ran a large confirmatory trial with 304 veterans, and it failed its primary endpoints. Prazosin still helps some people, and some clinicians prescribe it off-label with good results. The clean story of "block the norepinephrine, stop the nightmares" turned out more complicated than the early data suggested. It belongs on the list of things that might help rather than the list of things that reliably do.

The general shape: regulation first, integration second. The ratio matters more than any specific technique. Months of regulation, then careful integration, then more regulation, then more integration. You do not have to choose perfectly between modalities. You have to keep the sequence right.

6.6 The Cost Asymmetry, Named Once

Bar-Haim and colleagues confirmed this in a meta-analysis of nearly 180 studies: across every anxiety-related condition they measured, PTSD included, people showed a reliable attentional bias toward threat that non-anxious people did not. The bias is measurable in milliseconds. It is automatic.[5] Your Lifeguard is not choosing to look for threats. Her attention is being pulled there before choice is involved.

[5] Bar-Haim et al. (2007). Meta-analysis of nearly 180 studies on attentional bias to threat in anxiety-related conditions, PTSD included.

The problem is the priors. When her prior expectation of how often threats appear is set too high, she runs the math against a world that is not actually full of tigers, and the cost of her over-allocation falls on you.

She does not know that. She is doing what the data taught her to do.

6.7 When This Is Beyond Self-Help

If any of these apply, the next step is clinical support, not this book. For crisis resources, see the Introduction.

- You are losing time regularly or noticing others describing behavior you don't remember: this is a dissociation question that needs a clinician trained in dissociative disorders.
- Your sleep deprivation has crossed into perceptual disturbance or is affecting basic safety (driving, cooking): medical attention, not self-help.
- Rumination is touching suicidal ideation or anything resembling a plan: stop and get support now. The circuit can wait.
- There is active danger in your home environment: a cramped Lifeguard is reading the data accurately. The work begins after the situation changes, not before.

These are moments when the framework hands off to something else.

See Half a Second More (Ch.7) for the Lifeguard practice path; Borrowed Peace for borrowed-regulation patterns paired with this phenotype.

6.8 Coming Back to the Pool

There is a lifeguard in a chair at the edge of an indoor pool. She is wearing a red suit. She has a whistle around her neck. The pool is quiet. The pool is small. The water is treated. There are no sharks in the water. There have never been sharks in the water. The pool is in a building. The building is in a city. The city has weather and traffic and ordinary life happening around it. None of this contains a shark.

Your Lifeguard does not know that. She was trained somewhere else, in water that did contain something. She brought what she learned in that water to the chair at the edge of this pool, and she has been scanning ever since.

She scans because that is the job she was given.

What changes her is new data, given slowly, over time. You teach her that the pool is mostly safe by being in the pool, again and again, while keeping her supplied with what she needs to come down: rest, breath, the right people next to you, sometimes the right clinician, sometimes the right neurofeedback session. She does not stop being a Lifeguard. She becomes a Lifeguard who can sit in her chair without spending every moment of every shift looking for sharks in the indoor pool.

She still notices the kid who has been under too long and needs a check. She still reads the room. She still sees the changes nobody else saw. Those capacities do not go anywhere. They were always part of the same circuit.

She walked back into the same party six months later. The eyes still scanned. The scan was shorter. She found someone she knew near the kitchen and stood with him. Her shoulders dropped about an inch in the first ten minutes. Nobody else in the room could see that, including her, but I had been watching her nervous system for half a year and I could tell you the inch was real.

She told me later she had no idea what had changed. She said it had stopped feeling like she was at work when she was at a party. She said she had started enjoying her friends again. She said her sleep had come back. She said she still scanned the room when she walked in, and she added, with a small surprised laugh, that she thought she always would.

I told her she probably would. I told her that was fine. The circuit was doing its job. The volume had come down to where she could live in front of it instead of behind it. That was the work we had been doing, and she had done most of it.

She nodded. She picked up her bag. She walked out of the office. Her eyes did the door on the way out. The scan was a beat. Then she was gone.

Ch 7: The CEO Under Threat

It is 9:47 on a Sunday night. You are in bed. The light is off. You have a presentation in the morning. You should be asleep. Instead you are running, for the fourth time today, the same sixteen-second moment from Friday afternoon when your boss said the thing she said and you nodded the wrong way.

You replay it in her voice. You replay it in your voice. You try out the response you should have given. You try out a second response. You wonder if the first response would have made things worse. You re-litigate whether the original comment was even about you. You decide it probably was. You decide it probably was not. The light is still off. The presentation is still in the morning.

Or it is the song. You woke up with one chorus, sixteen seconds long, and it has been on a loop since 7:14 a.m. You did dishes to it. You walked the dog to it. You were on a phone call where you missed two whole sentences because the chorus came back and you could not push it out. You have not chosen to think about this song at any point in the last fourteen hours. It is just there, on a track underneath everything else, and you cannot find the off button.

Stuck on the wrong thing. That is the signature.

7.1 The Gift

The gift is what the cramped version distorts, and the gift is large.

The CEO is the circuit that makes long-term work possible. A book that takes three years, the training program that takes five, the marriage that survives a hard decade, the career arc that takes twenty. None of those is possible without a circuit that can hold a priority in working memory for months at a time, check it against incoming information, register when something is off, and update the plan. That is the CEO when he is working: holding the goal, tracking the gap between what you expected and what is happening, flagging errors, arbitrating conflict between competing demands, keeping the project alive across the months it takes to finish.

When the CEO is regulated, you do not notice him. You move from task to task. You finish things and forget about them. You let go of the comment from Friday because there is no actual conflict left to resolve. He has done his job and released the priority.

A high-functioning CEO is also the colleague who catches the typo in the contract that would have cost the firm half a million dollars. A high-functioning CEO is also the friend who notices when something is off in someone else's marriage and asks the right question. A high-functioning CEO is the one people count on. The cost of a stuck version is real, which is why the next section covers that cost; the Gift section covers the same circuit when it has room to breathe.

In the clinic I sometimes see Performers misread as people with character problems, when what they actually have is a CEO running survival-grade error-monitoring on a life that does not need that level of scrutiny anymore. The labels that get applied (OCD, generalized anxiety, perfectionism, type A, workaholic, overcontrolled) are accurate descriptions of the surface. They miss the circuit. Lynch (2018) gives the broader pattern a useful clinical name: overcontrol. Standard DBT was built for the opposite end, undercontrol, the impulsive emotionally flooded presentation most people picture when they hear the word trauma. The CEO is the overcontrolled end. The treatments are different, which is why the misread matters.

7.2 Where the CEO Lives

The CEO lives at the front midline of your brain. The anatomy most closely associated with his circuit is the anterior cingulate cortex, another large midline cortical sheet. A frontal-midline scalp pattern supports a coarse hypothesis about its involvement, though adjacent midline sources are hard to separate cleanly. On a QEEG report I read his pattern most clearly at Fz and FCz, just behind your forehead. The ACC has rich connections to the prefrontal cortex above it, to the limbic system below it, and to the posterior cingulate at the back, where the Lifeguard's post is.

I find it useful to think of the two midline circuits as a pair. The lifeguard at the back is asking what is happening out there. The CEO at the front is asking what am I doing, and is it the right thing. Both circuits can get loud. They get loud about different things, in different rhythms, and they need different work. A reader who walks into my clinic with a stuck CEO often also has a cramped Lifeguard, because the two systems were shaped by the same conditions and they learned the same lesson from those conditions, which is that letting go was not safe.

The ACC has a few well-described jobs. He monitors for conflict between competing responses. He tracks the gap between what you expected and what actually happened, which is one of the brain's main learning signals. He flags errors. He helps switch attention from one thing to the next. And he holds the current goal in a way that lets the rest of your cognition organize around it.

There are two flavors of stuck, and they look different on a brain map and they feel different from the inside.

The first flavor is theta-stuck. Theta is the slow rhythm that the front midline settles into when systems are working on simple recurring patterns. A theta-stuck CEO produces the simple loops: songs in your head, counting tics, tapping, repeating the same short sentence in your mind. The Obsessive-Compulsive Disorder signature is often theta-stuck at the front midline. The loops are short, rhythmic, and self-sustaining, often the same five seconds on repeat, the same six steps to the kitchen counted, the same prayer or phrase in cycles.

The second flavor is beta-stuck. Beta is the faster rhythm that fronts of brains use when they are doing effortful cognitive work. A beta-stuck CEO produces the elaborated loops. The seven possible interpretations of what your boss meant. The "what if" cascades that build whole hypothetical futures from one ambiguous comment. The intrusive narrative scenarios that play out in detail and then play again with slightly different parameters. The replays of yesterday's conversation, edited each time. Where the Lifeguard ruminates by checking the past for missed tigers, the CEO ruminates by trying to resolve unresolved goals. On a QEEG the beta-stuck CEO often shows elevated high-beta at frontal sites, the electrical signature of a system running effortful cognitive processing at a volume it was never meant to sustain.

Some people run mostly theta-stuck loops, some mostly beta-stuck, and many run both. The two patterns travel together more often than not, and what helps is similar in both cases.

7.3 What Trauma Does

Trauma teaches the CEO that the cost of letting a thing go before it is fully resolved is too high. So he does what the data taught him to do. He does not release. He holds the priority because the priority might not really be done, and if it is not done and you let it go, something bad might happen.

The bad thing was sometimes real. A child whose parent's mood determined whether the night would be safe learns to monitor the parent's mood with the precision of a CEO who never leaves the desk. A child who had to anticipate violence learns to play out scenarios in advance. A child who was punished for missing a detail learns that no detail is too small to track. The CEO who emerged from these conditions is a CEO who learned that error monitoring was survival.

You can take the child out of the conditions. The CEO does not always come with you.

This is where the Performer shows up. A Performer is a CEO who learned that the way to stay safe was to be high-functioning. To get the assignment done early. To never miss a deadline. To always be the one in the meeting who has read the document. To send the thoughtful follow-up email. To remember the friend's birthday. To never let anyone see the cost of all this remembering.

A Performer CEO does not look stuck from the outside. He looks impressive. He looks together. He looks like the person other people use as a comparison point for what is possible. Part of how the cost stays hidden is body dissociation. Bertsch and colleagues (2024) found that disconnection from bodily signals mediated more than sixty percent of the link between childhood trauma and impaired personality functioning, a finding that held across diagnostic groups from PTSD to depression to healthy controls. The performer runs on that mechanism. She overrides the body's signals that something is wrong because they would slow her down, and slowing down was never safe.

I see the cost in the clinic at three in the morning, in the patient's report from the night before. The loop runs and the body does not get to rest. I see it in the inability to let any task be unfinished, which means a real day off is not actually possible because there is always something unfinished. I see it in the relationship pattern, where the Performer cannot tolerate her partner's small mistakes because the CEO has learned that mistakes have consequences and cannot turn that learning off.

A trauma-driven CEO is not the same as someone with simply high standards. The marker is that the priority cannot be released. The work being done well is not enough; it has to keep being checked, monitored, defended against the possibility that it was not actually done well. The internal experience is not pride. The internal experience is brief relief followed by the next thing that has to be tracked.

The performer is the most clinically dangerous version precisely because the circuit that produces the cost is also the circuit that gets praised. The boss promotes the Performer. The performer's friends rely on her. The performer's family is held together by her invisible labor. There is rarely an external reason to slow down, and often a great deal of external pressure to speed up. The cost is not only emotional. Longitudinal data from the MIDUS study, tracking 2,471 adults across nine years, showed that lifetime trauma exposure predicted steeper declines in executive functioning and episodic memory over time (Lynch & Lachman, 2020). I see this arc in my clinic in the high-functioning CEO who arrives in her mid-forties, decades of invisible management behind her, now finding that she cannot do what she did at thirty-five without twice the effort. The high-functioning surface today may be paying a cognitive bill that will not arrive for years. The collapse, when it comes, often arrives later than it should, because the Performer was so good at hiding that anything was wrong.

The same circuit, in someone whose life has not given them the same resources, may show up less polished. As obsessive-compulsive symptoms. As severe anxiety. As religious scrupulosity. As compulsive checking. The presentation differs by person and context, but the underlying anatomy tracks the same anterior cingulate signature: the error-detection circuit running at the wrong volume for the current conditions.

The most clinically dangerous variation I see is when a stuck CEO produces depression-like symptoms and gets treated as primary depression. A CEO running at high volume for years, with the loops constantly underneath the surface, eventually exhausts the circuit. The exhaustion looks like depression, and the loops look like rumination. Standard antidepressant treatment may help with some of the secondary symptoms but does not address the underlying circuit pattern. The patient feels better for a while, then worse, then is told the medication has stopped working. The medication did its job on the secondary symptoms; the CEO is still stuck.

Here is the clinical picture this often produces: she is high-functioning, produces on deadline, and runs organizations while managing other people's crises alongside her own, and she is also exhausted in a particular way that she cannot explain to the people around her, because from the outside she looks fine. When she describes it, the description is always some version of, "I cannot turn it off." It is always running somewhere in the background, even when she is at a dinner she chose to attend, even when she is reading a book she likes, even when she is in bed trying to sleep. The first patient I worked with who really crystallized this for me described it as living in an open browser with too many tabs. Not metaphorically. As an exact account of how the inside felt: tabs she did not open, audio playing from one she could not find, the fan running.

That is an exact description of a theta-stuck loop pattern in the anterior cingulate: a CEO who learned that the cost of letting go was too high, in a context that no longer existed, running a monitoring program that had never received the memo that the original threat was past.

7.4 What Helps

Before the CEO can loosen any loop, the alarm underneath it has to come down. Regulation before integration. A CEO is hard to retrain when the underlying nervous system is at high arousal, because the arousal feeds the stuck. Chapter 15 covers the sequencing principle.

Once there is some baseline regulation, the CEO has his own tools.

Loop labeling. This is a deceptively simple practice that targets the mechanism directly. When you notice a loop running, you name it. Not "I am ruminating again," which is just another loop. The label is shorter and more functional: *theta loop*, or *ACC loop*, or just *the song again*. The act of naming the loop appears to engage prefrontal regions that can release it in a way that fighting it cannot. You do not stop the song. You name the song. The loop often releases on its own once you have named it, because the ACC gets the signal that the loop has been recognized as a loop. Try this for the next loop you catch. Three words. Out loud if you can. Then return to whatever you were doing without arguing with the loop.

Open-monitoring meditation. This is a meditation style that suits a stuck CEO better than focused-attention meditation does. Focused attention asks the CEO to hold one object, the breath or a mantra, and to return whenever the mind wanders. For a stuck CEO, that is just more priority-holding. Open monitoring asks the practitioner to allow whatever arises to arise, notice it, and let it pass, without holding any single object. This appears to engage a different mode of frontal regulation that can loosen the CEO's grip on his current contents. Open monitoring is not appropriate for everyone. The adverse-effects literature on intensive meditation, documented by Lindahl and Britton and colleagues (2017), makes clear that trauma populations need careful screening and sequencing before intensive practice. For a cramped

Lifeguard with a lot of trauma activation, open monitoring can flood. For a regulated CEO, it is often the meditation style that helps.

N-acetylcysteine. NAC is a glutamatergic-modulating amino acid supplement that has shown reasonable evidence in controlled trials for OCD-spectrum conditions including trichotillomania and skin-picking. The proposed mechanism involves glutamate balance in cortico-striatal-thalamic loops that include the ACC. This is one of the few supplements with controlled-trial evidence for stuck-loop conditions, and it is generally well-tolerated. Dosing should come from a clinician who has reviewed the current literature rather than from a consumer book; the evidence base has been evolving and the conversation with a prescriber is worth having. It is not a substitute for clinical care, but for some people it is one of the more useful adjuncts to it.

Targeted neurofeedback. A QEEG-guided neurofeedback approach for a stuck CEO usually involves working at frontal midline sites, with the protocol depending on whether the dominant pattern is theta-stuck or beta-stuck. Theta-stuck patterns often respond to protocols that decrease frontal midline theta and support flexible engagement. Beta-stuck patterns sometimes respond to calming work at the rostral ACC, or to alpha-enhancement protocols that support the CEO's ability to come off the priority. This is clinical work and benefits from a provider who can explain why they are starting where they are starting and what they expect to see.

Strategic external offloading. The performer CEO often runs loops because she is holding more priorities than working memory can manage. Externalizing the priorities, on paper, in a list, in a calendar with explicit reminders, can take some of the load off the circuit. This is not a cognitive trick. When the CEO can trust that a priority will not be lost if she releases the active hold on it, the active hold becomes easier to release. The corollary matters: if you are already a Performer, do not adopt a more sophisticated productivity app on top of the one you have. The new app becomes another priority to track. What you need is a tool that lets you release things, not one that helps you hold more.

Sleep, like everywhere. A stuck CEO without adequate sleep is harder to retrain than a stuck CEO with sleep. The basic regulation rests on a foundation of decent sleep. If the loops are keeping you up, the loops have to come down before sleep can come up, which means the tools above all become foundational. There is a chicken-and-egg situation here that has to be solved by working on both ends at once.

Radically Open DBT. Lynch's modality was built specifically for overcontrol (Lynch, 2018). Where standard DBT teaches distress tolerance and emotion regulation for undercontrolled presentations, RO-DBT targets the rigidity and suppressed emotional signaling that keep an overcontrolled CEO locked in position. The core move is learning to tolerate being seen, to let some of the control go without the CEO reading that as catastrophe. For a Performer who has spent years making sure no one sees the cost, this is often the intervention she resists most.

A few things to avoid.

Trying to stop thinking the thought. This is the most common reflexive response and the least effective one. Suppression of an active loop usually amplifies it. The classic experiment of trying not to think of a white bear is the actual mechanism. The CEO's loops are susceptible to suppression backfire because the suppression instruction is itself a held priority that the CEO then has to monitor.

Self-criticism as a motivator. The CEO is already running an error-monitoring loop. Adding more on top of it (calling yourself a procrastinator, beating yourself up for the rumination, blaming yourself for the song) only feeds the circuit that produces the loops in the first place. The performer in particular tends to use self-criticism as a productivity tool, and the productivity tool is also the trauma-amplification tool.

7.5 When This Is Beyond Self-Help

If any of these apply, the next step is clinical support, not this book. For crisis resources, see the Introduction.

- Intrusive thoughts of harming yourself or others: these are OCD-spectrum presentations with their own evidence base.

The loop is the CEO on the wrong thing, not a character reading. Specialist clinician involvement helps.
- Performer pattern has crossed into physical breakdown (chronic insomnia, autoimmune flare, fatigue that does not resolve): medical evaluation. The trauma framework still applies; it does not apply alone.
- Loops touching suicidal ideation or planning of any kind: the CEO is not a reliable assessor of its own life's value when stuck. Stop and get support now.

These are moments when the framework hands off to something else.

See Gifted & Tortured (Ch.5) for the CEO baseline-temperament version; Half a Second More (Ch.7) for the practice path.

7.6 Releasing the Priority

A stuck CEO does not retire when she reads a chapter about herself. The performer who has been on duty for thirty years does not stop running her quiet daily audit of who needs what, what is unfinished, where the next failure could come from. What changes is the volume, the cost, and whether, six months from now, you get a real Sunday afternoon where the loops are quiet enough that you can sit on the couch with a book and not be doing anything, not be planning the next thing, not be replaying the last conversation, and just be in the chair with the book and no priority active.

I had a patient finish a year of work with me on a stuck CEO. She came in at the end of the year for what we both knew would be one of the last sessions. I asked her what was different. She thought about it. She said:

"I closed the tabs. I did not even know I was the one who had to close them."

The afternoon she described, sitting on the couch with the book, the quiet behind her eyes, the sense that nothing was running underneath, came a few weeks later, unremarkable, and that unremarkableness was the proof.

Ch 8: The Princess and the Pea

You walk into the kitchen and your partner says hi. You hear something in the way he said it. You do not know what. You only know that you heard it. By the time you have answered, you have already cycled through five interpretations of one syllable. Maybe he is annoyed. Maybe he is tired. Maybe he is hiding something. Maybe nothing.

You sit through a meeting where someone says your idea is interesting. You spend two hours afterward trying to figure out whether *interesting* meant interesting or whether it meant the polite thing people say when they think the idea is bad. Nobody else in the meeting seems to be running this calculation. You cannot tell whether they are not running it because there is nothing to calculate, or because they cannot read what you can.

You go to the grocery store on a Sunday. The fluorescents have a frequency you can feel. The music is too loud. A shopping cart squeaks. The person behind you in line is wearing a perfume you can taste. By the time you reach the car you are flattened, in a way that someone who does not live in your nervous system would not believe is possible from an errand. You sit in the driver's seat for ten minutes before you can drive.

That is the phenotype.

The fairy tale is older than the diagnosis and is a better entry point. The princess sleeps on twenty mattresses with a single pea under the bottom one. She does not know there is a pea. She just knows she did not sleep. The pea is real. Her capacity to feel it is what the story is about. Walk through your life with that image in mind and a great deal of what has been called *too sensitive* starts to make sense.

The princess is not a personality. She is a circuit. Her post is at the right temporoparietal junction, at the back-and-right of your brain, and her job is high-resolution social and sensory processing. She reads micro-expressions, hears micro-shifts in tone, catches the half-second pause before someone answers a question. She picks up that the room got colder, that the air pressure changed, that the energy between two people shifted in the last thirty seconds. These are not imagined. Other brains are processing the same signals at lower resolution. Your Princess processes them at higher resolution. Her gain is turned up.

When she is well-regulated, the gain is a gift. You read rooms accurately. You know what people need before they ask. You hear the song under the song in a conversation. You write the friend the right message on the right day because you knew, somehow, that today was the day.

When she is cramped, the gain is a problem. Every facial twitch gets appraised. Every shift in tone is a possible meaning. Every sensory overload day adds to a baseline you cannot reset. Rejection lands as annihilation rather than as feedback, because the Princess is processing the social cue at the same intensity she would process a literal threat to your body.

This chapter is about that circuit. What trauma did to yours. What helps when the gain has been paired with constant alarm for too long. The room with the right lamp is one piece. There are several more.

8.1 Where the Princess Lives

Her circuit runs through the right temporoparietal junction, abbreviated rTPJ. On a brain map I read her pattern near the electrode sites P4, T6, and TP8. She sits at the convergence of the temporal lobes (which handle sound and language and emotional meaning), the parietal lobes (which handle spatial attention and the sense of where your body is in space), and the higher visual areas (which handle face and motion). She is the meeting place of these systems on the right side, and her question is: *what does this person mean? what does this room contain? where do I end and the other person begin?*

Like the Lifeguard, she is a back-of-brain system, an outside-world processor. She is not scanning for tigers. She is scanning for meaning. Well-calibrated, she gives you accurate readings of other people and of the spaces you walk into, with an effort cost low enough that you do not notice the work.

Several specific functions live here. Theory of mind, the capacity to represent what another person is thinking, was localized to rTPJ by Saxe and Kanwisher in 2003. Embodied perspective-taking, the capacity to imagine yourself in another's position with felt sense rather than just cognitively, was shown to depend causally on rTPJ in a 2020 study by Martin and colleagues that combined fMRI with transient transcranial magnetic stimulation of the region: when they disrupted it, people made more errors on tasks that required mentally inhabiting another viewpoint.[1] Self-other distinction was elaborated by Decety and Lamm in 2007. They reviewed how rTPJ hypoactivation produces excessive mirroring, the kind that blurs the line between your own agency and someone else's intentions. What this looks like in the clinic is the client who cannot enter a difficult conversation without absorbing the other person's distress as if it were her own, and who leaves the meeting not quite sure whose feeling she has been carrying.

Early trauma changes this system directly. Cracco and colleagues in 2020 found that early interpersonal trauma predicted reduced rTPJ activation during spontaneous mentalizing tasks, with the reduction correlating with dissociation scores. The more severe the early history, the more blunted the automatic social-reading system became. Stimulation of the same region in neurosurgical patients can reproduce out-of-body experiences (Blanke and Arzy, 2005). The boundary between self and not-self lives, in part, here. When the boundary is intact, you know where you end. When the Princess is reading every micro-cue and routing it through your own emotional system without filter, the boundary blurs. You start feeling the other person's mood as if it were your mood. You experience rejection as if it had happened to your body.

---

[1] Saxe and Kanwisher (2003); Martin and colleagues (2020); Decety and Lamm (2007); Cracco and colleagues (2020); Blanke and Arzy (2005); Aron and Aron (1997); Greven and colleagues (2019); Paulus and Stein (2010); Aron and colleagues (2012); Garfinkel and colleagues (2015); Khalsa and colleagues (2018); Price and Hooven (2018); Mehling and colleagues (2012).

A well-regulated Princess gives you exquisite social information at low cost. A cramped Princess gives you the same information at a cost that flattens you by the end of the day.

The 1.5x framing is useful. Most people experience the social and sensory world at 1x volume. A princess phenotype experiences it at something like 1.5x. The number names the difference rather than measuring it, and there is a real trait underneath. The literature on sensory processing sensitivity (SPS) describes a real, partially heritable pattern of heightened central nervous system responsiveness to physical, social, and emotional stimuli, characterized by deeper processing and easier overstimulation. Aron and Aron first described the trait in 1997; Greven and colleagues in 2019 reviewed the broader environmental-sensitivity literature and noted that SPS-like patterns appear evolutionarily conserved across many species. The population estimate (15 to 20 percent) should be held lightly. The general finding that a meaningful minority of people process at higher gain is well-supported.

The 1.5x is a phenotype. Some Princesses are simply built with the higher gain, and they have arranged their lives around it: no open offices, no loud restaurants, a small deep friend group, a rich inner life. The non-traumatized Princess often becomes the person who reads everyone in the room with a precision the room does not realize it is being read by.

The traumatized Princess is something different. The gain is the same. The context is not.

8.2 What Trauma Does to a Princess

Trauma teaches the Princess that the high-resolution data she is picking up is dangerous. The micro-expression on the parent's face used to predict the next several hours. The shift in the partner's tone used to predict whether the night was going to be safe. The way the room got quiet used to predict that something was about to be wrong. So she learned that her capacity to read these signals was survival, not just a useful skill.

Once that learning is in, scanning locks in. Every social and sensory micro-cue gets processed for threat potential alongside meaning. The same circuit that, in a non-traumatized Princess, produces high-resolution empathy produces, in a traumatized Princess, high-resolution threat detection. You read the room at 1.5x and you read the room as dangerous.

A few specific patterns show up. They are the same circuit doing the same job in different states.

Rejection lands as annihilation. This is the rejection-sensitivity-dysphoria pattern, and it is one of the more reliable signatures of a cramped Princess. A friend takes a day to text back, and your body responds as if she has ended the friendship. A mild critique from a coworker lands as if you have been told you should not be in this job, in this field, in this life. You can usually see, in the moment, that the reaction is bigger than the cue. The seeing does not make the reaction smaller. The princess is processing the social cue at the intensity of a literal threat to the body, because the data she was trained on taught her that social cues *were* body threats.

Sensory overload hits earlier and lasts longer. Lights, sounds, crowds, and smells all hit earlier and harder than they do for most people. Particular sounds (chewing, breathing, repetitive clicking) can produce a body-level alarm that seems disproportionate to the trigger. Part of why this happens is interoceptive. Paulus and Stein in 2010 described an anticipatory-insula model in which the anterior insula, the brain region that maps body states into conscious feeling, becomes hyperactive after trauma. It begins overweighting body signals under threat, predicting that bad sensations are coming before they arrive. Your heart rate ticks up in the grocery store and the insula reads it as confirmation that something is wrong, which sends arousal higher, which generates more body signal, which the insula reads again. The loop is fast and largely automatic. The result is the "everything is too much" experience that flattens you by the time you reach the car. The flattening is real, and it is a prediction engine running hot in a body that learned prediction was survival.

Emotional contagion flattens you in a different way. You spend a day with someone in a bad mood and carry their mood for the rest of the week, after they have moved on. You sit with a friend in crisis and feel her grief in your own body, in a way that does not abate when you go home. Every face in a long day of meetings is rich data, and rich data is expensive; some Princesses describe a particular exhaustion from high-face-count days that other people do not seem to feel. The boundary between your emotional experience and other people's is permeable, and the trauma history has made the permeable boundary more permeable. You are not codependent. You are a Princess whose self-other distinction circuit is doing its job under conditions that overload it.

The body itself becomes unreliable. This is a quieter version of the problem and easy to miss. The problem is not feeling too much from the outside world; you cannot trust what your own body is telling you. Garfinkel and colleagues in 2015 proposed a three-dimensional model of interoception that makes this precise. They distinguish interoceptive accuracy (how well you actually detect body signals, measured by tasks like counting your own heartbeat), interoceptive sensibility (how much you *believe* you feel your body), and interoceptive awareness (the metacognitive match between the two). In a well-calibrated system the three align. In a trauma-shaped system they split. The princess pattern often looks like high sensibility with low accuracy. You feel overwhelmed by body sensation. You are certain your body is telling you something urgent. When tested objectively, your detection of actual signals is no better, and sometimes worse, than average. The alarm is loud. The signal underneath is unclear. This mismatch, feeling too much while reading too little accurately, is one of the reasons the Princess can feel simultaneously hyperaware and confused about what is actually happening in her own body.

Khalsa and colleagues in 2018 distinguish between people who get too much body signal (the flooding pattern) and people who get too little (the numb, disconnected-from-body pattern). The princess can present either way depending on where she is sitting in the trauma-response cycle. During hyperarousal she is flooded. During dissociation she is absent. Both are disruptions of the same system.

You may recognize one of these. You may recognize several. The princess who has been traumatized is processing at the volume she was built for, in a world her training taught her was not safe.

On a brain map, a cramped Princess does not produce a single reliable signature. The EEG and imaging literature on trauma consistently shows that individual patterns vary considerably. What the research does show is that early maltreatment is associated with structural and functional changes at right temporal-parietal sites, including reduced activation during social-processing tasks (Cracco and colleagues, 2020). Aron and colleagues in 2012 describe amplified limbic and insula activation in high-SPS individuals during emotional face processing, consistent with the clinical picture of high gain. The combination of high posterior alpha variability, elevated right temporal engagement with affective stimuli, and salience-network responsiveness is clinically recognizable, even if it is not reducible to a single topographic signature.

8.3 What This Misreads As

A cramped Princess is often misread because the surface features that are most visible map onto other clinical categories. Social anxiety, borderline personality disorder, autism spectrum, highly sensitive person in the popular sense: each of these labels describes something real at the surface and misses the circuit underneath. The most clinically consequential misread is borderline personality disorder, because the intensity, the rejection sensitivity, the all-or-nothing relational quality, and the rapid emotional shifts can look like BPD on the surface, and the label tends to stick once applied in ways that color all subsequent treatment. Some people who carry a BPD diagnosis have a Princess phenotype with significant trauma history. Sorting it out matters because the treatments are different.

The most common non-clinical misread is character. *You're just too sensitive.* This advice is unfollowable in any practical sense, because the gain is not under conscious control. Telling a Princess to be less sensitive is like telling someone with excellent hearing to hear less. What changes is not the gain. What changes is the gating and the threat appraisal that sit downstream of the gain, and changing those takes real work.

8.4 The Gift

In the clinic, I watch princesses do things that most nervous systems cannot do: the gain is there, and they have learned how to use it.

The simplest version of the gift is affective empathy. Not the cognitive kind, which most people have to some degree. The kind where, sitting next to a friend who is grieving, you feel some shape of her grief in your own chest, without effort, and you stay there with her, and she knows. A stabilized Princess is often the person the room turns to in a crisis: the parent whose kid feels known, the colleague who notices the team member who is about to quit and has the conversation that keeps her.

The high-resolution sensory processing that overwhelms her in a grocery store does something else when she is rested and the environment matches her. She notices the way the light hits the corner of the room. She notices the wrong note in a piece of music half a beat before anyone else does. She notices the texture of a fabric, the silence in a room before someone says something true. A great many of the people I have worked with who write, design, compose, or direct are Princesses. The cost is real and so is what comes out the other side.

Then there is the social-discernment piece. A stabilized Princess reads micro-cues that most nervous systems do not register, and with enough regulation the readings become more useful and less catastrophic. The cue is real, and the reader's experience is real. Its meaning may be accurate, exaggerated, or wrong, so the reading remains a hypothesis to check rather than a verdict. In the clinic she is often the patient who, after some recovery, comes back and tells me her last several decisions were better than any she made in the previous decade. The reading was always there. It is finally being tested against the world rather than running the world.

She also tends to be the person other people unconsciously consult about environments. She arranges a room and people sit longer in it. She picks the restaurant and the conversation is easier. She walks into a friend's home and suggests moving the lamp, and the room works. None of this is decorative talent in the magazine sense. It is environmental sensitivity, which becomes useful when you can use it without being mauled by it.

The gain did not come from the trauma. The gain was already there. What the trauma did was pair the gain with a threat-detection prior that flattened the use of the gift. Address the trauma layer and the gift remains. The princess does not become someone else. She becomes a Princess who can use what she has.

8.5 What Helps

The high-gain system needs a quieter environment before it can recalibrate. That is sequencing. So the autonomic work (breath, HRV, sleep, basic regulation) comes first, and the sensory environment is part of that foundation. Chapter 15 covers the sequencing principle.

The princess has her own particular set of moves.

Sensory environment design. Start here, tonight. Pick one room. Replace anything that flickers at sixty hertz with something that does not. Turn off the overhead. Put one lamp at a low angle. Sit for fifteen minutes and notice what your shoulders do. Most of what helps a Princess starts with the room around her. It requires nothing more sophisticated than taking the gain seriously. You arrange your life around the fact that your nervous system processes at 1.5x. You do not work in open offices if you can avoid them. You wear noise-canceling headphones in environments you cannot control. You schedule recovery time after social events instead of treating recovery time as a weakness. You light your home with bulbs that do not flicker at sixty hertz. You build a life in which the sensory world does not constantly outrun your capacity to process it. Call this calibration. A princess who has built the right sensory environment can usually access *more* of the world because she is not flattened by the parts of it she chose not to subject herself to unnecessarily.

Loving-kindness and self-compassion practice. These specific meditation styles tend to help cramped Princess patterns more than focused-attention meditation does. Clinically, I have watched Princesses do poorly with breath-focused concentration when the nervous system is already running hot (the inward focus can amplify interoceptive alarm) and do better with loving-kindness and open-awareness styles that include an outward relational dimension. The evidence base for loving-kindness in anxiety and trauma-adjacent populations is decent.

Interoceptive rehabilitation. If the Garfinkel split applies to you (high sensibility, low accuracy; loud alarm, unclear signal), targeted body-awareness work can recalibrate the system. Price and Hooven in 2018 described Mindful Awareness in Body-Oriented Therapy (MABT), which titrates interoceptive exposure. You practice noticing body sensations in small, supported doses rather than being thrown into the full flood. The approach builds what clinicians call "body listening" and "body trust," measured on the MAIA (Multidimensional Assessment of Interoceptive Awareness; Mehling and colleagues, 2012). The key insight of MABT is the body-awareness paradox: trauma survivors benefit from reconnecting with body signals for regulation, but unstructured body-focus risks flooding or dissociation when sensations map onto trauma memory. The titration is what makes it different from generic mindfulness. You go slowly, with a trained guide, and you stop when the window of tolerance narrows. For the Princess who is overwhelmed by sensation but cannot tell what the sensation actually means, this is often the missing piece between stabilization and recovery.

Targeted neurofeedback. When the Princess is the dominant pattern, the neurofeedback move usually involves working at right posterior sites, with protocols aimed at supporting alpha rhythms in the right TPJ region and reducing over-activation of the right-temporal-salience cluster. The exact protocol depends on what the QEEG actually shows for the individual. The map contributes to protocol selection alongside the clinical picture; whether it improves outcomes over competent symptom-guided selection remains an open question.

Boundary practices that respect the gain. Standard boundary-setting advice often assumes you can decide to be less affected by other people's emotional states. This is not how a Princess works. Boundary practice for a Princess is more about timing and sequencing than willpower. You spend a focused day with the friend in crisis, then you spend the evening alone. You take the work call, then you do not take the next one. You go to the wedding, then you do not go to brunch the next morning. The boundary works as a rhythm. A princess can do enormous amounts of high-empathy work if she is allowed to recover between bouts.

Rejection-sensitivity protocols. When the rejection-sensitivity pattern is severe, there are specific tools. The first is the time delay: when something has landed as annihilation rather than feedback, do not respond from the annihilation. Wait. The reactivity tends to come down within hours if you do not feed it by acting on it. The second is the reality-check, with a person whose appraisal you trust: *did this comment mean what my body is reading it as meaning, or am I reading something in?* The third is medication, in some cases. When the arousal component of severe rejection sensitivity is disabling, a prescriber may consider pharmacological options. Clonidine and guanfacine, the alpha-2 noradrenergic agonists, are among the medications some clinicians use for this presentation, particularly in ADHD-spectrum contexts. The decision is the prescriber's, based on the full clinical picture rather than the phenotype pattern alone. It warrants a careful conversation with someone who understands both the trauma context and the medication profile.

Co-regulation with calmer nervous systems. Spending time with people whose autonomic baseline is lower than yours helps. This is the parent-infant physiological synchrony research applied to adult relationships. A princess's nervous system entrains to the systems around it, and being around regulated people gives her something to entrain to. Choosing your friends partly for autonomic compatibility is deliberate design for a high-gain nervous system.

What does not help, or sometimes makes things worse:

Pushing through the sensory overwhelm. Forcing a Princess to keep working in the loud open office, to keep going to the parties, to keep showing up to the high-stimulation environments, in the name of being normal or being tough. This systematically degrades her capacity. The recovery time is not optional. Skipping it does not toughen the system. It depletes it.

Just don't take it personally. The princess cannot decide to take things less personally. She can decide to wait before responding. She cannot decide to feel less.

Telling her her perception is wrong. This is what the people in her life often default to. *That's not what he meant. You're imagining things. You're being dramatic.* Sometimes the perception is partially wrong. Often it is partially right and the trauma layer is amplifying it. Either way, telling a Princess her perception is wrong is the opposite of what helps. The useful move is helping her sort the signal from the alarm, which is appraisal work.

Long stretches of solitude after a sensory-overwhelm event without any co-regulation. Some solitude is recovery. Too much can become rumination. The princess often needs both: time alone to come down, then time with a regulating presence to update the system. Either alone is incomplete.

8.6 When This Is Beyond Self-Help

If any of these apply, the next step is clinical support, not this book. For crisis resources, see the Introduction.

- Rejection sensitivity has cost you relationships you wanted to keep, or social paranoia has crossed into fixed beliefs that people are organized against you: trauma-competent clinician with highly-sensitive-population experience, not self-help work.

- Sensory overwhelm has crossed into agoraphobia (stopped going to the grocery store, the outside world): the avoidance is organizing your life. Structured, titrated re-engagement with clinical support.
- Emotional contagion is so severe you cannot tell where you end and another person begins, especially in a relationship where the other person uses your contagion: there may be a coercive-control dynamic that needs separate clinical attention.
- Suicidal ideation during sensory-overload crashes or all-or-nothing bad days: the Princess's reactivity can produce thoughts that do not survive the cooldown. They are still worth treating as signals that you need more support. Stop and get it.

These are moments when the framework hands off to something else.

See Gifted & Tortured (Ch.8) for the Princess baseline-temperament version; Half a Second More (Ch.8) for the practice path.

8.7 Where to Start

The world is not getting quieter. You can learn to filter.

The right lamp is one filter. The friend whose nervous system runs calmer than yours is another. The two hours of nothing after the wedding. The calendar pruned to one social event. You will be building that stack for the rest of your life, and over time the stack itself becomes the regulation. The pea will still be there. The mattresses get to do their job.

Ch 9: The Fog & the Tide

You wake up and your brain is wrapped in cotton. Words are on the tip of your tongue and will not come. You read the same paragraph three times and absorb none of it. You drive to the meeting on autopilot and arrive without remembering most of the route. People are talking and you are nodding and a part of you is somewhere else, behind a thin wall of glass, watching this happen.

You did not stay up late. You had your coffee. You are not sick, exactly. You are just not here.

Or you are here, but you are tired in a way that no amount of sleep solves. You sleep ten hours and wake up at the same level of tired you went to bed at. The body is heavy. Tasks that should take twenty minutes take two hours. You used to write a paragraph in five minutes and now the paragraph takes an afternoon, and at the end of the afternoon you are not sure the paragraph is good. The world has slowed down or you have. You cannot tell which.

Or it comes in waves. You are clear for an hour and then you are not. You have a good morning and then by two in the afternoon the cotton is back. You feel sharp in the conversation with the friend and then thirty minutes later, sitting alone in the car, the sharpness is gone and you are not sure it was ever there.

That is the Fog. And the wave pattern, when it works the way it is supposed to, is the Tide.

The two go together. The tide is the healthy version. The fog is the Tide stuck.

I have read several thousand brain maps of foggy patients over twenty-five years, and the most important thing I can tell you about this phenotype is that the underlying mechanism is almost never what people assume it is. The brain is supposed to cycle. Energy ebbs and flows across a day. There are bright stretches where you are clear and sharp, and there are slow stretches where the nervous system is doing maintenance work and you are not at peak. That cycling is the design. Sleep cycles, ultradian cycles, hormonal cycles, attention cycles, all of them rise and fall on their own clocks. A healthy nervous system tides. The fog rolls in for an hour or a morning or a recovery day, the brain does what it needs to do, and the fog burns off and you come back.

Stuck in the fog is different. Stuck in the fog means the cycling pulled offline and could not come back. The maintenance crew showed up and forgot to leave. The cycling that should have rotated you back to clarity stopped rotating, and you are running every day from the same low-tide condition that was supposed to be a brief recovery state.

The tide is normal. Everyone tides. The fog is what happens when the Tide breaks.

This chapter is about both. About the cycling, why it matters, and what it gives you when it works. And about the stuck state, what makes it stuck, and how to give the brain back the capacity to come up for air.

9.1 What the Tide Actually Does

The tide is your brain's protective rhythm. It cycles you between clarity and rest, performance and recovery, on time scales that range from seconds to weeks. The basic mechanism is older than your species. Every nervous system that does sustained complex work has a cycling structure built into it, because sustained complex work depletes resources that have to be replenished, and the replenishment cannot happen at the same time as the work.

You can think of the tide as rhythms layered on top of each other: the daily circadian cycle anchored to light; the ultradian ninety-minute attentional rise and fall through the waking day; hormonal cycles that modulate mood and energy across days or weeks; and slower seasonal or menstrual arcs, plus the recovery stretch after illness or stress.

A well-tided brain is sharp at the right times and recovering at the right times, not always on. The mid-afternoon dip is part of the design. The slow Tuesday morning after a hard Monday is part of the design.

The day off after a week of intense work is part of the design. The body builds the next sharp stretch out of the rest stretch. You cannot have one without the other.

This is the gift the Tide gives you when it is working. Your morning peak. Your second wind in the late afternoon. The hour of clear writing on a Saturday after a long walk. The recovery you did not quite trust at the time, that turned out to be the thing that made the next breakthrough possible. The tide is what makes long arcs of work sustainable. People who get to use their Tide well do not appear to be doing anything special. They are just letting the cycling work.

The tide also gives you depth. The fog stretches, the slow processing stretches, and the quiet recovery stretches are when the brain integrates and when the slow insights arrive that the high-intensity stretches do not have room for. The slow stretches are part of how the bright ones get made. A nervous system that is not allowed to cycle eventually stops being able to cycle. The cycling becomes brittle, and then it stops, and then you have a Fog problem.

9.2 What the Fog Looks Like

The fog is the Tide stuck at low tide. You are missing your morning peak and your second wind. Running every day from the same low-energy, low-clarity condition that was supposed to be a brief trough.

The fog has a particular paradox to it that is one of its signatures: **racing thoughts in slow motion**. Your processing is slowed even though your mind is still active. You are still thinking, still cycling through the day's loops, still anxious about the things you are anxious about. The slowness is in the throughput. The activity is still there. This is part of what makes the Fog so exhausting. The frontal cortex is working hard and producing very little, like a car with the engine racing and the gears slipping.

Another signature: **the cost of the fog is hidden until it isn't**. You can run in fog for a long time before you notice. The first weeks, you assume you are just tired. The first months, you adjust. You compensate. You drink more coffee. You work longer hours to produce the same output. You stop doing the things that take real cognitive load (the deep reading, the difficult writing, the complex social work) and tell yourself you are just busy. Then one day, often after some final straw, you realize you have not had a clear hour in months. You realize you cannot remember the last time you read a book all the way through. You realize the friendships you used to be present in have become smaller. The fog has been organizing your life and you did not see it.

The fog has many drivers. It is one of those phenotypes that is the same final pattern arriving from many different upstream conditions. Common drivers include chronic sleep deprivation, post-viral states (including but not limited to long COVID), chronic fatigue syndrome and ME/CFS, hormonal dysregulation including thyroid and perimenopause, chronic inflammation, mold exposure in some cases, persistent insomnia, post-concussive states, and the burnout pattern that results from running too hot for too long without adequate recovery. Trauma is one of the drivers. It is not the only one.

A fog presentation should not be assumed to be one thing. The same pattern of slowed processing, frontal compensation, and stuck cycling can come from a thyroid problem, a sleep apnea problem, an undiagnosed mild traumatic brain injury, or a trauma history. Sorting out which driver or drivers are present is the first clinical task. In my clinic, perhaps one in three Fog presentations turns out to have a medical contributor that the previous workup missed.

9.3 What Trauma Does

Trauma is one of the most reliable drivers of a stuck-Fog pattern, and it produces it through a few distinct mechanisms.

The first is the **dissociative shutdown** mechanism. When the nervous system has been running at high alarm for too long, it has a self-protection reflex that pulls the system offline. This is design. The posterior cingulate cortex and precuneus, the same midline structures that sit at the core of the default mode network and handle your ongoing sense of being you in your life, are among the first regions to shift under stress. Vanhollebeke and colleagues (2023) showed that even mild psychosocial stress (negative peer feedback in a lab setting) was enough to increase alpha power in bilateral precuneus and right PCC, a pattern reflecting decreased cortical activity in these self-referential hubs. Standard frontal EEG measures did not pick it up. Only source-level analysis revealed the disruption. The self-location system went quieter, and you would not have seen it on a standard recording. The concept is not new. Pierre Janet described dissociation in the 1890s, a decade before Freud redirected psychiatry toward repression, as a structural splitting of personality under conditions the brain could not survive intact. Freud's framework dominated the next century, but Janet's account of what actually happens in a traumatized brain has aged better. The brain has limits to how long it can sustain the high-alarm state, and when those limits are crossed, it drops to a low-arousal protective state. From the outside, this looks like depression or fog or just being checked out. From the inside, it can feel like a wall of glass between you and your life.

Van der Hart, Nijenhuis, and Steele call this the structural dissociation of the personality: an *apparently normal part* that goes to work, answers email, smiles at the right moments, and an *emotional part* that stays locked in the threat (van der Hart et al., 2004). You can run in the apparently normal part for years. You can look functional. But the emotional part is running underneath, shaping your Fog, your reactivity, your sense of watching your life from behind glass. The lifeguard who has been running at twelve out of ten for too many days drops to zero, and the drop is not voluntary. The fog is what living in that drop looks like from day to day.

The second is the **chronic-load** mechanism. Trauma keeps the autonomic nervous system in a low-grade state of hyperarousal even when nothing acute is happening. The chronic load is metabolically expensive. The autonomic nervous system is burning fuel constantly that should have been available for cognition, and after years of this, the brain runs out of margin. The fog that results is, in part, the metabolic cost of running a nervous system that has not had a real rest in years. This is the burnout pattern, and trauma populations get to burnout faster than non-trauma populations because the baseline load is higher.

The third is the **disrupted-sleep** mechanism. Trauma fragments sleep. The lifeguard does not let the brain go offline during the night, the autonomic nervous system runs hot during what should be deep sleep, the REM stretches get truncated or distorted, and the recovery work that sleep is supposed to do does not get done. After enough nights of insufficient deep sleep, the brain's processing speed slows. The fog is in part the cognitive signature of chronic sleep insufficiency, and trauma is one of the most common drivers of chronic sleep insufficiency.

The fourth is more direct. Trauma's protective freeze response, when triggered, produces a literal slowing of the processing system. This is the freeze part of fight-flight-freeze, and it is not metaphorical. The body goes still, the mind goes blank, the time sense distorts, the processing speed drops. In acute moments this is the brain's deepest emergency response. In chronic activation, it can leave a trace pattern of partial freeze that runs underneath ordinary daily function. People who carry developmental trauma often describe a default low-grade freeze that is hard to push out of.

The tide can break under non-trauma conditions too. The thyroid problem can do it. The post-viral syndrome can do it. The chronic insomnia can do it. The trauma layer is one path. But when it is the path, the Fog has a particular feel: the dissociative quality, the sense of being behind glass, the slow-motion replays of past events that the slowed system cannot keep up with. Recognizing the trauma layer is part of what tells you which interventions to try first.

9.4 What Shows Up on a Brain Map

A stuck Fog tends to show up on a brain map with a recognizable cluster of patterns. When I see this cluster on a map, the client sitting across from me is usually describing a week that felt like walking through wet concrete, a month they can barely account for, a sense that the thing they used to be able to do quickly now takes two to three times as long. The map and the story match.

The first signature is slowed alpha peak frequency. Alpha is the dominant rhythm of the resting brain, normally cycling at around ten cycles per second; a slowed-alpha brain cycles at eight or nine instead. Alpha frequency is a marker of overall cortical processing speed, and the slowing is global. The cause can be genetic (the COMT genotype produces lifelong slower alpha) or acquired through post-viral state, sleep deprivation, hormonal shift, or chronic fatigue. This signature has a critical clinical implication discussed in the next section.

The second signature is frontal beta overactivation: when the back of the brain is slowed, the front compensates by working harder. This is the racing-thoughts-in-slow-motion paradox at the QEEG level, the back slow and the front racing. People with this pattern often describe feeling tired and wired at the same time, and they are right about both.

The third is coherence degradation: the communication between brain regions becomes less efficient, the regions that should be working together rhythmically are out of sync, and the functional consequence is that everything feels harder because the orchestra is not playing in time even when each individual instrument is fine. The fourth is delta dysregulation: excess delta during the day (the *I could fall asleep standing up* feeling) or deficient delta during sleep (the brain unable to drop into the deep restorative states even when given the time for them), either pattern meaning the brain's restorative work is not getting done.

These patterns travel together more often than they appear separately. The picture is recognizable across many causes, long COVID, chronic fatigue, post-concussive syndrome, severe burnout, trauma, because the brain has a limited number of ways to fail, and a failed Tide tends to produce these signatures regardless of what broke it.

9.5 A Critical Distinction: Frontal Slow Versus Slowed Alpha

I see this distinction missed all the time, and it changes treatment.

There are two completely different brain patterns that can produce the symptom of "I have trouble focusing and starting tasks." They look similar from the outside. They are very different on a brain map. What helps one of them often makes the other worse.

Frontal Slow is excess slow activity (theta and delta) specifically in the frontal motor regions of the brain. This is a classic ADHD pattern. The phenotype is a Stabilizer pattern in the larger phenotype framework, and it shows up as task-initiation difficulty, impulse-control problems, and the elevated theta-to-beta ratio that the ADHD literature has been describing for decades. Frontal Slow is the pattern most closely associated with classic ADHD, and stimulant medication is the standard pharmacological treatment for that presentation. Neurofeedback for Frontal Slow involves theta suppression and beta enhancement. The treatment is well-established.

Slowed Alpha is something else entirely. The dominant rhythm of the brain itself is slower, globally, not just in frontal motor regions. The genotype association is COMT, not the dopaminergic markers associated with classic ADHD. The phenomenology is *I process information slowly; I need more time than other people; everything feels like wading through mud,* which is different from *I cannot start tasks; I am restless; my attention bounces.* Slowed peak alpha frequency is a nonspecific EEG finding and does not determine whether stimulant medication is appropriate. If attention symptoms coexist with anxiety or poor sleep, those vulnerabilities belong in the prescriber conversation. A qualified prescriber should weigh the full picture.

The clinical pattern that comes through my office most often with this confusion: someone is diagnosed with treatment-resistant ADHD. They have been on three stimulants in succession. None of them worked, or each worked briefly and then stopped, or each made them more anxious without making them more focused. The conclusion is that they have unusually severe ADHD or some atypical variant. The actual situation, often, is that the underlying pattern is Slowed Alpha rather than Frontal Slow. The two patterns call for different conversations with a prescriber and different neurofeedback protocols.

The theta-suppression and beta-enhancement work that helps Frontal Slow ADHD (Lubar et al., 1995) addresses a different EEG architecture than Slowed Alpha does. Once alpha-frequency training begins rather than theta suppression, the picture often changes. The distinction is a clinical QEEG observation at this point rather than a controlled-trial comparison between the two protocols, but it is one that clinicians with QEEG-guided practices report consistently. Medication may be appropriate when a separately assessed condition or symptom cluster warrants it, but this phenotype framework does not establish a medication indication. A qualified prescriber should make that decision from the full diagnostic and medical picture.

A third pattern also mimics ADHD: the cramped Lifeguard. A Lifeguard running at high volume looks distracted, restless, unable to focus. She cannot focus because she is focusing on threat scanning, not on the task in front of her. The clinical move that helps is quieting the threat scanner. Three different presentations. Three different clinical conversations. The symptom is "can't focus." The circuit underneath is different each time, and the medication question belongs to a prescriber who can weigh each one.

The consequences of misdiagnosis are not minor. Years of unsuccessful stimulant trials. The conclusion that one's brain is somehow defective in a way that medication cannot fix. A QEEG can distinguish Frontal Slow from Slowed Alpha in a single recording, and a clinical history can flag the Lifeguard pattern. Treatment differs accordingly.

If you tried stimulants and they did not work or made you worse, this section is worth flagging for your next clinical conversation.

9.6 The Trauma-Driven Fog Has Some Particular Features

A fog with trauma underneath is not exactly the same as a Fog from post-viral state or sleep apnea, even though the QEEG signatures overlap markedly. Frewen and Lanius describe four dimensions of conscious experience that shift when trauma produces the dissociative altered state: time, thought, body, emotion. Your sense of time distorts. Your thoughts may lose their first-person quality. Your body stops feeling like yours. Your emotions flatten. These shifts are the brain reorganizing around threat. The default-mode-network vulnerability to stress appears specific to PTSD in a way that distinguishes it from depression: stress-induced connectivity drops in vmPFC and precuneus occur in PTSD populations but not in matched depression groups.[1]

The features that suggest trauma is part of the picture include:

- A dissociative quality to the Fog. Absent, with the sense of being behind glass.
- A pattern of triggers that seem to bring the Fog on or worsen it: certain people, certain conversations, certain rooms.
- Memory gaps, specifically around emotionally loaded material. Recent neuroimaging shows that dissociative amnesia severity correlates with reduced volume in the CA1 region of the hippocampus, the structure that time-stamps and binds autobiographical memories (Dimitrova et al., 2023). When that structure is compromised, the filing system loses its index.
- A history of switching between hypervigilance and Fog (the Lifeguard breaker pattern from the previous chapter), rather than a steady chronic Fog. Lanius and colleagues describe these as two forms of emotion dysregulation running on opposite circuits (Lanius et al., 2010; Nicholson et al., 2017). In undermodulation, the emotional brain overwhelms the prefrontal cortex from the bottom up, and you get re-experiencing, flooding, hyperarousal. In overmodulation, the prefrontal cortex clamps down on the emotional brain from the top down, and you get the numbness and detachment of the dissociative Fog. The switchers cycle between the two. The steady-fog people are stuck in overmodulation.

---

[1]Averill and colleagues (2024) on DMN connectivity under stress in PTSD vs MDD; Herringa (2017) on developmental differences in DMN connectivity in pediatric PTSD; Frewen and Lanius (2014) on the four-dimensional model of conscious experience in trauma; Vanhollebeke and colleagues (2023) on precuneus/PCC alpha increase under mild psychosocial stress; Lanius et al. (2010) and Nicholson et al. (2017) on overmodulation vs undermodulation circuits; Dimitrova et al. (2023) on CA1 hippocampal volume and dissociative amnesia.

- A history of childhood circumstances that would have required protective shutdown: chronic unsafety, violence, neglect, or chaos.
- The presence of other phenotype patterns alongside the Fog (a cramped Lifeguard, a stuck CEO, a high-volume Princess) that fit a trauma profile.

The neuroimaging evidence confirms that these dissociative states are not performance or imagination. Apparently normal parts and emotional parts show measurably different patterns of neural activation when scanned; simulators asked to fake the switching cannot reproduce the signatures.[2] The parts are neurobiologically distinguishable states.

When trauma is part of the picture, recovery involves both Fog-specific interventions and trauma-specific interventions. The fog tools alone are necessary but not sufficient. The trauma processing alone is risky if the brain is too foggy to engage with it. The sequence matters.

9.7 What Helps

A clinical picture that I see often enough to describe. A man comes in describing what sounds, on the surface, like depression. The heaviness, the low motivation, the cognitive slowing. He has tried two antidepressants. The first one helped somewhat for a month, then plateaued. The second made him more anxious without clearing the fog. He is now managing on caffeine and momentum and is noticeably running out of both. He also mentions, when I ask, that he has never felt fully rested no matter how many hours he sleeps. He mentions that his attention went sideways after a period of sustained stress several years ago and never quite came back. He mentions that he used to write easily and now the writing takes forever and feels wrong.

His QEEG shows slowed alpha peak frequency across the posterior cortex. A brain whose dominant rhythm is running slow, distinct from anxiety or classic frontal-asymmetry depression, with the frontal beta compensation that develops when the back of the brain is not doing its job at typical speed. He had tried stimulants as well; they produced

[2]Reinders (2008); Schlumpf and colleagues (2014); Brand and colleagues (2021).

more anxiety without clearing the fog. We do alpha-frequency training, a sleep evaluation, and the unglamorous foundations. Several months later the writing is easier. The fog has loosened enough that it is no longer organizing his life.

The common thread in Fog presentations: the brain needs its rhythm back, and rhythm is patient.

Fog and Tide work is almost always slow work. That slow pacing is the system's own signal. The sequence matters: rhythm before processing, processing before integration. Chapter 15 covers the sequencing principle.

For a Fog of any cause, the foundation is the same, and it is unglamorous. **Sleep, light, and the recovery of basic rhythm.**

Consistent wake time matters more than consistent bedtime. Morning light exposure within thirty minutes of waking matters more than almost any single supplement or intervention. A solid morning routine that the body learns to expect is more useful for the Tide than the latest nootropic. These are the boring foundations and they are also the load-bearing ones. Anyone who skips them while chasing more sophisticated interventions is going to underperform what they could have gotten from doing the basics first.

Once the basics are in place, the interventions sort by what is driving the Fog.

For trauma-driven Fog, autonomic regulation is foundational. The lifeguard tools apply here (resonance-frequency breathing, HRV biofeedback, grounding, body-based co-regulation). The fog often improves as the chronic-load mechanism gets some relief. Stabilization first: you do not begin trauma processing while the brain is too foggy to integrate. You support the cycling first, then engage the deeper material.

For post-viral Fog, long COVID and ME/CFS patterns, pacing matters more than anything else. The pattern that worsens these conditions is push-and-crash: pushing through a high-energy day and then crashing for a week. The pattern that helps is staying just under the threshold that triggers the crash, even when the temptation is to use the good days hard. The literature on graded activity for post-viral fatigue is more complicated than older protocols suggested; aggressive graded exercise can backfire in some patients. Pacing under the crash threshold is the safer move.

For hormonal Fog, thyroid, perimenopausal, and other endocrine drivers should be evaluated medically before assuming the Fog is purely neurological. Thyroid in particular is one of the more common reversible causes of a Fog presentation, and standard primary-care thyroid panels sometimes miss patterns that a more thorough endocrinology workup catches.

For Slowed Alpha specifically, the targeted intervention is alpha-frequency training: a neurofeedback protocol that specifically supports the brain's dominant rhythm in moving toward a more typical frequency. This is a clinical intervention and requires a provider who understands the distinction from theta-down work. Improvements are usually slow (measured in months) but can be substantial. If stimulants are being considered alongside a slowed-alpha finding, discuss the full picture with a prescriber who can weigh the attention symptoms, the anxiety and sleep profile, and the EEG pattern together.

For everyone, the load-bearing foundations remain the same: sleep, movement tolerable to the system, and reasonable glucose regulation through meal timing. Nootropics and supplements have thinner evidence bases than their marketing suggests; evaluate against personal experience over a few weeks rather than the testimonial of someone whose physiology is not yours.

What makes a Fog worse: pushing through rather than pacing; medication decisions made without sorting Frontal Slow from Slowed Alpha (the distinction matters and the prescriber conversation should include it); high-stimulation environments without recovery time built in; and self-criticism. The fog often arrives with a layer of *I should be able to do this.* The self-criticism is itself cognitively expensive. The brain does not need more load. It needs the load it already has to come down.

9.8 When This Is Beyond Self-Help

If any of these apply, the next step is clinical support, not this book. For crisis resources, see the Introduction.

- Fog persistent more than six months without identifiable cause, significantly affecting function: medical workup first (sleep study, thyroid, B12, ferritin, metabolic panel). A QEEG can then clarify the pattern.
- Head injury history and Fog that has not resolved: ask whether a post-concussive picture is contributing. The literature on chronic mild TBI is substantial.
- Fog with significant dissociation (losing time, outside-body, missing parts of your day): trauma-competent clinician with dissociative-population training. A generalist can inadvertently make this worse.
- Fog has produced bleakness crossing into thoughts of self-harm: stop and get support now. The fog's bleakness is a symptom of the Fog, not an accurate assessment.

These are moments when the framework hands off to something else.

See Half a Second More (Ch.5) for the Fog practice path; Borrowed Peace for borrowed-regulation patterns (alertness borrowed from caffeine and stimulants when the cycling won't return).

9.9 The Tide Coming Back

When the Tide is working, you do not notice it. You have a clear morning. You have a slow afternoon. You go for a walk. The walk loosens something. You come back to the desk and the work is easier than you remembered it being. You sleep that night and wake the next morning a little sharper than you went to bed. You have a foggy day on Tuesday and a clear day on Wednesday and that is fine. The cycling does what it does. You are not running on emergency reserves. You are running on rhythm.

Recovery from a stuck Fog is the recovery of cycling. It does not happen by trying harder. It happens by doing fewer things, doing them at the right times, and giving the brain the conditions under which it can begin to tide again.

It also does not happen quickly. The fog took a while to settle in, and the cycling takes a while to come back. The first signs are often small: a single clear hour where there used to be none. A morning when the words come without effort. A conversation where you were there. These small clear stretches are the cycling testing whether it can come up for air. It can. With time and the right conditions, it can come up for longer and longer, until the up time is more of the day than the down time, and then most of the day, and then enough of the day that you do not have to organize your life around the fog anymore.

On the brain map of a Fog patient six months into the right protocol, the alpha peak has moved. Eight and a half cycles per second has crept up to nine, then to nine and a half. The frontal beta has come down half a microvolt, because the front is no longer having to compensate quite so hard for what the back is finally doing on its own. The number on the screen is small. The change in the person sitting in front of it is not.

Ch 10: The Language Axis, Bard and Interpreter

You are at dinner. Someone tells a story you have heard before, with a different lilt than they used the last time. You catch the lilt. You are still trying to figure out what changed when the next person starts talking, and now you are watching their mouth and nodding and the words are arriving in your ears and somehow not turning into meaning. The sentence ends. You do not know what was said. You ask for it back. You feel the cost of asking, because for everyone else the sentence was simple, and for you it has just become a small puzzle you cannot solve in the time available.

Two circuits ran in that minute. The first one read the music. The second one tried to read the words and could not. They live on opposite sides of the back of your brain, and they take turns failing under trauma in particular ways. This chapter is about both of them.

The right side reads tone. How it was said. The half-step shift in pitch, the half-second hesitation, the vowel that landed too long, the sigh under the sentence. The right side is what tells you that *I'm fine* does not mean fine. This is the Bard.

The left side reads words. What was said. Phonemes into morphemes, morphemes into syntax, syntax into meaning. This is the Interpreter, the part of the brain that takes incoming sound waves and turns them into the experience of understanding what a person is talking about. Wernicke described it in the 1870s.

The two of them, working together, build the experience of hearing another person. You do not notice them as separate. You notice the fused experience: you got it. Or you did not.

I have watched these two systems fail on QEEG maps for twenty-five years, and the failures look different. The bard tends to fail loud. The interpreter tends to fail quiet. Most of my trauma clients have at least one of them constrained, and a meaningful subset have both.

The ones with both struggle in conversation in a way that is hard to describe to people who have not lost both the music and the words.

10.1 Where They Live

The bard's circuit runs through the right posterior superior temporal gyrus and sulcus, with strong connections to the right temporoparietal junction (the Princess, in the previous chapter) and to the limbic systems that handle emotional valence. On a brain map I read her pattern around T6 and P8. The interpreter's circuit runs through the left posterior superior temporal cortex and the left temporoparietal junction; I read her pattern around T5 and P7. They are anatomical mirrors. The bard's job is *how*. The interpreter's job is *what*.

The bard's job is paralinguistic processing. Speech arrives at your ears in two streams. The linguistic stream is the words themselves. The paralinguistic stream is the carrier: pitch contour, stress, rhythm, tempo, voice quality, emotional tone. The bard reads the carrier. She reads sarcasm by hearing the deliberate mismatch between word and tone. She reads humor that depends on timing. She reads the music in vocal range, in melody, in chord change, because the same right-temporal systems that process prosody process music.

A well-regulated Bard is the friend who knows when the phone call is not really about what the friend is calling about. She is the parent who notices that the kid's *I'm fine* is not fine. She catches charisma without thinking about it. She makes the speaker feel met, because she is not just receiving the words; she is receiving the meaning the speaker hoped someone would receive.

The interpreter's scope is the full architecture of language comprehension. She does four things in parallel. She handles phonological processing, the segmentation of sound into the units of language. She handles semantic processing, the connection of words to meaning. She handles syntactic processing, the parsing of who did what to whom. And she handles social-pragmatic processing, the layer of meaning that lives in context: the *I'm fine* that does not mean fine, the request phrased as a question, the joke that depends on shared reference. The bard reads the *I'm fine* for tone. The interpreter reads it for pragmatics. They check each other. When I see left-temporal involvement on a QEEG, the intake almost always maps back across these four: someone who mis-hears words in conversation, someone who loses the thread of complex sentences, someone who reads factual content accurately but keeps missing what was meant underneath.

She also shares neural real estate with the medial-temporal memory systems, the hippocampus and adjacent structures. Language and episodic memory are not separate. A well-functioning Interpreter helps you encode events with enough verbal scaffolding to retrieve them later. A constrained Interpreter often travels with constrained autobiographical memory, especially for what was said.

10.2 What Trauma Does to the Bard

Trauma teaches the Bard that tone matters more than words. In the original learning environment this is often correct. A child whose parent's words were neutral but whose tone determined whether the next hour would be safe learns very fast that the tone is the load-bearing data. So the Bard learns to listen at high gain.

In adult life that high gain produces a threat-biased reading. Your colleague who is tired sounds dismissive. Your partner who is busy sounds annoyed. The cue the Bard picks up is real, and the reader's experience of it is real. Its meaning may be accurate, exaggerated, or wrong, so the reading remains a hypothesis to check. The trauma layer tilts the reading toward the threat end of the range, and then a catastrophizing layer takes the small signal and runs it up. A slightly clipped voicemail becomes evidence that something is wrong. You cannot un-hear what the Bard heard. The leap from what the Bard heard to the catastrophic conclusion is where the trauma layer lives.

The opposite pattern shows up in the same population for different reasons. In some trauma histories, the Bard learned that reading tone was too painful and the right temporal cortex shut the gain down. The result is an adult who hears words as words and misses the music. Sarcasm goes by. The joke does not land. The upset friend's voice does not register until the friend says, in flat words, *I am upset.* This is sometimes mistaken for autism-spectrum, and the two can co-occur, but a trauma-flat Bard has a different developmental signature. The flatness is a defense. The receiving channel has been turned down to protect against affective overload.

A related pattern is what I think of as protective vocal flatness. Bards who have been hyper-tuned to threat in incoming prosody often develop a particular outgoing prosodic style: a careful neutralizing of tone in their own voice, designed to avoid producing anything that could be read by another Bard as hostile. Or the opposite, a soothing-prosody style designed to keep the room calm at all times. Some clients with severe early relational trauma arrive in my office with voices that have had the affect carefully managed out of them. The voice is a self-protection. Watching the same voice loosen across months of work is one of the slower but more recognizable arcs in this phenotype.

In the most severe presentations, the Bard begins to generate prosodic signal where none exists. A temporal-lobe system under chronic load can produce internal output, from intrusive verbal fragments that feel like your own mind generating speech, to, less commonly, auditory-verbal hallucinations with sensory vividness approaching external sound. Intrusive verbal material and auditory-verbal hallucinations can be different experiences, but perceived location alone does not distinguish them. Assessment considers sensory vividness, perceived agency, controllability, insight, associated beliefs and mood symptoms, substances or medications, sleep, neurological features, functional impact, and safety. The fragments are common in this phenotype, and when the overall load comes down, they often quiet with it. When significant ADHD or autism is driving the sensitivity higher, they do not reliably respond to load-reduction work; the gain stays up because the source is not the trauma load alone. I sometimes see right-temporal slowing in clients who report these experiences, but it is nonspecific and cannot identify voice-hearing or its cause. Persistent focal temporal slowing belongs in a medical and neurological differential rather than being treated as a trauma signature. What I cannot tell from the map alone is whether the client has ever said it out loud to anyone.

There is also a network-level mechanism that helps explain why a misread tone can feel like it rewrites your entire standing with a person. The default mode network, the system that maintains your running sense of self across time, is stress-sensitive in PTSD in ways that differ from other conditions. Even a mild laboratory stressor reduces DMN connectivity in PTSD populations while leaving depression populations unaffected; the ventromedial prefrontal cortex and precuneus take the largest hit. When your Bard is running high-gain threat detection on every tone in the room, the network that should be holding a stable sense of who you are and where you are is simultaneously weakening under the load. The self gets less sturdy at the same moment the alarm gets louder. The continuity that would normally let you hold *the boss was probably tired today* against *the boss is contemptuous of me* is operating with less working memory than the contest requires.

10.3 What Trauma Does to the Interpreter

The interpreter fails differently. She tends to fail quiet, by going under-resourced. I have had clients describe years of comprehension difficulty before connecting it to their trauma, because the experience does not feel like a trauma symptom. It feels like having gotten dumber. That sentence comes up so often in my intake conversations that I have learned to ask about it directly.

Under acute stress, the higher cortical functions get less supply. You become less articulate. Words come slower. You lose the right phrase. You cannot remember the name of the colleague you have known for years. For someone with a chronic alarm running, the Interpreter operates with chronically reduced resource and the collapse becomes a baseline rather than a peak. Meetings exhaust. Long phone calls exhaust. The cost of listening is high in a way that is invisible to the people you are talking with, because they are not paying it.

A second pattern is narrative collapse. The trauma event itself often did not get encoded into a coherent verbal narrative, because the

Interpreter was offline during the event. You may have a strong memory of the trauma in fragments, a smell, an image, a body sensation, and a much weaker capacity to tell the story of it. The words were never quite encoded. This is one of the more reliable signatures of significant trauma. Williams and colleagues have described a related phenomenon called overgeneral autobiographical memory: trauma survivors, asked to recall a specific event, tend to retrieve vague summaries instead, *that year was bad* rather than *that Tuesday afternoon at the kitchen table.*[1] The recall has gotten coarser because the precision work of specific retrieval is competing for executive resource against the threat-scanning that has been running in the background for years. The result is that you may remember the feeling of a conversation but not what was actually said, which makes it harder to reality-check the Bard's reading after the fact. The two circuits become harder to coordinate when the memory layer underneath them has been coarsened by the load they have both been operating under.

A third pattern is dissociative auditory phenomena. Tinnitus that is worse during stress. Sounds that arrive as if from further away than they are. Auditory dullness during dissociative episodes, words arriving but not landing, as if through water. The temporal lobes handle a lot of the auditory-meaning processing, and they are also one of the dissociation-vulnerable regions. The phenomena travel together. Clients describe this in a few stable ways: the meeting where everyone sounded like they were underwater, the conversation that was happening in a room they could not quite enter, the inability to hold what someone was saying even though they were listening hard. None of it is laziness. The interpreter is in a state that does not allow comprehension.

A fourth pattern is the borrowing of regulation through substances or compulsive behavior. The cost of operating an Interpreter under chronic load is real, and an Interpreter that cannot make the world cohere will reach for whatever briefly quiets it. The drink after the draining meeting. The pill that makes the noise stop. The scroll that

[1]Williams et al. (2007) on overgeneral autobiographical memory as a transdiagnostic feature of emotional disorder, including trauma populations.

fills the gap where meaning was supposed to be. Epidemiological data shows the pattern at population scale: PTSD precedes substance-use disorder onset in most comorbid cases, with lifetime overlap running between twenty-five and fifty percent depending on the substance.[2] The borrowing works briefly. Then the load goes up, and the next round arrives sooner.

And a fifth pattern, the most clinically delicate, is the temporal-lobe symptom cluster proper: intrusive verbal fragments, *temporal-lobe dreams* during waking that carry an unusual vivid quality, and in some cases voice-hearing experiences that warrant clinical assessment. These can appear on the left-temporal side independently of the right-temporal Bard pattern, though they often travel together. They get misdiagnosed as primary psychosis more often than they should be, and the misdiagnosis is consequential.

If you are reading this and you have voice-hearing experiences you have never told anyone about, others carry the same experience, and you are not necessarily psychotic. If you recognize the experience of seeming like multiple distinct selves or of losing time, that is the severe end of the dissociative spectrum, and it belongs in this framework. It is a brain that organized itself around multiple configurations to survive rather than a sign of fabrication or manipulation. The clinical conversation is worth having, with someone who understands the trauma-related literature. The Hearing Voices community has resources, and Eleanor Longden's clinical work shows that when voice-hearers learn to relate to their voices as dissociated communications, the distress often drops and functional recovery follows.[3] The misdiagnosis falls disproportionately on some populations; Black Americans receive

[2]Kessler et al. (1995), National Comorbidity Survey. Reports lifetime PTSD-SUD comorbidity of roughly 27-52% across substance categories (alcohol, drugs) and sex. Temporal precedence of PTSD over SUD onset is established separately (Chilcoat and Breslau, 1998), not tested in this paper.

[3]Romme and Escher (2000) and Longden et al. (2012) on trauma-related voice-hearing as distinct from primary psychosis. Harricharan, McKinnon, and Lanius (2021) on temporal-lobe alterations in trauma.

psychosis diagnoses at significantly elevated rates compared to white Americans with similar presenting symptoms.[4]

10.4 When Both Are Loud

The two circuits are anatomical mirrors and they share a common load. The bard at high gain pulls resource from the same back-of-brain region the Interpreter draws on. The interpreter under chronic strain produces a kind of listening fatigue that bleeds into how the Bard reads tone, because tired systems threat-bias more readily. The two failure modes interact in ways the chapters could not show when they were separate.

Configuration one is loud Bard with quiet Interpreter. This is the client I see most often in this cluster: someone who hears every micro-shift in tone, catastrophizes the reading, and also cannot follow what was actually said. The conversation becomes pure threat-music with no words underneath. She comes out of the meeting unable to recall what was discussed but certain that her boss is angry with her. Both readings are wrong, in different ways. The tone-reading is overcalled. The word-reading never assembled.

Configuration two is quiet Bard with quiet Interpreter. Words do not land. Tone does not register. Conversations slide off. This is the dissociation-leaning pattern, often paired with the Fog phenotype in earlier chapters. The whole back-temporal language axis has been turned down.

Configuration three is loud Bard with relatively intact Interpreter. The words come in fine. The music is overcalled. You understand exactly what was said and you are also sure the person hated saying it.

Configuration four, less common, is intact Bard with quiet Interpreter. The music is read accurately, sometimes too accurately, and the words underneath are not assembling. You hear the warmth in

[4]Whaley (2001) and subsequent diagnostic-disparity research on elevated psychosis-diagnosis rates in Black Americans with comparable presenting symptoms.

the friend's voice and you cannot quite track what she said. The relationship side of the friendship works. The information side does not.

The reason this matters is that the routing changes. The loud-Bard work and the quiet-Interpreter work look almost opposite. One is appraisal work, layered on top of accurate perception. The other is structural work, restoring resource to an Interpreter that is operating on too little. Doing the wrong work for the wrong configuration tends to entrench the cramped one. I have watched clients spend years in well-meaning therapy that addressed the more visible of their two circuits while the quieter one stayed unread. The visible Bard got better. The interpreter, still under-resourced, kept producing the comprehension difficulties that the Bard work could not reach. Mapping both circuits before routing the work is what changes that.

10.5 What These Get Misread As

Trauma-shaped Bards and Interpreters tend to attract a small catalog of clinical labels, almost none of which engage the underlying circuit. Knowing which label has been applied to you can be useful for ruling out the actual condition the label names, but the label is not the mechanism.

A threat-biased Bard often gets called socially anxious. The standard social-anxiety treatment can miss the prosodic layer entirely. Sometimes she gets called paranoid, when the catastrophizing layer is loud, because the person is convinced others are upset with her and the readings are not always supported by external evidence. High-gain prosodic processing with a threat-biased prior can look like delusional thinking from the outside. The two can be distinguished, but they often are not.

A trauma-flat Bard often gets called on the autism spectrum. Some people in this presentation are autistic. Some are trauma-flat Bards who have shut down the receiving channel. Sorting it out requires attention to developmental history and to the specific shape of the social-cue difficulty. The support strategies differ.

A constrained Interpreter often gets called inattentive, and ADHD treatment may get considered. Sometimes the diagnosis fits. Sometimes the underlying issue is a normally-functioning Interpreter under chronic autonomic load, and the clinical question is whether the attention difficulty is primary or secondary to that load. She may also get called dyslexic when the reception problem is severe enough to affect reading; the dyslexia label fits some people in this group and not others, and the distinction matters because reading remediation looks different from trauma-load reduction.

A constrained Interpreter who is missing implications and reading things literally that were not meant literally sometimes gets called on the spectrum too, the way the trauma-flat Bard does. As above, some are autistic, some are trauma-flat, and some are both. The trauma-related pragmatic-processing constraint has a different developmental signature and softens under autonomic-load reduction; the autism-spectrum version does not soften that way.

The most clinically consequential misreads, when voice-hearing is present, run in both directions. Overdiagnosing primary psychosis in someone whose experiences are trauma-related carries significant downstream cost, and the misdiagnosis falls disproportionately on certain populations, which means a clinical error has become a structural one. The error in the other direction is equally consequential: explaining away psychotic, mood, substance, medication, sleep, or neurological conditions as trauma delays treatment that may be urgent. A reader with voice-hearing experiences needs clinical assessment regardless of the trauma context, and the assessment should hold both possibilities open.

A trauma-driven Interpreter who is borrowing regulation through alcohol, food, or compulsive behavior often gets called an addict, with primary-addiction treatment routed accordingly. The treatment that works best for this overlap addresses both the trauma and the substance use at the same time, rather than demanding sobriety first and deferring the trauma work to some later moment that never quite arrives.

The clinical descriptions that lay people use for the same patterns are not exactly wrong. *Reads too much into things. Always thinks people are upset. Cannot follow a conversation. Has gotten dumber.* The descriptions catch a real surface feature. They are unhelpful because they do not engage with the circuit underneath, and because they land on the person as further evidence that her own perception or capacity is not trustworthy, which feeds the trauma layer it is supposed to address.

10.6 The Gift, Bilateral

Both circuits, when they get their job back, give you something specific.

The bard at her actual job gives you the music of the social world. You hear the room. You catch the friend's pain before the friend finishes the sentence. You sense when the warmth is performance and when it is real, though the sense remains a hypothesis to check rather than a certainty to act on. The gain is on intensity. You read it in a voice, but also in a face, in posture, in the speed of a gesture. The prosodic circuitry is the anchor; the felt experience runs wider. That intensity is what makes you the person others come to when they need to be understood. When the gain runs too high, the same circuit reads threat or rejection in a signal that may carry nothing more than fatigue. The gift and the cost are the same mechanism. People with strong Bards often have strong musical sensibilities, even if they do not play; the right-temporal cortex that reads vocal prosody also reads melodic and emotional content in music. And the Bard supports the construction of redemption narratives, because she can hear the warmth and repair that followed a rupture. A cramped Bard tilts the story the other way: the tone was off, so the whole memory gets filed under threat, and the narrative becomes one of contamination.

The interpreter at her actual job gives you the long arguments, the dense paragraphs, the multi-step explanation, the joke that depends on a particular word. She is the reason you can read a difficult book and still know what page eighty was about when you get to page two hundred. People with strong Interpreters often become writers, editors, translators, lawyers, scholars. The capacity to receive language with care is a capacity that, given the right context, becomes craft. And because she shares neural real estate with the memory systems, when she is doing her job, you can remember what was said in the conversation, which lets you reality-check the Bard's reading later.

Together, the two circuits give you the full experience of being heard and of hearing another person. The bard hears what the speaker meant. The interpreter hears what the speaker said. The two readings cross-check each other in real time. When the friend says *I'm fine* in the tone that is not fine, the Bard registers the tone and the Interpreter registers the pragmatic mismatch, and the two readings together produce the experience of catching that the friend is not fine. Each circuit on its own only does part of the work. A loud Bard with a quiet Interpreter catches the tone but cannot hold what was actually said long enough to act on it. A quiet Bard with a loud Interpreter catches the words and misses the meaning underneath. The two together produce the experience that good listeners describe and the rest of the world enjoys being on the receiving end of.

These are the same gifts the chapter has been pointing at. The trauma did not give you any of this. The trauma cramped what was already there.

10.7 What Helps

The language axis cannot sort signal from noise until the autonomic noise floor comes down. The bard cannot reality-check her readings if the alarm is too loud. The interpreter cannot hold a sentence if there is not enough resource to hold it. Sleep, breath, basic regulation. These are the floor that everything else stands on. Chapter 15 covers the sequencing principle.

Past that, the work branches depending on which circuit is dominant.

If the Bard is the louder problem, start with appraisal. The reading is real. The leap from the reading to the catastrophic conclusion is where the trauma layer lives, and that is where the intervention goes. The prosody reality-check is the workhorse: after some time has passed, ask the person the actual question the reading raised. Not *did you mean to be dismissive,* which puts the speaker on the defensive and confirms nothing. The honest question. *I want to make sure I read you right earlier; were you frustrated about X?* Sometimes the answer is yes and the Bard was accurate. Sometimes the answer is no and the reading needs an update. Either way you are training the Bard to test her readings against external feedback rather than running the trauma-prior unchecked. The threat-bias softens because the data accumulates.

Expressive writing helps the Bard in particular. Pennebaker found that writing about emotional experiences for fifteen to twenty minutes a day, over three to four sessions, produces measurable improvements in distress and physical health markers.[5] For a Bard, the mechanism is specific: putting the right-temporal prosodic impression into written words forces it into a format the left hemisphere can examine. You heard something in the tone. Writing it down makes the reading explicit, which makes it testable. Emotional depth matters more than factual detail, and the benefit comes from integration.

Music as deliberate regulation works for this phenotype better than for most. The right-temporal systems that process tone also process music, and a high-gain temporal-lobe phenotype tends to be unusually responsive to it. Specific pieces, used as autonomic-regulation tools, can shift the baseline. The tool is mechanism-matched.

For a trauma-flat Bard, prosody training rebuilds the receiving channel. Speech-language therapists who work on social communication, with autism-spectrum populations, have protocols for this, and they can be adapted. Slow, repetitive listening to prosodic samples with feedback. Useful for clients who have shut the channel down to protect.

Affective context-management helps for the Bard too. The bard reads tone, and tone is always read against context. If you are spend-

[5]Pennebaker and Beall (1986) on expressive writing about emotional experiences and subsequent improvements in distress and physical health markers.

ing most of your time in environments where you do not know the people well, new workplaces, new social groups, new partners, the Bard has less context to interpret tone against, and the threat-prior dominates by default. Choosing some social environments where the people are stable, where context is known, where prosodic readings can be cross-referenced against accumulated history with the person, gives the Bard data to work with that is not all noise. The intervention is structural, at the level of who you spend time with.

Loving-kindness practice helps in this phenotype the way it helps the Princess. Ten minutes, three times a week, even when it feels mechanical at first. The literature on the practice in trauma populations is favorable on adverse-effect profile compared to more concentration-intensive practices.

If the Interpreter is the louder problem, reduce the load rather than retrain the reading. The interpreter is under-resourced.

Written, not just spoken. Ask for instructions in writing. Take notes. Follow verbal conversations with written summaries. Read agendas before meetings rather than absorbing them in real time. Pre-meeting prep is a tool that takes pressure off an Interpreter operating under pressure. Clients who institutionalize this in their work life often report a recognizable shift within a few weeks: less exhaustion after meetings, more carry-over of what was said into the next conversation, fewer of the surprise moments where everyone else seems to remember a detail you cannot retrieve.

Single-tasking the language. A constrained Interpreter does worse when she is also being asked to filter background noise or split attention with another task. The phone call while looking at email is not the same as the phone call alone. Reducing parallel demand helps her absorb the primary input.

Reading practice in small doses. For someone whose Interpreter has been constrained for a long time, reading often becomes effortful and gets avoided. The avoidance is reasonable in the moment and costly over time, because the Interpreter loses fluency from disuse. Short, regular reading in material you actually want to read. The reading does not have to be ambitious. It has to be regular.

Slow conversation. A friend or partner who can hold a slower conversation, with pauses long enough for the Interpreter to absorb and respond, is a different experience for an Interpreter than someone who runs fast. Choose some of your social environment for compatibility with your processing speed. The compatibility is matching the input rate to the circuit that has to process it.

Addressing the borrowed regulation, if it is part of the picture. A constrained Interpreter who is using alcohol or other substances to quiet the load is in a feedback loop: the substance briefly reduces the cost of listening and then raises the next round of cost when it wears off. Sobriety enforced before the trauma load has been addressed often does not last, because the underlying noise the substance was quieting is still there. The integrated approach, treating the trauma layer and the substance use at the same time, is the one with the best clinical outcomes for this overlap. The chapters on borrowed regulation in *Borrowed Peace* go into this in detail; the short version here is that the Interpreter under load is one of the circuits most reliably driving the borrowing, and the borrowing tends to ease when the Interpreter gets enough resource back.

If both circuits are involved: stabilization, then Interpreter structural support, then Bard appraisal work. The bard's appraisal work requires enough verbal working memory to hold the reality-check process. A quiet Interpreter cannot hold it. Trying to do the Bard work first when the Interpreter is still under-resourced produces frustration without movement.

Targeted neurofeedback applies to both circuits but at different sites. For a high-gain Bard with right-temporal involvement on the QEEG, alpha-supporting work over the right temporal cortex is often what helps; the protocol is similar to the Princess but at different sites. For a constrained Interpreter with left-temporal involvement, the work is left-temporal and the protocols vary depending on what the map actually shows. In my practice, the map contributes to protocol selection alongside symptoms, history, and clinical response. Whether QEEG-guided selection improves outcomes over competent symptom-guided selection has not been established in a head-to-head trial.

For voice-hearing specifically, see the clinical routing in "When This Is Beyond Self-Help" below. The short version: it is not automatically psychosis, and the Hearing Voices approach has evidence.

What does not help, on either side.

Telling a Bard her readings are wrong. Sometimes they are. A reading may contain a real cue, but its meaning stays a hypothesis until checked. *You are imagining things* is the wrong intervention. The right intervention is helping her sort the signal from the alarm.

Suppressing the readings, either side. The circuit is doing its job. Telling yourself to ignore what the Bard hears does not work, the way telling yourself to ignore what the Lifeguard sees does not work.

Pushing through a fatigued Interpreter. She runs out of resource and starts producing comprehension errors. Better to stop, recover, come back, than to push and produce a misread that has consequences.

Self-criticism on either side. The internal voice that says *you should be smart enough to follow this,* or *you are imagining things again,* is adding load to a circuit that is already overloaded. Neither circuit responds to criticism the way the criticizer hopes it will.

Forcing extended exposure to high-conflict environments. A Bard in a chronically hostile workplace is reading actual hostility while the trauma prior amplifies it. Sometimes the intervention is environmental. Sometimes a Bard does not need more therapy; she needs a different room.

10.8 When This Is Beyond Self-Help

If any of these apply, the next step is clinical support, not this book. For crisis resources, see the Introduction.

- Voice-hearing is frequent or distressing: clinician with experience in trauma-related voice-hearing who can distinguish this picture from primary psychosis. The Hearing Voices approach has evidence. Medication can be appropriate and is worth discussing with a qualified clinician.

- Voice-hearing includes commands to harm yourself or others: this requires immediate risk assessment rather than a scheduled appointment. Commands to harm self or others are a clinical emergency regardless of their source. Use the crisis resources in the Introduction and in Appendix A.
- Comprehension difficulty has crossed into an inability to reliably understand the people in your daily life: medical workup first. Hearing loss is the most common reversible cause. Neurological evaluation if the change has been rapid.
- Temporal-lobe symptoms beyond voice-hearing (new, recurrent, or stereotyped olfactory hallucinations; deja-vu spells; altered-time or impaired-awareness episodes; unexplained gaps in continuity): a neurology referral is warranted rather than optional. Temporal-lobe seizure activity can present without convulsions, and these symptoms should not be assumed to be trauma-related until a neurological evaluation has been completed.
- Threat-biased prosodic reading has produced a pattern of relational ruptures you did not want (friendships ended over micro-readings, partnerships frayed): trauma-informed relational therapy.
- Significant memory gaps (large stretches of childhood simply absent, recent time you cannot account for): trauma-competent clinician with dissociative-population experience.

These are moments when the framework hands off to something else.

See Gifted & Tortured for the Bard and Interpreter baseline-temperament versions; Half a Second More for the practice paths for each circuit.

10.9 The Music and the Words

The boss said *nice job* on her way out of the meeting, and you read something in it. You may have read what was there. You may have read what your trauma layer added. You will not always be able to tell in the moment. With time, with regulation, with the prosody reality-check used often enough to update the Bard's prior, you get to a place where you can wait and check, and not have your whole afternoon organized by a reading you were not certain of.

The colleague said something in the meeting that did not turn into meaning, and you did not catch it. You may need to ask, take notes, or use the slower room. With the autonomic load lower and the Interpreter carrying less weight, the words begin to land more often. Not all of them. More of them than before.

The two circuits come back at different speeds. In my clinic, the Bard usually responds first because the appraisal work moves faster than the structural work. The interpreter takes longer because she is operating downstream of the whole system's resource budget, and that budget changes slowly. By the time the Interpreter is doing her job again, the Bard's appraisal work is mostly internalized, and the two circuits are running together the way they were meant to: tone read accurately, words decoded accurately, the friend on the other end of the conversation actually heard.

The arc of recovery on these circuits is rarely linear. There are days when the Bard reads a tone correctly and the Interpreter holds the whole conversation and you walk out of the meeting feeling like a person who can do this. There are days when the autonomic load is up for reasons that have nothing to do with the relationships in the room, and both circuits go back to their cramped configurations and the meeting feels like the meetings used to feel. The frequency of the better days slowly increases. The intensity of the worse days slowly decreases. The shape of recovery on this axis looks less like a steady upward line and more like a noisy average with a real positive slope when you look at it across months rather than across days.

Both circuits are worth tracking. Which one is louder this week? Which one is getting the most in the way? Start there,

Ch 11: The Approach/Avoid Brain

You are at a dinner and someone says something cutting about a friend who is not in the room. You want to push back. You have words ready. The words are right there. And the words do not come out. You sit with your wine glass and feel the moment pass. Later, in the car, you find the perfect response, and you give it to the empty passenger seat, three hours too late.

That freeze is brutal and familiar. You froze because two systems in the front of your brain were both running loud at the same time, and they cancelled each other out. The wanting was there. The front of your brain could not resolve its own push-pull, and the words stayed in.

That is your Approach/Avoid Brain.

I have watched this exact configuration on brain maps for twenty-five years. It has a signature you can see, a felt experience that clients describe in almost the same words across years of clinical work, and a way of changing that is slow but reasonably predictable once the underlying pattern has been read accurately. Most of the trauma freezes that send people to my clinic, *I knew what to say and could not say it*, are this brain pattern. The freeze happens when the motivation circuits in the front of your brain have been shaped by an environment that taught them no action was safe.

This chapter is about the front of your brain. The earlier chapters spent their time at the back: the Lifeguard at the back midline, the Princess at the back-and-right, the Bard a little forward of her, the Interpreter at the back-and-left. The back is the outside world. That is where threat-tuned circuits live, because threat shows up in the world before it shows up in your appraisal of it. The front is the inside self. The front is where you decide what to do about what the back is sending up.

The front does not get to be neutral. The front has its own pair of opposing systems that negotiate with each other in something like the way the Lifeguard and the CEO negotiate the inside-outside attention split. The front pair is the **approach system** on the left and the **avoidance system** on the right. The two of them, working together, produce your moment-to-moment readiness to engage with what is in front of you. When one of them is dominant, you tilt one way. When the other is dominant, you tilt the other way. When they are balanced, you act.

When trauma changes the balance, and it almost always changes the balance, action stops being available the way it should be. You want to and you cannot. You should and you will not. You opened your mouth and you said something other than the thing you meant to say.

Your motivation system is in a particular post-trauma configuration. It can be named, mapped, and changed.

11.1 The Push and the Pull

The front-of-brain motivation system is built around a push and a pull. The push is the approach side, anchored in the left dorsolateral prefrontal cortex and the systems connected to it. The pull is the avoidance side, anchored in the right dorsolateral prefrontal cortex and its connected systems. These two systems do not exactly fight each other. They bias each other. The balance between them, moment to moment, shapes what you do next.

The approach side is the circuit that says *let's go*, the engine of curiosity, social engagement, and forward motion. It is what gets you out of bed when the morning is interesting. It walks you across the room to introduce yourself. It says yes to the new opportunity, asks the new question, takes the new conversation. When it is running well, the world looks like something to engage with.

The avoidance side is the circuit that says *not yet, watch out, that is going to be expensive*. Its function is effort-evaluation and cost-prediction. It notices the meeting that is going to drain you, the relationship that is going to demand more than it gives, the project that looks shiny but will not pay off. Pessimism is not the goal of the avoid side. Cost accuracy is. When it is running well, the avoid side gives you the discrimination to decline what is not worth doing.

You need both. A brain that has only the approach side will pursue every opportunity into exhaustion. A brain that has only the avoidance side will decline every opportunity into stagnation. The push-pull is how the brain integrates cost and benefit in real time, and that integration is what produces useful action.

The clinical literature has tracked this push-pull through a measure called **frontal alpha asymmetry**. Alpha is the resting rhythm of the cortex. The more alpha there is at a region, the less active that region is at the moment of measurement. So a brain showing more alpha on the right than on the left has the left side more active relative to the right, which means the approach side is dominant. A brain showing more alpha on the left than on the right has the right side more active, which means the avoidance side is dominant. The asymmetry is one of the more replicated EEG markers in the affective neuroscience literature.[1]

In my clinic, I see frontal alpha asymmetry on a QEEG every week. Most of my trauma clients carry some version of it. Some are mildly right-shifted at rest and the shift gets dramatic under emotional load. Some sit fairly balanced at rest and only show the asymmetry on cognitive challenge tasks. The asymmetry behaves as a context-dependent readout of the motivation balance, not as a trait number you can read off a single recording and call settled. The pattern becomes most visible when the front of the brain is being asked to do its job.

A balanced asymmetry, the left and right roughly equal, with the small variations that natural mood changes produce, corresponds to a flexible motivation system. You can engage when engagement makes sense. You can withdraw when withdrawal makes sense. You can act with reasonable confidence that the action you are taking is the

[1]López-Castro et al. (2023) found that PTSD was specifically associated with maladaptive frontal alpha asymmetry emerging under challenging emotional conditions. Under low-demand conditions, PTSD and trauma-exposed resilient groups showed similar frontal patterns; under a higher-demand inhibitory-control task, only the PTSD group maintained a maladaptive threat-approach configuration while the resilient group shifted adaptively.

one your motivation system has integrated, not the result of one side bullying the other.

A persistently right-shifted asymmetry, the avoid side dominant, corresponds to the chronic-withdrawal pattern that shows up in depression, in anxiety, and in trauma populations. Action becomes harder when the avoid side consistently outweighs the approach side, not because you have decided against action. This is a brain pattern. People with this asymmetry often describe themselves to me as lazy or unmotivated. What is actually happening is that their approach circuit is running quiet and their avoid circuit is running loud, and the actions that should feel possible are being damped at the level of basic motivation.

11.2 What Trauma Does

Trauma reshapes the asymmetry. The exact shape depends on the trauma history and the underlying temperament, but the general direction is consistent. Trauma quiets the approach side and inflates the avoid side. In the original learning environment, this is often correct. A child whose attempts to engage produced punishment, rejection, or pain learns to mute the approach side. A child whose environment punished mistakes learns to inflate the avoid side, because the avoid side is the circuit that keeps you from making mistakes. The asymmetry shifts rightward, and the shift can become a stable trait that persists long after the original environment has changed.

This produces a few specific phenotype expressions.

The happy little kid quiet. When the left-frontal approach side is running quiet, the circuit that produces forward motion runs out of fuel. You do not feel like getting out of bed because the *let's go* signal is missing, and you do not feel like reaching out to the friend for the same reason. The world looks like something to manage, get through, or wait out rather than something to engage with. This is part of what depression feels like at the level of the motivation circuit. The approach system has gone offline, and without it, the things that should feel attractive do not. The treatment literature supports this framing. Behavioral activation, which is the most reliable behavioral treatment for depression, works in large part by re-engaging the approach system through small, repeated acts of engagement that the left frontal cortex has been failing to initiate spontaneously. You move first, the approach side catches up.

The grumpy old man inflated. When the right-frontal avoid side is running loud, the cost-evaluation circuit becomes negative-biased. Every option starts to look expensive. Every opportunity starts to look like it has a hidden cost. The dread comes up before the engagement. You read the email and your first response is *this is going to be hard, this is going to be a problem, this is going to drain me.* You read the calendar for the week ahead and your stomach drops. You can see the friend's text and feel the cost of replying before you feel anything else. The presentation often gets read as pessimism as personality. Underneath it sits an inflated avoid system producing the affective signature of *that is going to be expensive* even when the actual cost-benefit math does not warrant the dread. On a brain map, I often see this as excess slow-wave activity at right frontal sites. The presentation is clinically recognizable on a brain map. The specific presentation in any given person needs to be confirmed on their own map rather than assumed from the phenotype description.

The simultaneous activation. This is the most disabling pattern, and it is the one that produces the freeze in the dinner-party scene at the start of this chapter. Both systems are running loud at the same time. The approach side wants to act. The avoid side is registering high cost. The two are activating simultaneously, neither winning, and the result is paralysis. You want to and you do not want to, in the same moment. You move toward and away at once. You open your mouth and the words do not come because the approach signal is calling for one action and the avoid signal is blocking it, and the executive system that should be arbitrating cannot get a clean signal from either side. *I want to but I'm scared* is the felt experience of this configuration. It is also the configuration that produces the trauma freeze response, the inability to act in moments where action was needed and where the push-pull, for a few critical seconds, could not resolve.

The simultaneous activation is common in trauma histories where the original environment punished both engagement and withdrawal, where you got hurt for speaking and you got hurt for staying silent, where you got hurt for going close and you got hurt for going away. The motivation circuit learned that no action was safe, and it shows up later as the inability to act in moments where action would actually be safe.

These are the front-of-brain trauma patterns. They look like depression, like anxiety, like avoidance, like the freeze, like the missed-opportunity life. They are all the same circuit, in different states of imbalance.

11.3 The Speaker, in Brief

Most of what this chapter covers is the motivation balance. One related circuit gets dragged into the trauma freeze in a particular way: the Speaker.

The Speaker is your speech-production circuit, anchored in Broca's area in the left frontal cortex, with the supporting motor and timing circuits in the surrounding regions and the left anterior insula. The interpreter on the back-and-left handles incoming language. The Speaker on the front-and-left handles outgoing language. She is what turns intention to speak into actual speech.

The Speaker is, in the larger character ecology, a left-frontal approach system. To produce speech is, in a real sense, to engage with the world. You are pushing words out into shared space. The same left-frontal regions that house the approach motivation house the production motor for speech. She is the production-side counterpart to the Happy Little Kid's general engagement signal.

When the left-frontal approach side gets quieted by trauma, the Speaker gets quieted too. When the simultaneous approach-avoid paralysis takes hold, the Speaker is one of the first things to freeze. The words do not come, because Broca's area is downstream of a motivation system that has failed to resolve its own push-pull.

A second mechanism affects the Speaker independently. Broca's area requires precise timing to produce fluent speech. It coordinates with the motor cortex and the insula on a millisecond scale, and the timing is fragile. When the back of the brain is flooded with arousal, when the Lifeguard is running at twelve, when the sensory cortex is screaming with overload, when the autonomic system is in alarm, the resources Broca needs to maintain her timing get pulled away. The result is the freeze, the stutter, the word-finding failure, the *I just couldn't think of what to say*. The Speaker has not failed because of any defect in the production circuit. The production circuit is operating with the wrong upstream conditions.

This is why the trauma freeze, in the moment when you need to speak and cannot, has a particular quality. The wanting to speak is intact. The system that produces speech has lost the upstream support it needs to produce. The intention is there. The motor circuit is there. The connection between them has gone offline because the nervous system as a whole is in a state that does not allow the connection to function.

This shows up most acutely in trauma reenactments, being asked questions about the trauma, being in conversation with the person involved in the trauma, being in environments that resemble the trauma context. It shows up in selective mutism in children. It shows up in adults who can speak fluently in some settings and cannot speak at all in others. It shows up in the courtroom where the survivor cannot testify, in the meeting where the employee cannot push back, in the bedroom where the partner cannot say the thing she has wanted to say for months.

The Speaker's freeze is the production circuit operating downstream of an autonomic and motivational state that does not support it. What helps the Speaker is rarely direct speech work. What helps is work on the upstream conditions that determine whether she can do her job.

11.4 The Synthesis: Why Both Loud Equals Stuck

Three failure modes map to those three patterns. The first is approach offline, avoid quiet (flat, nothing looks worth engaging). The second is approach baseline, avoid inflated (dread before every task, cost predictions overshoot). The third, and hardest, is both sides loud simultaneously (the push-pull cannot resolve; action stalls).

The third is the trauma-freeze presentation. Both regulation strategies are needed at once. The approach side needs support to keep showing up. The avoid side needs softening to let the action through. Most clients in this mode function adequately in low-stakes situations. The signature is the simultaneous activation when something matters (the meeting, the partner, the moment when the words need to come out), and the freeze hits exactly there. The asymmetry is mild at baseline; the high-stakes moment activates both systems hard, and the simultaneous activation produces the freeze.

11.5 What Helps

Approach/avoid work starts with getting the freeze loose enough to feel the fork. You cannot work the push-pull while the nervous system is still at high alarm, because high alarm activates both sides simultaneously and makes the freeze worse. Breath, sleep, baseline regulation. The foundation here is the same as everywhere. Chapter 15 covers the sequencing principle.

The approach/avoid brain also has its own particular set of tools, and they tend to be different from the back-of-brain tools.

Behavioral activation, deliberately. When the approach side is offline, action precedes feeling. You do not wait until you want to call the friend. You call the friend, and the want catches up. You do not wait until you feel like going to the gym. You go, and the approach side updates that this is something it does. The mechanism is structural rather than motivational at first. You are giving the approach side new data to integrate. With repetition over weeks, the approach side begins producing the want signal more reliably because it has accumulated evidence that the action produces an outcome worth wanting. Behavioral activation has evidence as a depression intervention precisely because it targets this mechanism.

Light and a minimum-viable morning routine. Bright light exposure within the first thirty minutes of waking has measurable effects on the approach side, mediated through circadian and dopaminergic pathways. The literature on bright light therapy for depression and seasonal affective disorder is substantial, and the effect is real and reasonably fast. For an Approach/Avoid Brain with the approach side quieted, morning light is one of the highest-value interventions available. I tell clients to get fifteen to thirty minutes of outdoor light within an hour of waking, every day, before screens. Most of the people who actually do this report a noticeable shift within two to three weeks. The light is also a good anchor for a small repeatable morning sequence: light, a short walk, one brief practice. The bar should be deliberately low. When the approach side is offline, an elaborate morning protocol is the last thing that will get done. A minimum-viable routine, timed to the circadian window, gives the approach system a consistent signal at the moment in the day when it is most ready to update.

Exercise, the kind that brings the heart rate up. Physical activity reliably activates the approach system, in a way that has been documented across many studies. Intensity should stay within what the body can tolerate. For some trauma populations, very intense exercise is destabilizing. But getting the body in motion regularly, at an intensity the body can tolerate, supports the approach side in a way that few other interventions match.

Loving-kindness practice for the avoid side. Loving-kindness meditation, repeated over weeks, has been associated with leftward shifts in frontal asymmetry in some studies, corresponding to a reduction in the right-frontal dominance pattern. The frontal-asymmetry evidence is preliminary, and the loving-kindness-specific findings are a small subset of it. The clinical direction is consistent, and the practice has a favorable adverse-effect profile for trauma populations compared to intensive concentration practices.

Focused-attention practice for the approach side. If the dominant pattern is approach-quiet, the left side responds well to sustained-attention and concentration practices. Focused-attention meditation, the kind where you hold one object of attention and return to it when the mind wanders, engages the left prefrontal cortex in a way that open-monitoring and loving-kindness practices do not emphasize. The two practices address different sides of the imbalance: loving-kindness softens the avoid side, concentration wakes the approach side. In my clinic the approach-quiet clients who take up a regular concentration practice, even five or ten minutes a day, tend to show earlier left-frontal gains on follow-up maps than those who rely on behavioral activation alone.

Movement-based concentration. Concentration practice does not require sitting still, and for some trauma populations stillness itself is activating (Chapter 15 covers this in detail). Yoga, tai chi, and walking are all forms of moving concentration when done with sustained attention to the body and breath. Walking in particular has a strong evidence base for neuroplasticity: a one-year moderate-intensity walking program increased anterior hippocampal volume by roughly 2 percent and raised serum BDNF, the growth factor most directly linked to new neuron production in the hippocampus.[2] The effect was specific to aerobic walking at moderate intensity; stretching controls showed continued volume decline. For the approach-quiet brain, a daily walk at a pace that raises the heart rate modestly is both a concentration practice and a plasticity intervention, two mechanisms in one action.

Targeted neurofeedback. When the asymmetry is significant and a QEEG confirms the pattern, neurofeedback at the frontal sites can help. The protocols vary depending on whether the dominant pattern is approach quiet (and needs left-frontal up-training, typically raising

[2]Erickson et al. (2011) randomized 120 older adults to a one-year moderate-intensity aerobic walking program or a stretching control. The walking group showed a 2% increase in anterior hippocampal volume and elevated serum BDNF; the stretching group showed continued age-related decline. A 2025 systematic review of 21 studies (Khalil, 2025) confirmed that walking at moderate to high intensity reliably increases circulating BDNF, the primary growth factor for hippocampal neurogenesis.

beta and reducing excess alpha) or avoid inflated (and needs right-frontal calming), or simultaneous activation (which needs both). This is clinical work and benefits from a provider who specifically does asymmetry work and can explain the reasoning behind the protocol.

For the freeze specifically. The trauma freeze, when it happens in the moment, often does not respond to cognitive intervention because the executive systems that would do the cognitive work are themselves part of what has frozen. What sometimes helps in the moment is a small sensory input that brings the autonomic system down a notch. A longer exhale. The touch of the floor under your feet. A glance at a familiar object across the room. The intervention is not designed to solve the freeze; it gives the autonomic floor a tiny recovery moment that may allow the resolution to happen. Over time, working with a trauma-competent clinician on the freeze response, sometimes through somatic approaches, sometimes through EMDR with attention to the freeze patterns, can reduce its frequency and intensity.

For the Speaker, indirectly. Direct speech-production therapy for trauma-related Speaker freezes is rarely the first move. Upstream regulation usually comes first. As the Lifeguard comes down, as the autonomic baseline settles, as the front-of-brain motivation system gets less reactive, the Speaker becomes able to do her job in the moments she previously could not. There are also somatic-experiencing protocols specifically designed to address the freeze, including the speech freeze, that can be useful with the right clinician.

What does not help:

Self-criticism for the freeze. The approach/avoid brain in the freeze configuration is operating at the limits of what the push-pull can do. Adding criticism on top (*I should have spoken up, I should have known what to do*) does not improve future function and may worsen it by adding load to the avoid side. The criticism is the avoid side talking. Listening to it longer is not the answer.

Forcing the action when both sides are loud. Sometimes the freeze is the avoid side telling you that the moment is not as safe as it looked, and the freeze is doing its job. Pushing through the freeze in the wrong moment can produce a worse outcome than letting the moment pass and trying again later, with more support. There is judgment involved here. Sometimes the freeze is dysfunctional and pushing through helps. Sometimes the freeze is appropriate and pushing through hurts. A clinician can help with the discrimination.

11.6 When This Is Beyond Self-Help

If any of these apply, the next step is clinical support, not this book. For crisis resources, see the Introduction.

- Freeze is preventing action in situations involving physical safety: trauma-competent clinician with freeze-response experience. The work requires a regulated relationship to revisit those moments.
- Approach-quiet pattern has crossed into depression severe enough to include thoughts of self-harm: stop and get support now. The approach/avoid brain in that state is not a reliable assessor of its own situation.
- Avoid-inflated pattern has crossed into phobic-level avoidance (world has gotten smaller, dread produces avoidance produces more dread): structured trauma-informed exposure work with a clinician. The sequencing matters but the literature is well-developed.
- Simultaneous activation has crossed into inability to make even small decisions day to day: a clinician can provide the scaffolding the push-pull needs while it is being worked on.

These are moments when the framework hands off to something else.

See Gifted & Tortured (Ch.1+2) for the Happy Little Kid and Grumpy Old Man baseline-temperament versions; Borrowed Peace for action-initiation borrowed from stimulants or compulsions.

11.7 The Words That Finally Came

The dinner where you did not push back on the cutting comment about the friend who was not there. The meeting where you did not say the idea. The conversation where you did not ask the question.

These are moments when an old motivation system, configured by an environment that taught it that engagement was punished and avoidance was punished, ran both sides loud at once and could not produce the action you intended. The Speaker froze because the upstream motivation circuit could not give her what she needed to speak. The freeze was real. The freeze was the push-pull doing what the data taught it to do.

Here is what I see when this changes. The asymmetry moves toward balance, slowly. The approach side gets some of its volume back, because you have been giving it data, small actions, small engagements, small reasons to come back online. The avoid side softens, because the autonomic baseline is lower, because the regulation work has eased the chronic load, because the loving-kindness practice has slowly updated the threat-prediction prior. The simultaneous activation eases, because both sides are less reactive, and the moments that used to produce freeze begin to produce action instead.

Not all the moments. Some will still produce freeze, especially the high-stakes ones, especially the ones that touch the original trauma context. The freeze may not entirely go away. What changes is the frequency, the intensity, and the quality of recovery from it. You freeze less often. The freeze lasts shorter when it happens. You come back from it with less self-criticism and more workable next steps.

If this is your pattern, the starting move is the smallest action you can commit to this week. Not the conversation, not the confrontation. Morning light. Ten minutes of walking. Three rounds of loving-kindness. When the freeze hits, lengthen one exhale and put your hand on something solid. Let the smallest action be the next one.

And one day you are at a dinner and someone says something cutting and you push back. The words come. They come at normal volume, with normal timing, in real time. You do not have to deliver them to the empty passenger seat in the car later. You deliver them in the room. The friend who was not there gets defended. The approach/avoid brain has integrated, in that moment, well enough to act.

That is what I am after with my Approach/Avoid clients. From the outside, it does not look like much. From the inside, it is the difference between a life where you watch yourself fail to show up and a life where you actually show up. The push and the pull are both still there. They do not cancel each other out anymore. They produce action.

Ch 12: The Problem Child

You have been holding it together all week. The work has been hard, the kid has been sick, you have not slept enough, you have been the reasonable one in three different conversations that did not ask you to be the reasonable one. Then on Friday night your partner says something small. The thing he said is not a big deal. You know it is not a big deal. You feel the response coming up out of your chest with a velocity that has nothing to do with the size of the comment, and you say something that is going to take an hour to walk back. Or you do not walk it back. You slam a door, you stand in the kitchen breathing, and you do not know exactly what just happened, only that it happened.

Most of my clients with significant trauma have a version of that Friday-night moment in their history. Many of them have several. Some of them came to my clinic because of that moment specifically: a thing said, a door slammed, a choice made at midnight that did not look like a choice from the inside but is now a consequence they are trying to clean up. They walk in ashamed and also, quietly, angry. The shame is real, and so is the anger. The anger is one of the things that makes them good at what they do, and the shame is one of the things that keeps them locked in the pattern that produced the moment they came in to talk about.

This is the chapter on the brake. What it does, why it fails, what trauma does to it, and what to actually do about it.

When the brake is doing its job, you have impulses and the impulses do not always become actions. You can be angry without being destructive, frustrated without being cutting, tempted without being foolish. The brake is not suppression; you are not stuffing the impulse down. The brake is what allows the impulse to register and then, before it becomes action, get evaluated against the rest of your priorities.

When the brake fails, the impulse becomes action without the evaluation step. The anger becomes the words you wish you had not said. The bad decision at midnight is the consequence you are still cleaning up.

This is the problem child phenotype. It is also a bridge chapter. The problem child is the phenotype that most often shows up alongside the patterns I cover in *Borrowed Peace*: the substances, the work, the food, the achievement, the borrowed regulation strategies that try to compensate for what the brake cannot do directly. The two books overlap here. I will hand off cleanly between them at the end.

12.1 Where the Problem Child Lives

The problem child's circuit runs through the right inferior frontal gyrus, with related activity in the right ventrolateral prefrontal cortex, the orbitofrontal cortex, and the connections those structures have to the basal ganglia and limbic systems. On a brain map I read his pattern around F8, FT8, and the lateral right-frontal region. His circuit is part of what neuroscience calls the **stop signal** system, the network that, in laboratory tasks designed to test impulse control, fires in the milliseconds between the urge to act and the action.

The right IFG has been studied extensively as the brain's response-inhibition system. When this region is damaged, even by small lesions, the result is often disinhibition. Patients who were not impulsive before become impulsive. Patients who were not socially inappropriate before become socially inappropriate. Patients who could exercise restraint before find that restraint harder to access. The problem child is an inhibitory circuit. He says *no*, in the moments where *no* is needed.

He is part of a family. The grumpy old man, in the previous chapter, was an avoidance and effort-evaluation system in the right dorsolateral prefrontal cortex. The problem child is a related inhibitory system, sitting just below and to the side. They work together. The grumpy old man does the slower, deliberative cost-evaluation work, asking *should I be doing this at all*. The problem child does the faster, in-the-moment inhibitory work, catching the moment to stop before the next thing happens.

When both are functioning well, they form a layered defense against impulse-driven action. The grumpy old man slows you down at the planning level; the problem child catches you at the action level. When the grumpy old man fails, you take on more than you should and arrive at the impulsive moment with depleted resources. When the problem child fails, the impulse becomes action without the brake.

There is a particular relationship between these two that matters for the trauma story: the grumpy old man, when chronically activated, exhausts the problem child. The system that has been running anxious overcontrol (saying no to things, holding the line, monitoring for cost) eventually runs out of inhibitory resource. When the inhibitory system is exhausted, it stops being able to do the in-the-moment brake work. The system that was running too tight collapses into a system that cannot run tight at all. The grumpy old man fatigues into the problem child.

This is one of the core dynamics of the problem child phenotype. The brake was not always broken. The brake was over-used, by a system trying to hold itself together against trauma load, until the brake gave out. The disinhibition you see in the problem child is often the downstream consequence of years of over-inhibition somewhere else.

12.2 What Trauma Does to a Problem Child

Trauma can produce a problem child phenotype through several routes. If more than one of them sounds like you, that is expected. They look different from the inside even though they share the final pattern of the brake failing.

The first route is **chronic overcontrol collapse**. As above. The person spent years over-controlling, holding everything in, never letting the anger out, performing the regulated child even in environments that warranted reaction, and then ran out of inhibitory resource. The problem child shows up later in life as a brake failure that comes seemingly out of nowhere, in someone who used to be reliable, calm, controlled. The presentation is often confusing to the person and to the people around them. *I used to be the responsible one. I do not know what is happening to me.* What is happening is that the inhibitory system is depleted and the impulse-control circuits no longer have the resource to maintain the brake.

The second route is **state-shifting need**. Trauma puts the nervous system in states that are uncomfortable to be in: hypervigilance, fog, dread, simultaneous-activation freeze. The problem child phenotype, in some people, is the system that breaks the state. The impulsive action interrupts the unbearable internal experience. The drink interrupts the dread. The text interrupts the freeze. The risky choice interrupts the fog. The fight interrupts the dissociation. From outside, this looks like impulse-control failure. From inside, it is a primitive form of state-regulation: doing something to feel something different. The brake is being deliberately, if not consciously, overridden because the cost of not overriding it is intolerable, not because the brake is broken.

This is the bridge to *Borrowed Peace*. Most of what that book treats as borrowed regulation (substances, sex, food, work, intensity) operates through this mechanism. The problem child is the phenotype that does the borrowing. The substance is the tool, but the circuit doing the borrowing is the right-IFG brake being deliberately disabled to allow the state-shifting action through.

The third route is **direct disinhibition from chronic load**. When the autonomic nervous system has been running hot for years, the cortical regions that handle inhibition lose function. The right-frontal inhibitory cortex needs adequate resource (sleep, stable arousal, decent metabolic support) to do its work. The chronically traumatized nervous system often does not have these conditions, and the inhibitory circuit operates at lower capacity than it would otherwise. The brake is weaker because chronic load has depleted the substrate, not because of any deliberate compensation.

The fourth route, in developmental trauma, is **the brake never fully developed**. The right-frontal inhibitory systems mature across childhood and into the early twenties. A childhood characterized by chronic threat or chaos often does not provide the conditions under which these systems mature optimally. The adult arrives with inhibitory capacity that was never built to its full potential, and the problem child phenotype is what daily life looks like for an adult brain operating with adolescent-level brake function.

These routes can co-occur. Many people I see with significant trauma have a problem child driven by some combination of chronic-overcontrol collapse, state-shifting need, depleted substrate, and incomplete development. The presentation looks similar across the routes. What needs to change differs depending on which is dominant.

A trauma-driven problem child often comes with specific patterns. Reactivity that is disproportionate to the trigger. The 0-to-100 quality of anger, with no in-between. Morning-after regret about choices made the night before. The relationship pattern of repeated explosive moments followed by repair followed by the next explosive moment. The sense of being unable to predict your own behavior, which is one of the more demoralizing experiences a person can have. The fatigue that accompanies the brake-failure pattern, because keeping the brake working at all takes effort, and the effort exhausts.

12.3 What This Misreads As

A problem child phenotype gets called many things, often in ways that miss the trauma layer.

He gets called **bipolar**. The mood reactivity, the impulsive choices, the rapid shifts between states can look like bipolar disorder, bipolar II. Some people with this pattern have bipolar disorder. Many have a problem child driven by trauma load, which presents differently in important ways: the shifts are usually more reactive to environmental triggers, the depressive periods are not the classic bipolar depression, and the response to mood stabilizers is variable. Sorting this out matters because the treatments differ.

She gets called **borderline personality disorder**. The reactivity, the relationship pattern, the impulsivity, the anger episodes can map onto BPD criteria. As with the Princess phenotype's BPD-overlap question, some problem children carrying a BPD diagnosis have a trauma-shaped impulse-control system rather than a personality disorder per se. The label tends to follow the person and color subsequent treatment. The trauma framing often opens treatment options that the personality-disorder framing closes.

He gets called **conduct disorder** or **antisocial**, in adolescents. The disinhibited behavior is real, the harm to others is real, the consequences are real. A trauma-shaped problem child is usually different from a primary antisocial pattern, with more remorse, more attempts at repair, more recognition that the behavior does not match the values. The diagnostic distinction matters for what the treatment looks like.

She gets called **an addict**, often with no acknowledgment of the trauma layer underneath. The substance use is treated as the primary problem, the brake-failure pattern is treated as the central pathology, and the underlying state-shifting mechanism (the trauma load that the substance is being used to manage) gets ignored. This is one of the more reliable ways to fail at addiction treatment. The addiction is the symptom; the trauma-driven problem child is the circuit; the autonomic load and the trauma history are the upstream conditions. Addressing only the surface produces a high relapse rate.

He gets called **lazy**, **selfish**, **out of control**, **a bad partner**, **a difficult person**. The folk descriptions catch the consequences. They are unhelpful because they do not engage the mechanism, and they tend to land on the problem child as further evidence that the person is bad. That feeds the shame layer, which feeds the state-shifting need, which fuels the next failure of the brake.

12.4 The Gift

The problem child has a gift that the cramped version distorts, and it is one of the more underappreciated gifts in the phenotype catalog.

A regulated problem child is the part of you that does not automatically defer. When the boss is wrong, you see it; when the institution is wrong, you see that too; when the rule does not match the situation, you see it again. The same circuit that fails as disinhibited reactivity is, in better calibration, the circuit that registers when something is wrong and refuses to accept it. The problem child does not let things slide that should not be let slide. He will not pretend the comment was fine, the policy fair, or the situation acceptable when they are not, and that refusal is a trait the world needs more of.

The same circuit produces protective anger. When someone you love is being mistreated, the problem child rises. The anger is the system doing its job. A well-regulated version of this circuit can be protective without being destructive, can step in for the friend, the kid, the colleague, with the right amount of force to address the situation and not so much that the situation gets worse. Many of the most loyal, most fiercely loving people I see in my clinic have strong problem child circuits. They are the people you want with you in a hospital corridor at 2am, in a courtroom, in any moment that demands someone willing to make the call.

In professional contexts, this same calibration looks like assertiveness without aggression. The capacity to say no clearly. The willingness to push back when push-back is warranted. The ability to advocate without becoming destructive or capitulating. People with strong problem child circuits, when those circuits are well-regulated, tend to be the people you want in negotiations, in difficult conversations, in moments where someone needs to draw a line and hold it.

These capacities do not require trauma. The trauma did not give you the brake. The trauma broke the brake, or built it incompletely, or exhausted it through chronic over-use. What you are working toward is a brake that holds, with the underlying capacity intact. The willingness to question authority, the readiness to protect, the capacity for clean assertiveness: those were always yours. They come back online when the circuit that holds them is no longer in collapse.

The clinical picture that shows this most clearly is the one I described in the opening. Someone whose problem child pattern has gotten him into trouble, the lost job, the damaged relationship, the thing said in the wrong moment to the wrong person, comes in ashamed and also, quietly, angry. The shame is real. So is the anger, and the anger is one of the things that makes him good at his job, that makes him fight for the people he loves, that makes him the person others call when something is wrong. My job is to give the anger a brake that actually works, so it can be accurate, well-timed, and appropriately sized. When that happens, something shifts in how he carries himself. He stops apologizing for existing and starts using what he has. It is one of the more satisfying trajectories I get to watch.

12.5 What Helps

The brake circuit does not retrain under pressure. It retrains under regulation. Every intervention below works better when the autonomic baseline is lower, which means the regulation work comes first and the brake work follows. Chapter 15 covers the sequencing principle.

The problem child responds well to a handful of interventions, and several of the standard trauma interventions matter here in specific ways.

Sleep, more than almost anywhere. The right-IFG inhibitory system is unusually sensitive to sleep deprivation. A sleep-deprived problem child is a problem child whose brake is operating at reduced capacity. Many of my clients with this pattern can track the relationship directly: when sleep is good, the reactivity is manageable. When sleep is poor, the brake fails. Restoring sleep is foundational. Trying to do everything else without addressing sleep tends to fail.

Autonomic regulation. The same breath, HRV, grounding work that helps the back-of-brain phenotypes helps here, by lowering the baseline arousal that the brake is working against. A regulated autonomic state gives the brake more room to operate. When the lifeguard is at a four instead of a nine, the brake does not have to work as hard to maintain inhibition.

State-shifting alternatives. When the problem child phenotype is driven by state-shifting need, what helps is giving the system other ways to shift state besides the impulsive action. This is the heart of harm reduction in addiction treatment, and it applies more broadly than the addiction context. The dread can be shifted by a long exhale and twenty minutes of walking; the freeze can be shifted by sensory input that brings the autonomic system down a notch; the unbearable internal experience can be eased, in many cases, by something other than the substance or the risky choice. Building a repertoire of state-shifting tools that do not have the cost of the impulsive ones is one of the central pieces of recovery for this phenotype.

The half-second pause. Specifically, training the system to insert a half-second between impulse and action. The half-second pause is a learnable skill that, with practice, becomes more reliable. The pause is created by attention, noticing the impulse as an impulse, naming it briefly, letting the pause exist before deciding what to do with the impulse. The pause does not have to be long; even a brief deliberate gap between *I want to* and *I do* is enough to allow the rest of the system to weigh in. This works best when the autonomic baseline is regulated; under high arousal, the half-second pause is hard to access. With practice and the right conditions, it gets reliable.

Targeted neurofeedback. When the problem child pattern is dominant and a QEEG confirms the right-frontal inhibitory weakness, neurofeedback at right-frontal sites can help. The protocols typically involve supporting the inhibitory rhythms in the right inferior frontal region. This is clinical work and benefits from a provider with specific expertise in inhibition-related protocols who can explain the reasoning behind the approach.

Behavioral approaches with structure. The problem child often functions better with external scaffolding that takes some of the load off the internal brake. Schedules that limit access to high-temptation situations during high-fatigue times. Decisions made in advance rather than in the moment. Environmental design that does not require the brake to engage in the first place. These are intelligent design for a circuit operating at reduced capacity. Offloading the inhibition to structure is a real intervention. I tell people this often, because many of them feel they should not need it.

For the bridge to Borrowed Peace patterns specifically. When the problem child is doing state-shifting through substances or behavioral patterns, the most reliable approach is to address both the trauma layer and the substance layer simultaneously. Integrated dual-diagnosis treatment is more effective than treating one and deferring the other. *Borrowed Peace* covers the substance and behavioral side in detail.

Medication, when a prescriber assesses it as appropriate. The reactivity, impulsivity, and autonomic substrate that show up alongside this phenotype sometimes respond to pharmacological intervention. Mood stabilizers, alpha-2 adrenergic agonists, and naltrexone are among the classes I have seen prescribers use in this population, each for a different aspect of the clinical picture. The decision belongs to a prescriber who can assess the full diagnostic and medical context rather than routing from the phenotype pattern. What this chapter can contribute to that conversation is a clearer description of the clinical picture the prescriber is treating.

What does not help:

Self-criticism for the brake failures. The problem child who hates himself for his brake failures is running on additional cognitive load, with no benefit. The self-criticism is the same circuit that, in an over-controlled phase, produced the grumpy old man pattern. Adding more of it does not fix the brake; it just feeds the cycle. What helps is a different relationship to the failures: learning from them, making repair where repair is possible, extracting the information about what conditions produced the failure, and moving forward without the additional layer of self-attack.

Punitive consequences as the primary intervention. A problem child treated punitively often gets worse. Adding more reasons to fear consequences does not strengthen the brake-failure pattern; the circuit is already operating at low inhibitory capacity, and adding fear adds load to the avoid side without adding capacity to the brake itself. This is why punishment-based approaches to disinhibited behavior in adolescents and adults often fail, while structural and supportive approaches sometimes succeed.

Pretending the impulse can be eliminated. The problem child's job, in his correct calibration, is to slow the impulse, not to extinguish it. People with this phenotype who try to be impulse-free generally fail and then experience the failure as evidence that they are broken. The more useful framing is that the impulse is information, the impulse will keep happening, and the goal is a reliable brake that can handle the impulse without being overwhelmed by it.

12.6 When This Is Beyond Self-Help

If any of these apply, the next step is clinical support, not this book. For crisis resources, see the Introduction.

- Brake-failure pattern has begun to produce harm to others (physical violence, severe verbal aggression, behavior that has crossed legal lines): clinician with impulse-control and trauma experience. There is real work that can be done; it requires more support than this book provides.
- State-shifting through substances at physical-dependence levels (alcohol, benzodiazepines, opioids): do not attempt withdrawal alone. Medical detox is a real medical intervention. *Borrowed Peace* covers this in detail.
- Impulsive choices have begun to involve serious self-harm or thoughts of self-harm: stop and get support now. The problem child in that state is not a reliable judge of what has permanent consequences.
- Brake failures have created a pattern of harm in a relationship: couples or family work with a clinician who understands trauma dynamics and can hold both nervous systems at once.

These are moments when the framework hands off to something else.

See Gifted & Tortured for the baseline-temperament disinhibited version; Half a Second More for the gap-training practice path; Borrowed Peace for borrowed-regulation patterns that sit on top of this phenotype.

12.7 A Practice for the Half-Second Pause

Try this in a low-stakes moment first, before you need it in a high-stakes one.

Pick something small and habitual that has a brief gap between impulse and action. Picking up your phone when you sit down at your desk. Reaching for the snack on the counter when you walk past it. Saying the next thing in a conversation when there is a small lull. Anything where you can notice the impulse before you act on it.

When the impulse arrives, notice it. Name it silently. *Impulse to pick up the phone. Impulse to grab the snack. Impulse to fill the lull.* Then hold the next half-second open. Do not decide yet whether you will act on the impulse or not. Just let the gap exist.

After the half-second, decide. The decision can be either way. Insert the gap; you can still act on the impulse afterward. Sometimes you will pick up the phone, and that will be fine. Sometimes you will not, and that will also be fine. What you are training is the gap itself.

Do this several times a day for a few weeks. The gap will start to come more easily. It will start to show up in places you did not put it. The high-stakes moment, when it arrives, will land in a system that has a little more practice at not collapsing the gap into action. The brake gets stronger by being used in moments where the stakes are low enough that using it does not feel like effort.

The brake comes back. Not in a week. Over months, with the right conditions, with the autonomic baseline coming down and the trauma load easing and the system learning that there are ways to manage state that do not require the brake to fail. The problem child who has been failing because the substrate is failing becomes a problem child who can do his actual job, which is to slow the impulse just enough that the rest of you can decide what to do with it. Start with the half-second. The rest follows.

Part III

Parts, States, and the Autonomic System

Ch 13: Your Parts Have Brain Patterns

If you have spent any time in trauma therapy in the last twenty years, you have probably been asked to talk to a part of yourself. The therapist asks where it sits in your body. She asks how old it is. She asks what it wants you to know. You answer, and the answer feels both made up and true at the same time. There is a part. The part has things to say. You are not crazy for hearing it.

You are also probably wondering, at some point, whether the part is real. Real in the sense of having a discrete existence, of being a small entity inside you that can be addressed and listened to as if it were another person. Or real in some other sense, a way of speaking that captures something that does not have any other available language.

The honest answer is the second one: parts are real, but probably not as separate selves living inside your skull, and not in the way the most enthusiastic versions of parts work suggest. They are something more interesting and, in some ways, more workable: state-dependent configurations of the same brain patterns we have been mapping for the last several chapters.

The Manager who runs your life from a desk in your head is not a small executive who lives in there. The Manager is your CEO, the front-midline conflict-monitoring circuit, in a particular trauma-shaped configuration. The Firefighter who shows up with the bottle of wine when the day has been too much is not a separate entity. The Firefighter is your Problem Child, the right-frontal brake circuit, doing state-shifting work in the way that circuit does state-shifting work. The Exile who carries the early grief that nobody knew what to do with is not a buried child waiting for rescue. The Exile is unintegrated affect and memory, held in the temporal-limbic systems that store affect and memory, separated from the rest of you because the conditions for integration have not been there.

Parts work is useful, and this chapter adds the brain-pattern layer underneath it rather than telling you to discard what already helps. The move opens up a way of relating to internal experience that pure cognitive frameworks miss. The reason this chapter exists is that the parts framework gets more useful when you can see what is underneath it, when you can recognize the brain patterns the parts language has been describing without naming.

The chapter also brings in something the most popular versions of parts work tend to leave out: the traditions that came before. Internal Family Systems did not emerge in a vacuum. Structural family therapy, the multigenerational model of Murray Bowen, and the experiential work of Virginia Satir were the family-of-origin traditions that taught a generation of clinicians how to think about subsystems, roles, boundaries, and the way patterns get passed down through relationships. On the multiplicity side, Hal and Sidra Stone's Voice Dialogue had been working with inner "selves" since the early 1970s, developing what the Stones called the Aware Ego process (a meta-position for observing your parts without being captured by any one of them) in the same years that family therapy and parts-work traditions were taking shape across the field.[1] IFS took the family systems moves and turned them inward, and added a transformation agenda (the unburdening and role-shifting) that Voice Dialogue intentionally avoids. What Schwartz built in the unburdening framework gave clinicians a clean operational sequence for what to do once a part has been identified, and IFS's clinical reach, through training programs, certification tracks, and a network of practitioners, has done more than any other parts-tradition to put multiplicity-aware therapy into general clinical use.

This is a bridge chapter. It connects the phenotype framework you have been learning to the parts language you may have already been working with, and to the family systems language that gives the whole picture its developmental context. Give yourself a more accurate map underneath parts work.

---

[1]Stone, H., & Stone, S. (1989). *Embracing Our Selves: The Voice Dialogue Manual.* New World Library.

13.1 What Parts Work Got Right

The most important thing parts work got right is the recognition that you are not one thing. Internal experience is multiple voices, sometimes in conflict, often pulling in different directions. The cognitive psychology of the mid-twentieth century, with its assumption of a unified rational decision-maker, was always wrong about this. Real people do not work that way. Real people contain multiple motivational configurations that show up in different contexts and that often disagree with each other.

Parts work makes this multiplicity explicit and gives you language for it. Instead of saying *I'm conflicted about this*, you can say *part of me wants to take the job, and part of me is afraid of taking it*. The framing helps because it does not collapse the conflict into a single confused self. It separates the strands. You can listen to each one. You can find out what each one wants. You can let them have a conversation, sometimes literally, and arrive at a decision that integrates more of the actual data than the unified-self framing would have allowed.

Parts work also gets right that some of these motivational configurations are protective, even when the protection has become costly. The Manager is trying to keep you safe. The Firefighter is trying to keep the day from breaking you. Both have been holding things together for years. The reason these configurations are hard to dislodge is that they are doing real work, even when the costs exceed the benefits. Telling them to leave does not work, because the function they serve still needs to be carried somehow.

Parts work also gets right that something underneath these configurations exists beyond the parts themselves. IFS calls it the Self: what is there when no part is captaining. It is the regulated baseline: the curiosity, calm, compassion, and connectedness that become available when the parts are not running the show. The Self is hard to describe in clinical language because it is more like the field in which the parts move, the ground under the figures, than a discrete thing. When you have been in the Self even briefly, you recognize it.

The framework, in its most workable form, says: you have parts, the parts are doing work, that work is partly protective and partly costly, and underneath the parts there is a Self that can hold the parts without merging with them. The therapeutic move is to bring the Self forward, listen to the parts from the Self, give the parts what they have been needing, and let them gradually return to a more integrated configuration.

This is useful clinically, and the research literature offers real but modest support. The first major randomized controlled trial, published in 2013, randomized 79 rheumatoid arthritis patients to an IFS group or an education control; the IFS group showed significant pain and depression reductions that held at one-year follow-up (Shadick et al., 2013). That study led SAMHSA's National Registry of Evidence-Based Programs and Practices to list IFS as an evidence-based practice in late 2015, rating it "effective" for general functioning and "promising" for depression and anxiety.[2] The registry was discontinued in 2018, and the listing rested on a single modest-sized trial. More recently, the PARTS study at a Harvard-affiliated center randomized 60 PTSD patients to an IFS-based group program or an active nature-based control; both groups showed large reductions in PTSD symptoms comparable to established trauma treatments, but no significant difference between the two arms (Joss et al., 2026). A pilot for comorbid PTSD and substance use showed similar early promise with small numbers.[3] The model is a clinical approach with real evidence and growing research attention. The controlled-trial base remains a handful of studies with modest samples, however, and the largest trial did not show IFS outperforming an active comparison. That is worth knowing as you decide how much weight to put on the framework.

What the model does not do, in most of its popular presentations, is tell you what is happening at the brain level. The parts feel real

[2]SAMHSA NREPP (2015). National Registry of Evidence-Based Programs and Practices listing for Internal Family Systems. Registry discontinued 2018.

[3]Ally et al. (2025). Pilot study of IFS-based intervention for comorbid PTSD and substance use.

because they are. They are what the brain looks like when the patterns we have been mapping run in particular configurations.

13.2 The Translation

Here is the translation, as cleanly as it can be made. Each row is a way of looking at something that the parts language has been describing without naming.

A **Manager**, in IFS terms, is the part that runs the show, keeps things organized, anticipates problems, tries to prevent bad outcomes. The brain-pattern correlate is mostly the CEO, the front-midline conflict-monitoring circuit, in a stuck or over-active configuration. The classic Manager presentation is what we covered in Chapter 7: stuck on the wrong thing, holding priorities that should have released, running monitoring loops because the system learned that letting go was unsafe. The performer subtype of the CEO is a particular flavor of Manager, the one whose external function is itself the protection.

A **Firefighter**, in IFS terms, is the part that shows up when an emotional crisis is breaking through and disrupts the situation by impulsive action: drinking, eating, dissociating, picking a fight, making the risky choice. The brain-pattern correlate is mostly the Problem Child, the right-frontal brake circuit, doing state-shifting work. The Firefighter is the brake being deliberately overridden because the unbearable internal experience needs to stop somehow, now. Chapter 12 covered this in detail. The bridge to *Borrowed Peace* is the Firefighter in its substance-using form.

An **Exile**, in IFS terms, is the part that carries the painful affect, the early grief, the unprocessed terror, the shame that nobody knew what to do with. The brain-pattern correlate is unintegrated affect and memory, held in the temporal-limbic systems, separated from the conscious-narrative-producing systems because the conditions for integration have not been there. This is partly the Interpreter side of the temporal-lobe story Chapter 10, partly the autonomic-state memory that lives in the body, and partly the implicit memory systems that store affect without verbal scaffolding. Exiles are not buried children.

Exiles are the affective and somatic data that the trauma response did not have the resource to integrate at the time.

A **Protector**, in IFS terms, is a part that watches for threat and intervenes to prevent harm. The brain-pattern correlate is usually some version of the Lifeguard, the back-midline environmental-scanning circuit. A Protector who scans the room for danger before any action is taken is a Lifeguard doing her job at high gain. Chapter 6 covered this circuit in detail.

A **Critic**, in IFS terms, is a part that delivers harsh internal commentary, often experienced as the voice of a parent or other authority figure. The brain-pattern correlate is some combination of the CEO running the error-monitoring loop, the Grumpy Old Man producing the avoidance and dread, and sometimes the Bard producing the prosodic content of the critical voice. The Critic is rarely a single circuit. It is a configuration of circuits running together to produce the experience of an internal critical voice.

A **dissociated part**, in IFS terms, is a part that is offline, hard to access, separated from the rest of the system in a particular way. The brain-pattern correlate is the Lifeguard's breaker-tripped state, the Fog & the Tide stuck-fog presentation, and sometimes the temporal-lobe disconnection covered in Chapter 10. The dissociation is the same circuits, in different states, with reduced communication between them.

These translations are not exact. Real internal experience is messier than this. A Manager in a particular person may involve more of the CEO than of the Lifeguard, or it may involve both. A Firefighter may have a particular signature involving the Problem Child plus the Princess plus a specific Bard pattern. Parts are configurations of brain patterns, and those brain patterns are the same ones we have been studying all along.

A small illustration of why this matters. In a session, someone recognizes his Manager for the first time: the hypervigilant planning and control, the monitoring-everything quality, the exhaustion underneath. His therapist asks: "How old is this part?" He thinks. He says: "Thirty-five years old. Same age as me." He means it as a joke but it lands as true. When you give him the brain-pattern translation, the CEO stuck in monitoring loops, the anterior cingulate doing error-detection continuously, something shifts. It is *less about me and more about my brain*, which, for some people, is exactly the permission they need to stop taking the Manager personally and start working with it practically. Both framings are handles on the same thing. The handle that opens the jar is the one worth using.

Mira comes to session saying "the Controller is loud today." Her therapist knows what that means in parts language: the Manager is running hard, anticipating all the ways the week could go wrong, holding her in a state of rigid pre-planning. When they look at the QEEG from three weeks earlier, they see frontal-midline beta elevation, the CEO stuck in its error-monitoring loop. Same thing, two handles. In parts language: "What does the Controller need to feel safe enough to step back?" In brain-pattern language: the anterior cingulate is over-firing its conflict-detection signal, and the move is to give it less to detect. Mira works both sides. In session, she talks to the Controller. On the neurofeedback couch, she trains the rhythm underneath it. The Controller does not vanish. It softens. It becomes the part of her that plans well rather than the part that cannot stop planning.

Dante does not use parts language. He says "the rage just shows up," a state shift so fast that by the time he notices it, his voice has already changed and his partner has already flinched. In IFS terms, a Firefighter, the part that breaks states to manage the unbearable. In brain-pattern terms, his right-frontal brake circuit (F8) is running at low arousal, the Problem Child signature. The impulse fires before the brake can catch it. His therapist tries both doors. From the parts side: "What is the Firefighter protecting you from feeling?" From the regulation side: sleep, HRV work, the half-second pause, all aimed at giving the brake more bandwidth. The two approaches reinforce each other. The parts conversation gives him a relationship with the state. The regulation work gives the circuit more room to function.

This recognition does several useful things. It tells you that working on parts is not separate from working on regulation. The Manager who has been holding everything together is not a different problem from the cramped CEO; she is the cramped CEO, in a slightly different framing. Working on her at the parts-language level and working on the CEO at the regulation level are the same work, approached from two angles. They cross-validate each other when both are being addressed.

It also tells you that some interventions are aimed at the configurations and some are aimed at the underlying circuits, and you usually need both. Parts-work conversations alone do not retrain the underlying brain patterns; they help with the conscious framing and the self-relationship work. Neurofeedback alone does not necessarily produce the integration that conscious self-work produces; it changes the substrate but does not always update the narrative. The most effective work tends to combine both, the substrate retraining and the self-relational work, in the same arc. Janina Fisher's clinical work makes this point directly, bridging the structural dissociation model (which maps how trauma splits the personality into apparently normal parts and emotional parts) with IFS parts language, while insisting on the sequencing: stabilization first, somatic awareness throughout, and integration only when the nervous system is ready.[4]

13.3 The Self, in Brain Language

The Self in IFS is the harder concept to translate, and the translation is more speculative.

When a person is described as being *in Self,* they are described as being curious, calm, compassionate, courageous, clear, connected, confident, and creative, the eight Cs of IFS. The state has a recognizable quality. The parts are still there, present without dominating. The Self is the field in which the parts can be held without collapsing into one of them.

[4]Fisher, J. (2017). *Healing the Fragmented Selves of Trauma Survivors: Overcoming Internal Self-Alienation.* Routledge.

In brain-pattern terms, this state corresponds to something like a regulated default-mode configuration with the prefrontal-limbic balance functioning well, with the autonomic system in a parasympathetic-dominant resting state, and with the various phenotype circuits running at low volume and in coordination rather than competition. No single circuit has captured the system, and the executive and self-referential networks have the bandwidth to hold multiple internal states without being captured by any of them.

This is a real neurobiological state. It can be measured, in part, through autonomic markers and brain network coherence patterns. It is also learnable, and the learning is what most contemplative traditions and most effective trauma therapies are aiming at. The contemplative traditions used different languages: presence, awareness, the witness, the awake mind. The phenomenology is similar across traditions because the underlying brain state is similar.

The clinical implication is that the goal of parts work (to bring the Self forward and hold the parts from the Self) is the same goal as autonomic regulation work, meditation training, neurofeedback that targets default-mode integration, and trauma processing aimed at integration of fragmented material. Different people need different angles, depending on phenotype configuration and history.

The Self is not a part. The Self is what becomes available when the parts are not running the show. You can practice it, and the practice changes the brain in ways that, over time, make the Self more reliably accessible.

13.4 Family Systems: The Layer Beneath

Internal Family Systems took the conceptual moves of family therapy and turned them inward. Before there was an internal family of parts, there was an actual family of subsystems, roles, boundaries, and patterns. The therapists who built the family systems traditions in the 1960s and 1970s (Bowen, Minuchin, Satir, and others) were working out how to think about systems of people in relationship. The same logic, applied to the configuration of subselves inside one person, became IFS.

This is worth knowing because the family-of-origin layer is often where the trauma actually lives. The cramped Lifeguard learned to scan in a household where scanning was useful. The stuck CEO learned to monitor in a household where mistakes were costly. The Firefighter Problem Child learned to break states in a household where state breaks were the only available regulation. The configurations inside you are the residues of the relational systems you grew up in. Working with the parts without engaging the family systems they came from misses part of the picture.

The earliest family-therapy traditions came from Bowen, Minuchin, and Satir, and each named something that remains clinically useful.

Bowen named differentiation of self: the developmental capacity to be in close emotional contact with others without losing your own internal regulation, and to maintain your own internal regulation without disconnecting from others. If you notice that certain family members can send you into a state within thirty seconds of walking through the door, that is low differentiation at work. The state shift is real. It is happening in your nervous system. Bowen also described the multigenerational transmission of emotional patterns, the way anxious states travel from parent to child to grandchild through specific relational mechanisms, often without anyone choosing to pass them on. The lifeguard who passed her scanning down the line was not doing it on purpose. That is how nervous systems in families work. The differentiation framework is directly relevant to the trauma work we have been doing: stabilization is, in part, the project of building enough internal regulation that you can be in contact with others without being captured by their states.

Minuchin named the structural view: families as systems with subsystems, separated by boundaries that could be too rigid, too diffuse, or appropriately permeable. A family where the parental subsystem is collapsed and a child is pulled in to function as a parent produces specific developmental consequences. A family where boundaries between members are too rigid produces emotional disconnection. A family where boundaries are too diffuse produces enmeshment.

Many trauma patterns we have been mapping have roots in these structural conditions. Configurations like the Performer CEO are often associated with parentified family roles, the kid who held things together while the adults could not. Configurations like the dissociative Fog are often associated with households where boundaries were too diffuse, where there was nowhere to go to be alone with one's own experience. Configurations like the Problem Child are often associated with family systems where the disturbance role became the only available one. The same family conditions produce different brain patterns in different children, and the same brain pattern can emerge from different conditions; these are tendencies in the clinical picture.

Satir named communication patterns: the stances family members took under stress, including placating, blaming, computing (going hyper-rational), distracting, and leveling (the integrated response). Satir's stances map onto trauma-shaped phenotype configurations. The placater is often a Princess with a Performer overlay. The blamer is often a Problem Child whose anger has organized into a relational style. The computer is often a CEO who has retreated into cognition because affect was unsafe. The distractor is often a Firefighter whose state-shifting has become the family's escape valve. The leveler is what becomes available when the configuration is regulated enough that direct, integrated communication is possible.

The family systems layer gives you recognition that the parts inside you came from somewhere. They were shaped by the relational system you grew up in. When you work with the parts now, you are also, in some sense, working with the family configuration that produced them. Some of that work can be done internally. Some of it benefits from relational work (couples therapy, family therapy, sometimes sibling work) that takes the systems thinking back into the relationships where the patterns continue to play out.

The trauma framework in this book sits on top of the family systems framework. They are layers of the same picture. The family system shaped the brain patterns, the brain patterns are what shows up in your daily life now, and the integration involves both: the patterns themselves, addressed through regulation work and trauma processing, and the relational dynamics that originated them and that often continue to maintain them.

13.5 What This Means for the Work

A few practical implications of holding the parts framework, the brain-pattern framework, and the family systems framework at the same time.

When you are working with a part, you are working with a configuration of brain circuits. Listening to the part, getting to know it, finding out what it has been protecting against: this conscious-level work activates the circuits we have been mapping. When the conscious-level work goes well, the substrate often shifts too. When it plateaus, sometimes the missing piece is substrate-level work that conscious access cannot quite reach. Adding regulation, neurofeedback, or somatic work can move the picture in ways that conscious-level work alone could not.

Working the other direction: when you are doing regulation work without an explicit parts framework, you are still working with parts. The lifeguard is your Protector. The CEO is your Manager. The problem child is your Firefighter. The phenotype names give you the brain-pattern handle. The parts names give you the relational handle. Many people benefit from holding both.

When you are working in family systems territory (couples work, work with parents or siblings, work with your own kids) the same circuits show up in the relational space. Your partner's cramped lifeguard is interacting with your stuck CEO. Your kid's problem child is interacting with your performer's exhaustion. Nervous systems regulate through other nervous systems; the regulation is happening at the brain level even when the conversation is happening at the verbal level.

The integration of these three frameworks (brain patterns, parts, family systems) is, in our experience, the most useful place to work from. None of them alone is sufficient. Together, they triangulate.

13.6 What Gets Misunderstood

A few common misunderstandings that the integration helps clean up.

Parts are configurations of brain patterns that, when activated, produce the experience of an internal voice or stance. The fact that the experience feels like a separate self is the brain doing what it does: generating coherent first-person experience from whichever circuits are currently dominant. Treating parts as real-but-not-literal is workable. Treating them as literal subselves can produce a kind of clinical confusion in which the therapist starts addressing the subself as if it were a separate entity, and the work can get stuck. Dissociation specialists like Richard Chefetz and Bethany Brand have raised a specific version of this concern: in clients with significant dissociative symptoms, persistently treating inner experience as populated by autonomous entities can deepen compartmentalization rather than resolve it.[5] The risk is not that parts work is wrong. The risk is that parts work applied without attention to the client's dissociative baseline can reinforce the fragmentation it is trying to heal.

People sometimes ask which part of them the Self is. It is none of them. The Self is what is there when no part is captaining. This is hard to describe and easy to recognize once you have been there. The clinical move is to make the Self more reliably accessible, not to identify it as a particular entity that can be conversed with.

After the parts have been heard, the brain patterns underneath also have to settle. The sequencing principle applies here exactly as it applies in every other part of this book: the question is whether the nervous system has the regulatory capacity to tolerate deeper parts

[5]Chefetz, R. A. (2015). *Intensive Psychotherapy for Persistent Dissociative Processes: The Fear of Feeling Real.* Norton.

work or memory processing, not whether a fixed period has elapsed. Chapter 15 covers the principle in detail. Many people leave parts work feeling that the inner work is done, then are surprised when the symptoms return because the substrate-level work was not done or the sequencing was wrong. The integrated approach addresses both the work itself and the order in which it happens.[6]

Severe relational trauma usually requires family systems work alongside individual work. The configurations inside you came from relational conditions. Working only on the inside, without addressing the outside relational patterns that continue to feed the inside, often produces incomplete results. This does not mean every trauma survivor needs family therapy. It means that the relational dimension of trauma is part of the picture, and that ignoring it has costs.

13.7 The Map and the Territory

The parts came from somewhere. They were shaped by the relational system you grew up in. The configurations inside you have a history, and the Translation section above mapped them to circuits: CEO, Problem Child, Lifeguard, temporal-limbic systems, regulated default-mode state.

Integration involves all three layers. Parts-language work when that handle opens the jar. Substrate work (regulation, neurofeedback, somatic) when the underlying circuits need retraining. Relational and family-systems work when the patterns that produced the inside are still active in the outside. None alone is sufficient. Together they triangulate.

You are not one thing, and you are not many things. You are a configuration of circuits that, in different arrangements, produce the experience of different selves. The clinical move is to develop the kind of regulation that allows the configurations to shift fluidly, to honor what each part has been doing, to update the patterns that no longer

[6]ISSTD (2011). Guidelines for treating dissociative identity disorder in adults, third revision. *Journal of Trauma & Dissociation*, 12(2), 115–187.

serve, and to make the Self (the regulated, curious, compassionate baseline) more reliably accessible across more of your life.

The parts will keep being there. They are doing real work. What changes is that they stop running you, and start serving you. The Manager who was holding everything together becomes the CEO who can prioritize without holding. The Firefighter who was breaking states becomes the Problem Child who can register impulse without capturing the system. The Exile who was carrying the unbearable affect gets the integration that was not available before. The Protector who was scanning at twelve out of ten comes down to a working volume.

You become more of yourself in the sense of having more bandwidth, more flexibility, more access to your own capacities, not in the sense of performing authenticity. The parts get to be parts, and the Self gets to lead. The brain patterns make it possible. The relational systems made it necessary.

Here is what I see in the maps when parts work is doing its job. The frontal-midline beta that was holding the Manager together settles by about a point. The right-frontal brake that the Firefighter kept overriding starts to fire on its own. The temporal-limbic signature of the Exile's unintegrated affect loosens in the months after the memory has finally been held in Self. None of these are dramatic. All of them are visible. The parts have not left. They have come down to a volume at which the rest of the person can hear past them.

13.8 When Parts Work Needs a Clinician

Parts work done on your own (journaling to a Manager, noticing a Firefighter, sitting with an Exile's sadness) can be valuable and low-risk for many people. But some presentations require professional guidance, and pushing forward without it can destabilize a nervous system that is barely holding.

Seek a trained clinician if you experience any of the following: losing time or finding yourself in places without memory of how you arrived; parts that feel fully autonomous, making decisions you cannot override; rapid switching between states that leaves you disoriented or frightened; self-harm impulses that intensify when you engage with inner material; a part that holds suicidal content or intent; flashbacks or body memories that flood the system when a part is contacted; or derealization and depersonalization that worsen rather than ease when you do parts-oriented work. These are signs of significant dissociative organization, and the work needs a clinician trained in structural dissociation, not just basic IFS.

The ISSTD treatment guidelines are clear: stabilization first, processing second, integration third. A clinician who moves to deep unburdening or memory work before Phase 1 is solid is working out of sequence, regardless of credentials. If parts work is making you worse, more fragmented, more symptomatic, less functional, that is a sign the sequencing needs attention, and you need someone who knows how to hold the complexity.

If you are in crisis or experiencing active suicidal ideation from any part of your system, contact the 988 Suicide and Crisis Lifeline (call or text 988) before continuing any internal work.

Ch 14: Polyvagal: Useful Language, Imperfect Biology

If you have spent any time in a trauma therapy office in the last twenty years, you have probably been introduced to the polyvagal model. The therapist drew the ladder for you. At the top, ventral vagal, social engagement, safety. In the middle, sympathetic, mobilization, fight-or-flight. At the bottom, dorsal vagal, immobilization, freeze and shutdown. She asked which rung you were on right now. She gave you tools for moving up the ladder. She used phrases like *neuroception, co-regulation, window of tolerance*. The vocabulary felt useful. It gave you a map.

The trouble is that the map is partly wrong, in places the trauma-therapy world is only now beginning to grapple with. The vocabulary has done real clinical work. Some of the underlying biological claims have not held up to careful scrutiny. The working position: keep the bedside map, update the phylogeny story. That is what this chapter does.

The chapter is also not a tribal exercise. The polyvagal world has gotten polarized in the last few years, with proponents defending the theory in increasingly strong terms and critics dismissing it in equally strong terms. Neither extreme is helpful. Most of the people who have benefited from polyvagal-informed work, clients, therapists, somatic practitioners, were not making detailed neurobiological claims. They were using a language that gave them traction on autonomic state, and the traction was real. The biology under the language can be updated without throwing out the language.

What this chapter aims to do is two things. First, give the clinical vocabulary in its useful form, so it can be used without having to defend or attack the contested parts. Second, offer the cortical-resource framework that has been running through this book as a more brain-specific alternative for the parts of the picture that the polyvagal map oversimplifies.

14.1 A note for readers coming from *Gifted & Tortured*

The companion volume *Gifted & Tortured* uses polyvagal-informed language in its stress-response chapter without flagging the contested status of the underlying biology. The vocabulary there is doing the same clinical work it does in many trauma settings, and the language is fine for that purpose. This chapter is the corrective. If you have read the Tortured stress-response chapter and want the more careful version of where polyvagal theory holds and where it does not, this is where that account lives. The clinical tools the other book recommends still work; the anatomical story should be held more loosely than the simpler treatment there suggests.

14.2 What Polyvagal Got Right

The first contribution is the recognition that **autonomic state matters for trauma work, in ways the talk-therapy traditions had not fully appreciated**. Before polyvagal language entered the vocabulary, much of the field treated trauma as a primarily psychological problem to be addressed through cognitive and narrative work. Polyvagal-informed approaches insisted that trauma was a body-state problem, that the autonomic nervous system had to be attended to in the moment, and that interventions had to engage the body as well as the mind. This was a clinically important shift. Many trauma survivors had been failed by treatments that ignored their nervous system state, and the polyvagal-informed approaches gave them a vocabulary for what had been failing.

The second contribution is the recognition that **state determines access to higher functions**. When the autonomic system is in a state of mobilization or shutdown, the cognitive and relational capacities that depend on a regulated baseline become harder or impossible to access. You cannot reason well from a state of high alarm. You cannot connect well from a state of collapse. The polyvagal frame gave clinicians a way to see that intervention had to start with state regulation before it could move to processing or integration. This sequencing principle is correct, and it is one of the central contributions of the framework.

The third contribution is the importance of **co-regulation**, the recognition that nervous systems regulate each other through interaction, that being in the presence of a regulated other shifts autonomic state, and that the therapeutic relationship is itself a primary intervention. The parent-infant synchrony literature is the strongest foundation here. Bidirectional heart-rate and respiratory synchrony in early infancy predicts secure attachment, and maternal contingent responsiveness buffers infant cortisol reactivity in well-replicated paradigms.[1] The therapist-client coupling literature suggests a more modest but real effect; physiological synchrony in therapy dyads correlates with alliance and outcomes at small-to-moderate effect sizes, though causality is not established. The clinical move of attending to one's own nervous system as a regulating presence for the client is well-grounded in the infant data, and the extrapolation to adult therapy is on softer empirical ground but is consistent with the available evidence.

The fourth contribution, in more recent applications, is the recognition of **the freeze and the shutdown as distinct from fight-and-flight**. Earlier trauma-response frameworks tended to collapse all stress responses into the fight-or-flight category. The polyvagal framework explicitly named the immobilization response as a different category, with a different physiological signature and different clinical implications. Many trauma survivors carry shutdown patterns that look nothing like fight-or-flight, and naming the immobilization response as a separate category gave clinicians language to address it.

These are real contributions. The framework has changed how trauma is treated, in many places for the better.

[1] Tronick & Beeghly (2011) on parent-infant synchrony and attachment outcomes.

14.3 What Polyvagal Did Not Quite Get Right

The contributions above are real, but they are accompanied by a set of more specific anatomical and evolutionary claims that have been challenged by careful examination, and the challenges have force.

The most prominent critique came from Paul Grossman in a 2023 *Biological Psychology* paper that argued five of the basic premises of polyvagal theory are *untenable or highly implausible* on the available evidence (Grossman, 2023). The paper is technical, but the core points are accessible.

The first contested claim is **the dorsal-vagal versus ventral-vagal distinction as the theory presents it**. Polyvagal theory locates the immobilization-and-shutdown response in the dorsal motor nucleus of the vagus and the social-engagement-and-safety response in the nucleus ambiguus. The neuroanatomy is more complicated than this. The dorsal motor nucleus and the nucleus ambiguus do exist as distinct structures, and they do contribute differently to autonomic regulation, but the cleanly separable functions the theory assigns to them, one for shutdown and the other for social engagement, are not well supported by the actual physiology. Both nuclei contribute to multiple autonomic functions in ways that the theory's clean two-system mapping does not capture.

The second contested claim is **the evolutionary timeline**. Polyvagal theory makes specific claims about when certain vagal circuits evolved and how they enabled mammalian sociality. The comparative-anatomy evidence does not support the timeline as the theory presents it. The myelinated vagal fibers the theory associates with the *new* social-engagement system are present in non-mammalian vertebrates, and the social behaviors the theory associates with this system appear in species that, on the theory's account, should not have the relevant circuitry.

The third contested claim is **respiratory sinus arrhythmia as an unbiased index of cardiac vagal tone**. RSA is the variation in heart rate that occurs with the breath cycle, and polyvagal theory uses it as a proxy for the activity of the social-engagement vagal system.

The trouble is that RSA is influenced by many factors besides vagal tone, including breathing rate, respiratory volume, posture, and other autonomic activity. Using RSA as a clean readout of vagal social-engagement function overreads what the measure actually shows.

The fourth contested claim is the **neuroception** construct, the idea that the brain has a specific subcortical detector that distinguishes safety from danger and decides which autonomic state to enter. The phenomenon being described, that the brain rapidly assesses safety and adjusts state accordingly, is real. The specific neural mechanism the theory proposes, with neuroception as a discrete process happening in particular subcortical structures, is more speculative than the theory presents it.

The fifth contested claim is the **hierarchical-ladder framing** of the three states. The theory presents ventral, sympathetic, and dorsal as a sequential hierarchy, with the system descending the ladder under increasing threat and ascending it under increasing safety. The actual data on autonomic state suggests that mobilization, immobilization, and engagement do not always operate in this strict hierarchy. They can co-occur, they can be mixed, and the transitions between them are more complicated than the ladder suggests.

These are not trivial critiques, and they have been taken seriously by autonomic-physiology researchers. A 2026 follow-up co-authored by thirty-nine international experts in vagal physiology and comparative neuroanatomy reached similarly critical conclusions, and Porges has responded in the same journal.[2] The scholarly debate is ongoing. A body-state regulation system clearly exists; the specific neuroanatomical and evolutionary story polyvagal theory tells is not well-matched to what the actual physiology appears to be doing, and the clinical vocabulary can be retained without committing to the contested biology.

[2]Grossman et al. (2026) thirty-nine-author critique in *Clinical Neuropsychiatry*; Porges (2026) reply in the same journal.

14.4 Why This Distinction Matters

Scientific credibility: a trauma book that builds its biology on contested anatomical claims becomes vulnerable to dismissal as the clinical world catches up to the research world, and the gap is closing fast. Clinical accuracy: the polyvagal simplifications can produce clinical errors when applied as load-bearing facts for treatment decisions. And the alternative is available: the cortical-resource framework running through this book gives a more granular, more empirically grounded account of what the autonomic state is doing in trauma. The vocabulary can stay. The specific anatomy can soften.

14.5 What to Keep, What to Update

Here is the working position this book takes, and that any clinician can take when using polyvagal-informed work without inheriting the contested biology.

Keep the state vocabulary. Mobilization, immobilization, engagement, regulation, dysregulation are clinically useful descriptions. They give handles on what is happening in a client or in oneself. They do not commit anyone to specific anatomical claims. The vocabulary works at the phenomenological level, and the phenomenology is real.

Keep the sequencing principle. Stabilization before processing. State regulation before deeper trauma work. This is one of polyvagal-informed work's central contributions, and it is correct. The sequencing principle does not depend on the contested anatomy; it depends on the more general observation that higher functions are state-dependent and that processing has to happen from a regulated enough state to support integration.

Keep co-regulation. The recognition that nervous systems regulate each other through interaction, and that the therapeutic relationship is itself a primary regulating presence, is well-supported and useful. The mechanisms are not entirely as polyvagal theory presents them, but the phenomenon is real, and the clinical implications are mostly correct.

Keep the recognition of immobilization as distinct from fight-or-flight. The dissociative shutdown response is a different thing from the mobilized stress response, and treating them as the same thing produces clinical errors. The polyvagal framework's insistence on this distinction is one of its more important contributions.

When it comes to the anatomy, the language should soften. *Mobilization* is fine. *Sympathetic activation* is fine. *Immobilization* is fine. *Dorsal-vagal-shutdown-with-collapse-of-the-myelinated-ventral-vagal-system* is overcommitted. The simpler versions hold up; the more elaborate versions do not.

The evolutionary story should be updated. There is good reason to stop telling clients that the social engagement system evolved with mammals to enable safety in groups. The story is appealing and probably partly wrong. Saying that the autonomic system has a state that supports social engagement, and that humans are good at it, is honest and sufficient.

The RSA story should be updated. RSA is influenced by many things, vagal tone among them, but it does not cleanly read out social-engagement-system activity. HRV biofeedback works through autonomic mechanisms, but the specific mechanism is more complicated than *toning the social-engagement vagus*. Saying that slow breathing supports parasympathetic activity and reduces autonomic arousal is honest and sufficient.

The neuroception concept should be held loosely. The brain does rapidly assess safety and adjust state. Whether this happens through a discrete *neuroception* process in particular structures, or through a more distributed appraisal across multiple systems, is not settled. Saying that the brain is constantly assessing safety in the background is honest. Saying that *your neuroception is detecting the threat* overcommits.

The ladder should be replaced with the resource map. When the question is what trauma did to a particular nervous system, the seven-resources framework gives a more accurate map than the three-state ladder. Some trauma patterns are about safety detection; some are about sensory gating; some are about self-location; some are about social meaning. The ladder collapses these into one dimension. The resource map keeps them separate, and the separations matter for treatment selection.

This is the working compromise. It keeps the polyvagal-informed approach doing what it does well. It declines to defend the parts of the theory that careful examination has weakened.

14.6 The Cortical-Resource Alternative

The cortical-resource framework running through this book offers an alternative that is more brain-specific than the polyvagal map.

The polyvagal framing consistently undersells one thing: the vagus nerve is mostly afferent. Roughly 80 percent of its fibers run upward, from body and viscera to brain.[3] What happens in the Vagus does not stay in the Vagus. The ascending traffic from gut, heart, and lungs is enormous, and the brain builds much of its state from reading that traffic. The descending fibers do real work on beat-to-beat cardiac timing, but they are the minority channel. A framework that emphasizes the descending story misses most of the wire.

When trauma changes a nervous system, what gets changed is not a single ladder rung. What gets changed is access to specific cortical resources, the systems that, in the brain covered in Chapter 2, do the work of detecting safety, gating sensation, locating self, contextualizing memory, inhibiting threat response, integrating social meaning, and coordinating state across the whole brain.

The autonomic state is part of how these resources operate. When the autonomic baseline is high, sensory gating is impaired, threat appraisal is biased, and the integration across resources falters. The polyvagal framework was right to insist that this autonomic dimension matters. What the cortical-resource framework adds is granularity about what specifically gets affected and how.

[3]Berthoud & Neuhuber (2000). Functional and chemical anatomy of the afferent vagal system; the ~80% afferent figure refers to fiber counts in the cervical vagus.

A cramped lifeguard is a particular pattern of posterior-cingulate over-engagement with environmental scanning, not simply a sympathetic-mobilized state, with associated effects on sleep, attention, and downstream cortical resources. A dissociated fog state shows slowed alpha, posterior-midline disengagement, and frontal compensatory beta rather than a generic dorsal-vagal shutdown, with associated effects on processing speed and self-location. A trauma-shaped approach/avoid brain is a particular configuration of frontal asymmetry that produces specific patterns of motivational paralysis, not just being *off the ladder*.

These differentiated patterns matter for treatment. A cramped lifeguard responds best to particular interventions, a dissociated Fog responds to different ones, an inflated avoid system responds to others again. The polyvagal ladder, applied as the primary map, can produce a one-size-fits-all approach to *bringing the client up the ladder* that misses these differences. The resource framework keeps the differences visible.

This does not mean the autonomic state work stops mattering. It still matters. The cortical resources operate within the context of autonomic state, and addressing the state is often part of restoring access to the resources. Breath work, HRV biofeedback, body-based co-regulation all address the autonomic substrate, and they help. They help differently for different phenotypes, but they help.

The regulation tools themselves have better evidence than the anatomical theory they often travel with. Cyclic sighing, a double inhale through the nose followed by a long exhale through the mouth done for five minutes a day, outperformed both box breathing and mindfulness meditation on mood and anxiety in a randomized trial of 114 adults, with effects building over twenty-eight days. Slow breathing at around six breaths per minute has well-documented effects on heart rate variability and autonomic balance. Resonance-frequency breathing, which finds an individual's optimal rate between roughly 4.5 and 6.5 breaths per minute, has shown effects on both HRV and inhibitory control even in anxious populations. HRV biofeedback, which trains the same physiology with real-time feedback, has enough evidence in PTSD populations to serve as a front-line stabilization tool, with a meta-analysis of military PTSD trials finding meaningful reductions in symptom severity.[4]

None of these tools require belief in a particular story about the ventral vagus. They work through autonomic mechanisms that do not depend on the contested parts of the polyvagal framework. The clinical tools survive the anatomical critique because they were always working through real physiology, even when the explanatory story wrapped around them was too specific.

The integration is straightforward. Use the autonomic state work. Drop the contested anatomy. Replace the three-state map with the resource framework when finer-grained guidance is needed. This is a workable position, and it has the advantage of being defensible against the critiques the standard polyvagal framing has accumulated. The framework does not discard polyvagal-informed practice. It distinguishes what is clinically strong from what the anatomy cannot yet support, and keeps both in proportion.

14.7 Window of Tolerance, Briefly

The **window of tolerance**, Daniel Siegel's framing for the range of arousal a person can experience while remaining able to think and function. Hyper-arousal is above the window, hypo-arousal is below, healthy regulation is staying within it.

The window-of-tolerance metaphor is clinically useful. It gives clients a way to think about their own state in real time. It gives therapists a framing for tracking state across sessions. The metaphor does not commit anyone to any specific anatomy.

The empirical content of the window-of-tolerance concept is thinner than the metaphor's clinical popularity suggests. There is no formal measurement of *window width* in the literature, and the construct sits

[4]Balban et al. (2023) on cyclic sighing; Zaccaro et al. (2018) systematic review of slow-breathing effects on HRV and autonomic function; Spalding et al. (2025) on resonance-frequency breathing; Kenemore et al. (2024) meta-analysis on HRV biofeedback in military PTSD populations.

more comfortably as a clinical metaphor than as an empirical entity. The arousal-regulation literature it draws from is real; the specific elaboration as *window* is more pedagogical than measurable.

This does not mean the metaphor should be dropped. It means it should be used as a metaphor, with the recognition that *staying in your window* is a useful clinical orientation but not a precise neurobiological description. The same critique that applies to other parts of the polyvagal vocabulary applies here. Useful at the clinical-handle level.

14.8 What This Means for Practice

Rena had been stuck for months, functional enough to go to work, but every evening she came home and went straight to the couch, lights off, phone face-down, speaking to no one. Her therapist drew the polyvagal ladder on a whiteboard. "You're spending your evenings here," she said, pointing to the bottom rung. "Your system is going into shutdown because the day used everything you had." Rena looked at the drawing and something shifted. Not the biology underneath it, just the recognition. She was neither lazy nor depressed in the way she had been told. Her nervous system was collapsing into immobilization because it had been running in mobilization all day and the only move left was down. The language gave her something to work with. Over the following weeks, the therapist taught her transition rituals between work and home; five minutes of slow breathing in the car, a brief walk around the block before going inside. Small inputs aimed at the autonomic state before the collapse could happen. Whether the shutdown was *dorsal vagal* in the strict anatomic sense mattered less than the fact that naming it let her intervene upstream of it. The polyvagal map was imprecise about the anatomy. It was precise about what Rena needed to hear: her body was doing something predictable, and there were moves she could make before it got there.

If you have been working with a polyvagal-informed therapist, this chapter asks you to hold her framework with a bit more lightness around the anatomical claims, and to add the resource framework as a more granular complement.

If you have been working with the polyvagal framework on your own, the same principle applies. The state vocabulary is useful. The autonomic regulation tools are useful. The sequencing principle is useful. The specific anatomy of the dorsal-versus-ventral vagal story does not have to be load-bearing for daily practice.

If you are a clinician using polyvagal-informed work, there is a clinical question worth sitting with. Is the framework's contested anatomy load-bearing for what you do, or is the clinical scaffolding what you actually rely on? In my experience, most polyvagal-informed clinicians use the framework primarily as clinical scaffolding, and the anatomical claims are background rather than foreground. If that is true for you, the updates this chapter suggests cost very little. The clinical scaffolding stays. The contested anatomy gets held more loosely.

14.9 The State Is Real Even When the Map Needs Work

The nervous system has states. Some make the rest of functioning possible. Some make it very difficult. The work of regulation is real. The sequencing of stabilization-before-processing is real. Use the autonomic state work. Drop the contested anatomy.

14.10 When Polyvagal-Informed Work Needs Stabilization First

If body-state work is making things worse rather than better, that is information. For crisis resources, see the Introduction.

- Attending to autonomic state produces flooding or panic rather than regulation: the nervous system is signaling it cannot safely observe its own states yet. Back up to basic containment with a phase-oriented clinician before returning to state work.
- Chronic shutdown pattern (flat, disconnected, can't-feel-anything): practices aimed at "moving up the ladder" can

produce destabilizing activation the system is not ready to hold. Titration with a clinician, not solo.
- Immobilization pattern includes active suicidal ideation, self-harm, or escalating substance-mediated state-shifting: body work comes after safety is established, not before. See the Introduction for crisis resources.

Chapter 15 covers the full sequencing principle in detail.

14.11 One Picture From the Clinic

A man came to me a few years ago who had spent eighteen months with a polyvagal-informed therapist. He had memorized the ladder. He could tell me, with conviction, that his evening collapse onto the couch was dorsal vagal shutdown. He could tell me, with the same conviction, that his morning anxiety was sympathetic mobilization. He could draw the diagram. He had a vocabulary for his nervous system that he had never had before. He also had a QEEG sitting in my inbox showing slowed alpha across the posterior midline, a frontal compensation pattern, and a sleep apnea referral pending from the previous month. The polyvagal map had given him a language. The language had not, by itself, told him that the dorsal-shutdown reading was sitting on top of an undiagnosed nighttime hypoxia that was responsible for half of what he was calling his nervous system. We adjusted the picture. He kept the language he had earned. He also went to the sleep clinic. The therapist, when I called her, was as relieved as he was.

The next chapter is on what happens when trauma work itself goes wrong, when well-intentioned interventions produce harm, when stabilization is skipped, when the sequencing principle is violated, when body work or memory work or deep-state work is done in the wrong order. The polyvagal framework was, in many ways, a response to the prior generation's tendency to bypass the body. The next generation has to address the current tendency to do body work without adequate sequencing. That is the safety chapter.

Ch 15: Why Some Trauma Work Makes People Worse

You went looking for help. You found a therapist who specialized in trauma, or you went on a retreat that promised deep healing, or you started a meditation practice you had heard could change everything, or you tried a body-based modality you had read good things about, or you signed up for the brain-based protocol your friend swore by. You went in trusting. You went in hoping. You went in because something inside you was hurting and you wanted it to hurt less.

And you came out worse.

Not always immediately. Sometimes the bad turn took weeks. Sometimes you felt great in the session and broke down in the parking lot, then again the next morning, and the wave kept coming for a month. Sometimes the work seemed to be working until something cracked open that you could not put back. Sometimes the dissociation got worse. Sometimes the sleep got worse. Sometimes the relationships you had been holding together started to come apart. Sometimes you found yourself in a state your nervous system had not been in for years, and you did not have a way to get back out of it.

The clinical picture is consistent enough to have a shape. Someone walks in carrying the original trauma and the additional layer of harm from a treatment that was supposed to help. They tell me about the EMDR that opened them up and left them open. The silent retreat they could not come down from. The somatic session that lifted a numbness they did not know was protecting them. The neurofeedback protocol that gave them sleep paralysis for six months. They are often more frightened of trauma work than they were before they started it, and they have good reason to be.

If that has happened to you, this chapter is for you. If you are afraid to start trauma work because of stories like the one above, this chapter is also for you. If you are a clinician who has watched it happen to clients and has not always known what went wrong, this chapter is for you too.

Trauma work, done in the wrong sequence or under the wrong conditions, can make people worse. The tools are real. They have helped real people. None of what follows discards what worked. It names why it worked for some nervous systems, failed for others, and sometimes caused harm when the sequencing was wrong. The tools are not the problem; the sequencing is. A generation of trauma-therapy enthusiasm has sometimes forgotten that.

If you are currently in a treatment that you suspect is destabilizing you, stop and stabilize before you read every word of this chapter. The routing information is at the end. If you need it now, skip to *When This Is Beyond Self-Help*, and come back to the rest later.

15.1 The Sequencing Principle

The single most important thing in this chapter is one principle, and I keep returning to it because everything else in the chapter is a consequence of it. Stabilization before excavation.

The over-prescribed first moves in trauma work are usually some version of the same mistake: digging into the past, going on a meditation retreat, writing a trauma narrative, attending to body sensations in detail, entering deep brain states. None of these is the place to start. You start by getting the alarm down. You give the nervous system enough regulation that it has somewhere stable to come back to. Then, once the baseline is regulated enough, you can begin the integration work.

If the alarm is at nine, you do not work on what set the alarm. You bring it to a four or a five. Then you can think about the rest.

This sounds obvious when stated. In practice, most of the harms I am about to describe come from violating this principle. The therapist who starts with EMDR on the active trauma material in the second session, before any stabilization has been done. The retreat that drops you into ten days of silent meditation without any assessment of your nervous system's capacity to handle silence. The somatic practitioner who has you attend to bodily sensations of activation before you have any tools for managing what comes up. The neurofeedback provider who runs alpha-theta as a starting protocol because she has heard it is the deep trauma work, before she has done the alert-state stabilization that should precede it.

In each case the underlying mechanism is the same. Work is being done from a state that cannot integrate work. The system is being asked to process material it does not have the resources to process. Processing without resources does not produce integration; it produces flooding, dissociation, retraumatization, or some combination of the three.

The sequencing principle is not new. The structural-dissociation tradition has been making this point for thirty years. Phase-oriented treatment, with its insistence on stabilization first, processing second, integration third, has been the standard of care for dissociative disorders since the early 1990s.[1] What has happened in the broader trauma-therapy world is that this sequencing has sometimes been bypassed in the enthusiasm for newer, more powerful techniques. EMDR works. Somatic experiencing works. Neurofeedback works. MDMA-assisted therapy works in the right contexts. The harm comes when they are deployed without the stabilization that is supposed to precede them.

The rest of this chapter walks through specific patterns of harm. They are the most common ones I see, and they share a structure that makes them recognizable.

15.2 When Memory Work Goes Wrong

The most documented kind of harm in trauma therapy comes from memory-focused work done at the wrong time.

I have seen this go wrong many times, and the shape is always similar. A client begins reprocessing work in the second or third session,

[1] Van Der Hart, Nijenhuis, Steele, & Brown (2004). Trauma-related dissociation and phase-oriented treatment; Steele, van der Hart, & Nijenhuis (2005). Phase-oriented treatment of structural dissociation in complex traumatization.

before any stabilization phase. The session feels intense but contained. The clinician feels that something is moving. Then the client crashes between sessions. The dissociation that had been mild becomes severe. Sleep falls apart. Intrusive imagery, sometimes of the original trauma and sometimes of new content the client cannot anchor anywhere, begins to colonize ordinary days. By the time the client gets back to my clinic, often months later, the original trauma is still there and now there is a second layer of harm on top of it.

The mechanism is straightforward. Traumatic memory, when activated, produces an autonomic and affective response that is in some sense a partial reactivation of the original trauma state. The reactivation is what makes the memory accessible. It is also what makes memory work potentially dangerous. If the reactivation is too intense, or if it happens without conditions for the memory to be re-encoded in a more integrated form, the result is retraumatization.

Memory reconsolidation theory gives a fairly precise picture of what makes memory work integrative versus retraumatizing. An activated memory enters a window of malleability during which new information can be integrated into it. If what arrives during that window is the original trauma reactivated again, the memory is reconsolidated more or less as it was, sometimes with the trauma signal amplified. If what arrives is the trauma in the context of present-moment safety, with someone regulated next to you, in a body that has resources to process it, the memory can be reconsolidated in a more integrated form. Same window, very different outcomes.

Memory work therefore needs the conditions for a corrective reconsolidation, not just for an activation. Activation alone is not therapy. Activation alone is exposure to the trauma, which is what produced the trauma in the first place.

Those conditions include a regulated autonomic baseline before the session begins, a relationship that can hold the activation without flooding, a clinician who can track the system in real time and back off when activation crosses into too-much territory, and a body that has enough regulation tools to come down when the session ends.

When these are present, memory work is one of the most powerful interventions available. When they are not, it tends to produce harm.

The kinds of memory work I see produce harm most often are unstructured trauma narrative writing in someone with significant dissociation, hypnotic or guided-imagery exploration of suspected trauma in clients without adequate grounding, EMDR or related reprocessing modalities started before any stabilization phase, and recovered-memory work as historically practiced. The recovered-memory tradition did particular damage by combining memory activation with suggestive techniques that sometimes produced vivid memories of events that, on careful examination, did not happen as remembered. Real abuse survivors had their accounts dismissed because of association with the false-memory cases, and people without abuse histories sometimes developed strong false beliefs that reorganized their families and their lives. The current trauma-therapy world has mostly moved away from active recovered-memory work, but the underlying issue, that memory is constructive and that the conditions of its retrieval shape what gets reconstructed, has not gone away.

Not every survivor needs to remember more. What helps is often less about retrieving additional content and more about integrating what is already accessible, in a regulated body, in present-moment safety, with someone who can hold it. When new retrieval is involved, it should happen with care, with sequencing, and with explicit attention to the conditions that make corrective reconsolidation possible.

15.3 When Body Work Goes Wrong

The second category of harm comes from body-based interventions used at the wrong time or in the wrong way.

The body-based trauma traditions share a premise. Trauma is held in the body. Body-level intervention is necessary for resolution. The premise is partly correct. Trauma does produce somatic patterns, and addressing them is often part of recovery. The risk comes when body work is done in a system that does not have the resources to tolerate body-level activation.

A chronically dysregulated nervous system has often developed adaptive numbness or distance from body sensation. The numbness is protective. The system is saying *we cannot afford to feel everything that is happening in here right now.* When this system is asked, in a body-based intervention, to attend to bodily sensation in detail, the protective numbness sometimes lifts before the nervous system has the resources to process what was underneath it. The result is flooding, a wave of sensation, emotion, and memory that can persist for hours or days after the session ends.

A client comes in after a body-scan-heavy mindfulness retreat. She had attended retreats before, with mild benefit. This one was longer and more intensive. On day four her chest opened up, and a flood of memory she had not had conscious access to arrived with it. She left the retreat early. By the time I saw her she had been sleeping four hours a night for two months and was afraid of her own body.

Body scans in mindfulness contexts are one of the most common sites of this pattern. The practice asks the practitioner to attend, in turn, to each part of the body, noticing sensation without judgment. For a regulated nervous system this is generally fine and often beneficial. For a dysregulated trauma survivor it can produce panic, dissociation, or intrusive memory in the middle of what was supposed to be a calming practice. The harm comes from applying the practice in a context it was not designed for.

Somatic experiencing and sensorimotor psychotherapy, done by trained practitioners with attention to titration, are generally safer because they build dosing into the protocol. Touch activation, return to neutral, touch again. A competent practitioner does not push past what the system can tolerate. The harm I see in these modalities tends to come from less-trained practitioners who have learned the techniques but not the dosing principle, or from situations where the client's dysregulation exceeds what the modality can hold.

Trauma-informed yoga has similar issues. Yoga can be a powerful regulation tool for some trauma survivors. It can also produce flooding when the body is asked to attend to sensation that has been protectively held offline. Carefully developed protocols (the Trauma Center yoga work, the Hakomi tradition) include explicit attention to these issues. Generic yoga classes generally do not, and a trauma survivor who is told yoga will help and walks into a class without preparation may end up worse rather than better.

Going into the body is not universally safe instruction. For many trauma survivors, those with significant dissociative patterns, the body has been a difficult place to be. Returning to it needs to happen gradually, with support, with regulation tools available, and with respect for the protective function the distance from the body was serving.

15.4 When Meditation Goes Wrong

Meditation has been one of the more enthusiastically promoted interventions of the last two decades, and the enthusiasm has sometimes outrun the evidence on adverse effects.

I have seen plenty of meditation-related harm in the clinic. Almost always it follows the same pattern. A trauma survivor reads about meditation as a healing practice. She tries a brief practice and it seems fine. She decides to do more. She signs up for a longer retreat, or she increases her daily sit from ten minutes to an hour, or she takes on a Vipassana intensive she has been told will be transformative. Somewhere in the deeper practice the protective architecture of her ordinary mind lifts. What comes through is more than she can hold. She comes out of the retreat depersonalized, or with intrusive imagery she did not have before, or with autonomic dysregulation that takes months to settle.

The cleanest research on this comes from the Lindahl and Britton line of work, which has documented the range of adverse effects that arise from intensive meditation practice. Their taxonomy is sobering: cognitive changes, perceptual changes including visual distortions and depersonalization, affective changes, somatic changes including involuntary movements and autonomic dysregulation, sense-of-self changes including ego dissolution that does not resolve, and social changes. Lindahl's sample was recruited for difficult experiences, so it maps the territory rather than the frequency. In pooled analyses about 8 percent of meditators report adverse effects; in survey samples the figure is closer to a third.[2]

Risk factors include prior trauma history, dissociative tendencies, psychosis-spectrum vulnerability, recent bereavement, undiagnosed bipolar features, and some physical-health conditions. Practices most associated with adverse effects include long silent retreats (Vipassana retreats are implicated in the case literature), advanced concentration practices, intensive body scans, and certain breath retention practices.

The trauma-therapy world has developed adapted approaches (trauma-sensitive mindfulness, compassion-based practice) that attempt to address these risks.[3] Whether the adaptations reduce harm is suggestive but not definitive. The general principle is that intensive meditation, silent-retreat meditation, is not appropriate for all trauma populations, and that careful screening and graduated exposure are warranted before sending a trauma survivor into deep meditation work.

This does not mean trauma survivors should not meditate. Many forms of meditation, used in appropriate doses, are useful. Loving-kindness practice tends to be among the safer practices for trauma populations. Brief mindfulness practices in the context of stabilization, five or ten minutes a day, tend to be safer than intensive practice. The risk concentrates in long, intensive, silent-and-deep practice, when undertaken without attention to the practitioner's history and capacity.

If you have tried meditation and it has made you worse, you are not failing at meditation. You are encountering a real phenomenon that is

[2]Lindahl et al. (2017) varieties of contemplative experience, mixed-methods study of meditation-related challenges; Britton et al. (2021) defining and measuring meditation-related adverse effects in mindfulness-based programs; Farias et al. (2020) systematic review of adverse events in meditation practices; Goldberg et al. (2022) population-based prevalence of meditation-related adverse effects in the US.

[3]Treleaven (2018). *Trauma-Sensitive Mindfulness*: adapting mindfulness practice for trauma populations, documenting how standard mindfulness can destabilize trauma survivors; Baer et al. (2019) on conceptual issues and empirical findings regarding harm in mindfulness-based programs.

well-documented and that the meditation-promotion world has often ignored. Trying harder is not the answer. Understanding what was happening is. Usually some combination of insufficient stabilization, wrong practice for your phenotype, or insufficient context. Consider whether a different practice in a different context, with a different teacher, would be a better fit.

If you have been reading this chapter and you have recognized your own treatment history in one of these sections, take a moment. Naming what happened is not the same as the treatment having failed. You went looking for help. The fact that a particular intervention was not the right intervention for your phenotype, or was the right intervention in the wrong sequence, is information. The rest of this chapter tells you what comes next, and there is a rest of this chapter.

15.5 When Forced Exposure Goes Wrong

The exposure-based therapies, prolonged exposure and cognitive processing therapy in particular, have evidence for PTSD treatment. They are first-line in many treatment guidelines and for good reason. They also have a more complicated story around dropout, deterioration, and adverse effects than their advocates always acknowledge.

Dropout rates in exposure trials for PTSD are often substantial, frequently in the twenty to forty percent range, and sometimes higher in real-world clinical populations.[4] Some researchers argue the dropouts are people who did not get to benefit, meaning the published efficacy figures overstate real-world impact. Others argue dropouts are not necessarily harmed; some leave because they got better, some because the treatment was not a fit. The honest reading is that high dropout is a real signal worth taking seriously, and that not every person who starts exposure-based therapy is helped by it.

The shape is recognizable when it happens. A client with complex trauma, significant dissociation, or fragile regulatory capacity is started on a manualized protocol that requires sustained engagement

[4]Imel et al. (2013) meta-analysis of dropout in treatments for PTSD, pooled dropout rates across modalities; Levinson et al. (2022) on dropout reduction with twice-weekly prolonged-exposure scheduling.

with trauma material. The sustained activation does not produce extinction. It produces destabilization the client is then expected to push through, because pushing through is part of the protocol, until she either drops out or completes the protocol in a worse state than she started it. Sometimes I see her two years later trying to recover from the recovery.

The mechanism is the same one running through this whole chapter. Insufficient stabilization before exposure leads to activation the system cannot integrate. Prolonged exposure and CPT involve sustained, repeated engagement with trauma material, and the engagement is supposed to lead to extinction of the conditioned fear response over time. For some clients this works well. For others, those with significant dissociation, complex trauma history, or fragile regulatory capacity, sustained activation can produce destabilization rather than extinction.

The Foa and McLean line of argument has emphasized that exposure therapies are underused due to clinician concerns that turn out, in some studies, to be empirically unsupported.[5] The argument has merit. Many clinicians have been overly cautious, and many trauma survivors have been deprived of effective treatment because of unfounded concerns. The counterpoint, increasingly voiced in the clinical literature, is that real harms in exposure trials may be underreported, inclusion criteria often exclude the most complex cases, and the populations who do best in published trials may not match the populations most clinicians actually see.

Exposure therapies are valuable. They are not universally safe. The same mechanism that explains their effectiveness when done well, sustained activation of the trauma memory until extinction or reconsolidation occurs, explains their harm when done with insufficient stabilization or with a nervous system that cannot hold sustained activation. A person with simple, single-incident PTSD and intact regulatory capacity is often well-served by prolonged exposure or CPT. A person with complex trauma, significant dissociation, or fragile regu-

[5] McLean & Foa (2024). State of the science on prolonged exposure therapy for PTSD.

latory capacity may need stabilization work before exposure becomes appropriate, or may benefit more from other modalities entirely. The sequencing principle applies here exactly as everywhere else.

15.6 When Alpha-Theta Goes Wrong

The neurofeedback world has its own version of this problem, and it concentrates on alpha-theta training.

Alpha-theta is a deep-state neurofeedback protocol that, in the right context, can support memory integration, affect resolution, and the kind of deeper processing associated with both addiction recovery and PTSD treatment. The original Peniston and Kulkosky work on alpha-theta for combat veterans and alcoholics produced striking results that have remained influential, even as questions about methodology and the mixed replication record have been raised over the decades. Chapter 18 has the full evidence review.

I have seen alpha-theta go wrong, and almost always the failure has the same shape. A client is referred to alpha-theta as her opening protocol, either because the provider has heard it is the deep trauma work or because she herself asked for it after reading about it. She has not done the alert-state stabilization that should come first. She drops into the deep state. Material that has been protectively held offline rises into accessibility. Her system does not have the resources to hold what arrives. She comes out with intrusive imagery she did not have going in, or with a dissociation that lasts days, or with sleep paralysis, or with the conviction that she has uncovered memories of events she cannot now stop turning over.

The Othmer evolution of trauma neurofeedback, which moved alpha-theta from an entry protocol to a later protocol after stabilization, was a response to exactly this. In my practice and in the clinicians whose work I trust, the sequence is alert-state regulation first (SMR training, sub-Hz training, autonomic stabilization), then deeper state work later, with alpha-theta reserved for clients who have demonstrated regulatory capacity. The safety reasoning is straightforward: a system that is not yet regulated cannot safely hold what the deep-state work surfaces.

If you are considering neurofeedback for trauma, asking the provider about her sequencing logic, when does she do alpha-theta, when does she not, what comes first, is one of the more important questions to ask. Appendix B has the full list.

15.7 The Iatrogenic Identity Problem

There is a more subtle harm that shows up across modalities. Trauma work, even when it does not produce the more dramatic harms above, sometimes produces an unintended consequence. It organizes the person's identity around the trauma in a way that becomes its own problem.

This happens when therapy, even good therapy, becomes the dominant frame for understanding the self. The client who entered because of one specific trauma comes out two years later with a worldview in which everything that goes wrong is about the trauma, every difficulty is a trauma response, every relationship is filtered through the trauma history. She used to be many things. Now she is primarily *a trauma survivor*.

I see this in the clinic and it is harder to address than the more dramatic harms because the client is often not in distress about it. She is in a sense doing well. She has language for what happened. She has a community. She has a framework. What she has lost is the part of herself that existed before the framework, and a way back to a life in which the framework is one chapter rather than the whole book.

This is not exactly the therapy's fault. Identity formation is what humans do, and a sustained focus on trauma can foreground it as a central organizing feature. The therapy can be good and the side effect can still be costly. The capacities and relationships and meanings that exist outside the trauma frame get less attention, and the frame becomes the dominant lens.

You are not your trauma. You are a nervous system whose patterns were shaped by trauma. The shaping was real and so is the capacity to change. The longer arc of what that change looks like, and who you are on the other side of it, is what Chapter 22 is about.

15.8 When This Is Beyond Self-Help

If treatment is making you worse, slowing down is the right move. For crisis resources, see the Introduction.

- New symptoms since treatment began (new dissociation, new intrusive imagery, new panic, new suicidal ideation, new substance use): these are not signs the treatment is working through something. They are signs something has destabilized. Stop and stabilize.
- Life is getting smaller (lost relationships, lost function, lost the ability to go to work) during the course of treatment: trauma work that is going well does not cost you the rest of your life. Get a second opinion from a clinician trained in dissociation or phase-oriented work.
- Treatment has touched suicidal ideation: get support from someone outside the treatment that may be destabilizing you. Name destabilization for safety, not as a challenge to your therapist.
- You are the clinician: the principles apply identically. Slow down. Sequence. Consult. The field has more wisdom about this now than it did at peak trauma-therapy enthusiasm in the 2010s.

These are moments when the framework needs to back up a rung.

15.9 The Safety Ladder, Named

Here is the sequencing principle as a working practice, plain enough to act on.

First, before anything else, name where you are on the ladder right now. Acute crisis, active suicidal ideation, ongoing victimization, severe substance use crisis, untreated medical conditions driving the nervous system: rung zero. Crisis support and stabilization of the basic life conditions come first. The 988 lifeline (or Trans Lifeline at 1-877-565-8860 or BlackLine at 1-800-604-5841 if you prefer a peer-run option; Trans Lifeline states a policy against nonconsensual active rescue, with exceptions for credible threats to others and mandated abuse or neglect reporting), a clinician who can hold acute risk, sleep medicine if the sleep is broken, an honest medication review if the medication picture is part of the load. The trauma work waits at rung zero, and waiting is the right move.

Second, when rung zero is settled, the autonomic baseline is the next rung. Slow breathing, resonance-frequency breathing, HRV biofeedback, body-based co-regulation, sleep, basic nutrition, predictable daily rhythms. The aim is to get the alarm from a nine down to a four or a five. For some people that takes a few weeks. For others, months. The question that governs when to proceed is capacity rather than the calendar: can the regulation tools hold under stress, and can the person maintain dual awareness while engaging difficult material? For some people, regulation is the whole treatment. The nervous system settles, the alarm stays down, and excavation is never needed. When dual awareness and recovery capacity are present, supported processing can begin alongside continued regulation work. But the two phases are not strictly sequential.

Third, when the baseline holds and the regulation tools are reliable under stress, integration becomes available. Phase-oriented trauma processing, parts work, EMDR, somatic experiencing in small doses, alpha-theta when it is appropriate, deep meditation in titrated form. The integration rung is what most people think of as trauma therapy, and it works because the lower rungs are supporting it.

Fourth, identity. The framework that has been useful is not meant to be permanent. Late-stage work involves expanding the lens back out, returning attention to the rest of the life the framework was always supposed to be in service of. The framework recedes; the life comes forward.

If your current treatment is working the rungs out of order, name that to the clinician. If the clinician dismisses the question, get a second opinion from someone trained in phase-oriented trauma work. If the work is destabilizing rather than supporting you, drop back a rung until the ground is solid again. The ladder is not linear. You will revisit lower rungs across the years. The order of the rungs is the principle that protects the work.

The framework's last job is to make itself unnecessary. What that looks like, and who you are when the ladder becomes background rather than foreground, is what Chapter 22 is about.

If you are at the end of this chapter and you are not okay tonight, you do not have to be okay tonight. You have to be safe tonight. The work is still here tomorrow, and so are you.

The next chapter is on neurofeedback, which is one of the modalities I take seriously and which the following several chapters explore in detail. The same sequencing principle applies there too. Done in the right order, it is one of the better tools available. Done in the wrong order, it joins the list of treatments this chapter has been about. My job in the chapters ahead is to help you tell the difference.

Part IV

Neurofeedback and State Repair

Ch 16: What Neurofeedback Can Do That Talk Cannot, and How Modalities Converge on the Same Brain

Marcus came to me after four years of good talk therapy. The kind where you feel understood, where your clinician gets it, where you leave the room with genuine insight about why you do what you do. He could explain his hypervigilance to me beautifully in our intake. He could trace it to the house he grew up in. He could name the part of him that scanned every room and tell me exactly when it started, what age, what the trigger had been. What he could not do, after four years of explaining it, was stop scanning.

The understanding lived in one layer of his brain. The scanning lived in another. The layer doing the scanning did not read English.

He sat in my recliner for his sixth session of neurofeedback. No talking. I put the sensors on his scalp, brought up the nature documentary on the screen, and started the recording. The video would play smoothly when his posterior cortex was producing the alpha rhythm I had set as the target, and pause when his beta surged. He could not have told me what he was learning. By session ten his wife said something to him he had never heard her say in eight years of marriage. *You seem like you're actually here tonight.* The scanning had not stopped. It had turned down because the rhythm underneath it had moved, not because he understood it better.

That is what this chapter is about. Not whether to train instead of talk. That is a false opposition. The real question is why you would train the rhythm underneath a pattern, rather than only work on the pattern from above. Some patterns do not respond to insight because they do not operate at the level where insight lives. They operate in the electrical rhythms that produce your moment-to-moment brain state. Training reaches those rhythms directly. Talk reaches them indirectly.

This chapter introduces Part IV. It is also where the book's claim about modality convergence lives. The trauma-therapy modalities are different doors into the same set of rooms. The right modality is the one your nervous system can use, given where you are, what your phenotype is doing, and what doors are available to you.

16.1 Why Training Reaches What Talk Does Not

Start with what makes neurofeedback distinct from cognitive or insight-based talk therapy.

Most of the clients who walk into my clinic have done substantial talk therapy by the time they get to me. They can explain their patterns to me. The explaining is real and it is useful. It has not, by itself, retrained the rhythm. Talk therapy operates on the cortical-narrative level. You bring an experience to language. Your therapist helps you understand it, reframe it, integrate it, set new intentions about it. The mechanism is conscious meaning-making, with downstream effects on the underlying systems through repeated practice and through the relational regulation that happens in good therapy alongside the verbal work.

That is real. That can be substantial. It is also limited by what conscious meaning-making can reach. Some of the patterns this book describes do not respond well to cognitive intervention because they operate below the level where cognition can engage them. The cramped Lifeguard does not get less cramped because you understand intellectually that the past is past. I have seen this in the clinic year after year. The princess does not get less amplified because you tell yourself the cue was probably benign. The fog does not lift because you decide to focus harder.

Neurofeedback operates at the rhythm level, where talk reaches more slowly and less reliably. The training works without conscious understanding, verbal articulation, or insight. It works by giving the brain real-time information about its own activity and rewarding the brain when it moves toward a target pattern. The brain learns. The learning happens at the level of the underlying rhythms, often without the person being able to describe what is being learned. That is what makes neurofeedback reach patterns talk does not. The operative level is below the cortical-narrative level, in the rhythmic substrate that produces the cortical activity that produces the experience.

I have a client at the moment, a woman in her forties with a chronically activated autonomic baseline, who has been in psychodynamic therapy for eleven years. She has more insight into her trauma history than most of my colleagues have into theirs. The activation has not budged. After thirty sessions of neurofeedback the activation is measurably lower on every autonomic marker I track. She still cannot tell me what shifted. The shift shows up in the underlying rhythms.

Talk therapy still matters. The reverse is also true. I have had clients spend two years in neurofeedback with me, shift the underlying rhythms markedly, and still need cortical-narrative work to integrate what the change in baseline made newly possible. The two levels do different things. The most effective recovery work I do usually involves both, with attention to the sequencing that allows them to support each other rather than interfere.

16.2 What Neurofeedback Actually Does

The basic mechanism is operant conditioning of brain rhythms. The brain produces electrical activity continuously. The neurofeedback equipment reads that activity in real time, identifies specific features of it (particular frequencies, particular patterns, particular relationships between sites), and gives the trainee feedback when those features move in the target direction. The feedback might be visual, a video that plays smoothly when the target is being met and pauses when it is not. It might be auditory, a tone that sounds when the target is met. It might be both. The brain, given the feedback, learns to produce more of the target pattern, often without the trainee being able to describe what they are doing differently.

The technique started with Joe Kamiya in the 1960s training the alpha rhythm, and with Barry Sterman training the sensorimotor rhythm. Sterman's epilepsy work was the first major clinical demonstration that neurofeedback could produce durable changes in brain function with measurable downstream effects on a serious clinical condition. The field expanded from there. ADHD. Anxiety. Depression. Chronic pain. Peak performance. Eventually trauma.

The trauma applications have several lineages. The Peniston and Kulkosky alpha-theta protocol in the late 1980s, with combat veterans and alcoholics, produced striking results that have stayed influential even as questions about replication and methodology have followed the original studies.[1] The history matters to me because the original findings came from populations that the rest of the field had largely written off, and what those findings established is that the rhythms underneath intractable presentations can move. Sebern Fisher's developmental-trauma work brought neurofeedback into the trauma-clinical mainstream with detailed case work on populations that other modalities had not adequately reached. The Othmer infra-low-frequency line, reviewed systematically by Bazzana and colleagues, represents a distinct theoretical and clinical approach with its own accumulating literature.[2]

One fMRI-neurofeedback finding has changed how I think about what to target. Lieberman and colleagues (2023) ran a pilot study directly comparing two fMRI-neurofeedback targets in PTSD: the posterior cingulate cortex versus the amygdala. Participants learned to downregulate activity in their assigned target while viewing personalized trauma words. The PCC group showed significantly greater PTSD symptom reduction, even within a single session. The amygdala group showed no significant change. When the PCC group successfully downregulated, the effect cascaded across multiple systems, reducing activation in bilateral precuneus, primary visual cortex, superior parietal lobule, and right temporoparietal junction. The amygdala group showed no unique decreases beyond its own target. Training the self-referential hub produced widespread neural recalibration. Training the threat-alarm region did not.

---

[1] Peniston & Kulkosky (1989); Bazzana et al. (2022) systematic review of infra-low-frequency protocols.

[2] Fisher (2014); Bazzana et al. (2022).

I have been watching this finding closely because it matches what I see on QEEG in the dissociative-presentation cluster. The PCC is the Lifeguard's self-location partner, the node where the default mode network holds your sense of being you. Targeting it appears to reach deeper into the trauma architecture than targeting the amygdala alone. Nicholson and colleagues (2022) showed that PCC downregulation in PTSD patients recruited compensatory connections to the amygdala, posterior insula, and anterior default-mode regions that healthy controls did not show.[3] The PTSD brain is doing different work during the same task. The implication for what to train, in the dissociative phenotypes from Chapter 9, is becoming clearer with each replication.

The randomized-controlled-trial evidence base for neurofeedback in trauma is real and more modest than the clinical adoption suggests. Van der Kolk's group ran a PLOS ONE trial of an alpha-desynchronization protocol that demonstrated effects on PTSD symptoms and dissociation larger than waitlist control. Several subsequent trials have shown similar patterns. The Askovic systematic review found effects across EEG-neurofeedback trials with considerable heterogeneity in study designs, calling for larger studies with more rigorous control conditions.[4]

The most serious challenge to neurofeedback's evidence base comes from the condition where the evidence runs deepest: ADHD. Schönenberg and colleagues (2017), publishing in *The Lancet Psychiatry*, ran a triple-blind randomized trial of EEG-neurofeedback in adults with ADHD. Triple-blind: participants, trainers, and outcome assessors all blinded to condition. Both the active neurofeedback and the sham feedback groups improved significantly. There was no statistically significant difference between them. This is the most methodologically rigorous sham-controlled neurofeedback trial in the literature, and the null result lands harder for being in ADHD than it would in a PTSD-specific trial. If sham performs as well as active neurofeedback in the field's most studied indication, the question extends

[3]Lieberman et al. (2023); Nicholson et al. (2022).

[4]van der Kolk et al. (2016) PLOS ONE alpha-desynchronization RCT; Askovic et al. (2023) systematic review and meta-analysis.

to every indication. A fair reading has to hold the positive results from the Van der Kolk pilot and subsequent PTSD trials alongside the Schönenberg null. My clinical read is that the protocols differ in ways that matter and that the null result most plausibly reflects a protocol design that was not optimally matched to the underlying patterns, rather than evidence that neurofeedback as a class does not work. The direct comparison between protocols, QEEG-guided versus protocol-standardized targeting in a sham-controlled design, has not been run. That is the trial the field needs. Until it exists, honest practice means naming the Schönenberg result and holding it seriously. I do not know that I would get different results. I believe the QEEG-guided individualization is the reason I do, but belief and evidence are not the same thing.

The honest framing is that neurofeedback for trauma has a growing evidence base, that clinical practice runs ahead of the controlled trials in some respects, and that responsible practice means recognizing both the genuine clinical utility and the limits of what the current trial literature can establish. I tell my clients this in our intake. The framework I use is well-supported by the underlying neuroscience and by twenty-five years of clinical pattern. It is not the same thing as a treatment manual with a randomized evidence base. They deserve to know both.

What neurofeedback does, when it is doing its job, is train the underlying rhythms in ways that can shift autonomic baseline, support sensory gating, restore alpha rhythms, modulate default-mode network function, and address specific phenotype-related patterns. Different protocols target different things. The QEEG-guided approach, which the next chapter covers in detail, is how I match the protocol to the brain pattern in front of me.

16.3 Two Sessions in My Clinic

Two composite clients. Both real in the sense that the clinical picture is, with details changed to protect identities.

Janelle came to me Lifeguard-dominant. I targeted her posterior midline, Pz, the site where her beta was running hottest and her alpha had gone quiet. The screen showed a nature documentary. When her posterior cortex produced alpha in the target range, the video played smoothly; when the beta surged, the picture dimmed. The instruction I gave her was *don't try*. For the first three sessions, the video stuttered the entire time. Her brain kept producing the scanning rhythm. By session seven I started seeing stretches, thirty seconds, a minute, where the video ran uninterrupted. She did not notice. I did. After session ten she told me she had fallen asleep on the couch with the TV on, which she had not done in years. Her Lifeguard was learning that the room did not need scanning.

Owen came to me Approach/Avoid-dominant. His left-frontal alpha was elevated. The approach system running quiet, the avoid system dominant. I trained the asymmetry: left-frontal activation up, reward for the hemisphere to wake. The training felt like nothing to him, with no insight, no emotional shift, no sense that anything was happening. Three weeks in, his wife told him he was initiating things, a text to a friend, a plan for the weekend, without the agonizing lead-up that used to precede any forward movement. The asymmetry was shifting. The freeze that locked him before action had loosened because the rhythm underneath it had moved, not because he understood the freeze better.

I see this every week. The shift shows up in the rhythm that produces the story, not in the story they tell about themselves.

16.4 EMDR and the Temporal-Lobe Crossover

Eye Movement Desensitization and Reprocessing has been one of the better-studied trauma therapies. The RCT base is substantial. The WHO and APA guidelines support EMDR as first-line treatment for PTSD. Clinical adoption is widespread. EMDR works for many trauma survivors with single-incident PTSD and for some with more complex presentations.

The mechanism is contested. Several proposals have empirical support: working-memory taxation (bilateral stimulation competes with visual working memory, allowing re-encoding at lower affective intensity), orienting response (bilateral stimulation engages an investigative response that interrupts threat-response cycling), REM-mimicry (eye movements recruit REM-sleep-like consolidation, including depotentiation of overstrengthened amygdala circuits), and interhemispheric coupling (bilateral stimulation increases transcallosal communication supporting integration of affective and linguistic aspects of trauma memory).[5] None is exclusively correct. The mechanism is probably not single.

A separate strand, less prominent in the standard EMDR-mechanism conversation, suggests EMDR engages temporal-lobe processing. Imaging studies of pre-versus-post EMDR have shown changes in temporal-lobe activation and in connectivity between temporal regions and other systems. The Pagani group's EEG-during-EMDR work, across a series of studies from 2012 to 2017, identified oscillatory signatures of successful EMDR processing involving temporal-region activity, low-frequency synchronization consistent with memory consolidation. The claim that follows: part of what EMDR does is engage temporal-lobe plasticity in ways that support reorganization of trauma-related memory and meaning networks.

This is where the modality-convergence claim becomes specific, and where I am drawing on what I have seen across years of running both modalities with the same clients. If EMDR's mechanism includes temporal-lobe plasticity, then several modalities that engage temporal-lobe systems by different routes are doing related work.

Phenotype-matched neurofeedback at temporal sites, sub-Hz training over temporal cortex, coherence training across temporal-temporal or temporal-frontal sites, and protocols targeting right temporal regions associated with social-meaning processing, engages the same systems by direct rhythmic training. When I run these protocols with clients who have also done EMDR, the maps show changes in

[5]Engelhard et al. (2010) on working-memory taxation; MacCulloch & Feldman (1996) on orienting response; Stickgold (2002) on REM-mimicry.

the same temporal regions EMDR appears to be reaching. The convergence is visible in the brain map and in the clinical reports clients give me about what has shifted.

The bard chapter (Chapter 10) covered the temporal-lobe phenotypes in detail. Voice-hearing, prosodic threat-bias, narrative collapse: all signatures of temporal-lobe systems running under chronic load. The modalities that address those phenotypes well share that temporal-lobe reach even when surface techniques look different.

This is one of the more speculative claims in this book. The combined-protocol literature is small and the mechanistic story is suggestive rather than established. The picture, to those of us who work across modalities, has become increasingly visible.

16.5 Somatic Experiencing and Sensorimotor Psychotherapy

The body-based trauma traditions, Peter Levine's somatic experiencing and Pat Ogden's sensorimotor psychotherapy, share the premise that body-level intervention is necessary for trauma resolution, with somewhat different theoretical frameworks and clinical techniques. The empirical base for SE has been growing; the Brom 2017 RCT showed effects on PTSD symptoms larger than waitlist, and several subsequent studies have replicated. SP has a thinner controlled-trial base and clinical adoption, in attachment-focused trauma work.[6] What I see in clients who move through SE and then into neurofeedback is a recognizable sequence: the body work shifts the relationship to sensation in a way that makes the QEEG training go faster, because the client can notice internal states rather than defending against them. The clinical convergence is real, whatever the mechanism story turns out to be.

The mechanism overlaps with what neurofeedback does, by different routes. Both engage the autonomic regulation systems through body-level intervention. SE's emphasis on titrated activation and pendulation is autonomic-regulation training delivered through body awareness rather than through equipment. The vagal afferent path-

[6] Brom et al. (2017) somatic experiencing RCT.

ways that respond to slow breathing and slow movement are the same pathways that respond to HRV biofeedback. The interoceptive engagement that SE and SP build is operating on the same insular and salience-network systems that neurofeedback protocols can target directly.

The convergence here is at the autonomic-regulation level. Different doors, same set of rooms, the rooms where the autonomic baseline lives, where the interoceptive predictions get updated, where the chronic-load patterns can ease. SE's approach is body-led. HRV biofeedback is breath-and-rhythm-led. Certain neurofeedback protocols approach the same systems through their cortical correlates. The convergence is not metaphor. The Brom 2017 RCT that demonstrated SE's effects on PTSD symptoms was measuring change in the same autonomic and affective regulation systems that HRV biofeedback and neurofeedback protocols also target. The surface techniques are different. The downstream systems are not.

Brainspotting, developed by David Grand in 2003, has a thinner evidence base than EMDR or SE, and the mechanism story is less well-developed. The technique uses sustained gaze fixation on particular visual points to access trauma material, with the theoretical framing that gaze position engages subcortical orienting-system processing related to where trauma material is held. The primary controlled comparison is a pilot study by Hildebrand, Grand, and Stemmler, seventy-six adults in a between-groups design, that found both modalities produced significant PTSD symptom reduction, with EMDR showing somewhat larger effect sizes.[7] More than 20,000 clinicians have been trained in brainspotting. The ratio of trained practitioners to peer-reviewed trials is steep. The honest framing is that brainspotting is a widely used clinical modality with a mechanism story that is plausible in parts and speculative in others, with an evidence base developing more slowly than the clinical adoption.

[7]Hildebrand, Grand, & Stemmler (2017); EMDR effect sizes Cohen's d 1.19–1.76 versus 0.74–1.04 for brainspotting.

16.6 HRV Biofeedback and What It Buys You

HRV biofeedback deserves particular attention. It has stronger evidence than most neurofeedback protocols for some specific applications, and it is one of the most accessible and inexpensive interventions in the trauma toolkit.

The Lehrer and Vaschillo resonance-frequency tradition has shown that breathing at approximately six breaths per minute, the resonance frequency for most adults, aligns respiratory-driven vagal modulations with the baroreflex and cardiac-vagal regulatory system to maximize HRV oscillations and baroreflex gain (Lehrer et al., 2003). Sustained practice over weeks raises resting HRV, which is one of the more reliable autonomic markers of regulatory capacity I track in my clinic.

The applications to trauma populations are well-supported. A 2024 meta-analysis of HRV biofeedback for military PTSD found significant symptom reduction effects across five trials, with notably low dropout rates compared to conventional PTSD treatments.[8] The combination of HRV biofeedback with other trauma interventions appears to enhance both, and I often use it as the autonomic-foundation work that other interventions sit on top of.

The reason HRV biofeedback belongs in a chapter on neurofeedback is that, in mechanistic terms, it is a form of feedback training. The trainee gets real-time information about autonomic state, and the brain learns to modulate state through respiratory and attentional engagement. The substrate is different from EEG neurofeedback. Cardiac rhythms rather than cortical rhythms. The principle is the same: real-time biological feedback used to train regulation.

For many of my clients, HRV biofeedback is the most accessible starting point for autonomic regulation. It can be done with inexpensive equipment, a chest strap or finger sensor and a phone app. It does not require a clinician once the basic technique is learned. It fits into daily life in ten or fifteen minute sessions. The effects accumulate. I

[8]Kenemore et al. (2024) meta-analysis of HRV biofeedback for military PTSD.

recommend it to almost every trauma client who walks into my clinic, often before any neurofeedback begins.

There is a sequencing principle within sessions that matters. Some clients arrive too activated for the EEG training to land. The nervous system is running so loud that the brain cannot settle into the learning the neurofeedback asks for. When I see this, I do not push through. I start the session with HRV biofeedback or a breathing exercise, bring the autonomic baseline down, and then move to the EEG work. Sometimes the entire first portion of a session is autonomic regulation and the neurofeedback occupies the second half. This is the stabilization principle from Chapter 15 applied within a single hour. The nervous system that cannot learn at nine can learn at four. For some of my clients, this within-session sequence is the difference between sessions that produce measurable change and sessions that produce nothing. The HRV work makes the neurofeedback possible.

16.7 Emerging Neuromodulation

Several emerging interventions (TMS, transcutaneous auricular vagus nerve stimulation, photobiomodulation, light-flicker entrainment) are being investigated for trauma applications. None are ready for first-line clinical recommendation. The field is moving, and several may become more central in the coming years. Ask any provider you work with whether and how they track the evolving evidence in this space.

16.8 The Convergence Framework

Looking at the modalities together, the field has been working on a relatively common set of brain systems by a relatively diverse set of techniques. The convergence is not random. Trauma affects particular systems, and the modalities that work tend to engage those systems even when surface techniques look completely different.

Autonomic regulation work: HRV biofeedback, slow breathing, body-based co-regulation, certain neurofeedback protocols, somatic experiencing. All address the autonomic substrate.

Temporal-lobe work: EMDR, temporal-site neurofeedback, voice-hearing-informed approaches, certain forms of memory integration. These address the temporal-lobe systems that handle prosody, semantic processing, and trauma-related auditory phenomena.

Default-mode and self-referential work: meditation, PCC-targeted fMRI neurofeedback, some forms of insight-oriented therapy. These address the systems that handle self-location and self-narrative.

Frontal-asymmetry work: loving-kindness practice, behavioral activation, certain neurofeedback protocols, light therapy, exercise. These address the approach-avoid balance.

These are not exhaustive categories, and many modalities cut across them. Thinking about which modality to use is more useful when you ask *which set of rooms does my phenotype need to access* rather than *which is the best modality*. The second question rarely has a meaningful answer. The first one can.

16.9 How Modality Gets Matched to Phenotype

The short version: autonomic regulation tools (HRV biofeedback, breath, co-regulation) apply to all phenotypes as the foundation, and specific modalities match specific circuits. For a cramped Lifeguard, posterior-midline neurofeedback after the baseline has stabilized. For a Fog pattern with slowed alpha, alpha-frequency training targeting the slowed rhythm. For temporal-lobe patterns (Bard, Interpreter), temporal-site neurofeedback and EMDR tend to engage the relevant systems.

Chapter 19 develops the full phenotype-to-modality routing framework with specific sequencing, timeline guidance, and decision rules.

Regardless of phenotype: I would not refer a family member to a trauma-informed clinician who knew only one modality. A clinician who can match modality to the brain in front of them usually serves a client better than a clinician who has one approach and uses it on everyone. Ask any prospective provider what they are trained in, how they decide which modality to use when, and what they do when the primary modality is not working. The answers tell you a lot.

16.10 The Talk Is Still Important

Nothing in this chapter argues against talk therapy. The relational work in good talk therapy is itself a regulating intervention, and the cortical-narrative work is part of how trauma material gets integrated into a workable life narrative. Talk is not replaced by training. They do different things, and the most effective recovery work I see usually involves both, often alongside other modalities.

A clinician who only does talk therapy is leaving substantial tools on the table. A clinician who only does neurofeedback is doing the same. Most of my clients benefit from a combination that addresses both the cortical-narrative level and the rhythmic-substrate level, with sequencing that allows each to support rather than interfere with the other.

The next chapter is about reading the brain map, the QEEG that lets me see what the underlying patterns are rather than guess from symptoms alone. The QEEG is a hypothesis-generation tool that helps match what I do to the brain in front of me, not a diagnostic tool in the strict sense. The chapter after that covers alpha-theta, the deep-state work that has been part of trauma neurofeedback's most ambitious applications, with attention to the sequencing principles that determine when alpha-theta is appropriate and when it is not.

16.11 When to Seek a Certified Provider, and When to Be Cautious About Home Training

Neurofeedback is not a regulated title in most jurisdictions. Anyone can buy equipment and call themselves a neurofeedback practitioner. The quality variance is enormous. When you are choosing a provider, credentials are a starting point rather than a destination. BCIA awards the BCN neurofeedback credential; the International QEEG Certification Board separately awards QEEG credentials. Either tells you someone met a coursework and exam standard. Neither is a professional license, and certification is a floor rather than a ceiling.

I have remediated work from uncredentialed providers, sometimes years of it. But some of the most skilled providers I know do not hold

BCIA certification, and some who do are average at best. What matters more is how a provider thinks about your specific pattern: how they select protocols, how they handle a session that goes sideways, whether they adjust when something is wrong. Asking a provider to walk through their reasoning reveals information a credential alone cannot.

Questions worth asking any provider you are considering. What is your training background? How do you select protocols, symptom-based heuristics or QEEG-guided? What database do you use for QEEG comparison, and what is its normative sample? How do you handle a session that produces adverse effects? What is your plan if the work is not producing change after a reasonable trial?

Home neurofeedback devices have become widely available. Some are legitimate tools with clinical evidence behind them. Others are consumer gadgets with marketing that exceeds their capabilities. Red flags I tell my clients to watch for: a device that claims to treat specific conditions without clinician oversight; a system that encourages you to select your own protocols without professional clinical guidance; training that produces new symptoms (increased anxiety, sleep disruption, headaches, emotional instability) that persist past the session. If home training is producing adverse effects, stop and consult a qualified clinician before continuing. Neurofeedback trains the brain in the direction you point it. Pointing it in the wrong direction, even with good intentions, can make things worse. I have seen this in the clinic more than once.

16.12 What I See When Neurofeedback Works, and What I Do When It Doesn't

Here is what I see when neurofeedback is doing its job. The maps move in the direction I targeted. The autonomic markers I track between sessions move with them. The clinical reports change in the way the brain change predicts. The lifeguard's posterior beta comes down, and the client tells me she can sit in a restaurant without watching the door. The Approach/Avoid asymmetry shifts, and the partner notices initiation that was not there before. The PCC quiets, and the dissociation lifts in a way that the prior years of insight-oriented work had not been able to lift. None of these clients can usually tell me what they did to make the change happen. That is the point. The change happened below the level where they could narrate it.

Here is what I see when neurofeedback is not working. The maps do not move. The clinical reports do not change. The protocol is targeting the wrong thing, or the protocol is right but the dose is wrong, or the client is producing a state-dependent rhythm that looks like the target but is actually the brain finding a clever workaround. When I see this I stop. I reread the map. I ask whether something medical is driving the pattern that I missed. I check whether the client's sleep, alcohol use, medication, or trauma load has changed in a way that is competing with the training. I change the protocol or I change the modality or I refer out. Neurofeedback is one door. When the door is not opening I find a different door.

That is what I do for a living. I find the door that opens for the brain in front of me, given what it has been through, and I walk the client through it in the order the architecture allows.

Ch 17: Reading the Trauma Brain Map and Sequencing the Work

Dara is sitting in my office watching her brain map come up on the second screen. Blue patches over the posterior cortex. A hot red band across the top of the head at the high-beta frequencies. I rotate the image and point. "See this? Your sensory cortex is running cold in alpha. Your gating system is underperforming. And this red strip up here? That's the compensation. Your brain is working overtime to manage what the back isn't filtering."

She is quiet for a moment. Then: "That's why everything is so loud." Not a question. A recognition. Twenty years of feeling like the world's volume knob was broken, and here it is, a specific pattern of a specific brain doing a specific thing. The map did not tell her who she was. It told her what her brain was doing, and for the first time, the doing had a shape she could see.

That is what a brain map is for, in the cases when it is for anything: a specific shape where there was only a felt quality, and a place to start from rather than a wall.

This chapter is about reading those pictures, what they can show, and how the reading shapes the work. It is also about sequencing: the principle that determines when which interventions are appropriate, because the map and the intervention sequence inform each other at every stage.

One thing first. QEEG has been over-promised in some quarters. Claims have been made about brain maps that exceed what the technique actually delivers. I run QEEGs daily, I have read or supervised the reading of around 25,000 of them, and I will tell you straight: the map is a useful tool for hypothesis generation about brain patterns. It is one input among many in a thoughtful clinical assessment. It should not be used as a stand-alone diagnostic device, and anyone selling it that way is overselling what they have.

17.1 What a QEEG Actually Is

The technique is straightforward. I place electrodes on the scalp at the standard 10-20 positions, sometimes with a higher-density array if the question warrants it. I record the electrical activity at each electrode for about twenty to forty minutes, with eyes-open and eyes-closed segments, sometimes with a few cognitive-task segments depending on what I'm looking for. The raw recording gets processed to compute the features I read maps for: absolute power at each frequency band at each site, relative power, peak frequency in the alpha band, coherence between sites, amplitude asymmetry between hemispheres, phase-lag relationships, and a half-dozen other derived measures. The features are then compared to a normative database, a reference distribution built from hundreds to thousands of recordings of people without known brain conditions, age-matched. The comparison produces z-scores, each indicating how much a given feature deviates from what is typical for that age band.[1]

A z-score of +2 at a particular site means that feature is two standard deviations above the age-matched average. What the z-score does not tell you is *why*. The excess could reflect a trauma pattern, a medication effect, poor sleep the night before, or something else entirely. The database gives me a statistical comparison against the selected reference sample. I provide the meaning.

The output is a set of color-coded brain maps showing the deviations from norm. A site running very high in beta for its age shows up red on the beta map. A site running very low in alpha for its age shows up blue on the alpha map. I read the maps for patterns: clusters of related deviations that together suggest specific functional configurations.

I read maps in a standard order. First the eyes-closed alpha map: that tells me whether the brain's idle rhythm is doing its gating job.

[1] Hughes & John, 1999; Ko et al., 2021.

Then the eyes-open beta: that tells me what the system is recruiting to manage the world. Then theta, which tells me about frontal regulation and about state-shifts. Then peak alpha frequency at each posterior site, because alpha that's running too slow is a different problem than alpha that's suppressed. Then the asymmetry maps, the coherence patterns, the connectivity measures. The dominant pattern usually presents itself by the third map. The rest is confirmation or complication.

The information the maps provide is real. The technique has been refined over decades, the normative databases are substantial, and the patterns reproduce across recordings of the same person. The technique also does not show what cannot be shown. You cannot read someone's thoughts or memories from a QEEG. You cannot reliably diagnose specific psychiatric conditions. You cannot make confident predictions about an individual's behavior from the map alone. What you can do, with appropriate humility, is generate hypotheses about what the brain is doing in ways that match or do not match the clinical presentation, and use the hypotheses to guide treatment selection. That is what *hypothesis generation* means. The map suggests possibilities. I integrate the map with the clinical history, the symptoms, the patient's experience, the response to past interventions, and other available data, to arrive at a working understanding that informs what to try next.

How much spatial information can a recording from the scalp actually deliver? The question matters because this book names brain structures from scalp electrode data.

The technique faces what is called the inverse problem. Signals from millions of neurons mix as they pass through cerebrospinal fluid, skull, and scalp on the way to the electrodes, so more than one arrangement of sources could produce the same surface pattern. A single electrode cannot tell you where a signal originated. Source analysis addresses this. LORETA and related inverse methods combine all electrodes with a head model and mathematical constraints to produce a regularized, model-dependent estimate of cortical current density. This is one solution to the inverse problem rather than a unique answer, and the estimate is smoothed by the constraints the model imposes. With clean multichannel data, a posterior-midline pattern can support a coarse hypothesis that medial parietal generators, including PCC and precuneus, contribute; a frontal-midline pattern can support an analogous hypothesis involving medial frontal and cingulate cortex. The electrode itself does not identify the structure, and adjacent midline sources remain difficult to separate, especially with nineteen channels and a template head model. Those structures are large, coherently oriented cortical sheets whose electrical fields project clearly to the scalp, which is why the hypotheses about them are better supported than hypotheses about smaller or deeper sources.

With nineteen electrodes and a template head model, localization is centimeter-scale and spatially blurred; accuracy varies with source depth, recording quality, and modeling assumptions. Source analysis will localize artifact as brain activity if the data were not cleaned first. A surface-Laplacian display is complementary: it emphasizes relatively local superficial generators and reduces broad volume-conducted activity. It does not solve the inverse problem or confirm a deep midline source. Between these approaches, the technique can support hypotheses about large cortical generators with reasonable confidence. What it cannot resolve is anything deep and small. The section below on what the map cannot show covers that boundary, including the amygdala, hippocampus, and brainstem.

One more point about the z-scores. A deviation from the norm does not mean something is wrong. It can reflect genetic variation, adaptive specialization, or a brain that is configured unusually and works fine. People are weird. Their brains are weird in specific, repeatable ways. The map shows how unusual you are rather than what is wrong with you. That is the real reason a map cannot diagnose, and it is a better reason than any disclaimer.

17.2 Seeing Yourself on the Screen

Nadia is sitting across from me. The color-coded maps are rotating on the monitor between us. She has already told me her story, the childhood chaos, the decades of managing, the exhaustion she cannot explain to anyone who has not lived it. Now I am showing her what her brain is doing underneath all of that.

I point to a deep blue patch at the back of the head on the eyes-closed alpha map. "This should be your brain's idle state. The gating rhythm that filters sensation so you're not overwhelmed by everything at once. Yours is suppressed. It is suppressed below what this site needs."

She nods slowly. She had thought for years it was just her. That some people were built for this pace and she was not.

I rotate to the beta map and point at a red cluster at the posterior midline. "And this is your scanning system running at high gain. Your brain is using beta, the work rhythm, where it should be using alpha, the rest rhythm. So you're working to process the room even when there's nothing in the room that needs processing."

"I thought everyone felt like this."

"That's a big part of it. Your brain is doing twice the work it should be doing, all day, every day. The plan is to help the alpha come back up and the beta come back down. Not all at once. Systematically."

She looks at the map for a long time. Later she will tell me that seeing the brain map was the first time the tiredness felt like something she could *work with* rather than something that was simply wrong with her. The map did not fix anything. It made the fixing imaginable.

17.3 The Patterns We Have Been Mapping

Throughout this book, we have been describing brain patterns that correspond to phenotype configurations. In my practice, each phenotype tends to show up with characteristic features on the QEEG. The features are not invariant; real brains are messier than schematic descriptions, and the same features can appear in people whose clinical picture does not match the phenotype. These are recurring clinical associations rather than validated diagnostic clusters.

The features I associate with each phenotype in Part II run like this. The cramped Lifeguard: suppressed posterior alpha with elevated beta at the posterior midline (Pz in a standard nineteen-channel recording; CPz and POz in an expanded montage), and frontal beta compensation. The princess: suppressed posterior alpha more broadly. The fog: slowed alpha peak frequency with frontal beta compensation. The CEO: elevated frontal midline theta (simple loops) or beta (elaborated loops). The bard: right-temporal. The interpreter: left-temporal. The Approach/Avoid pattern: frontal asymmetry. The problem child: low arousal at right-frontal inhibitory sites.

The research base behind these patterns is real but unevenly distributed.[2] Frontal theta excess and posterior alpha suppression are the most commonly reported QEEG features in PTSD. They are not unique to trauma; the same features appear in depression, anxiety, ADHD, and other conditions. The patterns reproduce in trauma populations. They are pattern descriptions.[3] A real brain map usually shows several patterns at varying intensities. My job is to identify the dominant patterns, their relationships, and what that picture implies for what to try first.[4]

The QEEG is most useful when paired with the clinical history. A map that shows posterior-midline beta elevation in someone whose presenting complaint is hypervigilance and sleep disturbance is not surprising, and the map confirms what the history suggested. A map that shows the same pattern in someone whose presenting complaint is something else might suggest a Lifeguard component the clinical interview has not yet surfaced. The map and the history inform each other.

---

[2]Clancy et al., 2017.

[3]Butt et al., 2019 (frontal theta and posterior alpha across PTSD studies); Wahbeh & Oken, 2013 (peak alpha frequency in combat veterans); Shim et al., 2017 (network efficiency).

[4]Newson & Thiagarajan, 2018.

17.4 What the Map Cannot Show

The QEEG has real limits, and anyone considering a brain map should know them.

The QEEG does not reliably distinguish among DSM diagnoses. Two people with the same DSM-5 PTSD diagnosis can have very different QEEG patterns, and two people with very similar QEEG patterns can have different DSM diagnoses or no diagnosis at all. The map operates at a different level of description than the diagnostic system, and the two do not cleanly map onto each other.

Individual treatment response is not reliably predictable from a map. Population-level patterns exist, and certain QEEG features are associated with better response to certain interventions on average. Individual prediction is more uncertain than the strongest QEEG-marketing claims have suggested.

Stimulant appropriateness in particular cannot be inferred from a phenotype description or a QEEG finding. A brain map may clarify whether attention complaints coexist with anxiety, sleep disruption, or autonomic features that belong in the prescribing conversation. The decision to prescribe, adjust, or discontinue a stimulant is a diagnostic and medical judgment made from the full clinical picture.

Subcortical activity is not directly visible. The technique is sensitive to cortical electrical activity. Subcortical structures, the amygdala, the hippocampus, the brainstem, contribute to the cortical activity but are not directly read in a standard QEEG. Some of what the QEEG seems to show about subcortical function is inferred from cortical correlates, and the inference is approximate.

Structural brain changes are also not visible on a QEEG. For that you need neuroimaging, an MRI or a CT. A QEEG that looks unusual could reflect functional patterns or could reflect underlying structural changes that the QEEG cannot distinguish from. When structural causes are clinically suspected, neuroimaging is the appropriate next step.

The trauma-versus-TBI question matters more than most people realize, and the QEEG does not solve it on its own. Mild TBI and

PTSD co-occur in an estimated 30 to 50 percent of combat veterans, and the symptom overlap is substantial: cognitive fog, concentration problems, sleep disruption, irritability.[5] Both conditions can produce theta excess and alpha disruption on a QEEG. The direction and location sometimes differ; mTBI tends to increase frontal and temporal slow-wave activity, while PTSD more often shows posterior changes. In any individual the overlap is enough to confuse the reading. When a client of mine has a history of concussion, blast exposure, or repetitive head impacts, I want a neurological workup before neurofeedback begins. Training against a brain pattern that has a structural basis will not produce the same results as training against a functional one. Other medical conditions produce QEEG profiles that look like trauma patterns too: sleep apnea, thyroid dysfunction, chronic Lyme, migraine syndromes, and autonomic disorders like POTS all have their own EEG signatures that overlap with what I might otherwise read as trauma. The map does not tell me the cause. It tells me what the brain is doing.

Trauma history is not specifically visible either. A trauma history produces certain patterns, but the same patterns can be produced by other conditions, post-viral states, sleep disorders, certain genetic patterns. The map alone cannot tell me that the cause was trauma.

Comorbid psychiatric conditions shift the picture in ways that can mislead the reading if I do not account for them. Depression tends to increase frontal theta and reduce posterior alpha, mimicking some of the patterns associated with trauma. Anxiety can elevate beta broadly, compounding whatever beta excess the hypervigilance itself is producing. Substance use histories leave their own marks: chronic alcohol use tends to flatten the power spectrum, chronic stimulant use can alter alpha peak frequency, and active benzodiazepine use increases fast-frequency beta in ways that mask the underlying pattern.[6] I do not read a brain map without knowing the full medication, substance, and medical history. Doing so reads with critical context missing.

---

[5]Dolan et al., 2012 (mTBI/PTSD co-occurrence); Thatcher, 1998; Duff, 2004 (mTBI versus PTSD QEEG signatures).

[6]Newson & Thiagarajan, 2018.

None of this is an argument against using QEEG. It is an argument for using it within its appropriate scope, as one tool among many, in a thoughtful clinical assessment.

17.5 The Sequencing Principle, From the Map

The sequencing principle belongs to Chapter 15, where the full ladder lives. In my practice, the map contributes to target selection alongside symptoms, history, and response to treatment. It helps me form hypotheses about which targets to address first and whether the autonomic substrate can support deeper work.

If a map shows grossly elevated baseline arousal, severe sensory-gating disruption, or a significant dissociation pattern, I am in Phase 1 (stabilization). The right tools are HRV biofeedback, sleep restoration, body-based co-regulation, and alert-state neurofeedback protocols. The more powerful protocols wait.

If the baseline has settled and the map shows specific phenotype patterns, I am in Phase 2 (targeted integration). The lifeguard pattern gets posterior-midline alpha-supporting work. The fog with slowed alpha gets alpha-frequency-supporting work. EMDR, somatic work, and parts work join the picture here. Alpha-theta belongs in this phase for clients who have demonstrated regulatory capacity.

Phase 3 (consolidation) is when the patterns are shifting, the work is largely done, and the job becomes tracking stability and supporting the broader life rather than running protocols. Less time on the training. More time on what the training made possible.

The phases are not strictly linear. People cycle back through stabilization. The spiral is normal. The order of the phases is the principle that protects the work.

17.6 Where QEEG Fits In

In this scheme, QEEG is most useful at two specific points.

The first is at the beginning, as part of the assessment that informs initial protocol selection. The map gives me a baseline picture of what patterns are dominant and helps me form hypotheses about what to address first. If the map shows substantial Fog signature with slowed alpha, I focus the early work on the conditions producing the Fog and consider alpha-frequency training. If the map shows a Lifeguard pattern with disrupted posterior alpha, I focus on autonomic regulation and posterior-alpha-supporting protocols. The map is one input into protocol selection. Whether QEEG-guided selection improves outcomes over competent symptom-guided selection has not been established in a head-to-head trial. What the map gives me is a starting hypothesis I can test against the clinical response.

The second is at follow-up. I repeat QEEGs at intervals on most of my clients, usually six months, sometimes earlier if the clinical picture shifts faster than I expected. The 2023 RCT from Nicholson and colleagues showed, at the trial level, the same pattern shift I see at the clinic level: when alpha-desynchronization neurofeedback is working in PTSD, the targeted patterns shift, with measurable alpha resynchronization in the same default-mode regions that were abnormally low at baseline, while sham controls do not show that shift. In the experimental group, the normalization tracked with symptom reduction; sixty percent no longer met PTSD diagnostic criteria at three-month follow-up, compared with thirty-three percent of the sham group. The between-group difference on the primary outcome did not reach statistical significance.[7] The repeat map tells me a story the symptoms either confirm or do not. If the patterns are not shifting, the protocol may need to change. If the patterns are shifting but the symptoms are not, the relationship between the patterns and the symptoms may not be as direct as my initial reading suggested. Either way, the follow-up data informs the next phase.

The QEEG is less useful as a one-time diagnostic that produces a verdict about the brain. It is more useful as part of an ongoing assessment process that informs and tracks treatment over time.

[7] Nicholson et al. (2023). Double-blind sham-controlled RCT (N=40); 60% experimental vs 33% sham no longer meeting PTSD criteria at three months; between-group CAPS difference not statistically significant.

17.7 When QEEG Is Worth Doing

Not every trauma client of mine gets a QEEG. The technique is more useful in some situations than others.

A QEEG earns its cost when the symptom picture is unclear or previous interventions have not worked as expected; when neurofeedback is being considered and protocol selection needs a map; when the differential between similar-presenting patterns matters for treatment (especially the Frontal Slow versus Slowed Alpha distinction from Chapter 9); when there is a history of head injury, concussion, or blast exposure; or when significant dissociation constrains what the clinical interview can access.

It is less essential when the clinical picture is clear, the response to standard interventions has been good, and additional information would not change the plan. In those cases, the cost of the QEEG (which is real, the technique is not cheap, and access varies by region) may not be justified.

When QEEG is being recommended, the questions worth asking are the same questions that apply to any neurofeedback work, and Appendix B has the full list. Briefly: who is reading the map, what is their training, how does the QEEG inform protocol selection, what is the plan for follow-up, and how do they handle situations where the map and the clinical picture do not match.

The Marcu finding. A 2025 study by Marcu and colleagues in adolescent populations with complex childhood trauma did not find significant group differences in several of the QEEG features the trauma-neurofeedback literature has emphasized. Total EEG power was lower in the trauma group, but specific posterior-alpha and alpha-asymmetry markers did not separate trauma from control groups.[8] One technical point with clinical implications: *relative* alpha excess on a map may actually reflect globally reduced cortical activation, not overactive alpha rhythms, if total power is reduced across the board. A 2026 methods paper

[8]Marcu et al., 2024; Marcu et al., 2025.

confirmed that relative and absolute power capture different things.[9] Since the Marcu paper I say *this is a pattern I see in clients with trauma history* rather than *this is a trauma marker.* The QEEG is hypothesis generation. A map that does not show these patterns does not rule out a trauma history.

17.8 What the Brain Map Tells You About Treatment

When I interpret the map carefully and integrate it with the clinical picture, what it tells me about treatment is something like this:

What patterns are currently dominant. Which phenotype configurations appear to be most active. Where the highest-impact targets are likely to be. Whether the autonomic picture, together with the clinical assessment, suggests the substrate is regulated enough to support deeper work or whether more stabilization is needed first. Whether the neurofeedback has specific targets that match the clinical picture. Whether the picture suggests other clinical considerations, sleep evaluation, neurology consultation, medical workup, that might be relevant.

What the brain map does not tell you: who you are, what your trauma was, what the meaning of your experience is, what you should do with your life, or what your prognosis is in any deterministic sense. Those questions belong elsewhere. The map is one input.

17.9 Putting It Together

A worked example, composite. She is in her late thirties, referred by a therapist who has been working with her for two years without the traction either of them expected. The presenting history includes a childhood that involved chronic emotional unpredictability, not physical abuse, but a parent whose moods were the weather system everyone else organized around. She has been functional, high-functioning in many ways, and she has also been exhausted for longer than she can remember. Sleep is bad. Focus is intermittent. She describes a sense

[9] Sandre & Troller-Renfree (2026).

of being slightly disconnected from herself, most of the time, that has been there so long she assumed it was normal.

She has tried EMDR. It helped somewhat with specific incidents but did not change the underlying tone. She has tried medication, SSRIs for anxiety and depression, both with partial effects that wore off. She describes herself as someone who "tries hard but can't quite get there," and there is a flatness in how she says it, more like a conclusion she has reluctantly accepted than outright defeat.

My clinical interview points me toward a Lifeguard-dominant pattern: the chronic environmental scanning, the sleep maintenance difficulty, the difficulty letting guard down even in objectively safe environments. There is also something that looks like the Fog, the chronic low-grade processing difficulty, the sense of slight unreality. The combination is recognizable. Unstabilized hypervigilance eventually trips the breaker. She has been running hot for so long that her nervous system has begun cycling between high alert and protective offline-holding.

I run a QEEG.

The map confirms what the interview suggested, with some additions. Posterior midline beta elevation, the Lifeguard signature, the sensory cortex running too hot, the alpha rhythms that should be gating input disrupted and unstable. A frontal beta compensation pattern: the front of the brain working hard to manage what the back is sending up. And something I did not necessarily expect from the interview: the individual alpha peak frequency is measurably slowed across several posterior sites. In someone presenting with cognitive complaints, this matters. It means her cognitive load is at least partly neurological. Slowed peak alpha frequency is a nonspecific EEG finding and does not by itself determine whether stimulant medication is appropriate. Her previous clinician had briefly considered stimulants for her attention complaints; the slowed-alpha pattern, together with the anxiety and sleep disruption, was information I wanted a prescriber to weigh rather than a decision I could make from the map.

My reading: the dominant pattern is a cramped Lifeguard with sensory-gating disruption as the central feature. The frontal beta is compensatory. The slowed alpha is an independent contributor to the cognitive complaints. She is not treatment-resistant. She has been treated for the surface symptoms without addressing the underlying pattern.

I plan in phases. Phase one: HRV biofeedback daily, ten to fifteen minutes, as the autonomic foundation. Targeted neurofeedback at the posterior midline sites with alpha-frequency work specifically aimed at restoring alpha rhythm and supporting sensory gating. Sleep evaluation, with a referral to sleep medicine if the sleep does not respond to the autonomic work within six to eight weeks. The slowed-alpha finding goes on the chart with a note to discuss with her prescriber: the attention complaints coexist with anxiety and poor sleep, and those vulnerabilities should be weighed before any stimulant decision is made.

Phase two, eight to twelve weeks out: if the autonomic baseline has settled and the sleep has improved, the system will have more regulatory capacity for trauma-processing work. The EMDR her previous clinician tried was premature. There was not enough stable ground for the processing to land.

Phase three, months later: I will repeat the QEEG to see what shifted, and I will adjust accordingly.

At session twelve she says something I hear, in various forms, fairly often: "I feel like myself for the first time in years, and I don't quite trust it yet." The not-quite-trusting is appropriate. She has been in the old pattern for a long time. It takes longer to trust a shift than it takes to make one.

This is what informed sequencing looks like in my clinic. The clinical picture, the brain map, and the intervention plan all inform each other. We proceed in phases. I repeat the QEEG at intervals to track whether the patterns are shifting as expected. I adjust based on what is and is not working. Matching the map to the intervention is more demanding than running standard protocols on everyone. Whether it produces better outcomes than competent symptom-guided selection is an open question. What I can say is that the map gives me hypotheses I would not have formed from the clinical interview alone, and that the follow-up map tells me whether those hypotheses held.

17.10 When QEEG Should Come First, and When a Neurological Workup Comes Before That

Not everyone needs a QEEG before starting trauma work. In some situations the map adds information that changes what I would do; in others, the clinical picture is clear enough that additional data would not change the plan.

I want a QEEG before I start neurofeedback. Training a brain without knowing what it is doing is like prescribing glasses without checking the prescription: you might get lucky, and you might make things worse. That is my practice rather than a field standard. Competent clinicians select protocols from symptoms alone and get results doing it, and no head-to-head trial has told us how much the map is worth. It is why the routing in Chapter 19 is written to work without one.

Get a neurological workup *before* the QEEG when any of the following apply: a history of concussion, blast exposure, or repetitive head impacts that has not been formally evaluated; new or worsening cognitive symptoms progressing over time rather than stable; focal neurological signs, one-sided weakness, visual field changes, new-onset seizure-like episodes; headache patterns that have changed character recently; or a QEEG showing focal slowing or coherence patterns I cannot explain by trauma alone. In those cases, the next step is a neurologist rather than a neurofeedback protocol. Structural brain conditions can produce QEEG patterns that look like trauma but require medical rather than training-based intervention.

The sequencing matters. Clinical assessment comes first. If QEEG is indicated or chosen, obtain it before map-guided protocol selection. When structural brain involvement is suspected, neurological workup comes before either. Getting this order wrong means training against a pattern I do not fully understand, and the brain remembers what it is trained to do.

The next chapter is on alpha-theta, one of the more important and one of the more dangerous neurofeedback protocols, depending on when it is used and on what kind of nervous system. The sequencing principle this chapter has laid out applies there as much as anywhere. The right time matters.

If you were sitting in my chair right now, watching your own map come up on the second screen, here is the question I would ask you. What pattern do you suspect is loudest in your map? The cramped Lifeguard burning the back midline. The princess and the pea over-running the right temporal sensors. The fog slowing the alpha rhythm across the posterior cortex. The CEO stuck on the wrong loop. The Approach/Avoid asymmetry tilting the frontal balance. Sit with the question for a minute before turning the page. Whatever your guess is, that guess is information. The chapters that follow are partly about whether the map confirms what you already suspect.

Ch 18: (Alpha-Theta) The Door That Opens Later

She found a neurofeedback provider through a friend's recommendation. Came in with complex PTSD. He put her into alpha-theta sessions in her third visit, no QEEG, no stabilization work, no dissociation assessment. By session five she was losing time between sessions, waking up at night with intrusive imagery she did not have before treatment began. By session eight she stopped showing up. Eleven months later she arrived in my office, more symptomatic than when she had started, asking me to help her unwind what the protocol had opened and she could not close.

The protocol is not the problem. The sequencing is. Alpha-theta is a room you enter after the house has walls.

In the late 1980s, Eugene Peniston and Paul Kulkosky, working at the Fort Lyons VA Medical Center in Colorado, published a study that became one of the most influential and most contested papers in the history of clinical neurofeedback. Combat veterans with severe PTSD and chronic alcoholism, two populations the field had been failing. Extended sessions in a quiet room, eyes closed, audio tones tracking brain rhythms.

The published results were striking: sustained reductions in PTSD symptoms, sustained reductions in alcohol relapse, personality changes at long follow-up. The protocol became one of the foundational interventions in trauma-focused neurofeedback. It is also one of the protocols that, used wrongly, has hurt people. I have seen both outcomes. In my clinic I have run enough alpha-theta sessions to know what the protocol looks like when it is working, and I have done enough intake conversations with clients who came to me after it went wrong elsewhere. This chapter is about both.

18.1 What Alpha-Theta Does

The basic technique trains the brain to produce alpha and theta rhythms in particular ratios, with the client in a relaxed, eyes-closed state. Alpha runs around eight to twelve cycles per second and is often prominent when the eyes are closed and the mind is quiet. It has multiple generators and functions rather than being one unitary cortical resting rhythm. Theta is slower, around four to seven cycles per second, prominent in drowsy states and in the transition between waking and sleep. The alpha-theta state, in the protocol's framing, is a hypnagogic-like condition in which the brain produces significant theta while still maintaining some alpha. A particular borderline state between waking and sleep.

When sessions go well, clients enter a state of deep relaxation in which imagery, memories, and affective material arise spontaneously, without the effortful retrieval that other memory work involves. Practitioners have compared the state to certain meditation states, to hypnagogic imagery work, and to the deep imagery traditions that have been part of psychotherapy for decades. Material a person has been holding offline can become accessible in this state, often in ways that allow integration to happen without explicit cognitive effort on the material.

I cannot specify the mechanism. Several things appear to happen at once. The relaxed state allows the autonomic system to settle into a parasympathetic-dominant configuration that is rare in trauma populations during waking hours. The theta activity may engage hippocampal and medial-temporal systems in ways that support memory access and reconsolidation. The alpha activity provides a kind of cortical regulation that holds the system stable enough that the theta activity does not produce dysregulation. The combination, at its best, is a regulated body in which deep affective and mnemonic material can be accessed and worked with, without the forced retrieval that other memory work involves.

The Peniston protocol included specific sequencing. Preparatory work before the alpha-theta sessions began. Careful titration of session duration. Attention to the client's state at the end of sessions. The original results were obtained within that careful frame. The clinical use of alpha-theta in subsequent decades has not always preserved this care, and most of the harm I have seen has come from versions that skipped the preparation, the titration, or the post-session attention.

18.2 The Original Findings, Honestly

The Peniston studies have been celebrated and they have been criticized. Both deserve attention.[1]

The celebration is that the studies showed effects on populations the field considered treatment-resistant, with sustained improvement at long follow-up, and that they provided one of the first clear demonstrations that neurofeedback could produce meaningful clinical change in trauma populations. The protocol established a clinical model that has influenced decades of subsequent work. The findings, if they hold up, are some of the more important clinical results in the field.

The criticism is methodological. Small sample sizes. No double-blinding. Limited control conditions in some of the studies. The personality measures used to document the changes have been questioned for reasons that have to do with the measures themselves. Replication attempts have produced mixed results. Some replicated substantial effects. Others showed more modest effects. Some failed to replicate the dramatic findings of the originals. The honest framing is that the Peniston findings have not been as cleanly replicated as one would want for a treatment that has had this much clinical influence.

The current evidence base for alpha-theta in trauma populations is real but more modest than the protocol's reputation suggests. Several smaller studies have shown effects. The clinical case-series literature is substantial. The randomized controlled trial base is thinner. My

[1]Peniston & Kulkosky (1989, 1991); Saxby & Peniston (1995) for one of the positive replications; Scott, Kaiser, Othmer, & Sideroff (2005) for the most cited attempted replication that showed more modest effects; Trudeau (2000) and Moore (2000) for early methodological critiques; Sokhadze et al. (2008) for a broader review of the replication literature.

working position is the same one I take about most trauma modalities by now: alpha-theta is a clinically used protocol with growing but not definitive evidence, it has produced both substantial benefit and substantial harm depending on how it has been used, and responsible practice involves recognizing both. Alpha-theta shares with other trauma modalities the gap between clinical adoption and controlled-trial evidence, and it is somewhat unusual in the magnitude of harm that can result when the sequencing is violated.

18.3 When It Goes Wrong

The composite in the chapter's opening is the typical harm pattern. A second one shows the other outcome.

A Vietnam-era veteran came to me already destabilized from a different intensive trauma program. He was carrying PTSD, alcohol use that had returned after years of sobriety, and the kind of facial wariness I have learned to read as a system that is permanently bracing. He had heard that alpha-theta worked for veterans. He wanted me to start it that week. I told him no. We spent six months on alert-state stabilization first. We worked on sleep, on his alcohol use, on the autonomic baseline, on the relational ground that would let the deeper work matter. When I finally moved him to alpha-theta, the sessions went the way the original Peniston papers describe. Substantial imagery. Substantial integration. Substantial settling. He told me later, six months past the end of the alpha-theta arc, that he could hear his wife's voice in the morning without flinching for the first time since 1971.

The protocol was the same in both cases. The difference was the sequencing, and the sequencing was the difference between the room becoming available and the room becoming dangerous.

The mechanism of harm, when it happens, is the same one I describe throughout the safety chapter. Trauma material a brain has been holding offline has been held offline for a reason. The reason is usually that this person did not have the regulatory capacity to integrate the material when it was originally encoded, and the offline-holding has been a protective response to that limitation. When a deep-state intervention opens access before the regulation has been built, the offline-holding fails and the material floods through, but the integration that should accompany the access does not happen. The client ends up with the worst of both outcomes. The protective holding has been bypassed. The integration that bypassing it was supposed to allow has not occurred.

I have walked through enough of these unwindings to know how avoidable they are. The first composite did not need an alpha-theta provider with one year of training. She needed six to nine months of alert-state stabilization with a clinician who knew her dissociation profile. The trauma material she carried was real, the protocol can in principle help with it, and the sequencing failure was a clinical decision someone made on her behalf without examining whether she was ready.

The Othmer evolution of trauma-focused neurofeedback has been one of the more careful responses to this pattern. Siegfried and Susan Othmer, who have done substantial clinical work in trauma neurofeedback and have been part of the alpha-theta tradition since its early years, have explicitly described the evolution of their approach away from alpha-theta as an entry-level protocol and toward extensive alert-state stabilization work first, with alpha-theta reserved for clients who have demonstrated the regulatory capacity to use it. The infra-low-frequency protocol line that emerged from this evolution has its own growing evidence base.[2] The core clinical learning from the Othmer evolution is explicit. Physiological self-regulation comes first. Alert-state training carries the early load. Alpha-theta finds its appropriate place as a later integrative phase rather than an opening move.

This is what the sequencing looks like for alpha-theta and deep-state neurofeedback. I do some weeks of SMR or alpha training first, depending on the person's needs, stabilizing sleep, stress, attention, mood, anxiety. For some people that takes a few weeks. For others, months. The question that governs when to proceed is capacity rather

[2]Bazzana et al. (2022) on infra-low-frequency neurofeedback in trauma populations.

than the calendar: can she notice her feet on the floor while remembering the event. When she can, the deeper work is available. But the two phases are not strictly sequential. I run alpha-theta alongside SMR training when I need to, keeping sleep stable and grounding high. The whole process iterates. I test, I adjust, I move back to alert-state work when the picture changes. It does not go in one direction. The protocol has not been abandoned. The sequencing has been corrected.

18.4 What the Sessions Look Like

For a client who is appropriate for alpha-theta, treated by an experienced clinician, sessions have a recognizable shape.

The session typically begins with brief alert-state work. A few minutes of preparatory training that bring the client into a regulated state before the deeper protocol begins. This serves as warm-up and as assessment of how regulated she is on this particular day. If she is not regulated, the session changes. We do more alert work, or we postpone the alpha-theta entirely. I will end a session before it starts if the day is not right.

The client then transitions to the eyes-closed, lying-back position. Audio feedback continues, with tones that signal the alpha and theta rhythms. She relaxes into the state, often using guided imagery initially and increasingly letting whatever arises arise.

Sessions vary in length. Thirty to forty-five minutes of the alpha-theta state is typical. During the session, imagery, memories, affective material, and bodily sensations may arise. The client does not need to verbalize what is happening. The integration appears to happen at a state-level that does not require verbal processing.

The session ends with a transition back to ordinary waking state, often with a few minutes of orientation work to ensure the client is grounded before leaving the office. I check in about what came up, what she is taking from the session, and how she is doing in the moment. If she is leaving in a state I do not want her driving in, I keep her in the office longer or arrange a ride.

Between sessions, the client uses her stabilization tools as needed. Some clients have activation between sessions, in the early phase of alpha-theta work, and the activation is part of what the stabilization tools are managing. The activation should not be overwhelming. If it is, the protocol slows down or pauses.

A typical alpha-theta arc is one to two sessions per week, for somewhere between ten and thirty sessions depending on the protocol and the person. Treatment is not indefinite. There is usually a recognizable point at which deep-state training has done what it can do and the client moves into a different phase of treatment.

18.5 What Alpha-Theta Is (and When to Wait)

Alpha-theta is a clinical tool with the same kinds of limits and failure modes as other clinical tools. The original Peniston findings were striking, and the protocol has produced some of the more dramatic individual clinical changes I have seen in trauma neurofeedback. Framing it as a uniquely powerful intervention that bypasses every other modality has produced both unrealistic expectations and inappropriate sequencing.

The protocol does one thing well: support integration of trauma material in a deep-state context. It does not replace autonomic regulation work, relational repair, cognitive-narrative work, or daily-life stabilization. Clients who do alpha-theta well almost always do it as one phase inside a broader treatment arc that includes these other elements.

Every composite I have described in this chapter that went wrong went wrong for the same reason: alpha-theta used on an unstabilized nervous system before the regulatory infrastructure was in place. The sequencing principle applies here perhaps more than anywhere else in the book.

Some people are not suited to deep-state work, for various reasons I will name below. The clinician's job is to assess whether alpha-theta is appropriate for this client at this time, and to defer or decline when it is not. *Not yet* is a clinically correct answer that I give frequently.

Some clients on appropriate psychiatric medication can do alpha-theta well. Some medications change the brain's response to the protocol in ways that affect the work. The clinician needs to know the medication picture and adjust accordingly.

18.6 The Door That Opens Later

The metaphor in this chapter's title is the working position. Alpha-theta is a door. It opens into rooms that other interventions have trouble reaching. The rooms contain real value, for some trauma populations specifically and for the broader project of integration.

The door opens later: after the autonomic baseline is regulated, after the stabilization tools are reliable, after the client has demonstrated the capacity to handle what comes up, after the relationship with the clinician is solid enough to support what the protocol opens. That is when the door becomes available, not at the start of treatment and not before the house has the walls that allow the rooms to be safely entered.

If you are a clinician, alpha-theta is something you offer when the time is right. If you are a client and someone has told you that alpha-theta is your next step, the question to ask is whether the conditions are present. The right answer is sometimes yes. Sometimes the right answer is, not yet, let's do more stabilization work first, and revisit in three or six months. That answer is treatment.

Before this chapter closes, here is the routing decision in concrete form. These are the conditions I check, in order, before I move a client to alpha-theta in my clinic. Read them as a clinician's checklist or as a client's questions for a provider.

1. The autonomic baseline is regulated. The client can move between activation and relaxation with reasonable flexibility, uses basic stabilization tools effectively, and is not currently sitting in chronic high arousal or chronic dissociation.
2. The stabilization tools are reliable. When activation comes up between sessions, the client has practiced ways to bring it down. She

knows what to do when she gets flooded. The tools are accessible to her under stress, not just in the office on a good day.

3. The dissociation profile is known and stable. The client is not dissociating regularly in daily life. If she has a dissociative-spectrum history, we have worked with it directly, and her capacity to stay present with affective material is established.
4. No active crisis is consuming her capacity. Severe depression, active suicidality, ongoing victimization, acute substance use crisis. Any of these means the crisis is addressed first and alpha-theta waits.
5. No primary active psychotic-spectrum diagnosis. The alpha-theta state can produce experiences that resemble psychotic-like phenomena, and for clients with primary psychosis vulnerabilities the protocol can amplify rather than help.
6. The clinical relationship can hold what the protocol opens. There is substantial trust with the clinician, and the clinician knows alpha-theta specifically, understands the sequencing principles, has worked with trauma populations long enough to recognize a session going wrong, and is prepared to back off when material is too much.
7. The client's life context supports intensive integration. She has time for recovery between sessions, a support system she can lean on, and is not in the middle of an external crisis (medical, relational, occupational, financial) that is already consuming her stabilization capacity.
8. She wants to do this work. Alpha-theta is intensive. It produces experiences that are unfamiliar and sometimes disorienting. The client should be informed about what to expect and should be entering with full informed consent, not because someone recommended it and she did not feel free to say no.
9. Earlier treatment has plateaued in a place where deep-state integration is the plausible next move. Alpha-theta is rarely the right starting protocol. It is more often the right move after earlier modalities

have done what they can do, and the integration of remaining trauma material is the next phase.

When all nine are in place, alpha-theta can be one of the most effective interventions in the trauma-neurofeedback toolkit. When several are absent, the protocol waits. *Not yet* is the answer most worth practicing.

The rooms behind the alpha-theta door open into the broader life. The point of all of this has always been to make that life possible.

Part V

Recovery

Ch 19: The Phenotype-Matched Recovery Plan

Three people came through my clinic last spring, six weeks apart. All three carried a PTSD diagnosis. All three had been told, by competent prior clinicians, that they were treatment-resistant. None of them was treatment-resistant; each was routed to an intervention that made sense within a framework that did not have the phenotype layer to work with. A different framework, applied earlier, would have produced a different sequence. Here is what I saw.

Sofia. Mid-thirties, hypervigilant, six years of therapy and three modalities behind her. The trauma memories were vivid and intrusive and she wanted them gone, and she wanted to start EMDR the day she walked in. I read her map: cramped Lifeguard, posterior beta running hot, alpha gating offline, a baseline autonomic state so high I could see it in the resting recording. I told her what I tell most Lifeguards in her configuration. "Your autonomic baseline is so high that if we open those memories now, you won't be able to integrate them. We need to build the floor first." She resisted. She wanted the memories gone now. She complied anyway. Six weeks of cyclic sighing twice a day, the boring kind, no fireworks. Then posterior-alpha neurofeedback, twice a week. By month three her resting heart rate had dropped eight beats per minute and she was sleeping through the night for the first time in a decade. Only then did we begin EMDR. The processing landed because there was a floor underneath it to land on.

Andre. Late forties, high-functioning, a CEO presentation with the Performer overlay you see most often in eldest-children-of-immigrants and in physicians. He had tried CBT for the rumination, an SSRI for the mood, mindfulness for the spiral. The CBT helped him build a better internal argument with the thoughts. The SSRI flattened the spiral and his capacity to feel anything else. Mindfulness made the loop louder, because the focused-attention instruction was asking the part of him that had been monitoring the world since he was twelve to do more monitoring. The map showed it: frontal-midline theta stuck, anterior cingulate over-recruited, the conflict-monitor running like a fan that never spun down. I named the pattern directly. "Your brain's monitoring system has been stuck in the on position since you were twelve, and it's exhausting you." The first intervention I gave him was permission to stop performing. Leave one email unanswered. Let one task sit overnight. He came back the following week with a small surprised look. "I left the email," he said. "I kept waiting for something to go wrong." Nothing had. The anterior cingulate, given less to monitor, began to release its grip. Neurofeedback at FCz came second. Open-monitoring meditation came third. The performer did not vanish. It became something closer to a choice.

Luz. Late twenties, the chronic-load fog you see in survivors of long developmental trauma, plus an approach/avoid asymmetry that left her unable to leave her apartment some weeks. The weeks she could leave, she made a grocery list the night before. The weeks she could not, the list stayed on the counter. The previous clinicians had been routing this as treatment-resistant depression with a trauma history. I read her map and saw something else: alpha peak slowed to 8.2 Hz, frontal asymmetry tilted in the avoid-loud direction, and a Fog signature that did not look like trauma. I sent her for a medical workup first. The sleep study came back negative. The thyroid was borderline. The iron was low enough to matter. Supplementation alone brought her processing speed up inside a month. *Then* the work could start: alpha-frequency neurofeedback for the slowed peak, behavioral activation for the approach-quiet side, loving-kindness practice for the avoid-inflated pattern. The EMDR session that would have been wasted six months earlier worked at month eight because the Fog had cleared enough for her to be present to her own memories.

Three people, three configurations, three routings that no protocol manual would have written the same way. This chapter is about how I think when I see a map and a story and have to decide what comes next, and in what order, and what I tell the person sitting across from me when they ask the question they always ask first: *where do we start?*

19.1 Before the routing: what this framework can and cannot claim

The phenotype-matched routing framework in this chapter is clinically grounded, theoretically sound, and ahead of the empirical data. No biomarker panel currently exists that can tell a clinician *this patient needs this treatment* with the certainty I would like. The dissociative subtype of PTSD is the one phenotype with enough randomized data to say something specific about differential treatment response. For the rest, the routing draws on clinical pattern recognition, mechanism-of-action reasoning, and convergent indirect evidence rather than head-to-head biotype-by-intervention trials. That is where the field is. What follows is the best routing I know how to do, offered with appropriate honesty about what has and has not been demonstrated at scale.

A plan is a working hypothesis about what the next phase looks like, subject to revision as it unfolds. It is not a contract and it is not a protocol; if I am writing one with a client and we treat it as either, we have made a mistake we will have to back out of later. Held too rigidly, plans fail because nervous systems do not respond as predicted. Held too loosely, plans fail because they lose direction. The right level of commitment is enough to organize the next several months, with explicit attention to what would suggest the plan needs to change. That is the level I aim for in my own clinic, and the level I am writing toward here.

19.2 The general shape

Across phenotypes, the recovery plans I write tend to share a shape. Three phases, with porous edges.

Phase one: stabilization. The aim is the autonomic floor: sleep, basic safety, the regulatory tools that the rest of the work will rely on. The interventions are the basic kit. HRV biofeedback. Cyclic sighing five minutes a day. Sleep restoration in whatever form the client can tolerate. Body-based co-regulation. Sometimes alert-state neurofeedback. Sometimes medication for a specific symptom (sleep, anxiety, mood) that is interfering with the regulation work itself. Talk therapy in this phase tends to focus on present-moment functioning and the relational scaffolding that supports what comes later. For some people that takes a few weeks. For others, months. The question that governs when to proceed is capacity rather than the calendar: can the regulation tools hold under stress, and can the person maintain dual awareness while engaging difficult material? I have had clients spend a year in stabilization before integration could begin, and the year was not wasted.

Breath work and *HRV biofeedback* are vague enough to cover almost anything. The most evidence-backed starting point is cyclic sighing (double inhale through the nose, long exhale through the mouth, five minutes a day). Chapter 14 covers the specific evidence. Slow breathing at around six breaths per minute is the next tool I add. HRV biofeedback wraps the same physiology in real-time feedback and has the strongest evidence base for PTSD populations specifically. These are first-line state-regulation tools. Everything else I do later works better when the autonomic baseline is lower, and I have a long enough clinical track record on this point to say it without much hedging.

Phase two: targeted integration. Once the floor is reasonably in place and the regulatory capacity supports it, the phenotype-specific work becomes appropriate. EMDR. Somatic experiencing in deeper form. Parts work. Certain forms of CBT. Sometimes alpha-theta neurofeedback after substantial preparation. Sometimes MDMA-assisted therapy in qualifying contexts. This is when the trauma material gets worked through with explicit attention to integration. The pacing matters. I have watched well-intentioned clinicians, and a few less-well-intentioned ones, push integration too hard, too fast, and produce decompensation that took considerable time to walk back. Pacing is craft, and the difference shows up most clearly in this phase.

Phase three: consolidation and life-building. The integration has done what it can do, for the moment. The focus shifts toward consolidation of the gains and re-engagement with the broader life. Less time on processing. More time on relationships, work, the things that make a life. The trauma framework appropriately recedes from being the dominant lens. I check in periodically, especially when life produces new demands, but I am no longer the center of gravity for the client. Which is the point.

These phases are approximate, and their edges are porous. The transitions are governed by capacity rather than the calendar. Real timelines vary by trauma severity, developmental versus adult-onset history, phenotype configuration, access to good clinical work, and the rest of the life context. What the phasing captures is the general progression effective recovery tends to follow. Stabilization bearing integration, integration bearing identity, each rung supporting the next. But the two phases are not strictly sequential. When dual awareness and recovery capacity are present, supported processing can begin alongside continued regulation work. I called this the Stabilization Ladder in Chapter 15 and I will keep calling it that.

19.3 How I route by dominant phenotype

The phenotype framework becomes most useful when it tells me what to do next. Below is how I think about each one. The voice in this section is the voice I use in my own clinical notes: not protocol, just routing.

When a *Lifeguard* is dominant, I start with autonomic regulation and I start the day she walks in. HRV biofeedback. Breath work. Sleep restoration. Grounding practices. Basic somatic work. Targeted neurofeedback at posterior midline sites if I have access to it. The reason for the order is not theoretical. The research literature backs this up (Soder et al., 2019, on resting HRV as a moderator of psychotherapy response), but the reason I do it is that I have watched what happens when Lifeguards are pushed into exposure-based work before the floor is built. The exposure does not land. Sometimes it makes things worse. After stabilization, I add EMDR for specific traumatic events, somatic experiencing for the autonomic patterns, sometimes alpha-theta after extensive preparation for deeper integration of developmental material. In consolidation I want to see her re-engaging with environments and relationships she had been avoiding, with the regulation tools still available. If the regulation tools fall away too quickly during re-engagement, I slow down.

For *CEO* presentations, my routing question is what to subtract. The performer brain has been doing too much for too long. Stabilization includes autonomic regulation, yes, but the more pointed intervention is loop-labeling practice plus deliberate incompletion. Sometimes NAC for the rumination patterns. Possibly frontal-midline neurofeedback for the theta-stuck or beta-stuck variants. Open-monitoring meditation rather than focused-attention, because focused-attention asks the over-monitor to monitor harder. Integration looks like parts work that engages the Manager directly. An examination of the family-of-origin conditions that produced the over-control pattern. Sometimes EMDR for specific events that have been driving the perfectionism. The performer subtype almost always needs particular attention to the relationship between external function and internal cost; the gap between what the client looks like and what she feels like is part of the data.

The *Princess* routing has to do two things at once. Support the high-gain system without flattening it. Soften the threat-biased prior. Stabilization is autonomic regulation, sensory environment design, loving-kindness practice, possibly right-temporal neurofeedback. Boundary practices that respect the gain rather than fighting it. Integration adds EMDR for specific rejection-sensitivity events that have been formative, somatic experiencing for the body-level overwhelm patterns, parts work that engages the Princess as a sensitive expert rather than a defective signal-receiver. When severe rejection-sensitivity is disabling, a prescriber conversation about medication may be warranted. Consolidation is what most Princesses I see actually want by the time they get to it: a life that respects the gain, appropriate sensory environments, appropriate social pacing, deliberate use of the gift in work and relationships.

When a *Fog* presents, my first move is almost always a medical workup. Sleep, thyroid, viral picture, iron, B12, sometimes a cardiology referral. I have caught enough unrecognized apnea and enough mild hypothyroidism and enough post-viral pacing failures to know that the Fog is not always trauma. Once medical contributors are addressed or ruled out, stabilization continues with sleep restoration, alpha-frequency neurofeedback if slowed alpha is present, pacing if the map shows a post-viral picture. If attention symptoms coexist with a slowed-alpha finding, I want the prescriber to weigh the full picture rather than routing the medication decision from the map alone. Integration addresses the trauma layer when present, with attention to the dissociative quality of the Fog and the need for grounding work alongside any deeper engagement. The tide and the Fog are twins, and I want to see the Tide coming back before I push integration hard.

For *Bard* presentations, the routing is about softening the threat-biased prosodic reading. Stabilization includes autonomic regulation, prosody reality-checking practice with trusted others (after some time has passed, ask the person the honest question: *I want to make sure I read you right; were you upset about X?*), sensory environment work, possibly right-temporal neurofeedback. Integration adds EMDR for specific events of misread prosody that have been formative, parts work that engages the Bard as an expert listener. Sometimes voice-hearing-informed work if the pattern includes voice-hearing experiences, which it does more often than is generally acknowledged. Music as a deliberate regulation tool. Consolidation looks like relationships and contexts that allow the gift to operate without constant alarm.

For *Interpreter* presentations, I want to give the language system back its resources and address any temporal-lobe symptom material. Stabilization is autonomic regulation, written-not-just-spoken accommodations, single-tasking the language load, basic comprehension practice in low-stakes material, possibly left-temporal neurofeedback. Integration addresses the trauma narrative as integration becomes possible, with explicit attention to the conditions for safe memory work. If voice-hearing is present, I want a clinician who works specifically with trauma-related voice-hearing rather than one who treats it as psychosis by default. Consolidation is re-engagement with reading and complex listening as the bandwidth returns.

For *Approach/Avoid* presentations, I am rebalancing the asymmetry and addressing the freeze. Stabilization includes autonomic regulation, behavioral activation if approach is offline, light therapy and exercise as foundations, loving-kindness practice for the avoid side, possibly frontal-asymmetry neurofeedback. Integration adds somatic work for the freeze patterns (ideally with a clinician who specifically works with the freeze response), EMDR or other modalities for events that have been driving the asymmetry, sometimes medication for severe presentations. Consolidation is deliberate practice of action in moments where the freeze used to dominate.

With the *Problem Child*, sleep is foundational here more than anywhere. Stabilization includes autonomic regulation, the half-second pause practice, possibly right-frontal neurofeedback, sometimes medication when a prescriber assesses the autonomic substrate as warranting it. If substances are involved, integrated dual-diagnosis treatment from the start, with attention to both the trauma layer and the substance use rather than the old sequence of "get sober first, then we can talk about trauma" that I have watched fail more times than I want to count. Integration adds parts work that engages the Firefighter, sometimes formal substance-treatment work in coordination with the trauma work, examination of the family-of-origin conditions that left the brake under-developed. Consolidation is building life structures that take some of the load off the internal brake.

Dissociation can co-occur with any of the phenotypes above, and when it does it changes my routing. For years the clinical assumption was that dissociative presentations required extensive stabilization before any trauma-focused work, and that exposure would trigger further shutdown rather than processing. The evidence has gotten more complicated. One recent finding deserves attention: dissociative-subtype PTSD did not moderate outcomes of intensive trauma-focused treatment in one cohort, with sixty-eight percent of dissociative-subtype participants no longer meeting criteria after treatment.[1] This does not mean stabilization is unnecessary. It means the old bright line was probably too conservative for many people. My current routing principle, after watching this play out: if dissociation is present, assess whether the client can maintain dual awareness during trauma-focused work. Concretely: can she notice her feet on the floor while remembering the event. If yes, the work can proceed with appropriate pacing. If trauma cues produce full depersonalization or derealization, build the grounding capacity first.

19.4 When clusters are the rule

Most real trauma survivors do not have a single dominant phenotype. They have a cluster. I see clusters more often than singletons. The routing for clusters is what most of my actual case formulations look like.

A configuration I see constantly in developmental-trauma populations: *Lifeguard plus Princess plus Performer-Manager*. The cramped Lifeguard, the high-gain Princess, the over-controlling Performer. They travel together because they often emerge from the same developmental conditions. Chronic threat that produced environmental scanning and high social-cue processing, paired with the over-control adaptation that managed the load. I route this cluster by addressing all three in stabilization (autonomic regulation, sensory environment design, loop-labeling), with the Lifeguard work usually leading because the autonomic baseline is the floor under everything else. Integration addresses each phenotype's specific patterns sequentially or in parallel depending on capacity. Consolidation builds a life that respects all three at once.

Another configuration I see often, in adults with significant developmental trauma and a substance-use history: *Fog plus Approach/Avoid plus Problem Child*. The chronic-load fog, the approach-quiet, avoid-inflated asymmetry, the brake-failure pattern. My routing here is

[1] Zoet, Wagenmans, van Minnen, & de Jongh (2018). In 168 PTSD patients (38 meeting dissociative-subtype criteria), the dissociative subtype did not moderate intensive trauma-focused treatment outcomes; 68.4% of dissociative-subtype participants no longer met subtype criteria after treatment.

stabilization first, with attention to whether the fog has reversible medical drivers (Chapter 20 covers this); careful integration with attention to the dual-diagnosis dimension if substances are involved; consolidation that includes the bridge to *Borrowed Peace* for the borrowed-regulation patterns this cluster tends to produce.

A third common cluster, the one I see in adults who grew up in households where social cues were dangerous and verbal scaffolding was unreliable: *Lifeguard plus Bard plus Interpreter.* Hypervigilant attention, threat-biased prosodic reading, constrained language reception. Stabilization across all three with autonomic foundation. Integration that addresses the temporal-lobe systems specifically, sometimes with EMDR, sometimes with temporal-site neurofeedback, sometimes with voice-hearing-informed work if present. Consolidation in relationships that allow the temporal systems to operate without chronic threat.

Real clusters vary. The point of naming clusters at all is to recognize that most of my plans involve working with multiple phenotypes simultaneously, with the order of attention shifting based on what is most disabling and where I think I can get the most movement first.

19.5 Decisions I get asked about constantly

Clients ask me about a handful of decisions every week. Three come up most often.

Should I do EMDR or neurofeedback first? Usually both, with neurofeedback first for stabilization and EMDR added as the client has capacity. For Lifeguard and Bard patterns, the temporal-lobe convergence I described in Chapter 16 means the two modalities work together well. For Fog patterns, neurofeedback usually takes priority and EMDR may be less central. I tell you this not to discourage neurofeedback. I use it daily and I see what it does. I tell you so that you can hold the decision with appropriate information about what has and has not been demonstrated at scale: the pooled effect sizes for neurofeedback in PTSD are large in the studies that exist. A 2024 systematic review covering seventeen studies and over six hundred patients rated the evidence as moderate-to-high certainty by GRADE for clinician-administered PTSD outcomes, with effects that increase at follow-up.[2] Two 2025 meta-analyses found converging effect sizes.[3] That is a meaningful upgrade from the uncertain picture of a few years ago. The honest caveats: the 2024 review attributed its positive signal primarily to newer fMRI-guided neurofeedback protocols rather than to the EEG-based protocols that most practitioners use, and the review was partially funded by a neurofeedback device company. Most of the pooled signal comes from comparisons to passive controls (waitlist, treatment-as-usual). In the smaller number of trials using active sham controls, the specific effect of the neurofeedback signal has been harder to isolate. The 2025 EEG-specific meta-analysis pushed back: its sham-controlled sub-analysis concluded that EEG-neurofeedback outcomes were not attributable to placebo, with effects sustained at three months. The evidence is genuinely contested, and it cuts in both directions depending on which controls you look at. Both the upgraded evidence and the remaining questions are worth holding.

Should I get a QEEG? It is not essential for anyone. If you are considering neurofeedback, I would want one, for the reasons in Chapter 17, where I have also said that this is my own practice rather than a settled standard. Outside neurofeedback, a map can help clarify an ambiguous symptom picture. The Frontal Slow versus Slowed Alpha question is the clearest example I know. Raise it with a prescriber rather than acting on it yourself.

Should I do an intensive retreat? Probably not, unless you have done stabilization work and the retreat is led by clinicians who understand trauma and adapt for it. Intensive retreats (meditation retreats,

---

[2] Voigt, Mosier, & Tendler (2024), systematic review and meta-analysis, *Frontiers in Psychiatry* 15:1323485. 17 studies (628 patients, 10 in the quantitative meta-analysis), GRADE: moderate-to-high for CAPS, PCL, and BDI outcomes. The review attributed its positive signal primarily to fMRI-guided neurofeedback; funded in part by GrayMatters Health; two of three authors held positions at consulting firms. Active-control sub-analysis: SMD 0.05.

[3] Berman et al. (2025), *Frontiers in Neuroscience* 19:1658652; Matsuyanagi (2025), *Applied Psychophysiology and Biofeedback* 50(3):329-348. Matsuyanagi's sham-controlled sub-analysis concluded EEG-neurofeedback outcomes were not attributable to placebo, with effects sustained at three months.

ayahuasca ceremonies, intensive trauma processing weekends) concentrate exposure in ways that some nervous systems cannot tolerate. I have seen the harm. If you are drawn to intensive work, the question I would have you sit with is whether you have the regulatory capacity to integrate what comes up between sessions.

The other questions that come up regularly (whether to see a psychiatrist, whether to do somatic work, whether to work on the family system, whether to tell your employer) are addressed in the phenotype routing sections above and in Chapter 15, which covers sequencing and safety.

19.6 When the plan needs to change

A plan is a working hypothesis. Several signals suggest revision.

The plan is not producing expected changes after a reasonable trial. If you have been in stabilization-phase work for six months and the autonomic baseline is not coming down, the protocol may need to change, or there may be unaddressed contributors (medical, environmental, relational) that need attention. The practical implication of the early-trajectory research: you do not always need to wait until the end of a treatment course to know whether it is working. If meaningful movement is not happening in the first several weeks, that is information worth using. I use it in my own clinic. I will tell a client at week six that what we are doing is not moving and we need to try something else.

The plan is producing harm rather than benefit. If new symptoms have emerged, if dissociation has worsened, if your function in daily life is decreasing rather than increasing, this is a signal to slow down and reconsider. Chapter 15 (safety) covers the patterns to watch for.

Life circumstances have changed in ways that affect the plan. A new relationship, a new job, a medical issue, a loss; these change the context the plan was written for. A good plan adjusts.

You have had a substantial breakthrough that opens new work. Sometimes a particular session produces an insight or integration that changes what is possible in the next phase. I want plans flexible enough to take advantage of those moments rather than rigidly continuing the previous protocol.

The clinician relationship is not working. Sometimes the modality is right but the clinician is not the right fit. Sometimes the clinician was the right fit at one phase and is not the right fit at another. Changing clinicians is sometimes the right move, and the trauma-recovery world's culture of clinician-loyalty should not prevent the change when it is warranted.

A periodic check-in, every six months or so, is a reasonable rhythm. The check-in does not have to produce major revision. Sometimes it confirms the plan is working and continuing is the right move. The point is to make revision possible by checking in deliberately rather than drifting forward.

19.7 What recovery looks like from here

Recovery is not a return to a pre-trauma state. The configurations recruited for survival get released. The resources that were diverted come back to flexible use. The trauma stops organizing the day.

In phenotype terms, that means: the Lifeguard that was running at twelve can hold at four. The stuck CEO can release a priority without a crisis forcing it. The fog can lift enough to have a Tuesday she remembers. The approach/avoid brain can speak when it matters. These are the patterns released to a working volume, enough that the rest of life can happen around them.

That is substantial. It is also not the same thing as becoming who you would have been if the trauma had not happened. That person is not available. The longer arc, what markers matter, what incomplete resolution means, what identity looks like after the framework has done its work, is what Chapter 22 is for.

19.8 If you don't have access to a QEEG

Most readers will not have a QEEG. A QEEG takes time and costs money, providers are unevenly distributed, and there is no guarantee the nearest certified provider is the right one for your pattern. The routing logic in this chapter is written to work without one. When a map is available, it contributes to protocol selection alongside symptoms, history, and clinical response; whether it improves outcomes over competent symptom-guided selection has not been established in a head-to-head trial. So here is what symptom-based routing looks like in the absence of a map, for each phenotype. Most of what follows in this chapter does not require one.

Lifeguard. Markers: scanning rooms, startling easily, cannot relax in safe environments, trouble falling or staying asleep. Starting point without QEEG: resonance-frequency breathing twice daily, HRV biofeedback if you can access it, sensory environment design. Avoid: EMDR as a starting move, intensive retreats, any modality that opens trauma material before the baseline has come down. The signal that the baseline is coming down: you can sit in a room for thirty minutes without tracking the exits.

CEO. Markers: rumination that will not stop, cannot release tasks or priorities, perfectionistic monitoring loop, exhausted in a way that does not match output. Starting point: one deliberate incomplete task per day. Open-monitoring meditation (not focused-attention). Breath work. Signal: a quiet Sunday that feels acceptable rather than threatening.

Princess. Markers: sensory overwhelm at lower thresholds than most people, rejection-sensitivity that lands in the body, emotional contagion that flattens. Starting point: sensory environment design, loving-kindness practice, HRV biofeedback, titrated social exposure with planned recovery time. Signal: a social event you attended without being flattened for the following day.

Fog and Tide. Markers: slowed processing, fogginess that no amount of sleep resolves, racing thoughts in slow motion. Starting point: consistent wake time, morning light within 30 minutes of waking, medical workup (thyroid, iron, sleep study) before assuming it is trauma-primary. Signal: a clear hour appearing where there used to be none.

Bard and Interpreter. Markers: reading threat in tones that may not carry it, missing what was said in conversations, comprehension fatigue. Starting point: autonomic regulation first (the Interpreter needs resource before it can function); written rather than verbal communication where possible; prosody reality-checking with trusted others. Signal: noticing you were wrong about a tone, and that the correction came in under an hour rather than a day.

Approach/Avoid Brain. Markers: wanting to move and finding yourself frozen, cycling between over-commitment and withdrawal, good opportunities producing anxiety. Starting point: behavioral activation in very small doses (one commitment per week that you follow through on). Frontal-asymmetry regulation through loving-kindness and approach-oriented daily action. Signal: initiating one thing without the agonizing lead-up.

Problem Child. Markers: impulses acting faster than the intention to stop them, reactions bigger than the cue, brake-failure pattern. Starting point: the half-second pause practice; autonomic regulation before any situation likely to activate the pattern; sleep (this phenotype degrades fastest on inadequate sleep). Avoid: exposure work or trauma processing before the pause is reliable. Signal: one instance in a week where the pause held.

For the cluster presentations (and most presentations are clusters), work the most impairing phenotype first, then add the second. The routing chapter's three-composite cases are the model: the sequencing matters more than the specific interventions.

19.9 What comes next in the book

The next three chapters extend this routing in specific directions.

Chapter 20 addresses the medical conditions that can produce trauma-like patterns or amplify them: sleep apnea, TBI, migraine, hormonal disruption, chronic pain. Treating these is sometimes part of the trauma plan. Sometimes it is the plan.

Chapter 21 is the bridge to *Borrowed Peace,* the patterns of borrowed regulation through substances, work, achievement, and other state-shifting strategies.

Chapter 22 closes with the longer arc of life after most of the work has been done.

If you have read this far and you are not sure which phenotype is loudest in your map, that is where I would have you start. Not with the plan. With the assessment. The plan only works if you know which one you are working with.

The last thing I want to leave you with is a sentence Sofia said to me at the end of her first session, before any of the routing decisions described above were made. She had finished telling me her history. She had named the modalities she had tried and the ways each had not landed. Then she sat back in the chair, looked at me, and said, "I don't even know what I'm asking for anymore. I just know whatever I've been doing isn't it."

That is the question this chapter is for. I cannot answer it in a book. But I can show you how I think about the answer when someone is sitting across from me asking it, and I can offer you the routing logic I would use if I were the one across from you. The rest is the work in front of you. Find the phenotype. Match the order. Begin.

Ch 20: When Medical Conditions Are Driving the Map

Clinical note: This chapter discusses specific medications, medical conditions, and laboratory findings in the context of trauma treatment. It is educational, not prescriptive. Do not start, stop, or adjust any medication based on this chapter without the guidance of a prescribing clinician. Benzodiazepine and alcohol tapers in particular carry medical risk and require physician supervision. If you have questions about any medication you are currently taking, direct them to your prescribing clinician.

Terri's brain map looked like a textbook Lifeguard. Posterior beta elevated, alpha suppressed, the signature of a nervous system stuck in scan mode. Her clinician started posterior-alpha neurofeedback. Standard protocol, well-matched to the pattern on the screen. Eight sessions in, nothing moved. Twelve sessions, still nothing. The alpha would not come up. The beta would not come down. The system was not responding the way a trauma-recruited Lifeguard responds when you give it the right training.

The question that finally opened the case was four words long. "Do you snore?" She did. Her partner had mentioned it for years, gently at first and then with the careful flatness of someone who had stopped expecting the conversation to go anywhere. A home sleep study showed severe obstructive sleep apnea, fifty-three oxygen desaturations per hour, every night, for who knows how long. Her brain was stuck in scan mode because it was being oxygen-starved every night, and no amount of neurofeedback was going to override the effects of chronic nocturnal hypoxia, regardless of how real the trauma pattern was.

Three months on CPAP. Then the same neurofeedback protocol. The alpha came up in four sessions. The map had not been wrong. The trauma pattern was real. The map had been showing her something else *on top of* the trauma, and until that something else was addressed, the trauma work could not land.

The conditions in cases like Terri's vary. Sleep apnea, an old motor-vehicle concussion no one ever wrote up, a thyroid panel that nobody had ordered in three years, a stimulant prescription that was not helping the attention complaint it was written for. The constant is the shape of the case. A reasonable trauma formulation, a reasonable trauma intervention, and a brain that will not budge because something underneath is feeding the pattern faster than the trauma work can drain it.

This chapter is about the medical conditions that produce trauma-like patterns, amplify trauma patterns when present, or block trauma work from gaining traction. It is a routing chapter. It tells you when to ask whether the map is showing you something beyond what the trauma framework alone can explain, and when to insist on the medical workup that trauma work alone will not provide.

When to suspect a medical contributor before assuming it is all trauma: sleep that is bad despite reasonable sleep hygiene (and your partner has mentioned snoring); a head-injury history that was never formally evaluated; mood or fog that did not respond to treatments that should have worked; thyroid that has not been checked in several years; medication that was added for attention or sleep but does not quite do what it was supposed to; pain that is chronic and systemic. These are signals that the map may be showing you something beyond what trauma alone explains.

20.1 Sleep Apnea

Obstructive sleep apnea is one of the most under-recognized contributors to trauma-like symptom presentations. The condition involves repeated partial or complete airway obstruction during sleep, producing oxygen desaturation, sleep fragmentation, and chronic autonomic activation that persists into waking hours.

The symptom overlap with trauma phenotypes is substantial. Daytime hypervigilance. Sleep that feels unrefreshing despite adequate hours. Cognitive fog and attention difficulty that look like the Fog phenotype. Mood symptoms that look like depression. Anxiety symptoms that look like generalized anxiety. Cardiovascular consequences that take years to develop but that begin accumulating from the first night.

Trauma populations have elevated rates of sleep apnea, partly through body-weight changes. The other contributing pathways are not established well enough to name. Combat veterans with PTSD have high rates, and the comorbid presentation has become a well-recognized clinical reality in VA and military medicine settings.[1]

I refer to a sleep doctor when I see a client whose sleep is bad despite reasonable sleep hygiene, who snores, whose partner reports breathing pauses, who wakes gasping, who has elevated cardiovascular risk markers, or whose daytime symptoms are not improving with appropriate trauma work. A home sleep test is cheap and tells you most of what you need to know. The in-lab polysomnography is there for the complex pictures.

Treatment of sleep apnea, when it is present, often produces substantial movement in symptoms that had been attributed to the trauma. CPAP is the standard first-line treatment, with mandibular advancement devices and surgical options for cases where CPAP is not tolerated. CPAP adherence in trauma populations is its own challenge. The mask can be claustrophobic for trauma survivors, and a trauma-informed introduction to CPAP often makes the difference between a client who quits in week two and a client who is sleeping seven hours a night by month three. The two treatments work together. The sleep treatment usually makes the trauma work more effective.

20.2 Traumatic Brain Injury

Traumatic brain injury, including the milder forms that often go undiagnosed, produces symptoms that overlap markedly with trauma presentations. Headache, fatigue, attention and memory difficulties,

[1]McCall & Watson (2022) narrative review of PTSD-OSA association; DeViva, McCarthy, & Santoro (2021) differences in sleep apnea prevalence among veterans with PTSD versus other mental health conditions.

sensory hypersensitivity, mood dysregulation, sleep disturbance, irritability. Each of these can be a TBI consequence, a trauma symptom, or both.

The combat populations have substantial overlap of TBI and PTSD; the polytrauma presentation is well-recognized in VA care.[2] Civilian populations have substantial unrecognized TBI history that may never have been formally diagnosed. Motor vehicle accidents. Assaults. Falls. Sports impacts. Childhood head injuries no one thought were serious enough to write up.

The pattern appears often enough to be worth naming as a pattern. Someone has been in trauma therapy for years and has never mentioned the car accident in 2008, because nobody told them the car accident in 2008 was relevant. The mTBI was never worked up. The post-concussive symptoms got folded into the trauma picture and stayed there.

The clinical picture worth flagging: any trauma client with a head-injury history that has not been formally evaluated, persistent post-concussive symptoms despite trauma-informed treatment, new cognitive symptoms after a known head injury, sensory hypersensitivity that does not respond to standard trauma work and has features (vestibular symptoms, oculomotor difficulty, characteristic headache patterns) suggestive of head-injury sequelae.

The workup for suspected chronic mTBI usually includes a careful history (often with the partner or family providing information the patient does not remember), neuropsychological testing, possibly diffusion-tensor imaging or other advanced neuroimaging, vestibular and oculomotor evaluation, and sometimes QEEG, which shows specific TBI-related patterns that look different from the trauma signatures we discussed earlier in the book. Treatment varies with what the evaluation shows. Vestibular and oculomotor rehabilitation. Graded return to activity. Neurofeedback for chronic cases. Pharmacological support for specific symptoms.

[2]Dolan et al. (2012). Neuropsychological sequelae of PTSD and TBI following war deployment among OEF/OIF veterans.

A client with combined TBI and trauma usually does better when both layers are worked. The TBI work happens alongside the trauma work; the timing and intensity may need adjustment based on TBI status, with attention to the cognitive load that trauma processing puts on a brain that is already coping with TBI sequelae.

20.3 Migraine and Chronic Pain

Migraine is one of the more common medical conditions in trauma populations, with rates higher than in non-trauma populations.[3] The mechanism likely involves central sensitization, in which repeated activation lowers the threshold for pain signaling, and changes in trigeminal sensory pathways. These overlap with the sensory-system patterns described in several of the phenotypes in this book.

Severe migraine can mimic or overlap with trauma presentations. Photophobia and sensory hypersensitivity that look like the Princess phenotype. Cognitive fog that looks like the Fog. Anxiety and depression that often accompany chronic pain. Sleep disruption that maintains the cycle.

Chronic pain more broadly has substantial overlap with trauma populations. The pain-PTSD comorbidity literature is well-developed, with bidirectional relationships: pain drives trauma symptoms (chronic pain is itself traumatizing), and trauma amplifies pain (chronic autonomic activation lowers pain thresholds and amplifies pain processing).[4] The salience network we named earlier in the book is also the network that processes pain, and its recruitment in trauma populations is part of what produces the amplification.

Treatment in trauma populations involves the standard medical approaches (preventive and acute migraine treatments, multidisciplinary pain management) alongside the trauma work, with attention to how each affects the other. Some trauma interventions help with

---

[3]Smitherman & Kolivas (2013). Trauma exposure versus PTSD: relative associations with migraine, finding PTSD diagnosis more strongly associated with migraine than trauma exposure alone.

[4]Asmundson, Coons, Taylor, & Katz (2002). Shared vulnerability and mutual maintenance models of PTSD and chronic pain comorbidity.

pain. HRV biofeedback has evidence for both PTSD and chronic pain. Targeted neurofeedback for both is increasingly available in clinics that do the assessment well. Integrated pain and trauma treatment is usually more effective than either alone.

20.4 Sleep More Broadly

Sleep apnea aside, the basic conditions for restorative sleep are often disrupted in trauma populations, and the disruption is often a substantial driver of the symptom picture independent of the trauma itself. Insomnia, both sleep-onset and sleep-maintenance variants. REM disturbance, including the nightmare patterns characteristic of PTSD. Reduced deep sleep, with consequences for cognitive function and mood. Restless legs syndrome, which has higher prevalence in trauma populations. Other parasomnias.

Sleep evaluation is one of the more useful medical workups in a trauma case where sleep is significantly disrupted. The evaluation often surfaces both sleep apnea (covered above) and other sleep disorders that are individually treatable. Treating the sleep disorders, when present, usually produces measurable improvement in the trauma symptom picture, because chronic sleep deprivation has been amplifying everything else.

The pharmacology of trauma-related sleep is worth its own attention. Prazosin, an alpha-1 adrenergic blocker, has been used extensively for PTSD-related nightmares and showed early positive results in randomized trials. Subsequent larger confirmatory trials have produced mixed results, and the evidence picture is more complicated than the initial enthusiasm suggested.[5] Trazodone is commonly used for trauma-related insomnia. Benzodiazepines, despite frequent use, have specific risks in trauma populations including dependence, tolerance, and sometimes paradoxical activation effects. The medication conversation about sleep is best held with a clinician who understands both the trauma context and the current state of the evidence.

[5] Raskind et al. (2003) initial placebo-controlled study showing nightmare reduction in combat veterans; Raskind et al. (2018) subsequent VA cooperative trial (N=304) that did not find prazosin superior to placebo on the primary outcome.

20.5 Hormonal Conditions

Several hormonal conditions produce trauma-like presentations or amplify trauma patterns. Thyroid dysregulation is the most common. Both hypothyroidism and hyperthyroidism can produce mood, anxiety, sleep, and cognitive symptoms that look like trauma manifestations. The standard thyroid panel sometimes misses subtle dysregulation; a more thorough endocrinology workup is sometimes warranted.

Perimenopause and menopause produce a cluster of symptoms that overlaps heavily with trauma presentations. Mood changes. Sleep disruption. Cognitive fog. Anxiety. Hot flashes that mimic anxiety responses. Trauma symptoms that had been well-managed sometimes resurface during perimenopause, and the resurfacing has biological drivers that respond to hormonal management as much as to additional trauma work.

Adrenal fatigue is not a diagnosis. HPA-axis dysregulation in chronic stress is a real pattern with a different name, and it produces specific symptom patterns that need attention. The popular adrenal-fatigue framing is not well-supported as a discrete diagnostic entity. The broader picture of HPA-axis dysregulation is well-documented.

The workup for suspected hormonal contributors involves the appropriate endocrinology evaluation, with attention to how the hormonal picture interacts with the trauma picture. Treatment of hormonal contributors, when present, often changes the trauma symptom picture without replacing trauma work.

20.6 Substances and Medications

This section is the explicit bridge to *Your Brain on Drugs*. Substances and medications produce specific patterns on a brain map and in clinical presentation, and those patterns can mimic trauma symptoms or amplify them.

Alcohol use, even at levels considered moderate by social standards, produces measurable effects on sleep architecture, autonomic function, and mood regulation that amplify trauma patterns. The cycle of nightly drinking to manage symptoms, followed by amplified symptoms the next day, is one of the more common patterns in trauma populations and one of the more difficult to interrupt.

Cannabis has complex effects on trauma symptoms. Some users find relief, from sleep disturbance and acute anxiety. Many users develop tolerance with diminishing benefit, withdrawal symptoms that mimic the conditions the cannabis was being used to treat, and amotivational patterns that look like depression. The medical-cannabis literature for PTSD is contested. What I see in the clinic is that long-term cannabis use complicates trauma treatment more often than it supports it.

Stimulant medications, prescribed or not, produce autonomic patterns that amplify trauma symptoms in some users. I have seen clients whose stimulant trials increased vigilance and anxiety without improving focus; when I mapped them, several had a hypervigilance component that had not been identified before the stimulant was prescribed.

Benzodiazepines, prescribed for anxiety or sleep, can produce dependence, rebound anxiety, and cognitive effects that complicate the picture considerably. Tapering benzodiazepines in trauma populations needs to be done carefully, in coordination with the prescribing clinician, with appropriate timeline and support. I have seen rapid tapers go badly. I have seen patient tapers, done with someone who knows what they are doing, go well.

SSRIs and SNRIs, the most commonly prescribed antidepressants, often help with some trauma symptoms (mood, anxiety, sleep) without addressing the underlying patterns. They can be useful adjuncts. They should not substitute for trauma work when trauma is the primary driver.

Newer medications are changing trauma pharmacology faster than this chapter can keep up with. Ketamine in its various forms. MDMA-assisted therapy, which showed large effect sizes in Phase 3 trials but as of this writing remains in investigational status after the FDA declined the initial NDA in 2024, citing concerns about the trial design and requiring additional study before approval. Psychedelic-assisted therapy for various indications. Several have shown promise in trials, several have unresolved safety and access questions, and the field is moving fast enough that current published guidance may be out of date by the time you read this chapter. The conversation about whether any of these is appropriate for your situation is best held with a current trauma psychiatrist who follows this evolving field.

A trauma framework that does not engage with the medication and substance picture is incomplete. The medication picture is part of the clinical picture.

20.7 Other Medical Drivers Worth Considering

A few more conditions worth flagging because they show up in trauma populations more than they should and often go unrecognized. I see versions of this several times a year: a treatment-resistant presentation that is not treatment-resistant at all, just held back by something the trauma framework alone did not surface. The following are the ones that appear most consistently on my radar.

Chronic infections. Some chronic infections with neurological involvement (Lyme disease and related tick-borne illnesses, viral persistence patterns such as Epstein-Barr reactivation, post-COVID conditions) produce neuropsychiatric symptoms that overlap with trauma presentations. The diagnostic status of some of these is contested. The clinical observation is that some patients labeled treatment-resistant turn out to have unrecognized chronic infection contributing to their picture.

Autoimmune conditions. Several autoimmune conditions affect the nervous system in ways that produce trauma-like presentations. The autoimmune workup is worth considering when the symptom picture is unusual or when there are other autoimmune indicators in the personal or family history.

Mast cell activation patterns. The mast cell activation literature has been growing, with some evidence that this category of immune dysregulation produces neuropsychiatric symptoms in ways that are not always recognized. The evaluation is more specialized. Worth keeping on the differential for difficult cases.

POTS and related dysautonomias. The autonomic dysregulation patterns in postural orthostatic tachycardia syndrome overlap with the autonomic dysregulation patterns in trauma. Some patients have both. Diagnostic distinction matters because the treatments differ.

Vitamin and mineral deficiencies. Iron, vitamin D, B12, magnesium, and others can produce specific symptom patterns that amplify trauma presentations. The basic nutritional workup is inexpensive and worth doing.

Other neurological conditions. Subclinical seizure activity (temporal-lobe), early-stage neurodegenerative changes in older patients, specific neurological conditions that can present like trauma. Neurological evaluation is warranted when the picture has features that suggest something beyond the trauma layer is contributing.

This is not exhaustive. The point is that a thoughtful trauma evaluation should include consideration of medical drivers, with appropriate workup when the clinical picture suggests they may be present.

20.8 When to Get the Medical Workup

A few general principles for when the medical workup is worth pursuing alongside trauma work.

If your symptoms have not responded adequately to a reasonable course of trauma-informed treatment, the medical workup is warranted. Treatment-resistant trauma often turns out to be trauma plus an unrecognized medical contributor.

If your symptoms began or worsened markedly in association with a specific medical event (illness, injury, hormonal transition, medication change), the medical contribution is worth investigating before assuming the trauma framework is the full answer.

If your symptom picture has features that do not fit the trauma framework cleanly, those features may be pointing at a medical contributor. Unusual sensory phenomena. Prominent cognitive symptoms beyond what trauma typically produces. Autonomic features that seem out of proportion. Atypical sleep patterns.

If you have a family history of conditions with neurological or psychiatric manifestations (early-onset dementia, autoimmune conditions, certain genetic conditions), the medical workup may be warranted as part of a thorough evaluation.

If the trauma work is producing changes in some symptoms but not others, and the symptoms that are not changing have features suggestive of a medical contributor, that is a signal to investigate the medical layer.

The principle is that thoughtful clinical evaluation includes both trauma considerations and medical considerations. Trauma-only evaluation that does not consider medical contributors misses cases. Medical-only evaluation that does not consider trauma contributors also misses cases. Integration produces the most useful clinical picture.

20.9 What This Means for Your Plan

If you are in trauma work and one or more of the medical drivers in this chapter resonates with your situation, the action item is usually a medical evaluation by an appropriate clinician. The trauma work does not have to stop. It usually continues alongside the medical workup. The medical findings inform the trauma plan. The trauma context informs the medical workup.

A few specific routes to consider.

A primary care physician who can do the basic workup and refer for specialist evaluation when warranted. The PCP relationship is one of the more useful resources for moving through the medical-trauma interface.

A sleep medicine evaluation if sleep is a substantial issue. Home sleep tests can screen relatively inexpensively for sleep apnea; in-lab polysomnography is available for more complex pictures.

A neurologist if there are features suggestive of neurological involvement, in TBI cases or in cases with seizure-like features.

An endocrinologist if hormonal contributors are suspected and the basic primary-care workup has not clarified the picture.

A trauma-informed psychiatrist if medication is part of the picture or being considered. The trauma-informed framing matters; psychiatric treatment that does not engage with the trauma context can produce treatment that misses the underlying pattern.

A functional medicine clinician for some integrative workups, with appropriate skepticism about the parts of functional medicine that have weaker evidence bases. The approach can catch contributors that conventional medicine sometimes misses. It can also include interventions with thinner evidence than they are sometimes presented with. Discrimination matters.

The medical workup is part of the trauma plan. The plan that includes both is usually the one that works best.

20.10 Coming Back to the Map

The principle Terri's case demonstrated: when something else is feeding the pattern faster than the trauma work can drain it, the trauma work will look like it is failing. Find the something else first. Then the trauma work has somewhere to land.

The next chapter is the bridge to *Borrowed Peace* and the borrowed-regulation patterns.

Ch 21: Building What Trauma Borrowed

The first time I understood the distinction was watching a client try to sleep without the wine.

She had been drinking two glasses every evening for nine years. She did not consider herself someone with a drinking problem, and on the surface metrics she wasn't. She held a senior job, ran a household, did not drink during the day, did not crave it in the morning. What she did was come home, pour the glass, and within forty minutes her shoulders would drop and her body would feel like it belonged to her again. Sleep would follow. Without the glass, sleep would not.

This is what borrowing looks like when it is working. The wine was producing a state her nervous system could not produce on its own. The state was real. The relief was real. Her trauma history (hypervigilant childhood, a Lifeguard that scanned every room she walked into) made the off-switch she needed the one thing her brain could not generate, and the alcohol gave her a chemical version of it for forty minutes a night. It was an intelligent solution to a real problem. It was also a solution with an interest rate.

When she tapered the wine, the off-switch did not come back. It had never been there in the first place. The wine had been standing in for a regulation capacity her brain had never built, and removing the wine left the hole where the capacity should have been. She slept two hours the first night. The room-scanning came back hard. The whole point of the borrowing had been not to live in that state, and now she was living in it again.

What helped her was not to put the wine back. What helped was building, slowly and with several specific tools, the off-switch her brain had never built. That building took eighteen months. At month nineteen she could fall asleep without the wine. At month twenty-two she stopped using it most evenings because she had something else now, and the something else was hers.

That is the distinction this chapter is about. *Borrowed* is something you use that comes from outside the nervous system: a substance, a behavior, a relationship, a metric. It produces, in the moment, a state the brain cannot produce on its own. *Built* is the same state, produced from inside, by a nervous system that now has the capacity. The first is rented, on a meter, with a bill that accumulates. The second is yours.

Most of the trauma survivors I have seen in twenty-five years of clinic work are doing some version of borrowing. The borrowing is intelligent. It is not weakness. The bill comes due anyway.

21.1 Where the distinction comes from

The lineage of this distinction matters.

I introduced the borrowed/built distinction in *Half a Second More* in the context of medication: medication holds the floor, meditation builds the capacity. *Gifted & Tortured* uses the same framework for the baseline-temperament versions of the phenotypes. *Borrowed Peace* extends it to substance use and the behavioral addictions in full, with the medical considerations, harm-reduction lineage, decision frameworks, and integrated dual-diagnosis models.

This chapter is the trauma version. If the borrowing is a part of your picture, *Borrowed Peace* is the next book on your shelf. Most of the people I see have something on both sides of that door.

21.2 What borrowing actually is

The most familiar form is substance. Alcohol borrowed for sleep, or for the social edge, or to interrupt the rumination. Cannabis borrowed for the dampening, for the body that will not soften, for the loop that will not quiet. Stimulants borrowed for the focus or the brightness the nervous system cannot generate. Opioids borrowed for pain that is half-physical, half-the-body's-record-of-the-trauma. Benzodiazepines borrowed for the calm a hypervigilant brain cannot produce. Each substance has a target state, and each substance produces it for a window of time, and each substance has a bill.

The less obvious forms are equally real. Achievement borrowed for the sense of being okay. The next promotion, the next milestone, the next external validation that produces the feeling a dysregulated brain cannot produce from inside. Work borrowed for the temporary relief from internal experience, the productivity that masks the dysregulation underneath. Food borrowed for comfort, for numbness, for the brief activation. Sex borrowed for the intensity that interrupts a flat or dissociated state. Relationships borrowed for co-regulation, the partner whose presence shifts you out of the bad place, the friend whose company does the regulation work your nervous system cannot do alone. Intensity itself borrowed; the drama, the conflict, the crisis that produces the sympathetic activation that, briefly, feels like being alive.

These are not all the same morally or clinically. The diagnostic systems are catching up: ICD-11 now treats gambling, gaming, and compulsive sexual behavior as addictive behaviors alongside substances; DSM-5-TR is more conservative and accepts only gambling fully. Imaging studies show the same ventral striatal activation and dopaminergic cue-reactivity in behavioral addictions as in substance use (Brand et al., 2019). Not every pattern that looks like addiction is. Grubbs and colleagues have shown that much of what presents as "sex addiction" in clinical settings is moral incongruence rather than addictive process, the distress of someone whose sexual behavior conflicts with their values (Grubbs et al., 2019). The distinction matters when you are sorting your own picture. What the genuine borrowing patterns share is a common structure: an external source producing a state-shift the nervous system cannot produce internally.

The cleanest way to recognize borrowing in yourself is to ask what happens when the source is removed. If you take away the wine, the achievement, the cannabis, the partner, the metric, what does the underlying state look like? If the underlying state is steady, the thing was a preference, a pleasure, or a relationship. If the underlying state collapses, the thing was holding something up.

21.3 What the borrowing costs

Borrowed states have to be paid back. That is what the underlying physiology does.

The first cost is tolerance. The drink that worked at one glass becomes two, becomes three. The achievement that produced relief at one level becomes the next level. The relationship that regulated at one intensity needs to keep producing the intensity. Tolerance is the body doing what bodies do; it adapts to the borrowed input and requires more to produce the same shift.

The second cost is rebound. When the borrowed state ends, the underlying baseline often returns worse than it was. The borrowed peace becomes owed anxiety, sometimes at higher intensity than the anxiety that drove the borrowing in the first place. The borrowed energy becomes owed exhaustion. The borrowed numbness becomes owed amplified sensation. The rebound is what drives the next round of borrowing, and the cycle intensifies.

The third cost is dependence, in the medical sense. Some borrowing sources produce physical dependence with withdrawal syndromes that can be medically dangerous: alcohol, benzodiazepines, opioids most prominently. Stopping the borrowing without medical management can produce serious harm. *Borrowed Peace* covers this in detail; for the trauma reader, the recognition is enough to know that some borrowing patterns require medical involvement to address safely, and that ill-considered cessation can be worse than the borrowing it was meant to address.

The fourth cost is the one that matters most for this book: the borrowing displaces the building. While alcohol holds the floor, regulation underneath it does not get built; while achievement produces the sense of being okay, the inside-out version of being okay does not get built; and while the relationship is doing the co-regulation, auto-regulation does not get built. The borrowing is a nervous system surviving. It is also years of not building, which costs you the skills the borrowing was standing in for.

The fifth cost varies by source. The substance use that has affected family relationships. The achievement borrowing that ate the time that would have gone to relationships. The relational borrowing that produced patterns the partner could not sustain. These vary so much by what was borrowed, at what intensity, over what period, that any general statement about them is wrong in particular cases; they are worth tracking in the specifics of a particular life rather than in the abstract.

21.4 How trauma drives the borrowing

Trauma changes the nervous system in ways that leave specific resources under-built. Chapter 2 named the seven. Chapters 6 through 12 walked through what happens to each one. Chapter 19 is the routing chapter, the one that names which phenotype tends toward which intervention. For the purposes of this chapter, the relevant claim is: the under-built resource is exactly the resource the borrowing is standing in for. The cramped Lifeguard's missing off-switch is what the alcohol is renting her. The stuck CEO's missing release from the loop is what the achievement is renting her. The princess's missing dampening is what the cannabis is renting her. The fog's missing brightness is what the caffeine is renting her. The approach/avoid brain's missing integrated motivation is what the impulsive action is renting it. Many phenotypes are associated with a recognizable regulation gap, and a brain looking for an off-switch tends to find the cheapest available rental for the state it cannot generate. The mapping is not universal, and the same trauma does not produce the same regulation gap in every brain; but when a borrowing pattern does align with a phenotype, it often aligns precisely with what the phenotype is missing.

If your borrowing pattern does not match the phenotype you suspect you are, you may be looking at the wrong phenotype, or you may be looking at a borrowed pattern that came from environment more than from biology (what was around in the developmental house, what is normalized in the social context). Either is worth tracking. The routing logic in Chapter 19 is the tool for sorting it.

21.5 The sequencing question

A common question in clients with significant borrowing patterns is whether to address the borrowing first or the trauma first. The dual-diagnosis literature has been working on this for decades, and the answer that has emerged is that neither pure sequence works as well as integration.

Treating the substance use first, with abstinence as the condition for trauma work, often fails because the substance use is being driven by the trauma layer. Removing the substance without addressing the underlying need leaves the nervous system in worse acute condition than the borrowing produced. The relapse rate for trauma populations sequenced into abstinence-first treatment is high.

Treating the trauma first, with the substance use treated as a side issue, often fails because the substance use is interfering with the trauma work. The autonomic dysregulation the substance produces makes the regulation work harder. The cognitive effects make the integration work harder. The ongoing consequences of the substance use continue to traumatize the nervous system in ways that complicate everything underneath.

The integrated approach treats both at once. The substance use is addressed with appropriate medical management, harm reduction when total abstinence cannot come first, and recognition that the substance has been doing real work that needs to be replaced rather than just removed. The trauma work proceeds in parallel, with attention to how each affects the other. The two are coordinated. This is what *Borrowed Peace* describes in detail for substance use, and the same logic applies to the behavioral borrowings: address both, in parallel, with attention to how each is affecting the other.

21.6 Building what was borrowed

Here is the move that turns the framework from description into work.

The borrowing is renting the state. The building is producing the state from inside. The two are sequential, with the renting paying for the time the building takes. The drink at five o'clock buys the off-switch tonight; the eighteen months of regulation work builds the off-switch for the next twenty years. The achievement buys the sense of being okay this quarter; the parts work and the loop-labeling and the autonomic regulation builds the inside-out version of being okay for the rest of your career.

The specific build for each phenotype is the routing logic of Chapter 19. To take one example: the cramped Lifeguard's build is autonomic regulation, targeted posterior-midline neurofeedback, and the trauma processing that updates the threat-detection prior. When those three things progress, the off-switch the alcohol was renting starts to become available from the inside. That is what the build looks like. The taper is its consequence.

The clinical version of this is straightforward. The borrowing does not have to be removed first. The building proceeds while the borrowing is still load-bearing. As the build comes online, the borrowing tapers because the underlying state is now generating on its own and the borrowed version becomes redundant. Sometimes the taper happens deliberately, on a schedule. Sometimes it happens by drift; the client realizes she has not had the drink in two weeks and did not notice. Either is fine. What matters is that the building has happened, so that the taper does not leave a hole.

For the borrowings that have produced dependence (alcohol at scale, benzodiazepines, opioids), the medical management of the taper is a separate piece of work from the building, and it is the piece *Borrowed Peace* covers in detail.

21.7 Achievement borrowing, the normalized version

One borrowing deserves a separate moment because it is so culturally normalized that it is often not recognized as borrowing: achievement.

The performer subtype of the CEO from Chapter 7 is, in many cases, an achievement-borrowing pattern. The Bergen Work Addiction Scale finds that about 8 percent of working adults meet criteria for workaholism (Andreassen et al., 2014), with meta-analytic estimates across populations closer to 15 percent (Andersen et al., 2023). These people score high on the same addiction components that define substance disorders: salience, mood modification, tolerance, withdrawal, conflict, relapse. The achievement produces the temporary relief from internal experience that the dysregulation has been generating. The next achievement is needed to maintain the relief. The cycle continues, with the metrics escalating, the costs accumulating, the dysregulation underneath unchanged.

This is one of the most under-recognized borrowing patterns in the trauma populations I see. Substance use crosses thresholds that get recognized; achievement borrowing is rewarded by the surrounding social system, even as the cost accumulates. The performer who is killing herself to maintain the high-functioning veneer is celebrated for productivity and respected for competence, while the dysregulation continues underneath and the body presents the bill in slow accumulating ways: chronic exhaustion, relationship attrition, eventual physical breakdown for many. The research base reflects the same blind spot. No randomized controlled trials exist for workaholism treatment specifically; what we know about addressing this pattern is inferred from the broader addiction and trauma literatures rather than tested directly.

In my clinic the achievement-borrowing client is often the hardest to engage in any kind of treatment, because the borrowing has been positively reinforced for decades. The workplace depends on the level of function she has been providing. The family depends on it. The friends do, sometimes. Scaling back the achievement encounters resistance from everyone around her. The recognition that the achievement is borrowing can be one of the more important early moves. After that the build can begin.

This pattern is common in late-diagnosed neurodivergent women with trauma histories, in oldest-daughter parentified patterns, in eldest-child role-fulfillment patterns, in the professional cultures of medicine and law and academia and finance that reward the borrowing while ignoring its cost.

21.8 Closing the bridge

The trauma framework and the borrowing framework are two views of related territory. The trauma layer leaves specific resources under-built. The under-built resources drive the borrowing. The borrowing has its own costs, which accumulate, and which eventually present a bill. An integrated approach addresses both: builds the under-built resource, manages the taper of the borrowing as the build comes online, and treats the bill the borrowing has produced as its own clinical question.

If the borrowing is a part of your picture, *Borrowed Peace* is the book that goes into the specifics. The substances and the behavioral patterns and the decision frameworks for what to do about each are there. The harm-reduction lineage is there. The medical considerations are there. The integrated treatment models are there. The framework you have been reading in this book applies on the other side of that door, and the framework on the other side applies back on this one.

I have one composite I think about often when I write this chapter. He came in for the Problem Child pattern, brake-failed, alcohol at fifty drinks a week, multiple DUIs, two estranged children. The build took four years. Most of the first year was harm reduction and medical taper. Most of the second was autonomic regulation and the half-second pause practice. Year three was the trauma layer, which he had not known was underneath. Year four was his older daughter agreeing to a phone call. He still drinks. Not the way he used to. He calls himself a recovered alcoholic in conversation, which is not a description I would use for him clinically but which is the description that fits the life he is now living. What got built was not abstinence. What got built was a nervous system that no longer needed the borrowing to do the thing the borrowing had been doing for thirty years.

The next chapter is the final chapter of this book. It addresses what life looks like after most of the building has been done, when the trauma framework recedes from being the lens you use every day, and the question of who you are without the trauma starts to become a real question.

Ch 22: The Life After Survival

This is the last chapter of the book. The honest question it has to address is the one the rest of the book has been building toward: what does the life look like after most of the recovery has been done? The life itself. The Tuesdays. What everything else was for.

The framework I have been laying out rests on a few convictions. Recovery is real. Recovery is the return of the ordinary. The framework, having done its work, recedes. What becomes available when enough of the change has happened is what the rest of this chapter is about.

I want to be careful here. Recovery does not restore a pre-trauma self. That person is not available. Recovery does not look the same for everyone. Recovery is sometimes incomplete, and the practices are still worth doing when complete resolution does not arrive. Recovery is not always visible from the outside, and the life that follows it is its own substantial territory.

You carry a nervous system whose patterns were shaped by what you experienced. The patterns were real. The shaping was real. The patterns can change. What this chapter aims to do is show you what becomes available when enough of that change has happened, and what it takes to sustain it. The picture is integration rather than perfection. The aim is a life in which what happened is one chapter rather than the spine of the whole book.

22.1 What recovery actually looks like

A few practical definitions to clear ground.

Recovery leaves occasional symptoms in place. The lifeguard who used to run at twelve out of ten and now runs at four counts as a recovery, even though four is not zero. The dissociation that used to happen daily and now happens rarely counts. The freeze that used to dominate every important moment and now dominates only the highest-stakes ones counts. The standard of total symptom absence is unreasonable for many trauma histories and not always desirable; what remains is sometimes how the system knows its own limits.

Recovery is a state that takes ongoing maintenance, in lighter form. Configurations that were recruited can be released, and they can also be re-recruited under enough stress. People who have done the work keep doing regulation, often for the rest of their lives. The attention becomes part of how life is lived rather than the focus of the life itself.

Recovery does not require integrating every memory into a coherent narrative. Some memories integrate. Some integrate partially. Some stay fragmentary. People who have done good work think about their trauma history regularly, often in ways that are useful, informing choices, helping them understand themselves. The functional question is whether the memories are organizing your present in problematic ways; if they are not, the relationship to the thinking has changed in the way that counts, and complete integration is not required. Some recovered trauma survivors continue to have lives that look unconventional from the outside, fewer relationships than peers, work patterns that protect their nervous systems rather than improve career advancement. These are appropriate calibrations to the nervous system that has to live the life.

What does become available is calibrated, integrated, sustainable, and humane. Often undramatic, often slow, and real.

22.2 What becomes available

Here is what tends to become available.

Function in environments that used to be impossible. The phenotype chapters (Ch 6-12) mapped the specific failure modes; this is what success looks like for each one. The cramped Lifeguard can be at the party without tracking every exit. The stuck CEO can have a quiet Sunday. The princess can run an errand without being flattened by it. The fog can lift and the Tide can do its actual work. The approach/avoid brain can speak when speaking matters. These are not small things. People who arrive here often describe the experience as having their life back.

Relationships that hold. Relationships that were difficult or impossible during the active trauma period often become available in different form afterward. Intimacy that was unsafe becomes possible. Conflict that used to escalate becomes manageable. Friendships that used to cost too much become sustaining. The family relationships that produced the original trauma may or may not change in their own dynamics. The survivor's relationship to them changes, often in ways that allow more peace whether or not the family system itself updates.

The relational repair is sometimes the most important dimension. The trauma was often relationally shaped, and the relational rebuilding is often where the most substantial life-quality improvement shows up. The people I have seen who do the most thorough recovery point to their relationships when I ask what feels different.

Embodiment that does not feel like work. A body that has been a difficult place to be becomes a place to inhabit. The autonomic baseline settles enough that being in the body does not require constant management. Sleep restores. Pain reduces. Energy stabilizes. The somatic experience of being a person becomes available in ways it has not been for years or decades. The clients I have followed longest often tell me this one matters more than they expected; the cognitive shifts were easier to notice in the moment, but the embodied shift is the one that changes how the days feel.

The embodied recovery is often more substantial than the cognitive recovery. The body has been keeping a working record of the chronic conditions; as the conditions update, the record updates, and the felt sense of being in a body that is not constantly under low-grade alarm is one of the more meaningful changes anything can produce.

Cognitive bandwidth that was being consumed by the load. You read a paragraph and do not immediately re-read it. You complete a task without the doom-stacking that used to arrive midway through. The interpreter who could not absorb language because the system was running on chronic load gets her bandwidth back. The CEO who could not finish things because the loops were running gets her finishing capacity back. The fog who could not think clearly gets her clarity back. The cognitive recovery sometimes shows up dramatically: the book that could not be read becomes a book that can be read; the project that could not be completed becomes one that can be completed. The capacities were not new. They had been recruited by the trauma load and were not available for ordinary use. The release of them feels like a gift that was always there.

Identity that is larger than the trauma. The trauma framework that has been the dominant lens recedes. The framework served you. It explained what the nervous system was doing and why, and it organized the work. The point was always to make the framework unnecessary for daily life, not to replace your identity with it. Other dimensions of self come back into focus: vocation, relationships, interests, values, the identity that existed before the framework took over and that has been waiting underneath. The trauma is still part of the picture. It is no longer the whole picture. I know the timing of this shift varies enormously. For some clients it happens around the eighteen-month mark; for others it takes four or five years; for some it has not happened yet, and they are still doing good work.

This is the dimension the chapter has been pointing toward. Once it happens, the rest of who you are comes back into view.

22.3 Identity beyond the trauma

The identity work in late-stage recovery has its own particular shape.

It involves recognizing that the trauma framework, useful as it has been, has organized the self around a single lens, and that recovery requires expanding the lens back out. Dan McAdams' research on narrative identity captures what this looks like from the inside: you are always constructing a story about who you are, and trauma tends to turn that story into what he calls a contamination sequence, where the bad thing colors everything that follows (McAdams & McLean, 2013). Late-recovery identity work is the shift toward what McAdams calls a redemption sequence, where the suffering is real but the story keeps moving (McAdams, 2006). In phenotype terms, that shift is what flexibility looks like when it reaches the level of self-concept: the configurations that were recruited for survival stop organizing the story you tell about yourself.

None of this is a rejection of the trauma identity. The trauma identity has often been important. It gave language to suffering. It connected the survivor to a community of others with similar experiences. It allowed the recognition that the symptoms were not personal failure. It served a function. The function does not have to be discarded; the identity has to be put into proportion. Berntsen and Rubin's work confirms what I see in the clinic: when the trauma becomes the central organizing node of someone's life story and self-concept, PTSD symptoms tend to be worse and more persistent (Berntsen & Rubin, 2006). The distinction is between a life story organized around the wound and a life story that includes the wound without letting it run the whole narrative.

The healthy late-recovery position is something like: I am a person who experienced trauma. Not a trauma survivor, with the wound as the headline. Not someone who is "over it." A person who experienced something, did the work, and kept going. The language shift matters more than it might seem. "Survivor" keeps the trauma at the center of the sentence; "person who experienced trauma" puts the person first. I am also many other things. The trauma is one of the things that shaped me. It is no longer the most important thing about me right now.

This sounds simple. It is harder than it sounds, for people who have spent years in trauma communities, trauma therapy, trauma identity formation. The shift can feel disloyal: to the practices you have built, to the community, to the parts of self that needed the framework. The shift is itself part of recovery. The framework was always in service of the life.

Some specific markers of healthy late-stage identity work:

You can spend long stretches of time not actively engaged with trauma material. The attention that was sustained for years gives way to attention to other dimensions of life, with the trauma piece in the background, available when needed.

Your relationships are not primarily organized around the trauma. The friend you made through trauma community is now a friend, period. The partner who supported you through years of recovery is now your partner, in a relationship that is about the relationship. Your goals and dreams are not derivative of the trauma; you want what you want for reasons that are about who you are now.

You have access to capacities that were previously consumed by the load, and those capacities are doing their work in your life: your creative work, your professional work, your relational work, your contribution to whatever you contribute to. You can encounter trauma material, your own or someone else's, without being captured by it. The trauma is no longer the headline. It stays part of you, available when relevant, but no longer the first thing you tell new people about yourself.

These do not all arrive on the same day as the substantial work concludes. They develop over the years that follow. The years that follow are their own phase.

22.4 The continuing work

Some attention continues, in lighter form, for the rest of life. This is honest to name. I have stayed in touch with clients across decades, sometimes through occasional check-ins, sometimes through long gaps, and what I see consistently is that the work changes shape rather than ending.

The autonomic regulation tools that were foundational in early recovery often remain part of daily life. The breath practice that became a daily anchor in stabilization often stays a daily anchor, because it works. The sleep hygiene that was emphasized in early recovery often stays emphasized, because the system continues to be a system that does better with good sleep. The boundaries around high-stimulation environments often stay in place, because the gain is still there.

Periodic check-ins with clinical work are sometimes useful. Not weekly therapy for the rest of life, necessarily, but a relationship with a clinician who knows you and can be returned to when life produces new demands. A new job. A new relationship. A loss. A medical issue. Times when regulation that has been holding may need a hand to keep holding. I schedule six-month and twelve-month check-ins for many of my long-arc clients, and most of the time those sessions are brief and reassuring; sometimes they catch a drift early and let us adjust before it becomes a setback.

Continued attention to the patterns. The cramped Lifeguard who has come down to a working volume can re-cramp under enough stress. The stuck CEO who learned to release priorities can still get stuck on the wrong thing under enough load. The patterns have been updated. They are part of you, available to be recognized and worked with when they appear.

The continuing work runs lighter than the early-recovery work, more integrated into daily life, less the center of gravity. People who have done recovery often describe what continues as a small daily practice rather than a large ongoing project. The proportion has shifted.

This is what sustained recovery looks like in practice. The attention does not end. It changes form. The form it takes is one in which it supports the life rather than competing with the life for resources.

22.5 When recovery is incomplete

Some recovery is incomplete. The lifeguard comes down from twelve to four, not to zero. The fog returns periodically in lighter form. The CEO loops still appear, less often. The patterns have been updated. The honest framing is that improvement is itself a substantial outcome. Most of my clients who have stayed in touch describe it this way: a different relationship with the patterns. That is the real and more common version of recovery.

There are also trauma histories where the loss cannot be separated from the ongoing condition of the life. Bereavement, the death of someone central, is one of these. The trauma of loss does not always resolve into something the brain can update away from, because the loss itself does not change. The framework applies (the autonomic load, the phenotype pattern, the sequencing), and some of what was recruited in bereavement can be released. Some of it stays recruited in proportion to the size of what was lost. If your trauma is bereavement, the framework is for you. The timeline may be longer, and the picture of recovery may look different, and both of those things are allowed.

If you are reading this and you have not found meaning, or if you have not arrived at the Tuesday afternoon feeling described at the end of this chapter, you are not behind. There is no behind. The work runs on its own clock, for each person, in each life. If the patterns are more workable than they were, that is recovery. Even if the workable is partial and the ordinary is not yet here.

22.6 Meaning, when it comes

For some people, the trauma history becomes part of a meaning-making narrative. Growth is real for some people and unreliable as a general expectation.[1] If you are reading this and you have not found meaning in what happened to you, that is allowed. The absence of meaning is not a sign that recovery has failed. Some people find their trauma history shapes their work, their relationships, their contribution. Some find it is just something that happened. Both are outcomes. Neither requires justification.

22.7 Co-regulation, community, repair

The relational and community piece is what tends to protect the gains. The brain work and the body work matter, and they hold longer when there is someone holding them with you.

The trauma was often relationally shaped. The recovery is often relationally completed. People who do substantial trauma work in isolation can produce real change, but the change tends to be more

[1] Tedeschi & Calhoun (1996); Shakespeare-Finch & Lurie-Beck (2013) meta-analysis.

sustained when it includes some dimension of community. Other people who understand the territory. Relationships in which the recovery is supported and reflected. Sometimes formal support communities. Sometimes informal networks of peers who have done similar work.

The lifeguard who has come down to a working volume often comes down further, more sustainably, in environments that are co-regulating rather than activating. The princess whose gain is honored gets to use her gift in community with people who appreciate it. The bard who has been threat-tuned for years gets to read tone in friendships where the tone is mostly safe. The approach/avoid brain that has been freezing gets to act in groups that hold the action while it happens.

The community dimension is part of what makes late-stage recovery sustainable. Not as a permanent identity (the trauma-survivor identity that organizes everything), but as one of the connections that supports the broader life. The people who have a community of this kind often describe it as one of the most important elements of what made the recovery hold.

The relational repair also continues at the immediate-relationship level. The partnerships, friendships, family relationships that have been part of this are themselves part of what continues. The conversations that happen as both parties update. The recognition of patterns and the choice to not repeat them. The decision to stay in relationships that support you and to let go of relationships that drain you is the daily-life version of relational repair, and it continues for as long as the relationships do.

22.8 A last word

Most of the people I see, when they get to this point, do not announce it. There is no moment in the clinic when someone says, "I'm recovered now." What I see instead is a Tuesday afternoon. Someone walks in for a check-in I scheduled six months out because we had agreed we would. She tells me she is house-hunting. She tells me her sister is getting married and she is helping plan it. She tells me she was annoyed at her boss last week, and what she noticed was that she was annoyed, in the ordinary way, not flooded. She has read fewer trauma books this year than last year, and she said it almost apologetically, and I told her that is the point. The brain that built itself around what happened has been building itself around something else. The map I made of her in our first month is still on file. I rarely look at it anymore. Neither does she. If you are reading this at the end of a long book about your own nervous system, I want you to know that the Tuesday afternoon is the thing. Go have the Tuesday afternoon. That is what all of this has been for.

Before You Go: Your Reader Bonus

You read the argument. Here is the part you can put to work.

A free **Reader Bonus** goes with this book. It contains three appendices that did not fit in the printed interior but belong with the framework:

- A **Phenotype Self-Assessment**, thirty-five questions across the seven phenotype chapters. It is a self-recognition tool, not a diagnosis. Your highest-scoring clusters point you toward the chapters worth rereading, and toward the right conversation with the right clinician if clinical support is what you need next.
- Four **Decision Rubrics** consolidated in one place: the Safety Ladder from Chapter 15, the Alpha-Theta Readiness Checklist from Chapter 18, the Treatment-Stalling Differential, and the Provider Vetting Checklist from Chapter 17.
- **Conversations Worth Having**, three model openings for conversations that come up repeatedly in the clinical work this book describes: with your therapist about sequencing, with your prescriber about phenotype patterns, and with your clinician about destabilization.

The materials are free. The page asks for a first name and email so I can send them to you; that address is used only for delivery and occasional book-related updates, and you can unsubscribe at any time.

Scan with your phone's camera

or visit **peakbrainpress.com/trauma-book-bonus**

Appendix A: Trauma Red Flags and When to Get Clinical Help

This appendix is reference material. Use it when you need to know whether a particular pattern in yourself or someone you care about warrants clinical attention. The categories below describe situations where self-help work is not sufficient and where appropriate clinical care is the right next step.

This appendix guides you on when to seek a clinical evaluation; it does not replace one.

If You Are Supporting Someone Else

For another adult, begin with consent: ask whether they want listening, practical help, help finding care, or no action right now. Do not assign a phenotype, administer or score a screening tool, press for a trauma narrative, contact a provider, or choose a treatment without permission. Offer concrete help, transportation, child care, meals, insurance calls, a quiet place, or company at an appointment, while preserving privacy and the person's control.

When an adult's decision-making capacity is impaired or fluctuates, capacity is specific to the decision and the time; do not assume that one diagnosis removes the person's voice. Maximize supported participation, privacy, and assent, and use the least restrictive lawful option. Emergency action may be necessary for immediate danger, but ordinary care, guardianship, health-care authority, and confidentiality depend on local law and the person's circumstances. When authority is unclear, seek qualified local clinical and legal guidance rather than improvising it from this book.

Immediate danger is different. If someone may act on suicidal or violent intent, cannot maintain basic safety, is severely confused or medically unstable, or an overdose or other emergency is underway, seek live qualified help even when the person is ambivalent. Use the least coercive option that can keep people safe, and be honest about what you are doing. Reduce access to lethal means only when it can be done safely; do not put yourself in danger.

Do not mediate active abuse or use couples or family work when fear, stalking, coercive control, violence, or retaliation makes honest speech unsafe. Support confidential, survivor-centered safety planning. When a person has caused harm, compassion for trauma does not replace accountability, boundaries, or protection of others.

For a minor, use developmentally appropriate, licensed care and follow local consent, confidentiality, safeguarding, and mandatory-reporting requirements. Do not use this adult book to diagnose a child. A young person's voice, privacy, and assent still matter within the limits of safety and law.

Supporters also need boundaries. You can care, help make a plan, and seek consultation without becoming the person's clinician, sole crisis service, or monitor. If you are carrying more than you can safely hold, ask another qualified person or service to join the plan.

Crisis-Level Red Flags

These situations warrant immediate live support or urgent assessment. In the United States, call or text **988** or use 988lifeline.org for suicidal thoughts, emotional crisis, or concern about another person. Text **HOME** to **741741** for Crisis Text Line. Use **911** or an emergency department for imminent or in-progress danger, a serious attempt, severe medical symptoms, or when no less restrictive option can keep people safe. The 988 Lifeline seeks collaborative safety planning and may recommend emergency services when imminent or in-progress risk cannot be managed another way; privacy also has legal and safety limits.

Peer lines can be valuable but do not replace emergency assessment when danger is imminent. Trans Lifeline (**1-877-565-8860**) serves trans and questioning people and states a policy against nonconsensual active rescue, with exceptions for credible threats to others and mandated abuse or neglect reporting. BlackLine (**1-800-604-5841**) provides peer support centered on Black, Brown, Native, Muslim, and LGBTQ+ callers and describes its own privacy policy. Outside the United States, use **findahelpline.com** to locate a verified service and use the local emergency number for imminent danger. Routes and policies were verified July 16, 2026; confirm current availability with the service.

Suicidal thoughts or inability to stay safe. Do not wait for a plan or means. Current, recurrent, or escalating thoughts; intent; planning; preparation; access to lethal means; a recent attempt; intoxication; command experiences; or uncertainty about whether you can stay safe all warrant immediate live assessment. Ask directly, reduce access to lethal means when this can be done safely, and use a collaborative safety plan. A "no" to one question does not by itself establish safety.

Thoughts or threats of serious violence. Assess the target, intent, plan, preparation, access to weapons or other means, ability to resist, intoxication, command content, and current behavior. Protect potential victims and obtain immediate risk assessment. Use emergency services for imminent or in-progress danger.

New or intensifying psychotic or unusual perceptual symptoms. Prompt assessment is needed when voices, visions, fixed beliefs, disorganization, paranoia, or unusual sensory experiences are commanding, distressing, function-impairing, escalating, or accompanied by impaired reality testing or safety risk. Retained insight does not make the symptoms harmless. Trauma, psychosis, bipolar disorder, substances or medications, seizure, sleep disruption, delirium, and other medical causes can coexist or look similar; this book and QEEG cannot distinguish them.

Possible acute mania. Markedly reduced need for sleep combined with elevated or irritable mood, increased energy, pressured speech, racing thoughts, risky behavior, grandiosity, psychosis, or rapid functional decline warrants prompt psychiatric assessment. Use emergency care when safety, judgment, or basic self-care is failing.

Severe dissociation or altered awareness with safety implications. Losing time, finding yourself in places without memory of getting there, or being unable to maintain basic safety warrants dissociation-informed clinical and medical assessment. Do not drive, operate machinery, cook unattended, or care for dependents alone during unsafe episodes. New onset, injury, focal neurological symptoms, seizure-like episodes, or inability to remain safe requires urgent medical evaluation.

Active danger in the home or relationship. Domestic violence, stalking, sexual violence, threats, monitoring, retaliation, or coercive control calls for confidential, survivor-centered safety planning. The National Domestic Violence Hotline is **1-800-799-SAFE (7233)**, text **START** to **88788**, or use thehotline.org. Support, advocacy, medical care, housing and legal information, and trauma-informed therapy can begin while danger is ongoing. Leaving may be difficult and can temporarily increase risk. Do not begin with couples therapy when abuse or coercion makes honest disclosure unsafe.

Withdrawal, intoxication, or overdose risk. Sudden alcohol cessation after chronic heavy use can be life-threatening, and benzodiazepine withdrawal can cause seizures or delirium. Pregnancy, dehydration, medical illness, polysubstance use, prior severe withdrawal, hallucinations, confusion, seizure, severe agitation, or unstable vital signs increase urgency. Opioid withdrawal also needs individualized medical assessment; return to use after reduced tolerance creates high overdose risk. Detoxification without medication for opioid use disorder is not recommended. Obtain naloxone, use evidence-based ongoing treatment, and call emergency services for suspected overdose. SAMHSA's National Helpline is **1-800-662-HELP (4357)**.

Eating-disorder symptoms with possible medical compromise. Medical instability can occur at any body size; do not use BMI to self-clear. Rapid weight change, inability to maintain intake, severe restriction, repeated purging, fainting, chest pain, dehydration, severe weakness, abnormal temperature, pulse, blood pressure or orthostasis, electrolyte or organ abnormalities, ECG changes, suicidality, or clinician concern warrant urgent eating-disorder and medical assessment. The National Alliance for Eating Disorders offers treatment referrals at **866-662-1235** and allianceforeatingdisorders.com / find-treatment; it is not a substitute for emergency medical care. Route verified July 16, 2026.

Acute medical events. Chest pain, severe shortness of breath, signs of stroke, severe head injury, or other acute medical concerns. Emergency department or 911. Trauma context does not exclude medical emergency.

These situations take priority. Crisis care, medical care, protection, advocacy, and trauma-informed support can overlap; the person does not have to achieve a perfect baseline before deserving help.

Patterns Requiring Clinical Care

These are patterns that warrant clinical evaluation and ongoing professional support, even if they are not currently at crisis level.

Frequent dissociation. Regular episodes of losing time, depersonalization, derealization, switching between dramatically different states, or feeling like multiple distinct selves. The dissociative-disorders literature has substantial treatment frameworks, and the work requires a clinician with specific training.

Persistent self-harm urges or behaviors. Cutting, burning, hitting, or other deliberate self-injury needs clinical assessment, collaborative safety planning, and wound or medical care when indicated. Escalating lethality, suicidal intent, intoxication, inability to resist, or uncertainty about safety requires immediate live assessment.

Substance use with risk, loss of control, or concern. Do not wait for visible functional collapse. Assess quantity in standard units, pattern, impaired driving, overdose, withdrawal, tolerance, control, consequences, medical effects, prescribed and nonprescribed use, and the person's goals. Trauma and substance treatment can proceed together. Another book is not required to access essential safety information or care.

Eating-disorder symptoms. Restriction, bingeing, purging, compensatory behaviors, compulsive exercise, rapid change, significant distress, or medical symptoms warrant specialized assessment even when weight and daily function appear unchanged.

Severe sleep disturbance. Chronic insomnia despite reasonable sleep hygiene. Frequent nightmares that disrupt sleep significantly. Sleep apnea symptoms (snoring, witnessed pauses, gasping awakenings, severe daytime fatigue). Sleep medicine evaluation is warranted.

Persistent suicidal thoughts without a plan. Recurring thoughts of death or not wanting to be alive need prompt qualified assessment and a collaborative safety plan. Do not use a plan/no-plan split as a risk category. Current escalation, intent, preparation, access to means, inability to stay safe, intoxication, command experiences, or uncertainty requires immediate live help.

Severe rejection-sensitivity affecting relationships. Reactivity to perceived rejection that is producing relationship rupture or significant distress. Clinical support can assess trauma, mood, anxiety, neurodevelopment, attachment, current relationships, and other contributors without treating a high-gain-processing metaphor as a diagnosis or established treatment category. Supporters should use a metaphor name for another person only when that person chooses it.

Significant memory gaps. Recent time loss or gaps affecting safety require prompt clinical and medical assessment. Childhood gaps may have many causes and are not proof that a hidden event occurred. Use non-suggestive care; do not search for memories through leading questions, hypnosis, body sensation, or deep-state work.

Voice-hearing experiences. New, intensifying, frequent, distressing, commanding, function-impairing, or safety-relevant voices need prompt assessment across trauma, psychosis, mood, substance and medication, sleep, neurological, and medical causes. Trauma and psychosis can coexist. Commands to harm self or others require immediate risk assessment.

Symptoms that have not responded to a reasonable course of treatment. If you have done a substantial amount of self-help or therapy work and are not seeing the changes you would expect, evaluation by a different clinician or a clinician with different training may be warranted. Sometimes the framework or modality was wrong for your particular pattern.

Functional impairment. Difficulty maintaining work, relationships, or basic daily function at levels that have not improved with self-help work. The functional impact is itself a signal that more support is needed.

Patterns That Suggest Specific Types of Clinical Care

A few specific situations and the kind of clinician most likely to be useful.

Dissociative-spectrum patterns. Look for a licensed clinician with formal training and substantial supervised experience in dissociative disorders. ISSTD publishes professional guidelines and educational resources; do not assume society membership or a vaguely described "certification" establishes competence. Ask about differential diagnosis, non-suggestive memory practice, crisis planning, supervision, and coordination with medical care.

Complex PTSD. Look for familiarity with ICD-11 cPTSD, developmental trauma, dissociation, attachment, and current evidence-based PTSD treatments. Cognitive processing therapy (CPT), prolonged exposure (PE), and EMDR can be effective for people with complex presentations and do not universally require a preliminary phase. Ask how the clinician uses shared decision-making, adapts treatment, monitors outcomes and adverse effects, and offers alternatives when a method is not helping.

Substance use combined with trauma. Look for integrated or coordinated care that can address both conditions without automatically requiring one to be completed first. Acute intoxication, dangerous withdrawal, overdose risk, or immediate safety risk may change the order of care. Chapter 21 provides substance-specific safety routes.

Voice hearing or unusual perceptual symptoms. Look for culturally responsive, trauma-informed psychiatric and medical assessment that also considers mood disorder, substances and medications, seizure, sleep disruption, and other causes. Hearing Voices peer support may complement care. Antipsychotic medication can help or be indicated for some conditions; discuss benefits, risks, alternatives, and goals with a qualified prescriber.

Suspected unrecognized TBI. Start with standard medical assessment and use neurology, neuropsychology, vestibular, oculomotor, or rehabilitation referral when indicated. Routine QEEG is not validated to diagnose mild TBI or distinguish it from other conditions, and a map must not determine treatment.

Attention or processing-speed concerns. Seek standard clinical assessment for ADHD, sleep, mood, anxiety, trauma, substances or medications, neurological issues, and medical contributors. QEEG cannot diagnose ADHD or select medication. If QEEG is used for neurofeedback planning, the provider must explain its nonspecificity and remain within legal scope.

Complex developmental or relational presentations. Look first for an actively licensed clinician with competence in the presenting diagnoses and problems, current evidence-supported PTSD options, dissociation when relevant, cultural context, safety, and development. Relational or attachment-focused work may be one voluntary option; the history alone does not establish that a branded attachment modality is required.

Couples or family dynamics affecting the trauma picture. Require separate, confidential screening for abuse and coercive control before conjoint work. Do not use couples or family therapy while a person cannot speak freely or faces intimidation, stalking, retaliation, or violence. In safe relationships, look for a licensed couples or family therapist with trauma training.

Suspected medical contributors. Start with primary care for the basic workup, with referral to specialists (sleep medicine, neurology, endocrinology, rheumatology, infectious disease) as the picture indicates.

What to Ask When Looking for a Clinician

A few questions worth asking when interviewing potential clinicians:

What is your active license, legal scope, and training for the problem I am bringing? Verify good standing and ask about supervised experience, diagnosis and differential assessment, and competence in guideline-supported PTSD treatments such as CPT, prolonged exposure, or EMDR when PTSD is the target. A private modality certificate can document additional training but does not replace licensure, scope, competence, or evidence.

What is your approach to sequencing? Look for an individualized answer that covers current safety, dissociation, substance withdrawal, medical stability, preference, evidence-based options, monitoring, and how the plan changes if symptoms or function worsen. Skills can be preparatory, concurrent, or stand-alone; a fixed stabilization period is not required for everyone.

Which evidence-supported options do you offer, and when do you refer? Depth and fidelity in one supported treatment can be excellent care. Breadth is useful only when accompanied by competence. Look for shared decision-making, adaptation, measurement, and willingness to refer rather than a claim to match people perfectly to modalities.

How do you handle dissociation if it comes up? Look for thoughtful answers that include slowing down, grounding, and adjusting the work, rather than continuing the planned protocol regardless.

What is your scope, and when do you refer? Look for clinicians who are clear about what they do and do not do, and who have referral relationships with other clinicians for the situations beyond their scope.

What is your fee structure, and what about insurance? Practical question worth asking up front, both for budgeting and to understand the longer-term feasibility of the work.

How will we know if the work is helping? Look for clinicians who can articulate what changes they expect to see and on what timeline, and who are willing to revise the plan if the expected changes are not happening.

When self-help is and is not enough

Self-help may be appropriate for low-risk skills and education when the person can choose, stop, and notice adverse effects. Body-focused practices are optional and can worsen panic or dissociation for some people; use titration and external-orientation alternatives.

Self-help is not a substitute for active crisis care, severe dissociation affecting safety, dangerous intoxication or withdrawal, psychosis or mania, eating-disorder medical risk, serious violence, or other situations requiring professional support. When uncertain, an initial consultation can clarify the picture and does not commit you to ongoing care.

Trust yourself when you sense that more support is warranted. That sense is information worth honoring.

Appendix B, Questions to Ask a Neurofeedback Provider

If you are considering neurofeedback for trauma work, the provider matters more than the modality. A skilled provider can produce real results; an unskilled one can spend your money without producing change, or in some cases cause harm through inappropriate sequencing.

Many readers of this book are already working with a therapist on the trauma layer, using EMDR, brainspotting, or another trauma-informed approach. Neurofeedback is commonly added alongside that work. The live question is configuration: whether you want brain training and therapy from the same practitioner, or therapy with a therapist and brain training with a separate provider. When significant instability or complexity is plausible, make that decision with a licensed mental-health clinician with appropriate trauma expertise rather than relying on self-assessment alone. Those are different roles, and a good provider will be clear about which one they fill.

The questions below are not designed to interrogate. Most competent providers will be glad to answer them.

Training and experience

A credential is a minimum floor rather than a ceiling. BCIA awards the BCN neurofeedback credential. The International QEEG Certification Board separately awards QEEG credentials. Certification is not a professional license; ask what license, legal supervision, and scope rules apply where you live and who holds responsibility for clinical risk. Either credential tells you someone met a coursework and exam standard. It does not tell you how they think about your specific pattern, how they handle sessions that go sideways, how well they listen, or whether they have worked with clients like you. Some of the most skilled providers I know do not have BCIA certification. Some who do are average at best. Ask about credentials as one data point, then ask the questions below that reveal actual clinical thinking.

What matters more than any single credential:

- How does the provider explain what they would do for your picture specifically? Do they ask about your pattern, your history, what has and has not worked before? Or do they describe a standard protocol they use for everyone?
- Have they worked with clients whose histories resemble yours, including complex or developmental trauma, dissociation, prior failed treatments? What does that work look like?
- Do they individualize and adapt? Can they explain why they are starting where they are starting, and what they would change if the work is not producing expected results?
- Do they listen well? Can they explain what they are doing in plain language? Do they adjust when you say something is wrong, or do they push through?
- Do they coordinate with your other providers, or do they treat neurofeedback as the only thing you need?

These questions reveal information a credential alone cannot. Use them to surface clinical thinking rather than to collect certifications.

What is your scope of practice, and what sits outside it? Neurofeedback builds regulatory capacity. It is not therapy. What you want is a provider who can tell you clearly what they are equipped to do and what they are not, and who will refer rather than overreach.

What is your training in trauma specifically? Ask what it looks like in practice: how do they handle a session that opens material the client cannot manage? When do they slow down? What do they do the first time a client dissociates?

What is your training in QEEG? Reading a QEEG accurately requires substantial training. Ask how they learned, who trained them, and what they do when the map and the clinical presentation do not line up.

Approach and Philosophy

What is your approach to sequencing? Look for stabilization-first answers. The provider should be clear that early sessions focus on autonomic regulation and basic stabilization, with deeper protocols (alpha-theta in particular) reserved for later. I look for a provider who can explain the clinical reasoning behind the sequence and who has a plan for what happens if the client destabilizes. A provider who proposes alpha-theta as a starting protocol for trauma is skipping the stabilization step, and I have seen the harm that produces (Chapter 18).

Do you do QEEG-guided protocol selection or symptom-based protocol selection? These are two different approaches. QEEG-guided selection uses the brain map to form hypotheses about what to train and where; the map can surface patterns the clinical interview alone would not suggest. Symptom-based selection works from the clinical presentation and adjusts based on response. What matters more than which approach the provider uses is the thinking behind it: can they explain why they are starting where they are starting, and what they expect to see?

How do you handle dissociation during sessions? This is one of the more important questions. Look for answers that include slowing down, grounding, adjusting the protocol, and not pushing through. A provider who continues the planned protocol regardless of the client's state is a provider who is not appropriately responsive to what is happening.

How do you decide when to do alpha-theta? Look for criteria-based answers that include adequate stabilization, demonstrated regulatory capacity, and reasons to expect alpha-theta would help with what remains after other work. A provider who does alpha-theta on most clients early in treatment is skipping the sequencing step that, in my experience and in the Othmer evolution of trauma neurofeedback, protects the client from destabilization.

How do you coordinate with my other treatment providers? The most effective neurofeedback work usually happens in coordination with other clinicians (therapist, psychiatrist, primary care). A provider who insists on being the only treatment, or who discourages other treatment, is a flag.

Practical Logistics

How many sessions are typically needed for the kind of work you would propose for me? Look for honest answers. Initial courses for trauma work are usually twenty to forty sessions, sometimes more. A provider who promises results in five sessions is overpromising.

How often do sessions occur? Twice-weekly is common in early phases. Less frequent for maintenance. A provider who proposes much more frequent sessions early on (multiple times per week) may be appropriate for some intensive cases but warrants discussion.

What is the cost per session, and is insurance involved? Practical question. Costs vary widely by region; in many areas, sessions run several hundred dollars and are not covered by insurance. The total cost matters.

What equipment do you use? Brief answer is fine; the question lets you know whether the provider is using current equipment from established manufacturers or something less standard.

Where does the work happen? In-office is standard. Some providers offer home-use systems with remote supervision; this can be appropriate in some cases but requires careful provider involvement.

Tracking and Outcomes

How will we track progress? Look for clinical assessment at intervals (validated symptom measures, clinician evaluation), possibly periodic QEEG comparison, and explicit conversation about whether the work is producing the expected changes.

What would tell you the work is not helping, and what would you do then? This is one of the most important questions. A provider who has thought about what failure looks like and what to do about it is a provider who is doing reflective practice. A provider who has never considered failure is one who has not been paying attention to all of his cases.

How long do clients typically continue work, and how does it taper? The work should have an end, with the gains consolidated and maintenance sessions only as needed. A provider who keeps clients indefinitely without clear progression is one whose model may be more about ongoing revenue than about achieving recovery.

Specific Protocol Questions

What is your protocol for sleep issues, if I have those? If sleep is part of your picture, the provider should have specific approaches.

What is your protocol for the Frontal Slow versus Slowed Alpha distinction? This question lets you know whether the provider understands this distinction. The Slowed Alpha pattern responds to alpha-frequency training, not to the standard ADHD protocols. A provider who has not heard of this distinction may not be the right fit if your picture suggests Slowed Alpha is involved.

Do you do any work at temporal sites, and what for? The temporal lobe is involved in emotional reactivity and memory processing, and I see temporal-site involvement in many of the trauma presentations I map. The answer tells you how the provider thinks about site selection and whether their approach covers the sites your pattern may call for.

Do you do coherence training, and when? Coherence training is appropriate for some patterns and not others. A provider who does it routinely without QEEG indication may be over-applying it.

What is your approach if I am on psychiatric medication? Many neurofeedback clients are on medication. The provider should be comfortable working with this and have a sense of how medications interact with the protocols.

Red Flags

A few things that should make you cautious about a particular provider.

Promises of cure or guaranteed results. No clinician can guarantee outcomes. Promises of this kind reflect either marketing-driven practice or insufficient understanding of what the work can do.

Hostility to other modalities or other treatment providers. A provider who insists that neurofeedback alone is the answer, or who is dismissive of therapy or medication, is one whose model is not integrated.

Heavy upfront payment for a fixed package without flexibility. Some payment models are reasonable; large prepaid packages with no refund possibility for a treatment that may not fit are a flag.

Scope confusion: acting as therapist when they are not. A neurofeedback provider who frames what they do as therapy, who digs into trauma processing, parts work, or memory integration without clinical training, is operating outside what neurofeedback is. The training is the training. The therapy is the therapy. A good provider knows the difference and refers across that line when the work crosses it.

Equipment or protocols that have unusually large claims and unusual training requirements. The legitimate field has its variations, but unusual claims paired with high-cost training are sometimes a sign of marginal practice.

Pressure to make decisions quickly. A reasonable provider will give you time to consider. Pressure tactics are a flag.

Discomfort with questions. A provider who becomes defensive or evasive when asked about their training, their approach, or their reasoning.

Closing Note

The neurofeedback field has skilled, ethical, experienced providers, and it has providers whose practice does not meet the standards the field aspires to. Credentials help sort the obvious problems, but the clinical thinking is what you are actually hiring. A provider who can explain, in plain language, what they see in your pattern, what they would try first, how they would know it is working, and what they would do if it is not, that is the provider you want, regardless of what letters follow their name.

A provider who becomes defensive when asked these questions is showing you how the working relationship would proceed. Trust your read of it. You will be doing intimate work with this person, and the relational fit is part of the clinical fit.

Appendix C: Terms Worth Keeping, Terms to Handle Carefully

The trauma-therapy world has accumulated a vocabulary that is partly precise, partly metaphorical, partly contested, and partly diluted by overuse. This appendix walks through the terms that show up most often in trauma conversations, with a brief recommendation about how to use each one.

The categories are: **Keep** (precise terms with clinical utility); **Use carefully** (terms with utility but with limitations or contested elements); **Drop** (terms whose costs outweigh their benefits in current usage).

Keep

Post-traumatic stress disorder (PTSD). A specific clinical diagnosis with criteria. Useful when the criteria are met. Should not be applied loosely to any trauma history.

Complex PTSD (cPTSD). An ICD-11 diagnosis for PTSD plus disturbances in self-organization. It may fit some prolonged or repeated-trauma presentations; it is not automatically more accurate for every person with developmental trauma.

Phase-oriented treatment. A model emphasizing safety and skills, trauma processing, and integration. It is established in dissociative-disorder guidance and may help some complex presentations. Do not turn it into a fixed preliminary phase required before guideline-supported PTSD treatment for everyone.

Stabilization. A useful term for immediate safety, medical stability, crisis response, and skills that support tolerable treatment. It can be preparatory, concurrent, or a treatment focus; it is not a universal months-long gate before trauma-focused care.

Co-regulation. Social interaction and practical support can influence regulation, especially in caregiver-developmental contexts. Effects can be helpful, neutral, or harmful and are not necessarily reciprocal. The term does not mean one person can or must control another person's nervous system.

Window of tolerance. Daniel Siegel's metaphor for the range of arousal a person can experience while remaining functional. Useful clinical scaffolding. Hold as metaphor; do not treat as precisely measurable construct.

Memory reconsolidation. A neuroscience framework for how reactivated memories may update under some conditions. It is one mechanistic model, not proof that every effective therapy works through the same process. Reactivation or bodily sensation does not verify a memory.

Dissociation. Real clinical phenomenon with multiple presentations. Useful when used precisely. Covers everyday absorption and clinical dissociative-disorder symptoms, though taxometric evidence (Waller, Putnam & Carlson, 1996) suggests pathological dissociation may be categorically distinct from absorption rather than a more intense version of it. The question is not settled. Specify which is meant.

Hyperarousal / hypoarousal. Useful descriptive terms for autonomic states. Distinguish trauma-related hyperarousal from other conditions producing similar phenotypes.

Adverse Childhood Experiences (ACE). Useful population-level epidemiological tool. Limit to that use; do not treat as individual-level prediction.

Attachment classifications. The classic classifications arose from infant-caregiver assessment. Adult attachment constructs and measures differ, and "disorganized" attachment in adults is especially difficult to measure consistently. These are not diagnoses, fixed person labels, or brain patterns.

Polyvagal language at the clinical level (mobilization, immobilization, engagement, regulation). Useful descriptive vocabulary for autonomic state. Use without committing to the contested anatomy.

Embodiment. Useful for describing the felt-sense dimension of being in the body. General term that can accommodate various more specific approaches.

Integration. A broad term used differently across therapies for memory, identity, emotion, behavior, or continuity. Specify the model, the target, and how change will be recognized.

Use Carefully

Trauma. SAMHSA uses a broad framework involving events or circumstances experienced as harmful or threatening with lasting adverse effects. DSM PTSD uses a narrower exposure criterion. Name the intended framework; do not treat any stressor or any difficult response as diagnostically traumatic by definition.

Differentiation of self. A Bowen family-systems construct involving relationships among thought, feeling, autonomy, and emotional connection. It is a theoretical and research construct, not a precise measure of internal regulation or a diagnosis.

Polyvagal-specific anatomy (dorsal vagal, ventral vagal as discrete switchable systems). The clinical vocabulary is useful; the specific anatomical claims are contested. Use the state language without overcommitting to the anatomy. See Chapter 14.

Neuroception. Porges's term for the brain's below-awareness assessment of safety and threat. The phenomenon is real: the brain does rapidly assess safety and adjust autonomic state. The specific mechanism Porges proposes, a discrete subcortical detector in particular structures, is more speculative than the theory presents it. Use the concept loosely. See Chapter 14.

Vagal tone. Parasympathetic influence on the heart, often measured through respiratory sinus arrhythmia (RSA). RSA is influenced by breathing rate, volume, and other factors besides vagal activity (Grossman & Taylor, 2007), so it does not cleanly index a single autonomic channel. Useful as a general concept; hold loosely as a measure. See Chapter 14.

Trauma-informed care. Useful concept in principle (the SAMHSA framework with six principles is real). Has been diluted by overuse to the point of marketing label. When using, specify what trauma-informed actually means in the context.

Nervous system regulation / dysregulation. Useful when used precisely (with reference to specific autonomic and neural systems). Often used vaguely as a stand-in for "feeling distressed" or "feeling calm." Specify when possible.

Somatic. Useful as adjective for body-related work. Can be conflated with formal Somatic Experiencing (Levine's modality). Distinguish: *somatic* as general descriptor versus *Somatic Experiencing* as specific modality.

Parts (in the IFS sense). A useful clinical metaphor for some people. Do not treat parts as literal entities or validated QEEG configurations. Emergent images, sensations, voices, or apparent memories are not proof of events. See Chapter 13.

Inner child. Older psychological concept that has had mixed reception in the trauma literature. Useful for some clinicians and clients; carries a particular framework that not every trauma framework fits. Use with awareness of the framework it carries.

Reprocessing. Useful when referring to specific protocols (EMDR reprocessing, others). Can be used vaguely to mean any trauma-related therapeutic activity. Specify when possible.

Trigger / triggered. Useful terms when used precisely (trauma reminders that activate trauma-related responses). Have been diluted in casual usage to mean *anything that produces emotional discomfort*. Use carefully and specify.

Activation. Useful for describing autonomic and emotional engagement. Has been over-generalized to mean *any kind of strong emotion*. Use with attention to what is actually being activated.

Healing. Useful term, used widely. Carries some baggage from the wellness industry. Recovery work is what the term usually means; the term itself is not precise. Use without overpromising.

Empowerment. Useful concept, also widely diluted. Often functions as marketing language. Use sparingly and specifically.

Integrated. Sometimes useful as a descriptor for integrated treatment approaches. Often used loosely to mean *involving multiple things*. Specify what is integrated when possible.

Mindfulness. Useful when referring to specific practices and frameworks (MBSR, MBCT, traditional meditation traditions). Has been over-generalized in popular usage. Specify the practice.

Resilience. Useful concept in research literature; has been culturally weaponized in some contexts to imply that those who do not recover well lack resilience as a personal trait. Use carefully, with attention to social and material context.

Post-traumatic growth. Real phenomenon for some trauma survivors. Should not be applied coercively or framed as a goal that all survivors should reach. Use with attention to the survivor's own experience and pace.

Survivor, victim, person who experienced trauma. Identity-first and person-first language are both valid. Use the person's chosen term; survivor identity, advocacy, or trauma community can remain central without indicating stalled recovery.

Self-care. Useful in principle. Has been culturally captured by consumerist framings. Often functions as personal-responsibility framing for what should be broader social and clinical support. Use carefully.

Drop

The body keeps the score (as a literal claim). The phrase is in widespread cultural use and the original work is substantial. The literal version (trauma is stored in body tissue, retrievable through specific intervention) is not supported by current understanding. The state-ledger framing in Chapter 3 is more accurate. Use the original phrase if at all only with explicit framing about what it means and does not mean.

Re-traumatization (used without definition). Trauma-informed-care literature uses this term for several things, including systems or relationships that recreate traumatic conditions and experiences that produce renewed traumatic responses or additional harm. Define the intended meaning. Do not equate all discomfort, temporary distress, or trauma reminders with harm.

Toxic / detoxify (in psychological contexts). Often used as casual vocabulary. The terms imply specific medical processes that are not actually happening in the contexts they are usually applied to. Use precise vocabulary instead.

Gaslighting (used loosely). The term refers to manipulation that causes someone to doubt perceptions, experiences, or understanding. It is often used casually for disagreement or unwanted communication. Reserve it for manipulative reality-undermining behavior and use more precise language for ordinary conflict.

Narcissist / narcissism (as casual diagnosis). Has become culturally widespread as informal labeling of difficult people. Most usage is not clinically accurate, and the framing tends to produce more heat than light. Use the clinical term only when the clinical pattern is present.

Trauma response (used to label any negative emotional reaction). Can be specific and useful when referring to actual trauma reactivation. Has been loosened to label any negative emotion as a trauma response, which both inflates the trauma framework and obscures other things going on. Use with precision.

Manifesting / law of attraction (in trauma contexts). Carries spiritual-bypass framings that can be actively harmful in trauma populations. Drop in clinical and recovery contexts.

Cellular memory (as literal claim). Sometimes used to suggest that trauma memory is stored in cells throughout the body. Not supported. Drop.

Victim-blaming language. Drop language that transfers responsibility from a person who caused harm to the person harmed, including scrutiny of why the person did not leave, resist, report, or behave differently under threat. Disagreement alone is not victim blaming; displaced responsibility is the defining problem.

Vocabulary discipline

Precise vocabulary supports precise work. The recommendations above are not meant to police language but to support the careful thinking the trauma framework benefits from. Different settings warrant different vocabulary; clinical settings benefit from more precision than personal journaling does. The field is updating, and this appendix represents one current view rather than a final pronouncement.

The work itself is what matters. The vocabulary is in service of the work.

Resources

Crisis Support

988 Suicide and Crisis Lifeline Call or text **988** (United States) Available 24 hours a day, 7 days a week. Chat: 988lifeline.org

Crisis Text Line Text **HOME** to **741741** (United States) Text-based crisis support, 24/7. crisistextline.org

RAINN National Sexual Assault Hotline 1-800-656-HOPE (4673) Online chat available at rainn.org Available 24/7.

National Domestic Violence Hotline 1-800-799-SAFE (7233) | TTY: 1-800-787-3224 Text START to 88788 thehotline.org | Available 24/7.

Veterans Crisis Line Call 988 and press 1 | Text 838255 veteranscrisisline.net

Trevor Project (LGBTQ+ youth crisis support) Call 1-866-488-7386 | Text START to 678-678 thetrevorproject.org

---

Trauma Treatment Locators

Psychology Today Therapist Finder psychologytoday.com/us/therapists Filter by specialty (trauma, PTSD, EMDR, somatic, IFS, etc.), insurance, and location.

EMDRIA Therapist Locator (EMDR-trained clinicians) emdria.org/find-an-emdr-therapist

IFS Institute Therapist Directory (Internal Family Systems) ifs-institute.com/practitioners

Somatic Experiencing International Practitioner Directory traumahealing.org/find-a-se-professional

Sensorimotor Psychotherapy Institute Practitioner Directory sensorimotorpsychotherapy.org/find-a-practitioner

ISNR Neurofeedback Provider Directory (International Society for Neuroregulation and Research) isnr.org / find-a-provider

BCIA Certified Biofeedback and Neurofeedback Practitioners bcia.org / search / custom.asp

---

Screening Tools

PTSD Checklist for DSM-5 (PCL-5) A 20-item self-report measure of PTSD symptoms. Widely used in research and clinical settings. Available at ptsd.va.gov (search "PCL-5").

IES-R (Impact of Event Scale, Revised) A 22-item measure of PTSD symptoms. Widely available; ask your provider.

ACE (Adverse Childhood Experiences) Questionnaire The 10-item original ACE screen. Available through many trauma-informed primary care resources; see cdc.gov / aces.

ITQ (International Trauma Questionnaire) Measures ICD-11 PTSD and complex PTSD. Available at traumameasuresglobal.net.

PHQ-9 (Patient Health Questionnaire, 9) Depression screen commonly used alongside trauma assessment. Available at phqscreeners.com.

GAD-7 (Generalized Anxiety Disorder, 7) Anxiety screen. Available at phqscreeners.com.

These tools are for informational purposes only and are not a substitute for clinical assessment. Scores should be interpreted in consultation with a qualified clinician.

Education and Support Organizations

ISSTD (International Society for the Study of Trauma and Dissociation) isst-d.org, professional society; consumer resources and provider directory.

NASMHPD (National Association of State Mental Health Program Directors) nasmhpd.org, policy and system-level trauma-informed care resources.

NCTSN (National Child Traumatic Stress Network) nctsn.org, resources for childhood trauma, including parent guides and treatment summaries.

Cheetah House (meditation-related adverse effects support) cheetahhouse.org, support and resources for people experiencing difficulties related to meditation practice.

Hearing Voices Network, USA hearingvoicesusa.org, peer support and resources for people who hear voices, including trauma-related voice-hearing.

Further Reading

The Body Keeps the Score by Bessel van der Kolk, M.D. (Viking, 2014) The foundational trauma book for lay readers; strong on embodiment and the body's role in trauma.

Waking the Tiger by Peter Levine, Ph.D. (North Atlantic Books, 1997) Introduction to Somatic Experiencing; the animal model of trauma and its resolution.

Internal Family Systems Therapy by Richard C. Schwartz, Ph.D. (Guilford, 1995; revised 2020) The foundational IFS text for clinicians; lay-accessible sections available.

Trauma-Sensitive Mindfulness by David Treleaven (W.W. Norton, 2018) How to adapt mindfulness practice for trauma populations; important context for Chapter 15.

Complex PTSD: From Surviving to Thriving by Pete Walker (Azure Coyote, 2013) Widely recommended consumer resource for complex and developmental trauma.

The Polyvagal Theory in Therapy by Deb Dana (W.W. Norton, 2018) Clinical application of polyvagal-informed language; read alongside Chapter 14 for context.

For Clinicians

ISNR Continuing Education, isnr.org/education **BCIA Certification Pathways**, bcia.org/certification **EMDRIA Certification and Training**, emdria.org/emdria-approved-training **Somatic Experiencing Training**, traumahealing.org/se-training **IFS Level 1, 2, 3 Training**, ifs-institute.com/trainings

---

All URLs and phone numbers verified at time of manuscript completion. Please confirm currency before publication.

References

Abdallah, C. G., Averill, C. L., Ramage, A. E., Averill, L. A., Alkin, E., Nemati, S., et al. (2019). Reduced Salience and Enhanced Central Executive Connectivity Following PTSD Treatment. *Chronic Stress, 3*. https://doi.org/10.1177/2470547019838971

Abdallah, C. G., Averill, C. L., Ramage, A. E., Averill, L. A., Goktas, S., Nemati, S., et al. (2019). Salience Network Disruption in U.S. Army Soldiers With Posttraumatic Stress Disorder. *Chronic Stress, 3*. https://doi.org/10.1177/2470547019850467

Abdallah, C. G., Sanacora, G., Duman, R. S., & Krystal, J. H. (2015). Ketamine and rapid-acting antidepressants: a window into a new neurobiology for mood disorder therapeutics. *Annual review of medicine, 66*, 509-23. https://doi.org/10.1146/annurev-med-053013-062946

Acevedo, B. P., Aron, E. N., Aron, A., Sangster, M. D., Collins, N., & Brown, L. L. (2014). The highly sensitive brain: an fMRI study of sensory processing sensitivity and response to others' emotions. *Brain and Behavior, 4*(4), 580-594. https://doi.org/10.1002/brb3.242

Acheson, D. T., Gresack, J. E., & Risbrough, V. B. (2012). Hippocampal dysfunction effects on context memory: possible etiology for posttraumatic stress disorder. *Neuropharmacology, 62*(2), 674-85. https://doi.org/10.1016/j.neuropharm.2011.04.029

Adetunji, B., Mathews, M., Williams, A., Budur, K., Mathews, M., Mahmud, J., et al. (2005). Use of antipsychotics in the treatment of post-traumatic stress disorder. *Psychiatry (Edgmont (Pa. : Township)), 2*(4), 43-7. PMID: 21179651

Akiki, T. J., Averill, C. L., & Abdallah, C. G. (2017). A Network-Based Neurobiological Model of PTSD: Evidence From Structural and Functional Neuroimaging Studies. *Current Psychiatry Reports, 19*(11). https://doi.org/10.1007/s11920-017-0840-4

Akiki, T. J., Averill, C. L., Wrocklage, K. M., Scott, J. C., Averill, L. A., Schweinsburg, B., et al. (2018a). Default mode network abnormalities in posttraumatic stress disorder: A novel network-restricted topology approach. *NeuroImage, 176*, 489-498. https://doi.org/10.1016/j.neuroimage.2018.05.005

Akiki, T. J., Averill, C. L., Wrocklage, K. M., Scott, J. C., Averill, L. A., Schweinsburg, B., et al. (2018b). Topology of brain functional connectivity networks in posttraumatic stress disorder. *Data in brief, 20*, 1658-1675. https://doi.org/10.1016/j.dib.2018.08.198

Alexander, S. (2021). Trapped priors as a basic problem of rationality. *Astral Codex Ten*. https://www.astralcodexten.com/p/trapped-priors-as-a-basic-problem

Alkalame, L., Ogden, J., Clark, J. W., Porcheret, K., Risbrough, V. B., & Drummond, S. P. A. (2024). The relationship between REM sleep prior to analog trauma and intrusive memories. *Sleep, 47*(12). https://doi.org/10.1093/sleep/zsae203

Ally, D., Tobiasz-Veltz, L., Tu, K., Comeau, A., Bumpus, C., Blot, T., et al. (2025). A pilot study of an online group-based Internal Family Systems intervention for comorbid posttraumatic stress disorder and substance use. *Frontiers in psychiatry, 16*, 1544435. https://doi.org/10.3389/fpsyt.2025.1544435

Alting van Geusau, V. V. P., de Jongh, A., Nuijs, M. D., Brouwers, T. C., Moerbeek, M., & Matthijssen, S. J. M. A. (2023). The effectiveness, efficiency, and acceptability of EMDR vs. EMDR 2.0 vs. the Flash technique in the treatment of patients with PTSD: study protocol for the ENHANCE randomized controlled trial. *Frontiers in psychiatry, 14*, 1278052. https://doi.org/10.3389/fpsyt.2023.1278052

Alting van Geusau, V. V. P., Mulder, J. D., & Matthijssen, S. J. M. A. (2021). Predicting Outcome in an Intensive Outpatient PTSD Treatment Program Using Daily Measures. *Journal of clinical medicine, 10*(18). https://doi.org/10.3390/jcm10184152

Altunbas, F. D., Onen Unsalver, B., & Yasar, A. B. (2019). Aspects of cognitive performance relating to Theory of Mind (ToM) among people diagnosed with Post-Traumatic Stress Disorder (PTSD). *Neuropsychiatric disease and treatment, 15,* 2015-2025. https://doi.org/10.2147/NDT.S214595

American Psychological Association, Guideline Development Panel for the Treatment of Posttraumatic Stress Disorder in Adults. (2019). Summary of the clinical practice guideline for the treatment of posttraumatic stress disorder (PTSD) in adults. *American Psychologist, 74*(5), 596–607. https://doi.org/10.1037/amp0000473

Andersen, F. B., Djugum, M. E. T., Sjåstad, V. S., & Pallesen, S. (2023). The prevalence of workaholism: a systematic review and meta-analysis. *Frontiers in psychology, 14,* 1252373. https://doi.org/10.3389/fpsyg.2023.1252373

Andreassen, C. S., Griffiths, M. D., Hetland, J., Kravina, L., Jensen, F., & Pallesen, S. (2014). The prevalence of workaholism: A survey study in a nationally representative sample of Norwegian employees. *PloS one, 9*(8), e102446. https://doi.org/10.1371/journal.pone.0102446

Andrews-Hanna, J. R., Reidler, J. S., Sepulcre, J., Poulin, R., & Buckner, R. L. (2010). Functional-anatomic fractionation of the brain's default network. *Neuron, 65*(4), 550-62. https://doi.org/10.1016/j.neuron.2010.02.005

Andrews-Hanna, J. R., Smallwood, J., & Spreng, R. N. (2014). The default network and self-generated thought: component processes, dynamic control, and clinical relevance. *Annals of the New York Academy of Sciences, 1316*(1), 29-52. https://doi.org/10.1111/nyas.12360

Antony, J. W., & Paller, K. A. (2018). Retrieval and sleep both counteract the forgetting of spatial information. *Learning & memory (Cold Spring Harbor, N.Y.), 25*(6), 258-263. https://doi.org/10.1101/lm.046268.117

Aron, E. N., & Aron, A. (1997). Sensory-processing sensitivity and its relation to introversion and emotionality. *Journal of Personality and Social Psychology, 73*(2), 345-368. https://doi.org/10.1037//0022-3514.73.2.345

Aron, E. N., Aron, A., & Jagiellowicz, J. (2012). Sensory processing sensitivity: A review in the light of the latest evolutionary and neurobiological evidence. *Personality and Social Psychology Review, 16*(3), 262-282. https://doi.org/10.1177/1088868311434213

Askovic, M., Soh, N., Elhindi, J., & Harris, A. W. F. (2023). Neurofeedback for post-traumatic stress disorder: systematic review and meta-analysis of clinical and neurophysiological outcomes. *European journal of psychotraumatology, 14*(2), 2257435. https://doi.org/10.1080/20008066.2023.2257435

Asmundson, G. J. G., Coons, M. J., Taylor, S., & Katz, J. (2002). PTSD and the Experience of Pain: Research and Clinical Implications of Shared Vulnerability and Mutual Maintenance Models. *The Canadian Journal of Psychiatry, 47*(10), 930-937. https://doi.org/10.1177/070674370204701004

Auber, A., Tedesco, V., Jones, C. E., Monfils, M., & Chiamulera, C. (2013). Post-retrieval extinction as reconsolidation interference: methodological issues or boundary conditions?. *Psychopharmacology, 226*(4), 631-47. https://doi.org/10.1007/s00213-013-3004-1

Aupperle, R. L., Melrose, A. J., Stein, M. B., & Paulus, M. P. (2012). Executive function and PTSD: disengaging from trauma. *Neuropharmacology, 62*(2), 686-94. https://doi.org/10.1016/j.neuropharm.2011.02.008

Averill, C. L., Averill, L. A., Akiki, T. J., Fouda, S., Krystal, J. H., & Abdallah, C. G. (2024). Findings of PTSD-specific deficits in default mode network strength following a mild experimental stressor. *NPP, Digital Psychiatry and Neuroscience, 2*(1). https://doi.org/10.1038/s44277-024-00011-y

Azarias, F. R., Almeida, G. H. D. R., de Melo, L. F., Rici, R. E. G., & Maria, D. A. (2025). The Journey of the Default Mode Network: Development, Function, and Impact on Mental Health. *Biology, 14*(4). https://doi.org/10.3390/biology14040395

Bachrach, N., & Huntjens, R. J. C. (2025). Recent evidence-based developments in the treatment of DID. *Frontiers in psychiatry, 16,* 1650164. https://doi.org/10.3389/fpsyt.2025.1650164

Badre, D., & Nee, D. E. (2018). Frontal Cortex and the Hierarchical Control of Behavior. *Trends in cognitive sciences, 22*(2), 170-188. https://doi.org/10.1016/j.tics.2017.11.005

Baer, R., Crane, C., Miller, E., & Kuyken, W. (2019). Doing no harm in mindfulness-based programs: Conceptual issues and empirical findings. *Clinical psychology review, 71,* 101-114. https://doi.org/10.1016/j.cpr.2019.01.001

Balban, M. Y., Neri, E., Kogon, M. M., Weed, L., Nouriani, B., Jo, B., et al. (2023). Brief structured respiration practices enhance mood and reduce physiological arousal. *Cell Reports Medicine, 4*(1), 100895. https://doi.org/10.1016/j.xcrm.2022.100895

Bar-Haim, Y., Lamy, D., Pergamin, L., Bakermans-Kranenburg, M. J., & van IJzendoorn, M. H. (2007). Threat-related attentional bias in anxious and nonanxious individuals: A meta-analytic study. *Psychological Bulletin, 133*(1), 1–24. https://doi.org/10.1037/0033-2909.133.1.1

Barawi, K. S., Lewis, C., Simon, N., & Bisson, J. I. (2020). A systematic review of factors associated with outcome of psychological treatments for post-traumatic stress disorder. *European journal of psychotraumatology, 11*(1), 1774240. https://doi.org/10.1080/20008198.2020.1774240

Barrett, L. F. (2017). The theory of constructed emotion: an active inference account of interoception and categorization. *Social cognitive and affective neuroscience, 12*(1), 1-23. https://doi.org/10.1093/scan/nsw154

Baudinet, J., Simic, M., & Eisler, I. (2021). Formulation in eating disorder focused family therapy: why, when and how?. *Journal of eating disorders, 9*(1), 97. https://doi.org/10.1186/s40337-021-00451-3

Bazzana, F., Finzi, S., Di Fini, G., & Veglia, F. (2022). Infra-Low Frequency Neurofeedback: A Systematic Mixed Studies Review. *Frontiers in human neuroscience, 16,* 920659. https://doi.org/10.3389/fnhum.2022.920659

Beckers, T., & Kindt, M. (2017). Memory Reconsolidation Interference as an Emerging Treatment for Emotional Disorders: Strengths, Limitations, Challenges, and Opportunities. *Annual review of clinical psychology, 13,* 99-121. https://doi.org/10.1146/annurev-clinpsy-032816-045209

Bedny, M., Pascual-Leone, A., Dravida, S., & Saxe, R. (2012). A sensitive period for language in the visual cortex: distinct patterns of plasticity in congenitally versus late blind adults. *Brain and language, 122*(3), 162-70. https://doi.org/10.1016/j.bandl.2011.10.005

Belkin, M. R., & Schwartz, T. L. (2015). Alpha-2 receptor agonists for the treatment of post-traumatic stress disorder. *Drugs in Context, 4,* 212286. https://doi.org/10.7573/dic.212286

Berger, W., Mendlowicz, M. V., Marques-Portella, C., Kinrys, G., Fontenelle, L. F., Marmar, C. R., et al. (2009). Pharmacologic alternatives to antidepressants in posttraumatic stress disorder: a systematic review. *Progress in neuro-psychopharmacology & biological psychiatry, 33*(2), 169-80. https://doi.org/10.1016/j.pnpbp.2008.12.004

Berman, D. E., Cowansage, K. P., Bellanti, D. M., Nair, R., Boyd, C. C., Beech, E. H., et al. (2025). Systematic review and meta-analysis of neurofeedback training efficacy and neural mechanisms in the treatment of posttraumatic stress disorder. *Frontiers in neuroscience, 19*, 1658652. https://doi.org/10.3389/fnins.2025.1658652

Bernstein, A., Hadash, Y., & Fresco, D. M. (2019). Metacognitive processes model of decentering: emerging methods and insights. *Current opinion in psychology, 28*, 245-251. https://doi.org/10.1016/j.copsyc.2019.01.019

Berntsen, D., & Rubin, D. C. (2006). The Centrality of Event Scale: A measure of integrating a trauma into one's identity and its relation to post-traumatic stress disorder symptoms. *Behaviour Research and Therapy, 44*(2), 219–231. https://doi.org/10.1016/j.brat.2005.01.009

Berthoud, H.-R., & Neuhuber, W. L. (2000). Functional and chemical anatomy of the afferent vagal system. *Autonomic Neuroscience, 85*(1-3), 1-17. https://doi.org/10.1016/S1566-0702(00)00215-0

Bertsch, K., Göhre, I., Cottin, M., Zettl, M., Wienrich, C., & Back, S. N. (2024). Traumatic childhood experiences and personality functioning: effect of body connection in a cross-sectional German and Chilean sample. *Borderline Personality Disorder and Emotion Dysregulation, 11*(1). https://doi.org/10.1186/s40479-024-00266-z

Bethell, C. D., Newacheck, P., Hawes, E., & Halfon, N. (2014). Adverse childhood experiences: Assessing the impact on health and school engagement and the mitigating role of resilience. *Health Affairs, 33*(12), 2106–2115. https://doi.org/10.1377/hlthaff.2014.0914

Beutler, S., & Croy, I. (2023). Psychophysiological reactions during the trauma-film paradigm and their predictive value for intrusions. *European journal of psychotraumatology, 14*(2), 2281753. https://doi.org/10.1080/20008066.2023.2281753

Bick, J., & Nelson, C. A. (2016). Early Adverse Experiences and the Developing Brain. *Neuropsychopharmacology : official publication of the American College of Neuropsychopharmacology, 41*(1), 177-96. https://doi.org/10.1038/npp.2015.252

Bisson, J. I., Ehlers, A., Matthews, R., Pilling, S., Richards, D., & Turner, S. (2007). Psychological treatments for chronic post-traumatic stress disorder. Systematic review and meta-analysis. *The British journal of psychiatry : the journal of mental science, 190*, 97-104. https://doi.org/10.1192/bjp.bp.106.021402

Blanke, O., & Arzy, S. (2005). The out-of-body experience: Disturbed self-processing at the temporo-parietal junction. *The Neuroscientist, 11*(1), 16-24. https://doi.org/10.1177/1073858404270885

Boccia, M., Bonavita, A., Diana, S., Di Vita, A., Ciurli, M. P., & Guariglia, C. (2019). Topographical Disorientation: Clinical and Theoretical Significance of Long-Lasting Improvements Following Imagery-Based Training. *Frontiers in human neuroscience, 13*, 322. https://doi.org/10.3389/fnhum.2019.00322

Boccia, M., Piccardi, L., Cordellieri, P., Guariglia, C., & Giannini, A. M. (2015). EMDR therapy for PTSD after motor vehicle accidents: meta-analytic evidence for specific treatment. *Frontiers in human neuroscience, 9*, 213. https://doi.org/10.3389/fnhum.2015.00213

Bollimunta, A., Mo, J., Schroeder, C. E., & Ding, M. (2011). Neuronal mechanisms and attentional modulation of corticothalamic α oscillations. *The Journal of neuroscience : the official journal of the Society for Neuroscience, 31*(13), 4935-43. https://doi.org/10.1523/JNEUROSCI.5580-10.2011

Bolu, A., Akarsu, S., & Aydemir, E. (2017). Cortical Excitability and Post-Traumatic Stress Disorder. *Noro psikiyatri arsivi, 54*(2), 191-192. https://doi.org/10.5152/npa.2016.12539

Bonanno, G. A. (2004). Loss, trauma, and human resilience: Have we underestimated the human capacity to thrive after extremely aversive events? *American Psychologist, 59*(1), 20-28. https://doi.org/10.1037/0003-066X.59.1.20

Bonanno, G. A., Chen, S., Bagrodia, R., & Galatzer-Levy, I. R. (2024). Resilience and Disaster: Flexible Adaptation in the Face of Uncertain Threat. *Annual Review of Psychology, 75*, 573-599. https://doi.org/10.1146/annurev-psych-011123-024224

Bonanno, G. A., & Diminich, E. D. (2013). Annual research review: Positive adjustment to adversity, trajectories of minimal-impact resilience and emergent resilience. *Journal of Child Psychology and Psychiatry, 54*(4), 378-401. https://doi.org/10.1111/jcpp.12021

Bonn-Miller, M. O., Brunstetter, M., Simonian, A., Loflin, M. J., Vandrey, R., Babson, K. A., et al. (2022). The Long-Term, Prospective, Therapeutic Impact of Cannabis on Post-Traumatic Stress Disorder. *Cannabis and cannabinoid research, 7*(2), 214-223. https://doi.org/10.1089/can.2020.0056

Borah, R. M., Pathak, A., & Banerjee, A. (2025). Inhibition of thalamic relay nuclei scales the aperiodic and alpha band oscillations associated with arousal during naturalistic stimulus viewing. *Imaging neuroscience (Cambridge, Mass.), 3*. https://doi.org/10.1162/imag_a_00451

Bowen, M. (1978). *Family therapy in clinical practice*. Jason Aronson.

Boyer, S. M., Caplan, J. E., & Edwards, L. K. (2022). Trauma-Related Dissociation and the Dissociative Disorders:: Neglected Symptoms with Severe Public Health Consequences. *Delaware journal of public health, 8*(2), 78-84. https://doi.org/10.32481/djph.2022.05.010

Brand, B. L., Barth, M., Schlumpf, Y. R., Schielke, H., Chalavi, S., Vissia, E. M., et al. (2021). The utility of the Structured Inventory of Malingered Symptomatology for distinguishing individuals with Dissociative Identity Disorder (DID) from DID simulators and healthy controls. *European journal of psychotraumatology, 12*(1), 1984048. https://doi.org/10.1080/20008198.2021.1984048

Brand, B. L., Schielke, H. J., Putnam, K., Pierorazio, N. A., Nester, M. S., Robertson, J., et al. (2025). A randomized controlled trial assists individuals with complex trauma and dissociation in Finding Solid Ground. *Psychological trauma : theory, research, practice and policy, 17*(8), 1717-1727. https://doi.org/10.1037/tra0001871

Bremner, J. D. (2002). Neuroimaging of childhood trauma. *Seminars in clinical neuropsychiatry, 7*(2), 104-12. https://doi.org/10.1053/scnp.2002.31787

Bremner, J. D. (2006). Traumatic stress: effects on the brain. *Dialogues in clinical neuroscience, 8*(4), 445-61. https://doi.org/10.31887/DCNS.2006.8.4/jbremner

Bremner, J. D. (2007). Neuroimaging in posttraumatic stress disorder and other stress-related disorders. *Neuroimaging clinics of North America, 17*(4), 523-38, ix. https://doi.org/10.1016/j.nic.2007.07.003

Bressler, S. L., & Menon, V. (2010). Large-scale brain networks in cognition: emerging methods and principles. *Trends in cognitive sciences, 14*(6), 277-90. https://doi.org/10.1016/j.tics.2010.04.004

Britton, W. B., Lindahl, J. R., Cooper, D. J., Canby, N. K., & Palitsky, R. (2021). Defining and measuring meditation-related adverse effects in mindfulness-based programs. *Clinical psychological science : a journal of the Association for Psychological Science, 9*(6), 1185-1204. https://doi.org/10.1177/2167702621996340

Brom, D., Stokar, Y., Lawi, C., Nuriel-Porat, V., Ziv, Y., Lerner, K., et al. (2017). Somatic Experiencing for Posttraumatic Stress Disorder: A Randomized Controlled Outcome Study. *Journal of traumatic stress, 30*(3), 304-312. https://doi.org/10.1002/jts.22189

Brunet, A., Orr, S. P., Tremblay, J., Robertson, K., Nader, K., & Pitman, R. K. (2008). Effect of post-retrieval propranolol on psychophysiologic responding during subsequent script-driven traumatic imagery in post-traumatic stress disorder. *Journal of psychiatric research, 42*(6), 503-6. https://doi.org/10.1016/j.jpsychires.2007.05.006

Brunet, A., Saumier, D., Liu, A., Streiner, D. L., Tremblay, J., & Pitman, R. K. (2018). Reduction of PTSD Symptoms With Pre-Reactivation Propranolol Therapy: A Randomized Controlled Trial. *The American journal of psychiatry, 175*(5), 427-433. https://doi.org/10.1176/appi.ajp.2017.17050481

Bryant, R. A., Williamson, T., Erlinger, M., Felmingham, K. L., Malhi, G., Hinton, M., et al. (2021). Neural activity during response inhibition associated with improvement of dysphoric symptoms of PTSD after trauma-focused psychotherapy-an EEG-fMRI study. *Translational psychiatry, 11*(1), 218. https://doi.org/10.1038/s41398-021-01340-8

Bryant, T. (2022). *Homecoming: Overcome fear and trauma to reclaim your whole, authentic self.* TarcherPerigee.

Brzozowska, A., & Grabowski, J. (2025). Hyperarousal, Dissociation, Emotion Dysregulation and Re-Experiencing-Towards Understanding Molecular Aspects of PTSD Symptoms. *International journal of molecular sciences, 26*(11). https://doi.org/10.3390/ijms26115216

Burgess, C. R., Livneh, Y., Ramesh, R. N., & Andermann, M. L. (2018). Gating of visual processing by physiological need. *Current opinion in neurobiology, 49*, 16-23. https://doi.org/10.1016/j.conb.2017.10.020

Butt, M., Espinal, E., Aupperle, R. L., Nikulina, V., & Stewart, J. L. (2019). The Electrical Aftermath: Brain Signals of Posttraumatic Stress Disorder Filtered Through a Clinical Lens. *Frontiers in psychiatry, 10*, 368. https://doi.org/10.3389/fpsyt.2019.00368

Button, K. S., Ioannidis, J. P. A., Mokrysz, C., Nosek, B. A., Flint, J., Robinson, E. S. J., et al. (2013). Power failure: why small sample size undermines the reliability of neuroscience. *Nature reviews. Neuroscience, 14*(5), 365-76. https://doi.org/10.1038/nrn3475

Calhoun, L. G., & Tedeschi, R. G. (2013). *Posttraumatic growth in clinical practice.* Routledge. https://doi.org/10.4324/9780203629048

Calhoun, V. D., Lawrie, S. M., Mourao-Miranda, J., & Stephan, K. E. (2017). Prediction of Individual Differences from Neuroimaging Data. *NeuroImage, 145*(Pt B), 135-136. https://doi.org/10.1016/j.neuroimage.2016.12.012

Carmassi, C., Shear, K. M., Corsi, M., Bertelloni, C. A., Dell'Oste, V., & Dell'Osso, L. (2020). Mania Following Bereavement: State of the Art and Clinical Evidence. *Frontiers in psychiatry, 11*, 366. https://doi.org/10.3389/fpsyt.2020.00366

Carmichael, J., Ponsford, J., Gould, K. R., Tiego, J., Forbes, M. K., Kotov, R., et al. (2025). A Transdiagnostic, Hierarchical Taxonomy of Psychopathology Following Traumatic Brain Injury (HiTOP-TBI). *Journal of neurotrauma, 42*(7-8), 714-730. https://doi.org/10.1089/neu.2024.0006

Carter, R. T. (2007). Racism and psychological and emotional injury: Recognizing and assessing race-based traumatic stress. *The Counseling Psychologist, 35*(1), 13–105. https://doi.org/10.1177/0011000006292033

Carter, R. T., & Pieterse, A. L. (Eds.). (2020). *Measuring the effects of racism: Guidelines for the assessment and treatment of race-based traumatic stress injury.* Columbia University Press.

Castro Ribeiro, T., Sobregrau Sangrà, P., García Pagès, E., Badiella, L., López-Barbeito, B., Aguiló, S., et al. (2023). Assessing effectiveness of heart rate variability biofeedback to mitigate mental health symptoms: a pilot study. *Frontiers in physiology, 14,* 1147260. https://doi.org/10.3389/fphys.2023.1147260

Cattane, N., Rossi, R., Lanfredi, M., & Cattaneo, A. (2017). Borderline personality disorder and childhood trauma: exploring the affected biological systems and mechanisms. *BMC Psychiatry, 17*(1). https://doi.org/10.1186/s12888-017-1383-2

Caudle, M. M., Simmons, A. N., Moore, R. C., Thomas, M. L., & Bomyea, J. (2026). The association between childhood maltreatment and neural functioning during a working memory task in adults with internalizing disorders. *Brain imaging and behavior, 20*(2). https://doi.org/10.1007/s11682-026-01120-2

Cavanna, A. E., & Trimble, M. R. (2006). The precuneus: a review of its functional anatomy and behavioural correlates. *Brain : a journal of neurology, 129*(Pt 3), 564-83. https://doi.org/10.1093/brain/awl004

Chamberlin, D. E. (2019). The Predictive Processing Model of EMDR. *Frontiers in psychology, 10,* 2267. https://doi.org/10.3389/fpsyg.2019.02267

Chamberlin, D. E. (2022). The Active Inference Model of Coherence Therapy. *Frontiers in human neuroscience, 16,* 955558. https://doi.org/10.3389/fnhum.2022.955558

Chand, G. B., Wu, J., Hajjar, I., & Qiu, D. (2017). Interactions of the Salience Network and Its Subsystems with the Default-Mode and the Central-Executive Networks in Normal Aging and Mild Cognitive Impairment. *Brain connectivity, 7*(7), 401-412. https://doi.org/10.1089/brain.2017.0509

Chefetz, R. A. (2015). *Intensive psychotherapy for persistent dissociative processes: The fear of feeling real.* W. W. Norton.

Chen, J. A., Fortney, J. C., Bergman, H. E., Browne, K. C., Grubbs, K. M., Hudson, T. J., et al. (2020). Therapeutic alliance across trauma-focused and non-trauma-focused psychotherapies among veterans with PTSD. *Psychological services, 17*(4), 452-460. https://doi.org/10.1037/ser0000329

Chen, J., Fang, Z., Zhang, X., Zheng, Y., & Chen, Z. (2025). How Fear Memory is Updated: From Reconsolidation to Extinction?. *Neuroscience bulletin, 41*(6), 1054-1084. https://doi.org/10.1007/s12264-025-01367-7

Chen, W. G., Schloesser, D., Arensdorf, A. M., Simmons, J. M., Cui, C., Valentino, R., et al. (2021). The Emerging Science of Interoception: Sensing, Integrating, Interpreting, and Regulating Signals within the Self. *Trends in neurosciences, 44*(1), 3-16. https://doi.org/10.1016/j.tins.2020.10.007

Cherkin, D. C., Sherman, K. J., Balderson, B. H., Cook, A. J., Anderson, M. L., Hawkes, R. J., et al. (2016). Effect of Mindfulness-Based Stress Reduction vs Cognitive Behavioral Therapy or Usual Care on Back Pain and Functional Limitations in Adults With Chronic Low Back Pain: A Randomized Clinical Trial. *JAMA, 315*(12), 1240-9. https://doi.org/10.1001/jama.2016.2323

Chiamulera, C., Hinnenthal, I., Auber, A., & Cibin, M. (2014). Reconsolidation of maladaptive memories as a therapeutic target: pre-clinical data and clinical approaches. *Frontiers in psychiatry, 5,* 107. https://doi.org/10.3389/fpsyt.2014.00107

Choi, K. R., Seng, J. S., Briggs, E. C., Munro-Kramer, M. L., Graham-Bermann, S. A., Lee, R. C., et al. (2017). The Dissociative Subtype of Posttraumatic Stress Disorder (PTSD) Among Adolescents: Co-Occurring PTSD, Depersonalization/Derealization, and Other Dissociation Symptoms. *Journal of the American Academy of Child and Adolescent Psychiatry, 56*(12), 1062-1072. https://doi.org/10.1016/j.jaac.2017.09.425

Choi, Y., Choi, E., & Ko, E. (2023). Neurofeedback Effect on Symptoms of Posttraumatic Stress Disorder: A Systematic Review and Meta-Analysis. *Applied psychophysiology and biofeedback, 48*(3), 259-274. https://doi.org/10.1007/s10484-023-09593-3

Christianson, J. P., Fernando, A. B. P., Kazama, A. M., Jovanovic, T., Ostroff, L. E., & Sangha, S. (2012). Inhibition of fear by learned safety signals: a mini-symposium review. *The Journal of neuroscience : the official journal of the Society for Neuroscience, 32*(41), 14118-24. https://doi.org/10.1523/JNEUROSCI.3340-12.2012

Chung, S. W., Sullivan, C. M., Rogasch, N. C., Hoy, K. E., Bailey, N. W., Cash, R. F. H., et al. (2019). The effects of individualised intermittent theta burst stimulation in the prefrontal cortex: A TMS-EEG study. *Human brain mapping, 40*(2), 608-627. https://doi.org/10.1002/hbm.24398

Clancy, K., Ding, M., Bernat, E., Schmidt, N. B., & Li, W. (2017). Restless 'rest': intrinsic sensory hyperactivity and disinhibition in post-traumatic stress disorder. *Brain : a journal of neurology, 140*(7), 2041-2050. https://doi.org/10.1093/brain/awx116

Clancy, K. J., Albizu, A., Schmidt, N. B., & Li, W. (2020a). Intrinsic sensory disinhibition contributes to intrusive re-experiencing in combat veterans. *Scientific reports, 10*(1), 936. https://doi.org/10.1038/s41598-020-57963-2

Clancy, K. J., Andrzejewski, J. A., Simon, J., Ding, M., Schmidt, N. B., & Li, W. (2020b). Posttraumatic Stress Disorder Is Associated with α Dysrhythmia across the Visual Cortex and the Default Mode Network. *eNeuro, 7*(4). https://doi.org/10.1523/ENEURO.0053-20.2020

Coan, J. A., & Sbarra, D. A. (2015). Social baseline theory: The social regulation of risk and effort. *Current Opinion in Psychology, 1,* 87–91. https://doi.org/10.1016/j.copsyc.2014.12.021

Cohen, J. A., Mannarino, A. P., & Murray, L. K. (2011). Trauma-focused CBT for youth who experience ongoing traumas. *Child abuse & neglect, 35*(8), 637-46. https://doi.org/10.1016/j.chiabu.2011.05.002

Cole, P. M., Michel, M. K., & Teti, L. O. (1994). The development of emotion regulation and dysregulation: a clinical perspective. *Monographs of the Society for Research in Child Development, 59*(2-3), 73-100.

Colvert, E., Rutter, M., Beckett, C., Castle, J., Groothues, C., Hawkins, A., et al. (2008). Emotional difficulties in early adolescence following severe early deprivation: findings from the English and Romanian adoptees study. *Development and psychopathology, 20*(2), 547-67. https://doi.org/10.1017/S0954579408000278

Colvonen, P. J., Glassman, L. H., Crocker, L. D., Buttner, M. M., Orff, H., Schiehser, D. M., et al. (2017). Pretreatment biomarkers predicting PTSD psychotherapy outcomes: A systematic review. *Neuroscience and biobehavioral reviews, 75,* 140-156. https://doi.org/10.1016/j.neubiorev.2017.01.027

Connor, K. M., Sutherland, S. M., Tupler, L. A., Malik, M. L., & Davidson, J. R. (1999). Fluoxetine in post-traumatic stress disorder. Randomised, double-blind study. *The British journal of psychiatry : the journal of mental science, 175,* 17-22. https://doi.org/10.1192/bjp.175.1.17

Conrad, C. D. (2008). Chronic stress-induced hippocampal vulnerability: the glucocorticoid vulnerability hypothesis. *Reviews in the neurosciences, 19*(6), 395-411. https://doi.org/10.1515/revneuro.2008.19.6.395

Conway, A. R., & Engle, R. W. (1996). Individual differences in working memory capacity: more evidence for a general capacity theory. *Memory (Hove, England), 4*(6), 577-90. https://doi.org/10.1080/741940997

Corominas-Roso, M., Ibern, I., Capdevila, M., Ramon, R., Roncero, C., & Ramos-Quiroga, J. A. (2020). Benefits of EEG-Neurofeedback on the Modulation of Impulsivity in a Sample of Cocaine and Heroin Long-Term Abstinent Inmates: A Pilot Study. *International journal of offender therapy and comparative criminology, 64*(12), 1275-1298. https://doi.org/10.1177/0306624X20904704

Corrigan, F. M., & Hull, A. M. (2015). Neglect of the complex: why psychotherapy for post-traumatic clinical presentations is often ineffective. *BJPsych bulletin, 39*(2), 86-9. https://doi.org/10.1192/pb.bp.114.046995

Cracco, E., Hudson, A. R., Van Hamme, C., Maeyens, L., Brass, M., & Mueller, S. C. (2020). Early interpersonal trauma reduces temporoparietal junction activity during spontaneous mentalising. *Social cognitive and affective neuroscience, 15*(1), 12-22. https://doi.org/10.1093/scan/nsaa015

Crouch, E., Probst, J. C., Radcliff, E., Bennett, K. J., & McKinney, S. H. (2019). Prevalence of adverse childhood experiences (ACEs) among US children. *Child Abuse & Neglect, 92,* 209-218. https://doi.org/10.1016/j.chiabu.2019.04.010

Cross, D., Fani, N., Powers, A., & Bradley, B. (2017). Neurobiological Development in the Context of Childhood Trauma. *Clinical psychology : a publication of the Division of Clinical Psychology of the American Psychological Association, 24*(2), 111-124. https://doi.org/10.1111/cpsp.12198

Cuijpers, P., Veen, S. C. v., Sijbrandij, M., Yoder, W., & Cristea, I. A. (2020). Eye movement desensitization and reprocessing for mental health problems: a systematic review and meta-analysis. *Cognitive behaviour therapy, 49*(3), 165-180. https://doi.org/10.1080/16506073.2019.1703801

Cyders, M. A., Littlefield, A. K., Coffey, S., & Karyadi, K. A. (2014). Examination of a short English version of the UPPS-P Impulsive Behavior Scale. *Addictive Behaviors, 39*(9), 1372-1376. https://doi.org/10.1016/j.addbeh.2014.02.013

Danese, A., & Baldwin, J. R. (2017). Hidden wounds? Inflammatory links between childhood trauma and psychopathology. *Annual Review of Psychology, 68,* 517-544. https://doi.org/10.1146/annurev-psych-010416-044208

Dave, F., & Tripathi, R. (2023). The efficacy of neurofeedback for alcohol use disorders - a systematic review. *The world journal of biological psychiatry : the offi-*

cial journal of the World Federation of Societies of Biological Psychiatry, 24(6), 496-507. https://doi.org/10.1080/15622975.2022.2151043

Daw, N. W. (2009). The foundations of development and deprivation in the visual system. *The Journal of physiology, 587*(Pt 12), 2769-73. https://doi.org/10.1113/jphysiol.2009.170001

De Filippi, E., Marins, T., Escrichs, A., Gilson, M., Moll, J., Tovar-Moll, F., et al. (2022). One session of fMRI-Neurofeedback training on motor imagery modulates whole-brain effective connectivity and dynamical complexity. *Cerebral cortex communications, 3*(3), tgac027. https://doi.org/10.1093/texcom/tgac027

de Moraes Costa, G., Zanatta, F. B., Ziegelmann, P. K., Soares Barros, A. J., & Mello, C. F. (2020). Pharmacological treatments for adults with post-traumatic stress disorder: A network meta-analysis of comparative efficacy and acceptability. *Journal of psychiatric research, 130*, 412-420. https://doi.org/10.1016/j.jpsychires.2020.07.046

de Oliveira Matos, F., Vido, A., Garcia, W. F., Lopes, W. A., & Pereira, A. (2020). A Neurovisceral Integrative Study on Cognition, Heart Rate Variability, and Fitness in the Elderly. *Frontiers in aging neuroscience, 12*, 51. https://doi.org/10.3389/fnagi.2020.00051

de Voogd, L. D., Hashemi, M. M., Zhang, W., Kaldewaij, R., Koch, S. B. J., van Ast, V. A., Klumpers, F., & Roelofs, K. (2025). Amygdala hyperactivity in posttraumatic stress disorder: Disentangling predisposing from consequential factors using a prospective longitudinal design. *Biological Psychiatry, 98*(5), 427–435. https://doi.org/10.1016/j.biopsych.2025.02.894

Dębiec, J., Bush, D. E. A., & LeDoux, J. E. (2011). Noradrenergic enhancement of reconsolidation in the amygdala impairs extinction of conditioned fear in rats–a possible mechanism for the persistence of traumatic memories in PTSD. *Depression and anxiety, 28*(3), 186-93. https://doi.org/10.1002/da.20803

Debiec, J., & LeDoux, J. E. (2006). Noradrenergic signaling in the amygdala contributes to the reconsolidation of fear memory: treatment implications for PTSD. *Annals of the New York Academy of Sciences, 1071*, 521-4. https://doi.org/10.1196/annals.1364.056

Decety, J., & Lamm, C. (2007). The role of the right temporoparietal junction in social interaction: How low-level computational processes contribute to meta-cognition. *The Neuroscientist, 13*(6), 580-593. https://doi.org/10.1177/1073858407304654

Deen, A., Biedermann, S. V., Lotzin, A., Krüger-Gottschalk, A., Dyer, A., Knaevelsrud, C., et al. (2022). The dissociative subtype of PTSD in trauma-exposed individuals: a latent class analysis and examination of clinical covariates. *European journal of psychotraumatology, 13*(1), 2031591. https://doi.org/10.1080/20008198.2022.2031591

DeGruy, J. (2017). *Post traumatic slave syndrome: America's legacy of enduring injury and healing* (Rev. ed.). Joy DeGruy Publications.

Dehghani-Arani, F., Rostami, R., & Nadali, H. (2013). Neurofeedback training for opiate addiction: improvement of mental health and craving. *Applied psychophysiology and biofeedback, 38*(2), 133-41. https://doi.org/10.1007/s10484-013-9218-5

Delapaz, N. R., Hor, W. K., Gilbert, M., La, A. D., Liang, F., Fan, P., et al. (2021). An Emulation of Randomized Trials of Administrating Antipsychotics in PTSD Patients for Outcomes of Suicide-Related Events. *Journal of personalized medicine, 11*(3). https://doi.org/10.3390/jpm11030178

DeLaRosa, B. L., Spence, J. S., Didehbani, N., Tillman, G. D., Motes, M. A., Bass, C., et al. (2020). Neurophysiology of threat processing bias in combat-related post-traumatic stress disorder. *Human brain mapping, 41*(1), 218-229. https://doi.org/10.1002/hbm.24800

DeViva, J. C., McCarthy, E., & Santoro, G. M. (2021). Differences in sleep apnea among veterans with PTSD and other mental health conditions. *Psychiatry Research, 300*, 113909. https://doi.org/10.1016/j.psychres.2021.113909

Desmond, M. (2016). *Evicted: Poverty and profit in the American city*. Crown.

DiGangi, J. A., Gomez, D., Mendoza, L., Jason, L. A., Keys, C. B., & Koenen, K. C. (2013). Pre-trauma risk factors for posttraumatic stress disorder: A systematic review of the literature. *Clinical Psychology Review, 33*(6), 728-744. https://doi.org/10.1016/j.cpr.2013.05.002

Dimitrova, L. I., Dean, S. L., Schlumpf, Y. R., Vissia, E. M., Nijenhuis, E. R. S., Chatzi, V., et al. (2023). A neurostructural biomarker of dissociative amnesia: a hippocampal study in dissociative identity disorder. *Psychological medicine, 53*(3), 805-813. https://doi.org/10.1017/S0033291721002154

Dobrushina, O. R., Vlasova, R. M., Rumshiskaya, A. D., Litvinova, L. D., Mershina, E. A., Sinitsyn, V. E., et al. (2020). Modulation of Intrinsic Brain Connectivity by Implicit Electroencephalographic Neurofeedback. *Frontiers in human neuroscience, 14*, 192. https://doi.org/10.3389/fnhum.2020.00192

Dolan, S., Martindale, S., Robinson, J., Kimbrel, N. A., Meyer, E. C., Kruse, M. I., et al. (2012). Neuropsychological Sequelae of PTSD and TBI Following War Deployment among OEF/OIF Veterans. *Neuropsychology Review, 22*(1), 21-34. https://doi.org/10.1007/s11065-012-9190-5

Domingo-Fernández, D., Provost, A., Kodamullil, A. T., Marín-Llaó, J., Lasseter, H., Diaz, K., et al. (2019). PTSD Biomarker Database: deep dive metadatabase for PTSD biomarkers, visualizations and analysis tools. *Database : the journal of biological databases and curation, 2019*. https://doi.org/10.1093/database/baz081

Duda, J. M., Keding, T. J., Kribakaran, S., Odriozola, P., Kitt, E. R., Cohodes, E. M., et al. (2025). Exposure to unpredictable childhood environments is associated with amygdala activation during early extinction in adulthood. *Developmental cognitive neuroscience, 74*, 101578. https://doi.org/10.1016/j.dcn.2025.101578

Dudai, Y. (2006). Reconsolidation: the advantage of being refocused. *Current opinion in neurobiology, 16*(2), 174-8. https://doi.org/10.1016/j.conb.2006.03.010

Dudai, Y. (2012). The restless engram: consolidations never end. *Annual review of neuroscience, 35*, 227-47. https://doi.org/10.1146/annurev-neuro-062111-150500

Dukic, S., McMackin, R., Costello, E., Metzger, M., Buxo, T., Fasano, A., et al. (2022). Resting-state EEG reveals four subphenotypes of amyotrophic lateral sclerosis. *Brain : a journal of neurology, 145*(2), 621-631. https://doi.org/10.1093/brain/awab322

Dunbar, A. B., & Taylor, J. R. (2016). Inhibition of protein synthesis but not β-adrenergic receptors blocks reconsolidation of a cocaine-associated cue memory. *Learning & memory (Cold Spring Harbor, N.Y.), 23*(8), 391-8. https://doi.org/10.1101/lm.042838.116

Dutra, S. J., & Wolf, E. J. (2017). Perspectives on the conceptualization of the dissociative subtype of PTSD and implications for treatment. *Current opinion in psychology, 14*, 35-39. https://doi.org/10.1016/j.copsyc.2016.10.003

Dutton, M. A., Dahlgren, S., Martinez, M., & Mete, M. (2023). The holistic healing arts retreat: An intensive, experiential intervention for survivors of interpersonal trauma. *Psychological trauma : theory, research, practice and policy, 15*(5), 727-737. https://doi.org/10.1037/tra0001178

Eaton, E., Capone, C., Gully, B. J., Brown, Z. E., Monnig, M., Worden, M. S., et al. (2024). Design and methodology of the first open-label trial of MDMA-assisted therapy for veterans with post-traumatic stress disorder and alcohol use disorder: Considerations for a randomized controlled trial. *Contemporary clinical trials communications, 41*, 101333. https://doi.org/10.1016/j.conctc.2024.101333

Ecker, B., Ticic, R., & Hulley, L. (2012). *Unlocking the emotional brain: Eliminating symptoms at their roots using memory reconsolidation*. Routledge.

Eddie, D., Vaschillo, E., Vaschillo, B., & Lehrer, P. (2015). Heart rate variability biofeedback: Theoretical basis, delivery, and its potential for the treatment of substance use disorders. *Addiction Research & Theory, 23*(4), 266-272. https://doi.org/10.3109/16066359.2015.1011625

Ehlers, A., & Clark, D. M. (2000). A cognitive model of posttraumatic stress disorder. *Behaviour research and therapy, 38*(4), 319-45. https://doi.org/10.1016/s0005-7967(99)00123-0

Ehrenkranz, R., Agrawal, M., Nayak, S. M., & Yaden, D. B. (2025). Adverse Events Should Not Be Surprising in Psychedelic Research. *Psychedelic medicine (New Rochelle, N.Y.), 3*(1), 59-62. https://doi.org/10.1089/psymed.2024.0006

Ehret, M. (2019). Treatment of posttraumatic stress disorder: Focus on pharmacotherapy. *The mental health clinician, 9*(6), 373-382. https://doi.org/10.9740/mhc.2019.11.373

Elsey, J. W. B., Van Ast, V. A., & Kindt, M. (2018). Human memory reconsolidation: A guiding framework and critical review of the evidence. *Psychological Bulletin, 144*(8), 797–848. https://doi.org/10.1037/bul0000152

Engelhard, I. M., van Uijen, S. L., & van den Hout, M. A. (2010). The impact of taxing working memory on negative and positive memories. *European journal of psychotraumatology, 1*. https://doi.org/10.3402/ejpt.v1i0.5623

Erickson, K. I., Voss, M. W., Prakash, R. S., Basak, C., Szabo, A., Chaddock, L., et al. (2011). Exercise training increases size of hippocampus and improves memory. *Proceedings of the National Academy of Sciences, 108*(7), 3017-3022. https://doi.org/10.1073/pnas.1015950108

Escolano, C., Navarro-Gil, M., Garcia-Campayo, J., Congedo, M., & Minguez, J. (2014a). The effects of individual upper alpha neurofeedback in ADHD: an open-label pilot study. *Applied psychophysiology and biofeedback, 39*(3-4), 193-202. https://doi.org/10.1007/s10484-014-9257-6

Escolano, C., Navarro-Gil, M., Garcia-Campayo, J., & Minguez, J. (2014b). The effects of a single session of upper alpha neurofeedback for cognitive enhancement: a sham-controlled study. *Applied psychophysiology and biofeedback, 39*(3-4), 227-36. https://doi.org/10.1007/s10484-014-9262-9

Etkin, A., Egner, T., & Kalisch, R. (2011). Emotional processing in anterior cingulate and medial prefrontal cortex. *Trends in cognitive sciences, 15*(2), 85-93. https://doi.org/10.1016/j.tics.2010.11.004

Etkin, A., & Wager, T. D. (2007). Functional neuroimaging of anxiety: A meta-analysis of emotional processing in PTSD, social anxiety disorder, and specific phobia. *American Journal of Psychiatry, 164*(10), 1476–1488. https://doi.org/10.1176/appi.ajp.2007.07030504

Evans, G. W., & Schamberg, M. A. (2009). Childhood poverty, chronic stress, and adult working memory. *Proceedings of the National Academy of Sciences of the United States of America, 106*(16), 6545–6549. https://doi.org/10.1073/pnas.0811910106

Fan, L., & Kang, T. (2025). Early childhood trauma and its long-term impact on cognitive and emotional development: a systematic review and meta-analysis. *Annals of medicine, 57*(1), 2536199. https://doi.org/10.1080/07853890.2025.2536199

Farias, M., Maraldi, E., Wallenkampf, K. C., & Lucchetti, G. (2020). Adverse events in meditation practices and meditation-based therapies: a systematic review. *Acta psychiatrica Scandinavica, 142*(5), 374-393. https://doi.org/10.1111/acps.13225

Farrelly, S., Peters, E., Azis, M., David, A., & Hunter, E. C. (2016). A brief CBT intervention for depersonalisation/derealisation in psychosis: study protocol for a feasibility randomised controlled trial. *Pilot and feasibility studies, 2*, 47. https://doi.org/10.1186/s40814-016-0086-7

Feder, A., Costi, S., Rutter, S. B., Collins, A. B., Govindarajulu, U., Jha, M. K., et al. (2021). A Randomized Controlled Trial of Repeated Ketamine Administration for Chronic Posttraumatic Stress Disorder. *The American journal of psychiatry, 178*(2), 193-202. https://doi.org/10.1176/appi.ajp.2020.20050596

Feder, A., Parides, M. K., Murrough, J. W., Perez, A. M., Morgan, J. E., Saxena, S., et al. (2014). Efficacy of intravenous ketamine for treatment of chronic posttraumatic stress disorder: a randomized clinical trial. *JAMA psychiatry, 71*(6), 681-8. https://doi.org/10.1001/jamapsychiatry.2014.62

Feduccia, A. A., & Mithoefer, M. C. (2018). MDMA-assisted psychotherapy for PTSD: Are memory reconsolidation and fear extinction underlying mechanisms?. *Progress in neuro-psychopharmacology & biological psychiatry, 84*(Pt A), 221-228. https://doi.org/10.1016/j.pnpbp.2018.03.003

Fehr, B. S., Katz, W. F., Van Enkevort, E. A., & Khawaja, I. S. (2018). Obstructive Sleep Apnea in Posttraumatic Stress Disorder Comorbid With Mood Disorder. *The Primary Care Companion For CNS Disorders, 20*(4). https://doi.org/10.4088/PCC.18m02281

Fein, G., & Cardenas, V. A. (2015). Neuroplasticity in Human Alcoholism: Studies of Extended Abstinence with Potential Treatment Implications. *Alcohol research : current reviews, 37*(1), 125-41. https://doi.org/10.35946/arcr.v37.1.09

Felitti, V. J., Anda, R. F., Nordenberg, D., Williamson, D. F., Spitz, A. M., Edwards, V., et al. (1998). Relationship of childhood abuse and household dysfunction to many of the leading causes of death in adults. The Adverse Childhood Experiences (ACE) Study. *American journal of preventive medicine, 14*(4), 245-58. https://doi.org/10.1016/s0749-3797(98)00017-8

Férat, V., Seeber, M., Michel, C. M., & Ros, T. (2022). Beyond broadband: Towards a spectral decomposition of electroencephalography microstates. *Human brain mapping, 43*(10), 3047-3061. https://doi.org/10.1002/hbm.25834

Fernández, R. S., Boccia, M. M., & Pedreira, M. E. (2016). The fate of memory: Reconsolidation and the case of Prediction Error. *Neuroscience and biobehavioral reviews, 68*, 423-441. https://doi.org/10.1016/j.neubiorev.2016.06.004

Fischer, Q. S., Aleem, S., Zhou, H., & Pham, T. A. (2007). Adult visual experience promotes recovery of primary visual cortex from long-term monocular deprivation. *Learning & memory (Cold Spring Harbor, N.Y.), 14*(9), 573-80. https://doi.org/10.1101/lm.676707

Fisher, J. (2017). *Healing the fragmented selves of trauma survivors: Overcoming internal self-alienation*. Routledge. https://doi.org/10.4324/9781315886169

Fisher, S. F. (2014). *Neurofeedback in the treatment of developmental trauma: Calming the fear-driven brain*. W. W. Norton.

Fitzgerald, J. M., DiGangi, J. A., & Phan, K. L. (2018). Functional Neuroanatomy of Emotion and Its Regulation in PTSD. *Harvard review of psychiatry*, *26*(3), 116-128. https://doi.org/10.1097/HRP.0000000000000185

Fleming, L. L., Harnett, N. G., & Ressler, K. J. (2024). Sensory alterations in post-traumatic stress disorder. *Current opinion in neurobiology*, *84*, 102821. https://doi.org/10.1016/j.conb.2023.102821

Fonzo, G. A., Federchenco, V., & Lara, A. (2020). Predicting and Managing Treatment Non-Response in Posttraumatic Stress Disorder. *Current treatment options in psychiatry*, *7*(2), 70-87. https://doi.org/10.1007/s40501-020-00203-1

Förstner, B. R., Tschorn, M., Reinoso-Schiller, N., Maričić, L. M., Röcher, E., Kalman, J. L., et al. (2023). Mapping Research Domain Criteria using a transdiagnostic mini-RDoC assessment in mental disorders: a confirmatory factor analysis. *European archives of psychiatry and clinical neuroscience*, *273*(3), 527-539. https://doi.org/10.1007/s00406-022-01440-6

Foster, B. L., & Koslov, S. R. (2025). Functions of the posterior cingulate cortex and default network. *Current opinion in behavioral sciences*, *65*, 101560. https://doi.org/10.1016/j.cobeha.2025.101560 PMID: 41050212

Frazier, P., Tennen, H., Gavian, M., Park, C., Tomich, P., & Tashiro, T. (2009). Does self-reported posttraumatic growth reflect genuine positive change? *Psychological Science*, *20*(7), 912–919. https://doi.org/10.1111/j.1467-9280.2009.02381.x

Fremont, R., Brown, O., Feder, A., & Murrough, J. (2023). Ketamine for Treatment of Post-traumatic Stress Disorder: State of the Field. *Focus (American Psychiatric Publishing)*, *21*(3), 257-265. https://doi.org/10.1176/appi.focus.20230006

Frewen, P. A., & Lanius, R. A. (2006). Toward a psychobiology of posttraumatic self-dysregulation: reexperiencing, hyperarousal, dissociation, and emotional numbing. *Annals of the New York Academy of Sciences*, *1071*, 110-24. https://doi.org/10.1196/annals.1364.010

Frewen, P. A., & Lanius, R. A. (2014). Trauma-related altered states of consciousness: exploring the 4-D model. *Journal of trauma & dissociation : the official journal of the International Society for the Study of Dissociation (ISSD)*, *15*(4), 436-56. https://doi.org/10.1080/15299732.2013.873377

Friston, K. (2009). The free-energy principle: A rough guide to the brain? *Trends in Cognitive Sciences*, *13*(7), 293–301. https://doi.org/10.1016/j.tics.2009.04.005

Fujita, S., Mori, S., Onda, K., Hanaoka, S., Nomura, Y., Nakao, T., et al. (2023). Characterization of Brain Volume Changes in Aging Individuals With Normal Cognition Using Serial Magnetic Resonance Imaging. *JAMA network open*, *6*(6), e2318153. https://doi.org/10.1001/jamanetworkopen.2023.18153

Fuller, A., Jenkins, K., Kreutzer, K., House, A., Toleson, S., King, A., et al. (2026). The Impact of Error-Related Brain Activity and Parental Attachment on Youth Posttraumatic Stress Symptoms. *Psychophysiology*, *63*(4), e70295. https://doi.org/10.1111/psyp.70295

Furnari, F., Park, H., Yaffe, G., & Hampson, M. (2024). Neurofeedback: potential for abuse and regulatory frameworks in the United States. *Philosophical transac-*

tions of the Royal Society of London. Series B, Biological sciences, 379(1915), 20230099. https://doi.org/10.1098/rstb.2023.0099

Gainer, D., Alam, S., Alam, H., & Redding, H. (2020). A FLASH OF HOPE: Eye Movement Desensitization and Reprocessing (EMDR) Therapy. *Innovations in clinical neuroscience, 17*(7-9), 12-20.

Gallagher, M. W., & Resick, P. A. (2012). Mechanisms of Change in Cognitive Processing Therapy and Prolonged Exposure Therapy for PTSD: Preliminary Evidence for the Differential Effects of Hopelessness and Habituation. *Cognitive therapy and research, 36*(6). https://doi.org/10.1007/s10608-011-9423-6

Gao, Q., Ping, X., & Chen, W. (2019). Body Influences on Social Cognition Through Interoception. *Frontiers in psychology, 10*, 2066. https://doi.org/10.3389/fpsyg.2019.02066

Garfinkel, S. N., Seth, A. K., Barrett, A. B., Suzuki, K., & Critchley, H. D. (2015). Knowing your own heart: Distinguishing interoceptive accuracy from interoceptive awareness. *Biological Psychology, 104*, 65-74. https://doi.org/10.1016/j.biopsycho.2014.11.004

Garland, E. L., Pettus-Davis, C., & Howard, M. O. (2013). Self-medication among traumatized youth: structural equation modeling of pathways between trauma history, substance misuse, and psychological distress. *Journal of Behavioral Medicine, 36*(2), 175-185. https://doi.org/10.1007/s10865-012-9413-5

Gentzler, A. L., Santucci, A. K., Kovacs, M., & Fox, N. A. (2009). Respiratory sinus arrhythmia reactivity predicts emotion regulation and depressive symptoms in at-risk and control children. *Biological psychology, 82*(2), 156-63. https://doi.org/10.1016/j.biopsycho.2009.07.002

Genzer, S., Ong, D. C., Zaki, J., & Perry, A. (2022). Mu rhythm suppression over sensorimotor regions is associated with greater empathic accuracy. *Social cognitive and affective neuroscience, 17*(9), 788-801. https://doi.org/10.1093/scan/nsac011

Geraerts, E., Schooler, J. W., Merckelbach, H., Jelicic, M., Hauer, B. J., & Ambadar, Z. (2007). The reality of recovered memories: Corroborating continuous and discontinuous memories of childhood sexual abuse. *Psychological Science, 18*(7), 564-568. https://doi.org/10.1111/j.1467-9280.2007.01940.x

Gerhardt, A., Leisner, S., Hartmann, M., Janke, S., Seidler, G. H., Eich, W., et al. (2016). Eye Movement Desensitization and Reprocessing vs. Treatment-as-Usual for Non-Specific Chronic Back Pain Patients with Psychological Trauma: A Randomized Controlled Pilot Study. *Frontiers in psychiatry, 7*, 201. https://doi.org/10.3389/fpsyt.2016.00201

Geronimus, A. T. (1992). The weathering hypothesis and the health of African-American women and infants: Evidence and speculations. *Ethnicity & Disease, 2*(3), 207–221. PMID: 1467758

Geronimus, A. T. (2023). *Weathering: The extraordinary stress of ordinary life in an unjust society*. Little, Brown Spark.

Geronimus, A. T., Hicken, M., Keene, D., & Bound, J. (2006). "Weathering" and age patterns of allostatic load scores among Blacks and Whites in the United States. *American Journal of Public Health, 96*(5), 826–833. https://doi.org/10.2105/AJPH.2004.060749

Gerritsen, R. J. S., & Band, G. P. H. (2018). Breath of Life: The Respiratory Vagal Stimulation Model of Contemplative Activity. *Frontiers in human neuroscience, 12*, 397. https://doi.org/10.3389/fnhum.2018.00397

Geva, R., Zivan, M., Warsha, A., & Olchik, D. (2013). Alerting, orienting or executive attention networks: differential patters of pupil dilations. *Frontiers in behavioral neuroscience, 7*, 145. https://doi.org/10.3389/fnbeh.2013.00145

Gevensleben, H., Albrecht, B., Lütcke, H., Auer, T., Dewiputri, W. I., Schweizer, R., et al. (2014). Neurofeedback of slow cortical potentials: neural mechanisms and feasibility of a placebo-controlled design in healthy adults. *Frontiers in human neuroscience, 8*, 990. https://doi.org/10.3389/fnhum.2014.00990

Gilbert, K., Codd, R. T., Hoyniak, C., Tillman, R., Baudinet, J., Pires, P. P., et al. (2023). Processes of change in a randomized clinical trial of radically open dialectical behavior therapy (RO DBT) for adults with treatment-refractory depression. *Journal of Consulting and Clinical Psychology, 91*(2), 71-81. https://doi.org/10.1037/ccp0000795

Gilbert, P., Matos, M., Basran, J., Morter, K., Plowright, P., Ferreira, A., et al. (2025). Development of a multicomponent survey of experiences of tragedy-based and fear-based trauma in COVID-19 healthcare professionals. *Frontiers in psychology, 16*, 1513067. https://doi.org/10.3389/fpsyg.2025.1513067

Giridharan, S., Soumian, S., Kumar, N. V., & Godbole, M. (2025). The Impact of Vipassana Meditation on Health and Well-Being: A Systematic Review of Current Evidence. *Cureus, 17*(9), e93355. https://doi.org/10.7759/cureus.93355

Gitler, A., Bar Yosef, Y., Kotzer, U., & Levine, A. D. (2025). using non-invasive vagal neuromodulation: HRV biofeedback and SSP for cardiovascular and autonomic regulation (Review). *Medicine international, 5*(4), 1-13. https://doi.org/10.3892/mi.2025.236

Glazebrook, A., Shakespeare-Finch, J., Andrew, B., & van der Meer, J. (2023). Posttraumatic growth EEG neuromarkers: translational neural comparisons with resilience and PTSD in trauma-exposed healthy adults. *European Journal of Psychotraumatology, 14*(2). https://doi.org/10.1080/20008066.2023.2272477

Goldberg, S. B., Lam, S. U., Britton, W. B., & Davidson, R. J. (2022). Prevalence of meditation-related adverse effects in a population-based sample in the United States. *Psychotherapy research : journal of the Society for Psychotherapy Research, 32*(3), 291-305. https://doi.org/10.1080/10503307.2021.1933646

Goltermann, J., Winter, N. R., Meinert, S., Grotegerd, D., Kraus, A., Flinkenflugel, K., et al. (2025). Gray matter correlates of childhood maltreatment lack replicability in a multi-cohort brain-wide association study. *Nature Communications, 16*, 8290. https://doi.org/10.1038/s41467-025-62374-w

Gorantla, V. R., Tedesco, S., Chandanathil, M., Maity, S., Bond, V., Lewis, C., et al. (2020). Associations of Alpha and Beta Interhemispheric EEG Coherences with Indices of Attentional Control and Academic Performance. *Behavioural neurology, 2020*, 4672340. https://doi.org/10.1155/2020/4672340

Goyal, M., Singh, S., Sibinga, E. M. S., Gould, N. F., Rowland-Seymour, A., Sharma, R., et al. (2014). Meditation programs for psychological stress and well-being: a systematic review and meta-analysis. *JAMA internal medicine, 174*(3), 357-68. https://doi.org/10.1001/jamainternmed.2013.13018

Grech, R., Cassar, T., Muscat, J., Camilleri, K. P., Fabri, S. G., Zervakis, M., et al. (2008). Review on solving the inverse problem in EEG source analysis. *Journal of neuroengineering and rehabilitation, 5*, 25. https://doi.org/10.1186/1743-0003-5-25

Greven, C. U., Lionetti, F., Booth, C., Aron, E. N., Fox, E., Schendan, H. E., Pluess, M., Kumsta, R., Boele, S., Bijttebier, P., & Homberg, J. (2019). Sensory Processing Sensitivity in the context of Environmental Sensitivity: A critical review and development of research agenda. *Neuroscience & Biobehavioral Reviews, 98*, 287-305. https://doi.org/10.1016/j.neubiorev.2019.01.009

Grillon, C. (2008). Models and mechanisms of anxiety: evidence from startle studies. *Psychopharmacology, 199*(3), 421-437. https://doi.org/10.1007/s00213-007-1019-1

Gross, J. J. (1998). The emerging field of emotion regulation: An integrative review. *Review of General Psychology*, 2(3), 271–299. https://doi.org/10.1037/1089-2680.2.3.271

Grossman, P. (2023). Fundamental challenges and likely refutations of the five basic premises of the polyvagal theory. *Biological psychology, 180*, 108589. https://doi.org/10.1016/j.biopsycho.2023.108589

Grossman, P., Ackland, G. L., Allen, A. M., Berntson, G. G. B., Booth, L. C., Burghardt, G. M., et al. (2026). Why The Polyvagal Theory Is Untenable: An international expert evaluation of the polyvagal theory and commentary upon Porges, S.W. (2025). Polyvagal theory: current status, clinical applications, and future directions. Clin. Neuropsychiatry, 22(3), 169-184. *Clinical neuropsychiatry, 23*(1), 100-112. https://doi.org/10.36131/cnfioritieditore20260110 PMID: 41768017

Grossman, P., & Taylor, E. W. (2007). Toward understanding respiratory sinus arrhythmia: relations to cardiac vagal tone, evolution and biobehavioral functions. *Biological psychology, 74*(2), 263-85. https://doi.org/10.1016/j.biopsycho.2005.11.014

Gruzelier, J. (2009). A theory of alpha/theta neurofeedback, creative performance enhancement, long distance functional connectivity and psychological integration. *Cognitive processing, 10 Suppl 1*, S101-9. https://doi.org/10.1007/s10339-008-0248-5

Gruzelier, J., Egner, T., & Vernon, D. (2006). Validating the efficacy of neurofeedback for optimising performance. *Progress in brain research, 159*, 421-31. https://doi.org/10.1016/S0079-6123(06)59027-2

Gutner, C. A., Galovski, T., Bovin, M. J., & Schnurr, P. P. (2016). Emergence of Transdiagnostic Treatments for PTSD and Posttraumatic Distress. *Current psychiatry reports, 18*(10), 95. https://doi.org/10.1007/s11920-016-0734-x

Haase, L., Thom, N. J., Shukla, A., Davenport, P. W., Simmons, A. N., Stanley, E. A., et al. (2016). Mindfulness-based training attenuates insula response to an aversive interoceptive challenge. *Social cognitive and affective neuroscience, 11*(1), 182-90. https://doi.org/10.1093/scan/nsu042

Hackman, D. A., Farah, M. J., & Meaney, M. J. (2010). Socioeconomic status and the brain: Mechanistic insights from human and animal research. *Nature Reviews Neuroscience, 11*(9), 651–659. https://doi.org/10.1038/nrn2897

Haeyen, S. (2024). A theoretical exploration of polyvagal theory in creative arts and psychomotor therapies for emotion regulation in stress and trauma. *Frontiers in psychology, 15*, 1382007. https://doi.org/10.3389/fpsyg.2024.1382007

Hall, N. T., & Hallquist, M. N. (2023). Dissociation of basolateral and central amygdala effective connectivity predicts the stability of emotion-related impulsivity in adolescents and emerging adults with borderline personality symptoms: a resting-state fMRI study. *Psychological medicine, 53*(8), 3533-3547. https://doi.org/10.1017/S0033291722000101

Hammond, D. C. (2005). Neurofeedback with anxiety and affective disorders. *Child and adolescent psychiatric clinics of North America, 14*(1), 105-23, vii. https://doi.org/10.1016/j.chc.2004.07.008

Hanevik, E., Røvik, F. M. G., Bøe, T., Knapstad, M., & Smith, O. R. F. (2023). Client predictors of therapy dropout in a primary care setting: a prospective cohort study. *BMC psychiatry, 23*(1), 358. https://doi.org/10.1186/s12888-023-04878-7

Hansen, M., Robinson, M., & Armour, C. (2025). Investigating risk factors of dissociative and complex posttraumatic stress disorder across diagnostic systems and potential implications: Latent class analyses. *Psychological trauma : theory, research, practice and policy, 17*(8), 1680-1690. https://doi.org/10.1037/tra0001851

Hardy, K. V. (2013). Healing the hidden wounds of racial trauma. *Reclaiming Children and Youth, 22*(1), 24–28.

Harnett, N. G., Fleming, L. L., Clancy, K. J., Ressler, K. J., & Rosso, I. M. (2025). Affective Visual Circuit Dysfunction in Trauma and Stress-Related Disorders. *Biological psychiatry, 97*(4), 405-416. https://doi.org/10.1016/j.biopsych.2024.07.003

Harricharan, S., McKinnon, M. C., & Lanius, R. A. (2021). How Processing of Sensory Information From the Internal and External Worlds Shape the Perception and Engagement With the World in the Aftermath of Trauma: Implications for PTSD. *Frontiers in neuroscience, 15*, 625490. https://doi.org/10.3389/fnins.2021.625490

Hase, M., Balmaceda, U. M., Ostacoli, L., Liebermann, P., & Hofmann, A. (2017). The AIP Model of EMDR Therapy and Pathogenic Memories. *Frontiers in psychology, 8*, 1578. https://doi.org/10.3389/fpsyg.2017.01578

Hatzenbuehler, M. L. (2016). Structural stigma: Research evidence and implications for psychological science. *American Psychologist, 71*(8), 742–751. https://doi.org/10.1037/amp0000068

Haveman, M. E., Van Putten, M. J. A. M., Hom, H. W., Eertman-Meyer, C. J., Beishuizen, A., & Tjepkema-Cloostermans, M. C. (2019). Predicting outcome in patients with moderate to severe traumatic brain injury using electroencephalography. *Critical care (London, England), 23*(1), 401. https://doi.org/10.1186/s13054-019-2656-6

Hawn, S. E., Cusack, S. E., & Amstadter, A. B. (2020). A Systematic Review of the Self-Medication Hypothesis in the Context of Posttraumatic Stress Disorder and Comorbid Problematic Alcohol Use. *Journal of Traumatic Stress, 33*(5), 699-708. https://doi.org/10.1002/jts.22521

Hensch, T. K., & Bilimoria, P. M. (2012). Re-opening Windows: Manipulating Critical Periods for Brain Development. *Cerebrum : the Dana forum on brain science, 2012*, 11.

Herbert, J. D., & Mueser, K. T. (1992). Eye movement desensitization: a critique of the evidence. *Journal of behavior therapy and experimental psychiatry, 23*(3), 169-74. https://doi.org/10.1016/0005-7916(92)90033-f

Herkt, D., Tumani, V., Grön, G., Kammer, T., Hofmann, A., & Abler, B. (2014). Facilitating access to emotions: neural signature of EMDR stimulation. *PloS one, 9*(8), e106350. https://doi.org/10.1371/journal.pone.0106350

Herrero-Roldán, S., & Martín-Rodríguez, A. (2025). Neglect and Neurodevelopment: A Narrative Review Understanding the Link Between Child Neglect and Executive Function Deficits. *Biomedicines, 13*(7). https://doi.org/10.3390/biomedicines13071565

Herringa, R. J. (2017). Trauma, PTSD, and the Developing Brain. *Current psychiatry reports, 19*(10), 69. https://doi.org/10.1007/s11920-017-0825-3

Hertzberg, M. A., Butterfield, M. I., Feldman, M. E., Beckham, J. C., Sutherland, S. M., Connor, K. M., et al. (1999). A preliminary study of lamotrigine for the treatment of posttraumatic stress disorder. *Biological psychiatry, 45*(9), 1226-9. https://doi.org/10.1016/s0006-3223(99)00011-6

Hetrick, S. E., Purcell, R., Garner, B., & Parslow, R. (2010). Combined pharmacotherapy and psychological therapies for post traumatic stress disorder (PTSD). *The Cochrane database of systematic reviews, 2010*(7), CD007316. https://doi.org/10.1002/14651858.CD007316.pub2

Hildebrand, A., Grand, D., & Stemmler, M. (2017). Brainspotting, the efficacy of a new therapy approach for the treatment of posttraumatic stress disorder in comparison to eye movement desensitization and reprocessing. *Mediterranean Journal of Clinical Psychology, 5*(1), 1–15. https://doi.org/10.6092/2282-1619/2017.5.1376

Hirshberg, M. J., Goldberg, S. B., Rosenkranz, M., & Davidson, R. J. (2022). Prevalence of harm in mindfulness-based stress reduction. *Psychological medicine, 52*(6), 1080-1088. https://doi.org/10.1017/S0033291720002834

Ho, T. C., & King, L. S. (2021). Mechanisms of neuroplasticity linking early adversity to depression: developmental considerations. *Translational psychiatry, 11*(1), 517. https://doi.org/10.1038/s41398-021-01639-6

Hochschild, A. R. (1983). *The managed heart: Commercialization of human feeling*. University of California Press.

Hoeboer, C. M., De Kleine, R. A., Molendijk, M. L., Schoorl, M., Oprel, D. A. C., Mouthaan, J., et al. (2020). Impact of dissociation on the effectiveness of psychotherapy for post-traumatic stress disorder: meta-analysis. *BJPsych open, 6*(3), e53. https://doi.org/10.1192/bjo.2020.30

Hoffmann, J. A., Parikh, T. K., Lorenz, D., Goldman, M. P., Powers, E. M., Patel, S. J., et al. (2026). Clinically Significant Neuroimaging Findings Among Pediatric Patients Presenting to the Emergency Department With Symptoms of Psychosis: A Multicenter Retrospective Study. *Academic emergency medicine : official journal of the Society for Academic Emergency Medicine, 33*(1), e70155. https://doi.org/10.1111/acem.70155

Holmes, J. (2022). Friston's free energy principle: new life for psychoanalysis?. *BJPsych Bulletin, 46*(3), 164-168. https://doi.org/10.1192/bjb.2021.6

Hong, J., & Park, J. (2022). Efficacy of Neuro-Feedback Training for PTSD Symptoms: A Systematic Review and Meta-Analysis. *International journal of environmental research and public health, 19*(20). https://doi.org/10.3390/ijerph192013096

Hudays, A., Gallagher, R., Hazazi, A., Arishi, A., & Bahari, G. (2022). Eye Movement Desensitization and Reprocessing versus Cognitive Behavior Therapy for Treating Post-Traumatic Stress Disorder: A Systematic Review and Meta-Analysis. *International journal of environmental research and public health, 19*(24). https://doi.org/10.3390/ijerph192416836

Hughes, J. R., & John, E. R. (1999). Conventional and Quantitative Electroencephalography in Psychiatry. *The Journal of Neuropsychiatry and Clinical Neurosciences, 11*(2), 190-208. https://doi.org/10.1176/jnp.11.2.190

Humphreys, K. L., Nelson, C. A., Fox, N. A., & Zeanah, C. H. (2022). build care leads to sustained cognitive gains following severe early deprivation. *Proceedings of the National Academy of Sciences of the United States of America, 119*(38), e2119318119. https://doi.org/10.1073/pnas.2119318119

Imel, Z. E., Laska, K., Jakupcak, M., & Simpson, T. L. (2013). Meta-analysis of dropout in treatments for posttraumatic stress disorder. *Journal of consulting and clinical psychology, 81*(3), 394-404. https://doi.org/10.1037/a0031474

International Society for the Study of Trauma and Dissociation. (2011). Guidelines for treating dissociative identity disorder in adults, third revision. *Journal of Trauma & Dissociation, 12*(2), 115–187. https://doi.org/10.1080/15299732.2011.537247

Ioannidis, J. P. A. (2015). Failure to Replicate: Sound the Alarm. *Cerebrum : the Dana forum on brain science, 2015*. PMID: 27420921

Ironson, G., Freund, B., Strauss, J. L., & Williams, J. (2002). Comparison of two treatments for traumatic stress: a community-based study of EMDR and prolonged exposure. *Journal of clinical psychology, 58*(1), 113-28. https://doi.org/10.1002/jclp.1132

Janssen, T. W. P., Bink, M., Geladé, K., van Mourik, R., Maras, A., & Oosterlaan, J. (2016). A randomized controlled trial into the effects of neurofeedback, methylphenidate, and physical activity on EEG power spectra in children with ADHD. *Journal of child psychology and psychiatry, and allied disciplines, 57*(5), 633-44. https://doi.org/10.1111/jcpp.12517

Jia, Y., Ye, Z., Yang, F., Chai, J., Xu, H., Yang, J., et al. (2025). Pharmacotherapy for post-traumatic stress disorder: systematic review and meta-analysis. *Therapeutic advances in psychopharmacology, 15*, 20451253251342628. https://doi.org/10.1177/20451253251342628

Johannessen, K. N., Bakken, A., Hambrick, E. P., & Solbakken, O. A. (2024). Treatment Effects of Introducing the Neurosequential Model of Therapeutics in a Norwegian Residential Treatment Facility for Children Aged 7-13. *Children (Basel, Switzerland), 11*(5). https://doi.org/10.3390/children11050503

Johnson, K. E., & Brown, M. J. (2026). The long-term impact of adverse childhood experiences on episodic memory in mid- to late-life among US older adults. *Aging & Mental Health*, 1-11. https://doi.org/10.1080/13607863.2026.2621787

Johnstone, J., Gunkelman, J., & Lunt, J. (2005). Clinical database development: characterization of EEG phenotypes. *Clinical EEG and neuroscience, 36*(2), 99-107. https://doi.org/10.1177/155005940503600209

Jonsson, U., Johanson, J., Nilsson, E., & Lindblad, F. (2016). Adverse effects of psychological therapy: An exploratory study of practitioners' experiences from child and adolescent psychiatry. *Clinical child psychology and psychiatry, 21*(3), 432-46. https://doi.org/10.1177/1359104515614072

Joshi, S. A., Aupperle, R. L., & Khalsa, S. S. (2023). Interoception in Fear Learning and Posttraumatic Stress Disorder. *Focus, 21*(3), 266-277. https://doi.org/10.1176/appi.focus.20230007

Joshi, S., Manandhar, A., & Sharma, P. (2021). Meditation-Induced Psychosis: Trigger and Recurrence. *Case reports in psychiatry, 2021*, 6615451. https://doi.org/10.1155/2021/6615451

Joss, D., Comeau, A., Chevannes, R., Parry, G., Rea, H. S., Barria, J., et al. (2026). A randomized controlled trial of an online group-based internal family systems treatment for posttraumatic stress disorder: The Program for Alleviating and Resolving Trauma and Stress (PARTS) study. *Psychological trauma : theory, research, practice and policy*. https://doi.org/10.1037/tra0002089

Juster, R., McEwen, B. S., & Lupien, S. J. (2010). Allostatic load biomarkers of chronic stress and impact on health and cognition. *Neuroscience and biobehavioral reviews, 35*(1), 2-16. https://doi.org/10.1016/j.neubiorev.2009.10.002

Kapur, V. K., Auckley, D. H., Chowdhuri, S., Kuhlmann, D. C., Mehra, R., Ramar, K., & Harrod, C. G. (2017). Clinical practice guideline for diagnostic testing for adult obstructive sleep apnea: An American Academy of Sleep Medicine clinical practice guideline. *Journal of clinical sleep medicine, 13*(3), 479-504. https://doi.org/10.5664/jcsm.6506

Karatzias, T., Mc Glanaghy, E., & Cloitre, M. (2023). Enhanced Skills Training in Affective and Interpersonal Regulation (ESTAIR): A New Modular Treatment for ICD-11 Complex Posttraumatic Stress Disorder (CPTSD). *Brain sciences, 13*(9). https://doi.org/10.3390/brainsci13091300

Karpicke, J. D., & Blunt, J. R. (2011). Retrieval practice produces more learning than elaborative studying with concept mapping. *Science (New York, N.Y.), 331*(6018), 772-5. https://doi.org/10.1126/science.1199327

Kawai, H., Kishimoto, M., Okahisa, Y., Sakamoto, S., Terada, S., & Takaki, M. (2023). Initial Outcomes of the Safe and Sound Protocol on Patients with Adult Autism Spectrum Disorder: Exploratory Pilot Study. *International journal of environmental research and public health, 20*(6). https://doi.org/10.3390/ijerph20064862

Kearney, D. J., Malte, C. A., Storms, M., & Simpson, T. L. (2021). Loving-kindness meditation vs cognitive processing therapy for posttraumatic stress disorder among veterans: A randomized clinical trial. *JAMA Network Open, 4*(4), e216604. https://doi.org/10.1001/jamanetworkopen.2021.6604

Kedwany, A. M., Sayad, R., Jibril, N. S., Hawash, E. A., Anis, A. M., John Wadie Danial, N., et al. (2025). improving ketamine dosing strategies across diverse clinical applications: a comprehensive review. *Annals of medicine and surgery (2012), 87*(9), 5678-5687. https://doi.org/10.1097/MS9.0000000000003580

Kenemore, J., Benham, G., Charak, R., & Hernandez Rodriguez, J. (2024). Heart Rate Variability Biofeedback as a Treatment for Military PTSD: A Meta-Analysis. *Military Medicine, 189*(9-10), e1903-e1909. https://doi.org/10.1093/milmed/usae003

Kessler, R. C., Sonnega, A., Bromet, E., Hughes, M., & Nelson, C. B. (1995). Posttraumatic stress disorder in the National Comorbidity Survey. *Archives of General Psychiatry, 52*(12), 1048-1060. https://doi.org/10.1001/archpsyc.1995.03950240066012

Khalil, M. H. (2025). The Impact of Walking on BDNF as a Biomarker of Neuroplasticity: A Systematic Review. *Brain Sciences, 15*(3), 254. https://doi.org/10.3390/brainsci15030254

Khalsa, S. S., Adolphs, R., Cameron, O. G., Critchley, H. D., Davenport, P. W., Feinstein, J. S., Feusner, J. D., Garfinkel, S. N., Lane, R. D., Mehling, W. E., Meuret, A. E., Nemeroff, C. B., Oppenheimer, S., Petzschner, F. H., Pollatos, O., Rhudy, J. L., Schramm, L. P., Simmons, W. K., Stein, M. B., et al. (2018). Interoception and mental health: A roadmap. *Biological Psychiatry: Cognitive Neuroscience and Neuroimaging, 3*(6), 501-513. https://doi.org/10.1016/j.bpsc.2017.12.004

Khan, A., Mar, K. F., & Brown, W. A. (2021). Consistently Modest Antidepressant Effects in Clinical Trials: the Role of Regulatory Requirements. *Psychopharmacology bulletin, 51*(3), 79-108. https://doi.org/10.64719/pb.4412

Killeen, T., Hien, D., Campbell, A., Brown, C., Hansen, C., Jiang, H., et al. (2008). Adverse events in an integrated trauma-focused intervention for women in community substance abuse treatment. *Journal of substance abuse treatment, 35*(3), 304-11. https://doi.org/10.1016/j.jsat.2007.12.001

Kim, D., Kim, D., Lee, H., Cho, Y., Min, J. Y., & Kim, S. H. (2019). Prevalence and clinical correlates of dissociative subtype of posttraumatic stress disorder at an outpatient trauma clinic in South Korea. *European journal of psychotraumatology, 10*(1), 1657372. https://doi.org/10.1080/20008198.2019.1657372

King, A. P., & Fresco, D. M. (2019). A neurobehavioral account for decentering as the salve for the distressed mind. *Current opinion in psychology, 28*, 285-293. https://doi.org/10.1016/j.copsyc.2019.02.009

King, S., Zhang, Z., Robinson, L., Whelan, R., Nees, F., Bobou, M., et al. (2026). Characterising a stress-sensitive default mode network (DMN) deficit in major psychiatric disorders. *Communications biology*. https://doi.org/10.1038/s42003-025-09400-1

Kingyon, J., Behroozmand, R., Kelley, R., Oya, H., Kawasaki, H., Narayanan, N. S., et al. (2015). High-gamma band fronto-temporal coherence as a measure of functional connectivity in speech motor control. *Neuroscience, 305*, 15-25. https://doi.org/10.1016/j.neuroscience.2015.07.069

Kirk, H. W., & Dahl, M. G. (2022). Infra Low Frequency Neurofeedback Training for Trauma Recovery: A Case Report. *Frontiers in human neuroscience, 16*, 905823. https://doi.org/10.3389/fnhum.2022.905823

Kirlic, N., Cohen, Z. P., Tsuchiyagaito, A., Misaki, M., McDermott, T. J., Aupperle, R. L., et al. (2022). Self-regulation of the posterior cingulate cortex with real-time fMRI neurofeedback augmented mindfulness training in healthy adolescents: A nonrandomized feasibility study. *Cognitive, affective & behavioral neuroscience, 22*(4), 849-867. https://doi.org/10.3758/s13415-022-00991-4

Klatte, R., Strauss, B., Flückiger, C., & Rosendahl, J. (2018). Adverse effects of psychotherapy: protocol for a systematic review and meta-analysis. *Systematic reviews, 7*(1), 135. https://doi.org/10.1186/s13643-018-0802-x

Klatte, R., Strauss, B., Flückiger, C., & Rosendahl, J. (2025). Adverse events in psychotherapy randomized controlled trials: A systematic review. *Psychotherapy research : journal of the Society for Psychotherapy Research, 35*(1), 84-99. https://doi.org/10.1080/10503307.2023.2286992

Kleim, B., Wallott, F., & Ehlers, A. (2008). Are Trauma Memories Disjointed from other Autobiographical Memories in Posttraumatic Stress Disorder? An Experimental Investigation. *Behavioural and cognitive psychotherapy, 36*(2), 221-34. https://doi.org/10.1017/S1352465807004080

Klimesch, W. (2012). α-band oscillations, attention, and controlled access to stored information. *Trends in cognitive sciences, 16*(12), 606-17. https://doi.org/10.1016/j.tics.2012.10.007

Ko, J., Park, U., Kim, D., & Kang, S. W. (2021). Quantitative Electroencephalogram Standardization: A Sex- and Age-Differentiated Normative Database. *Frontiers in neuroscience, 15*, 766781. https://doi.org/10.3389/fnins.2021.766781

Koob, G. F., & Volkow, N. D. (2016). Neurobiology of addiction: a neurocircuitry analysis. *The lancet. Psychiatry, 3*(8), 760-773. https://doi.org/10.1016/S2215-0366(16)00104-8

Koss, K. J., & Gunnar, M. R. (2018). Annual Research Review: Early adversity, the hypothalamic-pituitary-adrenocortical axis, and child psychopathology.

Journal of child psychology and psychiatry, and allied disciplines, 59(4), 327-346. https://doi.org/10.1111/jcpp.12784

Kovacevic, N., Meghdadi, A., & Berka, C. (2025). Characterizing PTSD Using Electrophysiology: Towards A Precision Medicine Approach. *Clinical EEG and neuroscience, 56*(4), 305-315. https://doi.org/10.1177/15500594241309680

Kozlowska, K., Walker, P., McLean, L., & Carrive, P. (2015). Fear and the Defense Cascade: Clinical Implications and Management. *Harvard review of psychiatry, 23*(4), 263-87. https://doi.org/10.1097/HRP.0000000000000065

Kraus, S. W., Krueger, R. B., Briken, P., First, M. B., Stein, D. J., Kaplan, M. S., et al. (2018). Compulsive sexual behaviour disorder in the ICD-11. *World psychiatry, 17*(1), 109-110. https://doi.org/10.1002/wps.20499

Krause-Utz, A., & Elzinga, B. (2018). Current Understanding of the Neural Mechanisms of Dissociation in Borderline Personality Disorder. *Current behavioral neuroscience reports, 5*(1), 113-123. https://doi.org/10.1007/s40473-018-0146-9

Kreutzer, K. A., & Gorka, S. M. (2021). Impact of Trauma Type on Startle Reactivity to Predictable and Unpredictable Threats. *Journal of Nervous & Mental Disease, 209*(12), 899-904. https://doi.org/10.1097/NMD.0000000000001394

Krüger-Gottschalk, A., Kuck, S. T., Dyer, A., Alpers, G. W., Pittig, A., Morina, N., et al. (2025). Effectiveness in routine care: trauma-focused treatment for PTSD. *European journal of psychotraumatology, 16*(1), 2452680. https://doi.org/10.1080/20008066.2025.2452680

Kuhfuß, M., Maldei, T., Hetmanek, A., & Baumann, N. (2021). Somatic experiencing - effectiveness and key factors of a body-oriented trauma therapy: a scoping literature review. *European journal of psychotraumatology, 12*(1), 1929023. https://doi.org/10.1080/20008198.2021.1929023

Kuhl, P. K., Conboy, B. T., Coffey-Corina, S., Padden, D., Rivera-Gaxiola, M., & Nelson, T. (2008). Phonetic learning as a pathway to language: new data and native language magnet theory expanded (NLM-e). *Philosophical transactions of the Royal Society of London. Series B, Biological sciences, 363*(1493), 979-1000. https://doi.org/10.1098/rstb.2007.2154

Lamb, D. G., Porges, E. C., Lewis, G. F., & Williamson, J. B. (2017). Non-invasive Vagal Nerve Stimulation Effects on Hyperarousal and Autonomic State in Patients with Posttraumatic Stress Disorder and History of Mild Traumatic Brain Injury: Preliminary Evidence. *Frontiers in medicine, 4*, 124. https://doi.org/10.3389/fmed.2017.00124

Lane, R. D., Ryan, L., Nadel, L., & Greenberg, L. (2015). Memory reconsolidation, emotional arousal, and the process of change in psychotherapy: New insights from brain science. *The Behavioral and brain sciences, 38*, e1. https://doi.org/10.1017/S0140525X14000041

Lanius, R. A. (2015). Trauma-related dissociation and altered states of consciousness: a call for clinical, treatment, and neuroscience research. *European journal of psychotraumatology, 6*, 27905. https://doi.org/10.3402/ejpt.v6.27905

Lanius, R. A., Boyd, J. E., McKinnon, M. C., Nicholson, A. A., Frewen, P., Vermetten, E., et al. (2018). A Review of the Neurobiological Basis of Trauma-Related Dissociation and Its Relation to Cannabinoid- and Opioid-Mediated Stress Response: a Transdiagnostic, Translational Approach. *Current psychiatry reports, 20*(12), 118. https://doi.org/10.1007/s11920-018-0983-y

Lanius, R. A., Brand, B., Vermetten, E., Frewen, P. A., & Spiegel, D. (2012). The dissociative subtype of posttraumatic stress disorder: rationale, clinical and neurobiological evidence, and implications. *Depression and anxiety, 29*(8), 701-8. https://doi.org/10.1002/da.21889

Lanius, R. A., Vermetten, E., Loewenstein, R. J., Brand, B., Schmahl, C., Bremner, J. D., et al. (2010). Emotion modulation in PTSD: Clinical and neurobiological evidence for a dissociative subtype. *The American journal of psychiatry, 167*(6), 640-7. https://doi.org/10.1176/appi.ajp.2009.09081168

Lanius, R. A., Williamson, P. C., Boksman, K., Densmore, M., Gupta, M., Neufeld, R. W. J., et al. (2002). Brain activation during script-driven imagery induced dissociative responses in PTSD: a functional magnetic resonance imaging investigation. *Biological psychiatry, 52*(4), 305-11. https://doi.org/10.1016/s0006-3223(02)01367-7

Larsen, S. E., Wiltsey Stirman, S., Smith, B. N., & Resick, P. A. (2016). Symptom exacerbations in trauma-focused treatments: Associations with treatment outcome and non-completion. *Behaviour research and therapy, 77*, 68-77. https://doi.org/10.1016/j.brat.2015.12.009

Lee, J. L. C. (2009). Reconsolidation: maintaining memory relevance. *Trends in neurosciences, 32*(8), 413-20. https://doi.org/10.1016/j.tins.2009.05.002

Lee, J. L. C., Nader, K., & Schiller, D. (2017). An Update on Memory Reconsolidation Updating. *Trends in cognitive sciences, 21*(7), 531-545. https://doi.org/10.1016/j.tics.2017.04.006

Lee, Y., Park, S., & Cho, Y. (2026). Phase-based versus non-phase-based psychological interventions for complex PTSD: a systematic review and meta-analysis. *European journal of psychotraumatology, 17*(1), 2644112. https://doi.org/10.1080/20008066.2026.2644112

Leech, K., Stapleton, P., & Patching, A. (2024). A roadmap to understanding interoceptive awareness and post-traumatic stress disorder: a scoping review. *Frontiers in Psychiatry, 15*. https://doi.org/10.3389/fpsyt.2024.1355442

Leech, R., & Sharp, D. J. (2014). The role of the posterior cingulate cortex in cognition and disease. *Brain : a journal of neurology, 137*(Pt 1), 12-32. https://doi.org/10.1093/brain/awt162

Legarda, S. B., McMahon, D., Othmer, S., & Othmer, S. (2011). Clinical neurofeedback: case studies, proposed mechanism, and implications for pediatric neurology practice. *Journal of child neurology, 26*(8), 1045-51. https://doi.org/10.1177/0883073811405052

Lehrer, P. M., Vaschillo, E., Vaschillo, B., Lu, S., Eckberg, D. L., Edelberg, R., et al. (2003). Heart rate variability biofeedback increases baroreflex gain and peak expiratory flow. *Psychosomatic medicine, 65*(5), 796-805. https://doi.org/10.1097/01.psy.0000089200.81962.19

Leone, G., Postel, C., Mary, A., Fraisse, F., Vallée, T., Viader, F., et al. (2022). Altered predictive control during memory suppression in PTSD. *Nature communications, 13*(1), 3300. https://doi.org/10.1038/s41467-022-30855-x

Levinson, D. B., Halverson, T. F., Wilson, S. M., & Fu, R. (2022). Less dropout from prolonged exposure sessions prescribed at least twice weekly: A meta-analysis and systematic review of randomized controlled trials. *Journal of traumatic stress, 35*(4), 1047-1059. https://doi.org/10.1002/jts.22822

Lewey, J. H., Smith, C. L., Burcham, B., Saunders, N. L., Elfallal, D., & O'Toole, S. K. (2018). Comparing the Effectiveness of EMDR and TF-CBT for Children and Adolescents: a Meta-Analysis. *Journal of child & adolescent trauma, 11*(4), 457-472. https://doi.org/10.1007/s40653-018-0212-1

Lewis, B. R., & Byrne, K. (2023). A Review of MDMA-Assisted Therapy for Posttraumatic Stress Disorder. *Focus (American Psychiatric Publishing), 21*(3), 247-256. https://doi.org/10.1176/appi.focus.20220088

Lewis, C., Roberts, N. P., Andrew, M., Starling, E., & Bisson, J. I. (2020a). Psychological therapies for post-traumatic stress disorder in adults: systematic review and meta-analysis. *European journal of psychotraumatology, 11*(1), 1729633. https://doi.org/10.1080/20008198.2020.1729633

Lewis, C., Roberts, N. P., Gibson, S., & Bisson, J. I. (2020b). Dropout from psychological therapies for post-traumatic stress disorder (PTSD) in adults: Systematic review and meta-analysis. *European Journal of Psychotraumatology, 11*(1), 1709709. https://doi.org/10.1080/20008198.2019.1709709

Li, S., Teng, Z., Qiu, Y., Pan, P., Wu, C., Jin, K., et al. (2021). Dissociation Pattern in Default-Mode Network Homogeneity in Drug-Naive Bipolar Disorder. *Frontiers in psychiatry, 12*, 699292. https://doi.org/10.3389/fpsyt.2021.699292

Liang, M., Starrett, M. J., & Ekstrom, A. D. (2018). Dissociation of frontal-midline delta-theta and posterior alpha oscillations: A mobile EEG study. *Psychophysiology, 55*(9), e13090. https://doi.org/10.1111/psyp.13090

Lieberman, J. M., Rabellino, D., Densmore, M., Frewen, P. A., Steyrl, D., Scharnowski, F., et al. (2023a). Posterior cingulate cortex targeted real-time fMRI neurofeedback recalibrates functional connectivity with the amygdala, posterior insula, and default-mode network in PTSD. *Brain and behavior, 13*(3), e2883. https://doi.org/10.1002/brb3.2883

Lieberman, J. M., Rabellino, D., Densmore, M., Frewen, P. A., Steyrl, D., Scharnowski, F., et al. (2023b). A tale of two targets: examining the differential effects of posterior cingulate cortex- and amygdala-targeted fMRI-neurofeedback in a PTSD pilot study. *Frontiers in neuroscience, 17*, 1229729. https://doi.org/10.3389/fnins.2023.1229729

Lieberman, L., Funkhouser, C. J., Gorka, S. M., Liu, H., Correa, K. A., Berenz, E. C., et al. (2020). The Relation Between Posttraumatic Stress Symptom Severity and Startle Potentiation to Predictable and Unpredictable Threat. *Journal of Nervous & Mental Disease, 208*(5), 397-402. https://doi.org/10.1097/NMD.0000000000001138

Lindahl, J. R., Fisher, N. E., Cooper, D. J., Rosen, R. K., & Britton, W. B. (2017). The varieties of contemplative experience: A mixed-methods study of meditation-related challenges in Western Buddhists. *PloS one, 12*(5), e0176239. https://doi.org/10.1371/journal.pone.0176239

Linden, M. (2013). How to define, find and classify side effects in psychotherapy: from unwanted events to adverse treatment reactions. *Clinical psychology & psychotherapy, 20*(4), 286-96. https://doi.org/10.1002/cpp.1765

Linson, A., Parr, T., & Friston, K. J. (2020). Active inference, stressors, and psychological trauma: A neuroethological model of (mal)adaptive explore-exploit dynamics in ecological context. *Behavioural Brain Research, 380*, 112421. https://doi.org/10.1016/j.bbr.2019.112421

Little, A. L. (2025). The A52 Breath Method: A Narrative Review of Breathwork for Mental Health and Stress Resilience. *Stress and Health, 41*(4). https://doi.org/10.1002/smi.70098

Livint Popa, L., Dragos, H., Pantelemon, C., Verisezan Rosu, O., & Strilciuc, S. (2020). The Role of Quantitative EEG in the Diagnosis of Neuropsychiatric Disorders. *Journal of medicine and life, 13*(1), 8-15. https://doi.org/10.25122/jml-2019-0085

Longden, E., Madill, A., & Waterman, M. G. (2012). Dissociation, trauma, and the role of lived experience: Toward a new conceptualization of voice hearing. *Psychological Bulletin, 138*(1), 28–76. https://doi.org/10.1037/a0025995

López-Castro, T., Martin, L., Nickley, S., Saraiya, T. C., & Melara, R. D. (2023). Frontal Alpha Asymmetry in Posttraumatic Stress Disorder: Group Differences Among Individuals With and Without PTSD During an Inhibitory Control Task. *Clinical EEG and Neuroscience, 54*(5), 472-482. https://doi.org/10.1177/15500594211046703

Lubar, J. F., & Bahler, W. W. (1976). Behavioral management of epileptic seizures following EEG biofeedback training of the sensorimotor rhythm. *Biofeedback and self-regulation, 1*(1), 77-104. https://doi.org/10.1007/BF00998692

Lubar, J. F., Swartwood, M. O., Swartwood, J. N., & O'Donnell, P. H. (1995). Evaluation of the effectiveness of EEG neurofeedback training for ADHD in a clinical setting as measured by changes in T.O.V.A. scores, behavioral ratings, and WISC-R performance. *Biofeedback and self-regulation, 20*(1), 83-99. https://doi.org/10.1007/BF01712768

Lunkenheimer, E., Tiberio, S. S., Skoranski, A. M., Buss, K. A., & Cole, P. M. (2018). Parent-child coregulation of parasympathetic processes varies by social context and risk for psychopathology. *Psychophysiology, 55*(2). https://doi.org/10.1111/psyp.12985

Lupien, S. J., & Lepage, M. (2001). Stress, memory, and the hippocampus: can't live with it, can't live without it. *Behavioural brain research, 127*(1-2), 137-58. https://doi.org/10.1016/s0166-4328(01)00361-8

Lynch, K. S., & Lachman, M. E. (2020). The effects of lifetime trauma exposure on cognitive functioning in midlife. *Journal of Traumatic Stress, 33*(5), 773–782. https://doi.org/10.1002/jts.22522

Ma, J., Zhang, Z., Su, Y., Kang, L., Geng, D., Wang, Y., et al. (2013). Magnetic stimulation modulates structural synaptic plasticity and regulates BDNF-TrkB signal pathway in cultured hippocampal neurons. *Neurochemistry international, 62*(1), 84-91. https://doi.org/10.1016/j.neuint.2012.11.010

MacCulloch, M. J., & Feldman, P. (1996). Eye movement desensitisation treatment utilises the positive visceral element of the investigatory reflex to inhibit the memories of post-traumatic stress disorder: a theoretical analysis. *The British journal of psychiatry : the journal of mental science, 169*(5), 571-9. https://doi.org/10.1192/bjp.169.5.571

Maercker, A., & Zoellner, T. (2004). The Janus face of self-perceived growth: Toward a two-component model of posttraumatic growth. *Psychological Inquiry, 15*(1), 41–48. https://doi.org/10.1207/s15327965pli1501_02

Manchia, M., Pisanu, C., Squassina, A., & Carpiniello, B. (2020). Challenges and Future Prospects of Precision Medicine in Psychiatry. *Pharmacogenomics and personalized medicine, 13*, 127-140. https://doi.org/10.2147/PGPM.S198225

Mani, A., Mullainathan, S., Shafir, E., & Zhao, J. (2013). Poverty impedes cognitive function. *Science, 341*(6149), 976–980. https://doi.org/10.1126/science.1238041

Mansour, M., Joseph, G. R., Joy, G. K., Khanal, S., Dasireddy, R. R., Menon, A., et al. (2023). Post-traumatic Stress Disorder: A Narrative Review of Pharmacological and Psychotherapeutic Interventions. *Cureus, 15*(9), e44905. https://doi.org/10.7759/cureus.44905

Marcinkowska, A. B., Kucewicz, M. T., Szarmach, A., & Winklewski, P. J. (2025). The Dorsolateral Prefrontal Cortex: A High-level Hub for Allostatic Cardiovascular Control. *Current neuropharmacology, 23*(9), 1036-1046. https://doi.org/10.2174/011570159X340612241121072233

Marcu, G. M., Băcilă, C. I., & Zăgrean, A. (2024). Temporal-Posterior Alpha Power in Resting-State Electroencephalography as a Potential Marker of Complex Childhood Trauma in Institutionalized Adolescents. *Brain sciences, 14*(6). https://doi.org/10.3390/brainsci14060584

Marcu, G. M., Müller, A., & Kropotov, J. Y. D. (2025a). Event-related potentials associated with cognitive control in adolescents exposed to complex childhood trauma. *European journal of psychotraumatology, 16*(1), 2494363. https://doi.org/10.1080/20008066.2025.2494363

Marcu, G. M., Szekely-Copîndean, R. D., Dumbravă, A., Rogel, A., & Zăgrean, A. (2025b). qEEG Neuromarkers of Complex Childhood Trauma in Adolescents. *Clinical EEG and neuroscience, 56*(5), 468-482. https://doi.org/10.1177/15500594241309456

Marinova, Z., & Maercker, A. (2015). Biological correlates of complex posttraumatic stress disorder-state of research and future directions. *European journal of psychotraumatology, 6*, 25913. https://doi.org/10.3402/ejpt.v6.25913

Marlatte, H., Beaton, D., Adler-Luzon, S., Abo-Ahmad, L., & Gilboa, A. (2022). Scene Construction and Spatial Processing in Post-traumatic Stress Disorder. *Frontiers in behavioral neuroscience, 16*, 888358. https://doi.org/10.3389/fnbeh.2022.888358

Marshall, R. D., & Cloitre, M. (2000). Maximizing treatment outcome in post-traumatic stress disorder by combining psychotherapy with pharmacotherapy. *Current psychiatry reports*, 2(4), 335-40. https://doi.org/10.1007/s11920-000-0078-3

Martin, A. K., Kessler, K., Cooke, S., Huang, J., & Meinzer, M. (2020). The right temporoparietal junction is causally associated with embodied perspective-taking. *Journal of Neuroscience, 40*(15), 3089-3095. https://doi.org/10.1523/JNEUROSCI.2637-19.2020

Martinez, P., Grinand, M., Cheggour, S., Taieb, J., & Gourjon, G. (2024). How to properly evaluate cardiac vagal tone in oncology studies: a state-of-the-art review. *Journal of the National Cancer Center, 4*(1), 36-46. https://doi.org/10.1016/j.jncc.2024.02.002

Marzano, C., Ferrara, M., Mauro, F., Moroni, F., Gorgoni, M., Tempesta, D., et al. (2011). Recalling and forgetting dreams: theta and alpha oscillations during sleep predict subsequent dream recall. *The Journal of neuroscience : the official journal of the Society for Neuroscience, 31*(18), 6674-83. https://doi.org/10.1523/JNEUROSCI.0412-11.2011

Marzbani, H., Marateb, H. R., & Mansourian, M. (2016). Neurofeedback: A Comprehensive Review on System Design, Methodology and Clinical Applications. *Basic and clinical neuroscience, 7*(2), 143-58. https://doi.org/10.15412/J.BCN.03070208

Matko, K., & Van Dam, N. T. (2026). Beyond serenity: Adverse effects of meditation and mindfulness in clinical practice. *Current opinion in psychology, 67*, 102197. https://doi.org/10.1016/j.copsyc.2025.102197

Matsuyanagi, K. (2025). Can electroencephalography-based neurofeedback treat post-traumatic stress disorder? A meta-analysis study. *Applied Psychophysiology and Biofeedback, 50*(3), 329-348. https://doi.org/10.1007/s10484-025-09701-5

Mattson, E. K., Nelson, N. W., Sponheim, S. R., & Disner, S. G. (2019). The impact of PTSD and mTBI on the relationship between subjective and objective cognitive deficits in combat-exposed veterans. *Neuropsychology, 33*(7), 913-921. https://doi.org/10.1037/neu0000560

Mattson, M. P., & Arumugam, T. V. (2018). Hallmarks of Brain Aging: Adaptive and Pathological Modification by Metabolic States. *Cell metabolism, 27*(6), 1176-1199. https://doi.org/10.1016/j.cmet.2018.05.011

Mayo, O., Lavidor, M., & Gordon, I. (2021). Interpersonal autonomic nervous system synchrony and its association to relationship and performance: A systematic review and meta-analysis. *Physiology & Behavior, 235,* 113391. https://doi.org/10.1016/j.physbeh.2021.113391

McAdams, D. P. (2006). *The redemptive self: Stories Americans live by.* Oxford University Press. https://doi.org/10.1093/acprof:oso/9780195176933.001.0001

McAdams, D. P., & McLean, K. C. (2013). Narrative identity. *Current Directions in Psychological Science, 22*(3), 233–238. https://doi.org/10.1177/0963721413475622

McCabe, D. P., Roediger, H. L., McDaniel, M. A., Balota, D. A., & Hambrick, D. Z. (2010). The relationship between working memory capacity and executive functioning: evidence for a common executive attention construct. *Neuropsychology, 24*(2), 222-243. https://doi.org/10.1037/a0017619

McCall, C. A., & Watson, N. F. (2022). A Narrative Review of the Association between Post-Traumatic Stress Disorder and Obstructive Sleep Apnea. *Journal of Clinical Medicine, 11*(2), 415. https://doi.org/10.3390/jcm11020415

McConnell, G. C., So, R. Q., & Grill, W. M. (2016). Failure to suppress low-frequency neuronal oscillatory activity underlies the reduced effectiveness of random patterns of deep brain stimulation. *Journal of neurophysiology, 115*(6), 2791-802. https://doi.org/10.1152/jn.00822.2015

McEwen, B. S. (1998). Stress, adaptation, and disease: Allostasis and allostatic load. *Annals of the New York Academy of Sciences, 840*(1), 33–44. https://doi.org/10.1111/j.1749-6632.1998.tb09546.x

McEwen, B. S., & Stellar, E. (1993). Stress and the individual: Mechanisms leading to disease. *Archives of Internal Medicine, 153*(18), 2093–2101. https://doi.org/10.1001/archinte.1993.00410180039004

McIntosh, R. C., Hoshi, R., Nomi, J. S., Di Bello, M., Goodman, Z. T., Kornfeld, S., et al. (2020). Neurovisceral integration in the executive control network: A resting state analysis. *Biological psychology, 157,* 107986. https://doi.org/10.1016/j.biopsycho.2020.107986

McLaughlin, K. A., Sheridan, M. A., & Lambert, H. K. (2014). Childhood adversity and neural development: deprivation and threat as distinct dimensions of early experience. *Neuroscience and biobehavioral reviews, 47,* 578-91. https://doi.org/10.1016/j.neubiorev.2014.10.012

McLaughlin, K. A., Weissman, D., & Bitrán, D. (2019). Childhood Adversity and Neural Development: A Systematic Review. *Annual review of developmental psychology, 1,* 277-312. https://doi.org/10.1146/annurev-devpsych-121318-084950

McLean, C. P., & Foa, E. B. (2024). State of the Science: Prolonged exposure therapy for the treatment of posttraumatic stress disorder. *Journal of traumatic stress, 37*(4), 535-550. https://doi.org/10.1002/jts.23046

Meewisse, M.-L., Reitsma, J. B., de Vries, G.-J., Gersons, B. P. R., & Olff, M. (2007). Cortisol and post-traumatic stress disorder in adults: Systematic review and meta-analysis. *British Journal of Psychiatry, 191*(5), 387-392. https://doi.org/10.1192/bjp.bp.106.024877

Mehling, W. E., Daubenmier, J., Price, C. J., Acree, M., Bartmess, E., & Stewart, A. L. (2013). Self-reported interoceptive awareness in primary care patients with past or current low back pain. *Journal of pain research, 6,* 403-18. https://doi.org/10.2147/JPR.S42418

Mehling, W. E., Price, C., Daubenmier, J. J., Acree, M., Bartmess, E., & Stewart, A. (2012). The Multidimensional Assessment of Interoceptive Awareness (MAIA). *PLoS ONE, 7*(11), e48230. https://doi.org/10.1371/journal.pone.0048230

Meiers, G., Nooner, K., De Bellis, M. D., Debnath, R., & Tang, A. (2020). Alpha EEG asymmetry, childhood maltreatment, and problem behaviors: A pilot home-based study. *Child abuse & neglect, 101*, 104358. https://doi.org/10.1016/j.chiabu.2020.104358

Menakem, R. (2017). *My grandmother's hands: Racialized trauma and the pathway to mending our hearts and bodies.* Central Recovery Press.

Menon, V. (2011). Large-scale brain networks and psychopathology: A unifying triple network model. *Trends in Cognitive Sciences, 15*(10), 483–506. https://doi.org/10.1016/j.tics.2011.08.003

Mertens, Y. L., Manthey, A., Sierk, A., Walter, H., & Daniels, J. K. (2022). Neural correlates of acute post-traumatic dissociation: a functional neuroimaging script-driven imagery study. *BJPsych open, 8*(4), e109. https://doi.org/10.1192/bjo.2022.65

Meyer, I. H. (2003). Prejudice, social stress, and mental health in lesbian, gay, and bisexual populations: Conceptual issues and research evidence. *Psychological Bulletin, 129*(5), 674–697. https://doi.org/10.1037/0033-2909.129.5.674

Michopoulos, V., Norrholm, S. D., & Jovanovic, T. (2015). Diagnostic Biomarkers for Posttraumatic Stress Disorder: Promising Horizons from Translational Neuroscience Research. *Biological psychiatry, 78*(5), 344-53. https://doi.org/10.1016/j.biopsych.2015.01.005

Miller, D. R., Hayes, S. M., Hayes, J. P., Spielberg, J. M., Lafleche, G., & Verfaellie, M. (2017). Default Mode Network Subsystems are Differentially Disrupted in Posttraumatic Stress Disorder. *Biological psychiatry. Cognitive neuroscience and neuroimaging, 2*(4), 363-371. https://doi.org/10.1016/j.bpsc.2016.12.006

Mills, A. C., Badour, C. L., Korte, K. J., Killeen, T. K., Henschel, A. V., & Back, S. E. (2017). Integrated Treatment of PTSD and Substance Use Disorders: Examination of Imaginal Exposure Length. *Journal of traumatic stress, 30*(2), 166-172. https://doi.org/10.1002/jts.22175

Minuchin, S. (1974). *Families and family therapy.* Harvard University Press.

Mitchell, J. M., Bogenschutz, M., Lilienstein, A., Harrison, C., Kleiman, S., Parker-Guilbert, K., et al. (2021). MDMA-assisted therapy for severe PTSD: a randomized, double-blind, placebo-controlled phase 3 study. *Nature medicine, 27*(6), 1025-1033. https://doi.org/10.1038/s41591-021-01336-3

Modesti, M. N., Rapisarda, L., Capriotti, G., & Del Casale, A. (2022). Functional Neuroimaging in Dissociative Disorders: A Systematic Review. *Journal of personalized medicine, 12*(9). https://doi.org/10.3390/jpm12091405

Mohamed, A., Touheed, S., Ahmed, M., Hor, M., & Fatima, S. (2022). The Efficacy of Psychedelic-Assisted Therapy in Managing Post-traumatic Stress Disorder (PTSD): A New Frontier?. *Cureus, 14*(10), e30919. https://doi.org/10.7759/cureus.30919

Monfils, M., Cowansage, K. K., Klann, E., & LeDoux, J. E. (2009). Extinction-reconsolidation boundaries: key to persistent attenuation of fear memories. *Science (New York, N.Y.), 324*(5929), 951-5. https://doi.org/10.1126/science.1167975

Montag, C., & Davis, K. L. (2018). Affective Neuroscience Theory and Personality: An Update. *Personality neuroscience, 1*, e12. https://doi.org/10.1017/pen.2018.10

Moore, N. C. (2000). A review of EEG biofeedback treatment of anxiety disorders. *Clinical EEG (electroencephalography)*, *31*(1), 1-6. https://doi.org/10.1177/155005940003100105

Morales-Quezada, L., Martinez, D., El-Hagrassy, M. M., Kaptchuk, T. J., Sterman, M. B., & Yeh, G. Y. (2019). Neurofeedback impacts cognition and quality of life in pediatric focal epilepsy: An exploratory randomized double-blinded sham-controlled trial. *Epilepsy & behavior : E&B*, *101*(Pt A), 106570. https://doi.org/10.1016/j.yebeh.2019.106570

Moriyama, T. S., Polanczyk, G., Caye, A., Banaschewski, T., Brandeis, D., & Rohde, L. A. (2012). Evidence-based information on the clinical use of neurofeedback for ADHD. *Neurotherapeutics : the journal of the American Society for Experimental NeuroTherapeutics*, *9*(3), 588-98. https://doi.org/10.1007/s13311-012-0136-7

Moss, D., & Gunkelman, J. (2002). Task Force Report on methodology and empirically supported treatments: introduction. *Applied psychophysiology and biofeedback*, *27*(4), 271-2. https://doi.org/10.1023/a:1021009301517

Mullainathan, S., & Shafir, E. (2013). *Scarcity: Why having too little means so much*. Times Books.

Mullally, S. L., Hassabis, D., & Maguire, E. A. (2012). Scene construction in amnesia: an FMRI study. *The Journal of neuroscience : the official journal of the Society for Neuroscience*, *32*(16), 5646-53. https://doi.org/10.1523/JNEUROSCI.5522-11.2012

Murad, S. T., Hansen, A. L., Sim, L. A., & Murad, M. H. (2024). Heterogeneity in Treatment Effect in Posttraumatic Stress Syndrome Trials: A Meta-Regression Analysis. *Mayo Clinic proceedings. Innovations, quality & outcomes*, *8*(3), 301-307. https://doi.org/10.1016/j.mayocpiqo.2024.04.003

Murphy, R. J. (2023). Depersonalization/Derealization Disorder and Neural Correlates of Trauma-related Pathology: A Critical Review. *Innovations in clinical neuroscience*, *20*(1-3), 53-59. PMID: 37122581

Nader, K., Schafe, G. E., & LeDoux, J. E. (2000). Fear memories require protein synthesis in the amygdala for reconsolidation after retrieval. *Nature*, *406*(6797), 722-6. https://doi.org/10.1038/35021052

Navratilova, Z., Banerjee, D., Muqolli, F., Zhang, J., Gandhi, S. P., & McNaughton, B. L. (2026). Place field dynamics in retrosplenial cortex compared to hippocampus. *Progress in neurobiology*, *257*, 102867. https://doi.org/10.1016/j.pneurobio.2025.102867

Neale, Z. E., Bountress, K., Sheerin, C., Saenz de Viteri, S., Cusack, S., Chorlian, D., et al. (2024). Childhood trauma is associated with developmental trajectories of EEG coherence, alcohol-related outcomes, and PTSD symptoms. *Psychological medicine*, *54*(15), 4302-4315. https://doi.org/10.1017/S0033291724002599

Nejati, V., Mardanpour, A., Zabihzaheh, A., Estaji, R., Vaziri, Z. S., & Shahidi, S. (2023). The role of prefrontal cortex and temporoparietal junction in interpersonal comfort and emotional approach. *Scientific Reports*, *13*(1). https://doi.org/10.1038/s41598-023-48099-0

Nelson, C. A., Zeanah, C. H., Fox, N. A., Marshall, P. J., Smyke, A. T., & Guthrie, D. (2007). Cognitive recovery in socially deprived young children: the Bucharest Early Intervention Project. *Science (New York, N.Y.)*, *318*(5858), 1937-40. https://doi.org/10.1126/science.1143921

Neuhaus, E., Bernier, R. A., & Beauchaine, T. P. (2016). Children with Autism Show Altered Autonomic Adaptation to Novel and Familiar Social Partners. *Autism research : official journal of the International Society for Autism Research*, *9*(5), 579-91. https://doi.org/10.1002/aur.1543

Newson, J. J., & Thiagarajan, T. C. (2018). EEG Frequency Bands in Psychiatric Disorders: A Review of Resting State Studies. *Frontiers in human neuroscience, 12*, 521. https://doi.org/10.3389/fnhum.2018.00521

Nicholson, A. A., Densmore, M., Frewen, P. A., Neufeld, R. W. J., Théberge, J., Jetly, R., et al. (2023). Homeostatic normalization of alpha brain rhythms within the default-mode network and reduced symptoms in post-traumatic stress disorder following a randomized controlled trial of electroencephalogram neurofeedback. *Brain communications, 5*(2), fcad068. https://doi.org/10.1093/braincomms/fcad068

Nicholson, A. A., Densmore, M., Frewen, P. A., Théberge, J., Neufeld, R. W., McKinnon, M. C., et al. (2015). The Dissociative Subtype of Posttraumatic Stress Disorder: Unique Resting-State Functional Connectivity of Basolateral and Centromedial Amygdala Complexes. *Neuropsychopharmacology : official publication of the American College of Neuropsychopharmacology, 40*(10), 2317-26. https://doi.org/10.1038/npp.2015.79

Nicholson, A. A., Friston, K. J., Zeidman, P., Harricharan, S., McKinnon, M. C., Densmore, M., et al. (2017). Dynamic causal modeling in PTSD and its dissociative subtype: Bottom-up versus top-down processing within fear and emotion regulation circuitry. *Human brain mapping, 38*(11), 5551-5561. https://doi.org/10.1002/hbm.23748

Nicholson, A. A., Harricharan, S., Densmore, M., Neufeld, R. W. J., Ros, T., McKinnon, M. C., et al. (2020a). Classifying heterogeneous presentations of PTSD via the default mode, central executive, and salience networks with machine learning. *NeuroImage. Clinical, 27*, 102262. https://doi.org/10.1016/j.nicl.2020.102262

Nicholson, A. A., Rabellino, D., Densmore, M., Frewen, P. A., Steyrl, D., Scharnowski, F., et al. (2022). Differential mechanisms of posterior cingulate cortex downregulation and symptom decreases in posttraumatic stress disorder and healthy individuals using real-time fMRI neurofeedback. *Brain and behavior, 12*(1), e2441. https://doi.org/10.1002/brb3.2441

Nicholson, A. A., Ros, T., Densmore, M., Frewen, P. A., Neufeld, R. W. J., Théberge, J., et al. (2020b). A randomized, controlled trial of alpha-rhythm EEG neurofeedback in posttraumatic stress disorder: A preliminary investigation showing evidence of decreased PTSD symptoms and restored default mode and salience network connectivity using fMRI. *NeuroImage. Clinical, 28*, 102490. https://doi.org/10.1016/j.nicl.2020.102490

Nicholson, A. A., Ros, T., Frewen, P. A., Densmore, M., Théberge, J., Kluetsch, R. C., et al. (2016a). Alpha oscillation neurofeedback modulates amygdala complex connectivity and arousal in posttraumatic stress disorder. *NeuroImage. Clinical, 12*, 506-516. https://doi.org/10.1016/j.nicl.2016.07.006

Nicholson, A. A., Sapru, I., Densmore, M., Frewen, P. A., Neufeld, R. W. J., Théberge, J., et al. (2016b). Unique insula subregion resting-state functional connectivity with amygdala complexes in posttraumatic stress disorder and its dissociative subtype. *Psychiatry research. Neuroimaging, 250*, 61-72. https://doi.org/10.1016/j.pscychresns.2016.02.002

Niwa, M., Kato, T., Narita-Ohtaki, R., Otomo, R., Suga, Y., Sugawara, M., et al. (2022). Skills Training in Affective and Interpersonal Regulation Narrative Therapy for women with ICD-11 complex PTSD related to childhood abuse in Japan: a pilot study. *European journal of psychotraumatology, 13*(1), 2080933. https://doi.org/10.1080/20008198.2022.2080933

Noble, K. G., Houston, S. M., Brito, N. H., Bartsch, H., Kan, E., Kuperman, J. M., et al. (2015). Family income, parental education and brain structure in children and adolescents. *Nature Neuroscience, 18*(5), 773–778. https://doi.org/10.1038/nn.3983

Noble, N. C., Sendi, M. S. E., Merker, J. B., Linton, S. R., Webber, T. K., Toll, R. T., et al. (2025). Posttraumatic Stress Disorder-Related Differences in Neural Connectivity Among Female Trauma Survivors. *Biological psychiatry global open science*, *5*(4), 100491. https://doi.org/10.1016/j.bpsgos.2025.100491

Norman, S. B., Luciano, M. T., Panza, K. E., Davis, B. C., Lyons, M., Martis, B., et al. (2025). A Randomized Clinical Trial of Prolonged Exposure Therapy With and Without Topiramate for Comorbid PTSD and Alcohol Use Disorder. *The American journal of psychiatry*, *182*(5), 452-462. https://doi.org/10.1176/appi.ajp.20240470

Ölçüoğlu, R. (2025). Neurofeedback for ADHD: Exploring the Role of Quantitative EEG and Brainwave Modulation. *Brain and behavior*, *15*(8), e70714. https://doi.org/10.1002/brb3.70714

Onyeama, F., Melegkovits, E., Yu, N., Parvez, A., Rodrigues, A., Billings, J., et al. (2024). A systematic review and meta-analysis of the traumatogenic phenotype hypothesis of psychosis. *BJPsych open*, *10*(5), e146. https://doi.org/10.1192/bjo.2024.52

Oprel, D. A. C., Hoeboer, C. M., Schoorl, M., de Kleine, R. A., Cloitre, M., Wigard, I. G., et al. (2021). Effect of prolonged exposure, intensified prolonged exposure and STAIR plus prolonged exposure in patients with PTSD related to childhood abuse: A randomized controlled trial. *European journal of psychotraumatology*, *12*(1), 1851511. https://doi.org/10.1080/20008198.2020.1851511

Orndorff-Plunkett, F., Singh, F., Aragón, O. R., & Pineda, J. A. (2017). Assessing the Effectiveness of Neurofeedback Training in the Context of Clinical and Social Neuroscience. *Brain sciences*, *7*(8). https://doi.org/10.3390/brainsci7080095

Otgaar, H., Howe, M. L., Patihis, L., Merckelbach, H., Lynn, S. J., Lilienfeld, S. O., et al. (2019). The Return of the Repressed: The Persistent and Problematic Claims of Long-Forgotten Trauma. *Perspectives on psychological science : a journal of the Association for Psychological Science*, *14*(6), 1072-1095. https://doi.org/10.1177/1745691619862306

Otto, A. R., Raio, C. M., Chiang, A., Phelps, E. A., & Daw, N. D. (2013). Working-memory capacity protects model-based learning from stress. *Proceedings of the National Academy of Sciences of the United States of America*, *110*(52), 20941-6. https://doi.org/10.1073/pnas.1312011110

Packard, M. G., & Teather, L. A. (1998). Amygdala modulation of multiple memory systems: hippocampus and caudate-putamen. *Neurobiology of learning and memory*, *69*(2), 163-203. https://doi.org/10.1006/nlme.1997.3815

Pagani, M., Amann, B. L., Landin-Romero, R., & Carletto, S. (2017). Eye Movement Desensitization and Reprocessing and Slow Wave Sleep: A Putative Mechanism of Action. *Frontiers in psychology*, *8*, 1935. https://doi.org/10.3389/fpsyg.2017.01935

Pagani, M., Castelnuovo, G., Daverio, A., La Porta, P., Monaco, L., Ferrentino, F., et al. (2018). Metabolic and Electrophysiological Changes Associated to Clinical Improvement in Two Severely Traumatized Subjects Treated With EMDR-A Pilot Study. *Frontiers in psychology*, *9*, 475. https://doi.org/10.3389/fpsyg.2018.00475

Pagani, M., Di Lorenzo, G., Monaco, L., Daverio, A., Giannoudas, I., La Porta, P., et al. (2015). Neurobiological response to EMDR therapy in clients with different psychological traumas. *Frontiers in psychology*, *6*, 1614. https://doi.org/10.3389/fpsyg.2015.01614

Pagani, M., Di Lorenzo, G., Verardo, A. R., Nicolais, G., Monaco, L., Lauretti, G., et al. (2012). Neurobiological correlates of EMDR monitoring - an EEG study. *PloS one, 7*(9), e45753. https://doi.org/10.1371/journal.pone.0045753

Palmisano, A. N., Meshberg-Cohen, S., Petrakis, I. L., & Sofuoglu, M. (2024). A systematic review evaluating PTSD treatment effects on intermediate phenotypes of PTSD. *Psychological trauma : theory, research, practice and policy, 16*(5), 768-783. https://doi.org/10.1037/tra0001410

Pan, J., Zhan, L., Hu, C., Yang, J., Wang, C., Gu, L., et al. (2018). Emotion Regulation and Complex Brain Networks: Association Between Expressive Suppression and Efficiency in the Fronto-Parietal Network and Default-Mode Network. *Frontiers in human neuroscience, 12*, 70. https://doi.org/10.3389/fnhum.2018.00070

Pan, Y., Vinding, M. C., Zhang, L., Lundqvist, D., & Olsson, A. (2023). A Brain-To-Brain Mechanism for Social Transmission of Threat Learning. *Advanced science (Weinheim, Baden-Wurttemberg, Germany), 10*(28), e2304037. https://doi.org/10.1002/advs.202304037

Paulus, M. P., & Stein, M. B. (2010). Interoception in anxiety and depression. *Brain Structure and Function, 214*(5-6), 451-463. https://doi.org/10.1007/s00429-010-0258-9

Peddi, A., Sendi, M. S. E., Minton, S. T., Langhinrichsen-Rohling, R., Hinojosa, C. A., West, E., et al. (2025). Towards predicting posttraumatic stress symptom severity using portable EEG-derived biomarkers. *Scientific Reports, 15*, 5344. https://doi.org/10.1038/s41598-025-88426-1

Peniston, E. G., & Kulkosky, P. J. (1989). Alpha-theta brainwave training and beta-endorphin levels in alcoholics. *Alcoholism, clinical and experimental research, 13*(2), 271-9. https://doi.org/10.1111/j.1530-0277.1989.tb00325.x

Peniston, E. G., & Kulkosky, P. J. (1991). Alpha-theta brainwave neuro-feedback for Vietnam veterans with combat-related post-traumatic stress disorder. *Medical Psychotherapy, 4*, 47–60.

Pennebaker, J. W., & Beall, S. K. (1986). Confronting a traumatic event: Toward an understanding of inhibition and disease. *Journal of Abnormal Psychology, 95*(3), 274-281. https://doi.org/10.1037/0021-843X.95.3.274

Perry, B. D. (2006). Applying principles of neurodevelopment to clinical work with maltreated and traumatized children: The neurosequential model of therapeutics. In N. B. Webb (Ed.), *Working with Traumatized Youth in Child Welfare* (pp. 27-52). Guilford Press.

Peterson, D. S., Gera, G., Horak, F. B., & Fling, B. W. (2017). Corpus Callosum Structural Integrity Is Associated With Postural Control Improvement in Persons With Multiple Sclerosis Who Have Minimal Disability. *Neurorehabilitation and neural repair, 31*(4), 343-353. https://doi.org/10.1177/1545968316680487

Petro, N. M., Ott, L. R., Penhale, S. H., Rempe, M. P., Embury, C. M., Picci, G., et al. (2022). Eyes-closed versus eyes-open differences in spontaneous neural dynamics during development. *NeuroImage, 258*, 119337. https://doi.org/10.1016/j.neuroimage.2022.119337

Pigott, H. E., Cannon, R., & Trullinger, M. (2021). The Fallacy of Sham-Controlled Neurofeedback Trials: A Reply to Thibault and Colleagues (2018). *Journal of attention disorders, 25*(3), 448-457. https://doi.org/10.1177/1087054718790802

Poldrack, R. A. (2011). Inferring mental states from neuroimaging data: from reverse inference to large-scale decoding. *Neuron, 72*(5), 692-7. https://doi.org/10.1016/j.neuron.2011.11.001

Poli, A., Cappellini, F., Sala, J., & Miccoli, M. (2023). The integrative process promoted by EMDR in dissociative disorders: neurobiological mechanisms, psychometric tools, and intervention efficacy on the psychological impact of the COVID-19 pandemic. *Frontiers in psychology, 14,* 1164527. https://doi.org/10.3389/fpsyg.2023.1164527

Ponnusamy, R., Zhuravka, I., Poulos, A. M., Shobe, J., Merjanian, M., Huang, J., et al. (2016). Retrieval and Reconsolidation Accounts of Fear Extinction. *Frontiers in behavioral neuroscience, 10,* 89. https://doi.org/10.3389/fnbeh.2016.00089

Porges, S. W. (2021). Polyvagal Theory: A biobehavioral journey to sociality. *Comprehensive psychoneuroendocrinology, 7,* 100069. https://doi.org/10.1016/j.cpnec.2021.100069

Porges, S. W. (2023). The vagal paradox: A polyvagal solution. *Comprehensive psychoneuroendocrinology, 16,* 100200. https://doi.org/10.1016/j.cpnec.2023.100200

Porges, S. W. (2025a). Polyvagal Theory: Current Status, Clinical Applications, and Future Directions. *Clinical neuropsychiatry, 22*(3), 169-184. https://doi.org/10.36131/cnfioritieditore20250301 PMID: 40735382

Porges, S. W. (2025b). Polyvagal theory: a journey from physiological observation to neural innervation and clinical insight. *Frontiers in behavioral neuroscience, 19,* 1659083. https://doi.org/10.3389/fnbeh.2025.1659083

Porges, S. W. (2026). When A Critique Becomes Untenable: A Scholarly Response To Grossman Et Al.'S Evaluation Of Polyvagal Theory. *Clinical neuropsychiatry, 23*(1), 113-128. https://doi.org/10.36131/cnfioritieditore20260111 PMID: 41768026

Potharst, E. S., Holtkamp, P., Walliser, L., Dommerholt, A. H., van den Heuvel, M. E. N., Spierts, I., et al. (2025). Improving Infant Mental Health: A Pilot Study on the Effectiveness, Acceptability and Feasibility of Eye Movement Desensitization and Reprocessing (EMDR) Storytelling in Infants With Post-traumatic Distress After Medical Procedures. *Evaluation & the health professions, 48*(1), 55-70. https://doi.org/10.1177/01632787241268176

Price, C. J., & Hooven, C. (2018). Interoceptive Awareness Skills for Emotion Regulation: Theory and Approach of Mindful Awareness in Body-Oriented Therapy (MABT). *Frontiers in Psychology, 9,* 798. https://doi.org/10.3389/fpsyg.2018.00798

Rabinak, C. A., Kilgore, P. E., Lumley, M. A., & Rauch, S. A. M. (2026). Randomized trial of delta-9-tetrahydrocannabinol (THC) versus placebo to augment the effects of prolonged exposure therapy on fear extinction learning in post-traumatic stress disorder: Study rationale and protocol. *Contemporary clinical trials, 160,* 108148. https://doi.org/10.1016/j.cct.2025.108148

Racz, J. I., Bialocerkowski, A., Calteaux, I., & Farrell, L. J. (2024). Determinants of Exposure Therapy Implementation in Clinical Practice for the Treatment of Anxiety, OCD, and PTSD: A Systematic Review. *Clinical child and family psychology review, 27*(2), 317-341. https://doi.org/10.1007/s10567-024-00478-3

Radiske, A., Gonzalez, M. C., Rossato, J. I., Conde-Ocazionez, S., & Cammarota, M. (2025). Theta-encoded information flow from dorsal CA1 to prelimbic cortex drives memory reconsolidation. *iScience, 28*(7), 112821. https://doi.org/10.1016/j.isci.2025.112821

Rajkumar, R. P. (2023). Biomarkers of Neurodegeneration in Post-Traumatic Stress Disorder: An Integrative Review. *Biomedicines, 11*(5). https://doi.org/10.3390/biomedicines11051465

Ram, D., Manjunatha, N., & Bada Math, S. (2026). Negative events in psychotherapy: A narrative review. *Industrial psychiatry journal, 35*(1), 15-24. https://doi.org/10.4103/ipj.ipj_114_25

Rapp, P. E., Keyser, D. O., Albano, A., Hernandez, R., Gibson, D. B., Zambon, R. A., et al. (2015). Traumatic Brain Injury Detection Using Electrophysiological Methods. *Frontiers in Human Neuroscience, 9*. https://doi.org/10.3389/fnhum.2015.00011

Raskind, M. A., Peskind, E. R., Kanter, E. D., Petrie, E. C., Radant, A., Thompson, C. E., et al. (2003). Reduction of nightmares and other PTSD symptoms in combat veterans by prazosin: a placebo-controlled study. *The American journal of psychiatry, 160*(2), 371-3. https://doi.org/10.1176/appi.ajp.160.2.371

Raskind, M. A., Peskind, E. R., Chow, B., Harris, C., Davis-Karim, A., Holmes, H. A., et al. (2018). Trial of Prazosin for Post-Traumatic Stress Disorder in Military Veterans. *New England Journal of Medicine, 378*(6), 507-517. https://doi.org/10.1056/NEJMoa1507598

Razlighi, Q. R. (2018). Task-Evoked Negative BOLD Response in the Default Mode Network Does Not Alter Its Functional Connectivity. *Frontiers in computational neuroscience, 12*, 67. https://doi.org/10.3389/fncom.2018.00067

Reinders, A. A. T. S. (2008). Cross-examining dissociative identity disorder: neuroimaging and etiology on trial. *Neurocase, 14*(1), 44-53. https://doi.org/10.1080/13554790801992768

Reiter, K., Andersen, S. B., & Carlsson, J. (2016). Neurofeedback Treatment and Posttraumatic Stress Disorder: Effectiveness of Neurofeedback on Posttraumatic Stress Disorder and the Optimal Choice of Protocol. *The Journal of nervous and mental disease, 204*(2), 69-77. https://doi.org/10.1097/NMD.0000000000000418

Riaz, K., Suneel, S., Hamza Bin Abdul Malik, M., Kashif, T., Ullah, I., Waris, A., et al. (2023). MDMA-Based Psychotherapy in Treatment-Resistant Post-Traumatic Stress Disorder (PTSD): A Brief Narrative Overview of Current Evidence. *Diseases (Basel, Switzerland), 11*(4). https://doi.org/10.3390/diseases11040159

Roback, H. B. (2000). Adverse outcomes in group psychotherapy: risk factors, prevention, and research directions. *The Journal of psychotherapy practice and research, 9*(3), 113-22. PMID: 10896735

Rolling, J., Fath, M., Zanfonato, T., Durpoix, A., Mengin, A. C., & Schröder, C. M. (2024). EMDR-Teens-cPTSD: Efficacy of Eye Movement Desensitization and Reprocessing in Adolescents with Complex PTSD Secondary to Childhood Abuse: A Case Series. *Healthcare (Basel, Switzerland), 12*(19). https://doi.org/10.3390/healthcare12191993

Romme, M., & Escher, S. (2000). *Making sense of voices: A guide for mental health professionals working with voice-hearers*. MIND Publications.

Rossini, P. M., & Dal Forno, G. (2004). Integrated technology for evaluation of brain function and neural plasticity. *Physical medicine and rehabilitation clinics of North America, 15*(1), 263-306. https://doi.org/10.1016/s1047-9651(03)00124-4

Rothärmel, M., Benosman, C., El-Hage, W., Berjamin, C., Ribayrol, D., Guillin, O., et al. (2022). Efficacy and Safety of Intranasal Esketamine in Patients With Treatment-Resistant Depression and Comorbid Chronic Post-traumatic Stress Disorder: Open-Label Single-Arm Pilot Study. *Frontiers in psychiatry, 13*, 865466. https://doi.org/10.3389/fpsyt.2022.865466

Roullet, P., Vaiva, G., Véry, E., Bourcier, A., Yrondi, A., Dupuch, L., et al. (2021). Traumatic memory reactivation with or without propranolol for PTSD and comorbid MD symptoms: a randomised clinical trial. *Neuropsychopharmacology : official publication of the American*

College of Neuropsychopharmacology, *46*(9), 1643-1649. https://doi.org/10.1038/s41386-021-00984-w

Rousseau, P., El Khoury-Malhame, M., Reynaud, E., Boukezzi, S., Cancel, A., Zendjidjian, X., et al. (2019). Fear extinction learning improvement in PTSD after EMDR therapy: an fMRI study. *European journal of psychotraumatology*, *10*(1), 1568132. https://doi.org/10.1080/20008198.2019.1568132

Rubin, A., Geva, N., Sheintuch, L., & Ziv, Y. (2015). Hippocampal ensemble dynamics timestamp events in long-term memory. *eLife*, *4*. https://doi.org/10.7554/eLife.12247

Salazar-Castro, J. A., Peluffo-Ordonez, D. H., & Lopez, D. M. (2025). Advances in Electroencephalography for Post-Traumatic Stress Disorder Identification: A Scoping Review. *IEEE open journal of engineering in medicine and biology*, *6*, 332-344. https://doi.org/10.1109/OJEMB.2025.3538498

Samara, Z., Elzinga, B. M., Slagter, H. A., & Nieuwenhuis, S. (2011). Do Horizontal Saccadic Eye Movements Increase Interhemispheric Coherence? Investigation of a Hypothesized Neural Mechanism Underlying EMDR. *Frontiers in psychiatry*, *2*, 4. https://doi.org/10.3389/fpsyt.2011.00004

Sandel, M., Sheward, R., Ettinger de Cuba, S., Coleman, S. M., Frank, D. A., Chilton, M., et al. (2018). Unstable housing and caregiver and child health in renter families. *Pediatrics*, *141*(2), e20172199. https://doi.org/10.1542/peds.2017-2199

Sandre, A., & Troller-Renfree, S. V. (2026). Power struggles: Absolute vs. relative EEG power in developmental neuroscience. *Developmental cognitive neuroscience*, *79*, 101698. https://doi.org/10.1016/j.dcn.2026.101698

Sar, V. (2011). Developmental trauma, complex PTSD, and the current proposal of *DSM-5*. *European Journal of Psychotraumatology*, *2*(1). https://doi.org/10.3402/ejpt.v2i0.5622

Sartory, G., Cwik, J., Knuppertz, H., Schürholt, B., Lebens, M., Seitz, R. J., et al. (2013). In search of the trauma memory: a meta-analysis of functional neuroimaging studies of symptom provocation in posttraumatic stress disorder (PTSD). *PloS one*, *8*(3), e58150. https://doi.org/10.1371/journal.pone.0058150

Satir, V. (1964). *Conjoint family therapy: A guide to theory and technique*. Science and Behavior Books.

Savoy, R. L., Frederick, B. B., Keuroghlian, A. S., & Wolk, P. C. (2012). Voluntary switching between identities in dissociative identity disorder: A functional MRI case study. *Cognitive neuroscience*, *3*(2), 112-9. https://doi.org/10.1080/17588928.2012.669750

Saxby, E., & Peniston, E. G. (1995). Alpha-theta brainwave neurofeedback training: an effective treatment for male and female alcoholics with depressive symptoms. *Journal of clinical psychology*, *51*(5), 685-93. https://doi.org/10.1002/1097-4679(199509)51:5%3C685::AID-JCLP2270510514%3E3.0.CO;2-K

Saxe, R., & Kanwisher, N. (2003). People thinking about thinking people. The role of the temporo-parietal junction in "theory of mind." *NeuroImage*, *19*(4), 1835-1842. https://doi.org/10.1016/s1053-8119(03)00230-1

Schabus, M., Griessenberger, H., Gnjezda, M., Heib, D. P. J., Wislowska, M., & Hoedlmoser, K. (2017). Better than sham? A double-blind placebo-controlled neurofeedback study in primary insomnia. *Brain : a journal of neurology*, *140*(4), 1041-1052. https://doi.org/10.1093/brain/awx011

Schäflein, E., Mertens, Y. L., Lejko, N., Beutler, S., Sattel, H., & Sack, M. (2022). Altered frontal electroencephalography as a potential correlate of acute dissociation in dissociative disorders: novel findings from a mirror confrontation study. *BJPsych open, 8*(6), e196. https://doi.org/10.1192/bjo.2022.593

Scheeringa, M. S. (2021). Reexamination of diathesis stress and neurotoxic stress theories: A qualitative review of pre-trauma neurobiology in relation to posttraumatic stress symptoms. *International Journal of Methods in Psychiatric Research, 30*(2), e1864. https://doi.org/10.1002/mpr.1864

Schlosser, M., Sparby, T., Vörös, S., Jones, R., & Marchant, N. L. (2019). Unpleasant meditation-related experiences in regular meditators: Prevalence, predictors, and conceptual considerations. *PloS one, 14*(5), e0216643. https://doi.org/10.1371/journal.pone.0216643

Schlumpf, Y. R., Nijenhuis, E. R. S., Klein, C., Jäncke, L., & Bachmann, S. (2021). Resting-state functional connectivity in patients with a complex PTSD or complex dissociative disorder before and after inpatient trauma treatment. *Brain and behavior, 11*(7), e02200. https://doi.org/10.1002/brb3.2200

Schlumpf, Y. R., Reinders, A. A. T. S., Nijenhuis, E. R. S., Luechinger, R., van Osch, M. J. P., & Jäncke, L. (2014). Dissociative part-dependent resting-state activity in dissociative identity disorder: A controlled fMRI perfusion study. *PLOS ONE, 9*(6), e98795. https://doi.org/10.1371/journal.pone.0098795

Schmidt, U., & Vermetten, E. (2018). Integrating NIMH Research Domain Criteria (RDoC) into PTSD Research. *Current topics in behavioral neurosciences, 38*, 69-91. https://doi.org/10.1007/7854_2017_1

Schönenberg, M., Wiedemann, E., Schneidt, A., Scheeff, J., Logemann, A., Keune, P. M., & Hautzinger, M. (2017). Neurofeedback, sham neurofeedback, and cognitive-behavioural group therapy in adults with attention-deficit hyperactivity disorder: a triple-blind, randomised, controlled trial. *The Lancet Psychiatry, 4*(9), 673-684. https://doi.org/10.1016/S2215-0366(17)30291-2

Schreiner, T., Doeller, C. F., Jensen, O., Rasch, B., & Staudigl, T. (2018). Theta Phase-Coordinated Memory Reactivation Reoccurs in a Slow-Oscillatory Rhythm during NREM Sleep. *Cell Reports, 25*(2), 296-301. https://doi.org/10.1016/j.celrep.2018.09.037

Schulte, T., & Müller-Oehring, E. M. (2010). Contribution of callosal connections to the interhemispheric integration of visuomotor and cognitive processes. *Neuropsychology review, 20*(2), 174-90. https://doi.org/10.1007/s11065-010-9130-1

Schütze, M. D., & Junghanns, K. (2015). The difficulty of staying awake during alpha/theta neurofeedback training. *Applied psychophysiology and biofeedback, 40*(2), 85-94. https://doi.org/10.1007/s10484-015-9278-9

Schwartz, R. C. (1995). *Internal family systems therapy*. Guilford Press.

Schwarz, R., & Stapleton, P. (2026). Theoretical and clinical insights into the psychological mechanisms and active ingredients of emotional freedom techniques. *Frontiers in psychology, 17*, 1672132. https://doi.org/10.3389/fpsyg.2026.1672132

Scott, W. C., Kaiser, D., Othmer, S., & Sideroff, S. I. (2005). Effects of an EEG biofeedback protocol on a mixed substance abusing population. *American Journal of Drug and Alcohol Abuse, 31*(3), 455-469. https://doi.org/10.1081/ADA-200056807

Seeman, T. E., Singer, B. H., Rowe, J. W., Horwitz, R. I., & McEwen, B. S. (1997). Price of adaptation, allostatic load and its health consequences: MacArthur studies of successful aging. *Archives of Internal Medicine, 157*(19), 2259–2268. https://doi.org/10.1001/archinte.1997.00440400111013

Seidel, S., Beisteiner, R., Manecke, M., Aslan, T. S., & Wöber, C. (2017). Psychiatric comorbidities and photophobia in patients with migraine. *The journal of headache and pain, 18*(1), 18. https://doi.org/10.1186/s10194-017-0718-1

Sele, P., Hoffart, A., Cloitre, M., Hembree, E., & Øktedalen, T. (2023). Comparing phase-based treatment, prolonged exposure, and skills-training for Complex Posttraumatic Stress Disorder: A randomized controlled trial. *Journal of anxiety disorders, 100*, 102786. https://doi.org/10.1016/j.janxdis.2023.102786

Semmlinger, V., Leithner, C., Klöck, L. M., Ranftl, L., Ehring, T., & Schreckenbach, M. (2024). Prevalence and Predictors of Nonresponse to Psychological Treatment for PTSD: A Meta-Analysis. *Depression and anxiety, 2024*, 9899034. https://doi.org/10.1155/2024/9899034

Semmlinger, V., Takano, K., Wolkenstein, L., Krüger-Gottschalk, A., Kuck, S., Dyer, A., et al. (2025). Dropout From Trauma-Focused Treatment for PTSD in a Naturalistic Setting. *Clinical psychology in Europe, 7*(1), e14491. https://doi.org/10.32872/cpe.14491

Sendi, M. S., Fu, Z., Harnett, N. G., van Rooij, S. J. H., Vergara, V., Pizzagalli, D. A., et al. (2025). Brain dynamics reflecting an intra-network brain state is associated with increased post-traumatic stress symptoms in the early aftermath of trauma. *Nature. Mental health, 3*(2), 185-198. https://doi.org/10.1038/s44220-024-00377-0

Seok, J., & Kim, J. I. (2024). The Efficacy of Eye Movement Desensitization and Reprocessing Treatment for Depression: A Meta-Analysis and Meta-Regression of Randomized Controlled Trials. *Journal of clinical medicine, 13*(18). https://doi.org/10.3390/jcm13185633

Seth, A. K. (2021). *Being you: A new science of consciousness*. Dutton.

Seth, A. K., & Critchley, H. D. (2013). Extending predictive processing to the body: emotion as interoceptive inference. *The Behavioral and brain sciences, 36*(3), 227-8. https://doi.org/10.1017/S0140525X12002270

Seth, A. K., Suzuki, K., & Critchley, H. D. (2011). An interoceptive predictive coding model of conscious presence. *Frontiers in psychology, 2*, 395. https://doi.org/10.3389/fpsyg.2011.00395

Sevenster, D., Beckers, T., & Kindt, M. (2014). Prediction error demarcates the transition from retrieval, to reconsolidation, to new learning. *Learning & memory (Cold Spring Harbor, N.Y.), 21*(11), 580-4. https://doi.org/10.1101/lm.035493.114

Shadick, N. A., Sowell, N. F., Frits, M. L., Hoffman, S. M., Hartz, S. A., Booth, F. D., et al. (2013). A randomized controlled trial of an internal family systems-based psychotherapeutic intervention on outcomes in rheumatoid arthritis: a proof-of-concept study. *The Journal of rheumatology, 40*(11), 1831-41. https://doi.org/10.3899/jrheum.121465

Shahkaram, H., Bakhtiari, M., Ganjali, A., & Kianimoghadam, A. S. (2025). Effectiveness of trauma-focused cognitive behavioral therapy on quality of trauma-related memory, dissociative experiences, and body image dissatisfaction in adolescents with complex post-traumatic stress disorder: A randomized controlled clinical trial. *Journal of education and health promotion, 14*, 496. https://doi.org/10.4103/jehp.jehp_1014_24

Shakespeare-Finch, J., & Lurie-Beck, J. (2014). A meta-analytic clarification of the relationship between posttraumatic growth and symptoms of posttraumatic distress disorder. *Journal of Anxiety Disorders, 28*(2), 223–229. https://doi.org/10.1016/j.janxdis.2013.10.005

Shankar, P., Chung, R., & Frank, D. A. (2017). Association of food insecurity with children's behavioral, emotional, and academic outcomes: A systematic review. *Journal of Developmental & Behavioral Pediatrics, 38*(2), 135–150. https://doi.org/10.1097/DBP.0000000000000383

Shapiro, F. (1999). Eye Movement Desensitization and Reprocessing (EMDR) and the anxiety disorders: clinical and research implications of an integrated psychotherapy treatment. *Journal of anxiety disorders, 13*(1-2), 35-67. https://doi.org/10.1016/s0887-6185(98)00038-3

Sharma, A., Anand, S., Kooper, C. C., van Putten, M. J. A. M., Avramiea, A., Diachenko, M., et al. (2025). Dimensionality reduction of quantitative EEG and clinical profiles uncover associations with monogenic neurodevelopmental phenotypes in SNAREopathies. *Frontiers in neuroscience, 19*, 1725623. https://doi.org/10.3389/fnins.2025.1725623

Shayani, D. R., Canale, C. A., Sloan, D. M., & Hayes, A. M. (2023). Predictors of dropout in cognitive processing therapy for PTSD: An examination of in-session treatment processes. *Behaviour research and therapy, 171*, 104428. https://doi.org/10.1016/j.brat.2023.104428

Sheline, Y. I., Barch, D. M., Price, J. L., Rundle, M. M., Vaishnavi, S. N., Snyder, A. Z., et al. (2009). The default mode network and self-referential processes in depression. *Proceedings of the National Academy of Sciences of the United States of America, 106*(6), 1942-7. https://doi.org/10.1073/pnas.0812686106

Shetty, V. S., Reis, M. N., Aulino, J. M., Berger, K. L., Broder, J., Choudhri, A. F., et al. (2016). ACR Appropriateness Criteria Head Trauma. *Journal of the American College of Radiology, 13*(6), 668-679. https://doi.org/10.1016/j.jacr.2016.02.023

Shim, M., Hwang, H., & Lee, S. (2022). Impaired functional cortical networks in the theta frequency band of patients with post-traumatic stress disorder during auditory-cognitive processing. *Frontiers in psychiatry, 13*, 811766. https://doi.org/10.3389/fpsyt.2022.811766

Shim, M., Im, C., & Lee, S. (2017). Disrupted cortical brain network in post-traumatic stress disorder patients: a resting-state electroencephalographic study. *Translational psychiatry, 7*(9), e1231. https://doi.org/10.1038/tp.2017.200

Shulman, E. P., Smith, A. R., Silva, K., Icenogle, G., Duell, N., Chein, J., et al. (2016). The dual systems model: Review, reappraisal, and reaffirmation. *Developmental cognitive neuroscience, 17*, 103-17. https://doi.org/10.1016/j.dcn.2015.12.010

Sierra, M., & David, A. S. (2011). Depersonalization: a selective impairment of self-awareness. *Consciousness and cognition, 20*(1), 99-108. https://doi.org/10.1016/j.concog.2010.10.018

Simeon, D., Knutelska, M., Yehuda, R., Putnam, F., Schmeidler, J., & Smith, L. M. (2007). Hypothalamic-pituitary-adrenal axis function in dissociative disorders, posttraumatic stress disorder, and healthy volunteers. *Biological psychiatry, 61*(8), 966-73. https://doi.org/10.1016/j.biopsych.2006.07.030

Sloan, R. P., Schwarz, E., McKinley, P. S., Weinstein, M., Love, G., Ryff, C., et al. (2017). Vagally-mediated heart rate variability and indices of well-being: Results of a nationally representative study. *Health psychology : official journal of the Division of Health Psychology, American Psychological Association, 36*(1), 73-81. https://doi.org/10.1037/hea0000397

Smith, D. L., & Held, P. (2023). Moving toward precision PTSD treatment: predicting veterans' intensive PTSD treatment response using continuously updating machine learning models. *Psychological medicine, 53*(12), 5500-5509. https://doi.org/10.1017/S0033291722002689

Smitherman, T. A., & Kolivas, E. D. (2013). Trauma Exposure versus Posttraumatic Stress Disorder: Relative Associations With Migraine. *Headache: The Journal of Head and Face Pain, 53*(5), 775-786. https://doi.org/10.1111/head.12063

Smyke, A. T., Zeanah, C. H., Fox, N. A., & Nelson, C. A. (2009). A new model of build care for young children: the Bucharest Early Intervention Project. *Child and adolescent psychiatric clinics of North America, 18*(3), 721-734. https://doi.org/10.1016/j.chc.2009.03.003

Soder, H. E., Wardle, M. C., Schmitz, J. M., Lane, S. D., Green, C., & Vujanovic, A. A. (2019). Baseline resting heart rate variability predicts post-traumatic stress disorder treatment outcomes in adults with co-occurring substance use disorders and post-traumatic stress. *Psychophysiology, 56*(8), e13377. https://doi.org/10.1111/psyp.13377

Sokhadze, E. M., El-Baz, A. S., Tasman, A., Sears, L. L., Wang, Y., Lamina, E. V., et al. (2014). Neuromodulation integrating rTMS and neurofeedback for the treatment of autism spectrum disorder: an exploratory study. *Applied psychophysiology and biofeedback, 39*(3-4), 237-57. https://doi.org/10.1007/s10484-014-9264-7

Sokhadze, T. M., Cannon, R. L., & Trudeau, D. L. (2008). EEG biofeedback as a treatment for substance use disorders: review, rating of efficacy, and recommendations for further research. *Applied psychophysiology and biofeedback, 33*(1), 1-28. https://doi.org/10.1007/s10484-007-9047-5

Sonuga-Barke, E. J. S., Kennedy, M., Kumsta, R., Knights, N., Golm, D., Rutter, M., et al. (2017). Child-to-adult neurodevelopmental and mental health trajectories after early life deprivation: the young adult follow-up of the longitudinal English and Romanian Adoptees study. *Lancet (London, England), 389*(10078), 1539-1548. https://doi.org/10.1016/S0140-6736(17)30045-4

Sotres-Bayon, F., & Quirk, G. J. (2010). Prefrontal control of fear: more than just extinction. *Current opinion in neurobiology, 20*(2), 231-5. https://doi.org/10.1016/j.conb.2010.02.005

Sottile, R. J., & Vida, T. (2022). A proposed mechanism for the MDMA-mediated extinction of traumatic memories in PTSD patients treated with MDMA-assisted therapy. *Frontiers in psychiatry, 13*, 991753. https://doi.org/10.3389/fpsyt.2022.991753

Spalding, D. M., Ejoor, T., Zhao, X., Bomarsi, D., Ciliberti, M., Ottaviani, C., et al. (2025). Effects of A Brief Resonance Frequency Breathing Exercise on Heart Rate Variability and Inhibitory Control in the Context of Generalised Anxiety Disorder. *Applied Psychophysiology and Biofeedback, 50*(2), 213-233. https://doi.org/10.1007/s10484-025-09687-0

Steele, K., van der Hart, O., & Nijenhuis, E. R. S. (2005). Phase-oriented treatment of structural dissociation in complex traumatization: overcoming trauma-related phobias. *Journal of trauma & dissociation : the official journal of the International Society for the Study of Dissociation (ISSD), 6*(3), 11-53. https://doi.org/10.1300/J229v06n03_02

Steingrimsson, S., Bilonic, G., Ekelund, A., Larson, T., Stadig, I., Svensson, M., et al. (2020). Electroencephalography-based neurofeedback as treatment for post-traumatic stress disorder: A systematic review and meta-analysis. *European psychiatry : the journal of the Association of European Psychiatrists, 63*(1), e7. https://doi.org/10.1192/j.eurpsy.2019.7

Sterman, M. B. (2010). Biofeedback in the treatment of epilepsy. *Cleveland Clinic Journal of Medicine, 77*(7 suppl 3), S60-S67. https://doi.org/10.3949/ccjm.77.s3.11

Sterman, M. B., & Egner, T. (2006). Foundation and Practice of Neurofeedback for the Treatment of Epilepsy. *Applied Psychophysiology and Biofeedback, 31*(1), 21-35. https://doi.org/10.1007/s10484-006-9002-x

Stickgold, R. (2002). EMDR: a putative neurobiological mechanism of action. *Journal of clinical psychology, 58*(1), 61-75. https://doi.org/10.1002/jclp.1129

Stone, H., & Stone, S. (1989). *Embracing our selves: The voice dialogue manual.* New World Library.

Strehl, U., Aggensteiner, P., Wachtlin, D., Brandeis, D., Albrecht, B., Arana, M., et al. (2017). Neurofeedback of Slow Cortical Potentials in Children with Attention-Deficit/Hyperactivity Disorder: A Multicenter Randomized Trial Controlling for Unspecific Effects. *Frontiers in human neuroscience, 11,* 135. https://doi.org/10.3389/fnhum.2017.00135

Swick, D., & Ashley, V. (2020). The Specificity of Inhibitory Control Deficits in Post-Traumatic Stress Disorder: A Dissociation Between the Speed and Reliability of Stopping. *Journal of anxiety disorders, 75,* 102278. https://doi.org/10.1016/j.janxdis.2020.102278

Taylor, E. W., Wang, T., & Leite, C. A. C. (2022). An overview of the phylogeny of cardiorespiratory control in vertebrates with some reflections on the 'Polyvagal Theory'. *Biological psychology, 172,* 108382. https://doi.org/10.1016/j.biopsycho.2022.108382

Tedeschi, R. G., & Calhoun, L. G. (1996). The Posttraumatic Growth Inventory: Measuring the positive legacy of trauma. *Journal of Traumatic Stress, 9*(3), 455–471. https://doi.org/10.1002/jts.2490090305

Teicher, M. H., Andersen, S. L., Polcari, A., Anderson, C. M., & Navalta, C. P. (2002). Developmental neurobiology of childhood stress and trauma. *The Psychiatric clinics of North America, 25*(2), 397-426, vii-viii. https://doi.org/10.1016/s0193-953x(01)00003-x

Teicher, M. H., Andersen, S. L., Polcari, A., Anderson, C. M., Navalta, C. P., & Kim, D. M. (2003). The neurobiological consequences of early stress and childhood maltreatment. *Neuroscience and biobehavioral reviews, 27*(1-2), 33-44. https://doi.org/10.1016/s0149-7634(03)00007-1

Teicher, M. H., Anderson, C. M., Ohashi, K., & Polcari, A. (2014). Childhood maltreatment: altered network centrality of cingulate, precuneus, temporal pole and insula. *Biological psychiatry, 76*(4), 297-305. https://doi.org/10.1016/j.biopsych.2013.09.016

Teicher, M. H., Anderson, C. M., & Polcari, A. (2012). Childhood maltreatment is associated with reduced volume in the hippocampal subfields CA3, dentate gyrus, and subiculum. *Proceedings of the National Academy of Sciences of the United States of America, 109*(9), E563-72. https://doi.org/10.1073/pnas.1115396109

Teicher, M. H., & Samson, J. A. (2016). Annual Research Review: Enduring neurobiological effects of childhood abuse and neglect. *Journal of child psychology and psychiatry, and allied disciplines, 57*(3), 241-66. https://doi.org/10.1111/jcpp.12507

Tekeoğlu, U., Çöp, E., & Avcı, H. (2025). Measure of Impulsivity in Children (UPPS-P-C): Turkish Adaptation, Reliability, and Validity Study. *Turkish Journal of Psychiatry.* https://doi.org/10.5080/u27468

Tenke, C. E., Kayser, J., Alvarenga, J. E., Abraham, K. S., Warner, V., Talati, A., et al. (2018). Temporal stability of posterior EEG alpha over twelve years. *Clinical neurophysiology : official journal of the International Federation of Clinical Neurophysiology, 129*(7), 1410-1417. https://doi.org/10.1016/j.clinph.2018.03.037

Tenney, J. R., Gloss, D., Arya, R., Kaplan, P. W., Lesser, R., Sexton, V., & Nuwer, M. (2021). Practice guideline: Use of quantitative EEG for the diagnosis of mild traumatic brain injury: Report of the Guideline Committee of the American Clinical Neurophysiology Society. *Journal of clinical neurophysiology, 38*(4), 287-292. https://doi.org/10.1097/WNP.0000000000000853

Thayer, J. F., Hansen, A. L., Saus-Rose, E., & Johnsen, B. H. (2009). Heart rate variability, prefrontal neural function, and cognitive performance: the neurovisceral integration perspective on self-regulation, adaptation, and health. *Annals of behavioral medicine : a publication of the Society of Behavioral Medicine, 37*(2), 141-53. https://doi.org/10.1007/s12160-009-9101-z

Theis, T., Bolduan, U., Seuß, S., Spallek, J., Wandernoth, B., & Mayer-Pelinski, R. (2025). ILF-neurofeedback in clinical practice: examining symptom change and performance metrics across diagnostic groups. *Frontiers in human neuroscience, 19*, 1601187. https://doi.org/10.3389/fnhum.2025.1601187

Tomoda, A., Nishitani, S., Takiguchi, S., Fujisawa, T. X., Sugiyama, T., & Teicher, M. H. (2025). The neurobiological effects of childhood maltreatment on brain structure, function, and attachment. *European archives of psychiatry and clinical neuroscience, 275*(7), 1939-1958. https://doi.org/10.1007/s00406-024-01779-y

Tonhajzerova, I., Mestanik, M., Mestanikova, A., & Jurko, A. (2016). Respiratory sinus arrhythmia as a non-invasive index of 'brain-heart' interaction in stress. *The Indian journal of medical research, 144*(6), 815-822. https://doi.org/10.4103/ijmr.IJMR_1447_14

Trawalter, S., Richeson, J. A., & Shelton, J. N. (2009). Predicting behavior during interracial interactions: A stress and coping approach. *Personality and Social Psychology Review, 13*(4), 243–268. https://doi.org/10.1177/1088868309345850

Treleaven, D. A. (2018). *Trauma-Sensitive Mindfulness: Practices for Safe and Transformative Healing*. W. W. Norton.

Tronick, E., & Beeghly, M. (2011). Infants' meaning-making and the development of mental health problems. *The American psychologist, 66*(2), 107-19. https://doi.org/10.1037/a0021631

Trudeau, D. L. (2000). The treatment of addictive disorders by brain wave biofeedback: A review and suggestions for future research. *Clinical EEG (electroencephalography), 31*(1), 13-22. https://doi.org/10.1177/155005940003100107

Tschiesner, R. (2023). Infra-Low-Frequency Neurofeedback Treatment in Dysthymia: A Case Study. *Behavioral sciences (Basel, Switzerland), 13*(9). https://doi.org/10.3390/bs13090711

U.S. Department of Veterans Affairs & U.S. Department of Defense. (2023). *VA/DoD clinical practice guideline for management of posttraumatic stress disorder and acute stress disorder.* https://www.healthquality.va.gov/guidelines/MH/ptsd/

U.S. Food and Drug Administration. (2024, August 8). *Complete Response Letter: NDA 215455.* https://download.open.fda.gov/crl/CRL_NDA215455_20240808.pdf

Umemoto, A., Panier, L. Y. X., Cole, S. L., Kayser, J., Pizzagalli, D. A., & Auerbach, R. P. (2021). Resting posterior alpha power and adolescent major depressive disorder. *Journal of psychiatric research, 141*, 233-240. https://doi.org/10.1016/j.jpsychires.2021.07.003

Utevsky, A. V., Smith, D. V., & Huettel, S. A. (2014). Precuneus is a functional core of the default-mode network. *The Journal of neuroscience : the official journal of the Society for Neuroscience, 34*(3), 932-40. https://doi.org/10.1523/JNEUROSCI.4227-13.2014

van den Berg, D. P. G., de Bont, P. A. J. M., van der Vleugel, B. M., de Roos, C., de Jongh, A., Van Minnen, A., et al. (2015). Prolonged exposure vs eye movement desensitization and reprocessing vs waiting list for posttraumatic stress disorder in patients with a psychotic disorder: a randomized clinical trial. *JAMA psychiatry, 72*(3), 259-67. https://doi.org/10.1001/jamapsychiatry.2014.2637

Van Der Hart, O., Nijenhuis, E., Steele, K., & Brown, D. (2004). Trauma-Related Dissociation: Conceptual Clarity Lost and Found. *Australian & New Zealand Journal of Psychiatry, 38*(11-12), 906-914. https://doi.org/10.1080/j.1440-1614.2004.01480.x

van der Kolk, B. A. (2014a). *The body keeps the score: Brain, mind, and body in the healing of trauma*. Viking.

van der Kolk, B. A., Dreyfuss, D., Michaels, M., Shera, D., Berkowitz, R., Fisler, R., & Saxe, G. (1994). Fluoxetine in posttraumatic stress disorder. *Journal of Clinical Psychiatry, 55*(12), 517–522. https://pubmed.ncbi.nlm.nih.gov/7814344/

van der Kolk, B. A., Hodgdon, H., Gapen, M., Musicaro, R., Suvak, M. K., Hamlin, E., et al. (2016). A Randomized Controlled Study of Neurofeedback for Chronic PTSD. *PloS one, 11*(12), e0166752. https://doi.org/10.1371/journal.pone.0166752

van der Kolk, B. A., Pynoos, R. S., Cicchetti, D., Cloitre, M., D'Andrea, W., Ford, J. D., Lieberman, A. F., Putnam, F. W., Saxe, G., Spinazzola, J., Stolbach, B. C., & Teicher, M. H. (2009). *Proposal to include a developmental trauma disorder diagnosis for children and adolescents in DSM-V*. Unpublished proposal.

van der Kolk, B. A., Stone, L., West, J., Rhodes, A., Emerson, D., Suvak, M., & Spinazzola, J. (2014b). Yoga as an adjunctive treatment for posttraumatic stress disorder: A randomized controlled trial. *Journal of Clinical Psychiatry, 75*(6), e559–e565. https://doi.org/10.4088/JCP.13m08561

van Minnen, A., Harned, M. S., Zoellner, L., & Mills, K. (2012). Examining potential contraindications for prolonged exposure therapy for PTSD. *European journal of psychotraumatology, 3*. https://doi.org/10.3402/ejpt.v3i0.18805

van Schie, K., & van Veen, S. C. (2026). Adverse effects of Eye Movement Desensitization and Reprocessing therapy: A neglected but urgent area of inquiry. *Current opinion in psychology, 67*, 102155. https://doi.org/10.1016/j.copsyc.2025.102155

van Vliet, N. I., Huntjens, R. J. C., van Dijk, M. K., Bachrach, N., Meewisse, M.-L., & de Jongh, A. (2021). Phase-based treatment versus immediate trauma-focused treatment for post-traumatic stress disorder due to childhood abuse: randomised clinical trial. *BJPsych open, 7*(6), e211. https://doi.org/10.1192/bjo.2021.1057

Vanhollebeke, G., Kappen, M., De Raedt, R., Baeken, C., van Mierlo, P., & Vanderhasselt, M. (2023). Effects of acute psychosocial stress on source level EEG power and functional connectivity measures. *Scientific reports, 13*(1), 8807. https://doi.org/10.1038/s41598-023-35808-y

Verdi, E. K., Katz, A. C., Gramlich, M. A., Rothbaum, B. O., & Reger, G. M. (2023). Impact of dissociation on exposure therapy for PTSD outcomes and Adherence among U.S. Military service members. *Journal of psychiatric research, 166*, 86-91. https://doi.org/10.1016/j.jpsychires.2023.09.011

Voigt, J. D., Mosier, M., & Tendler, A. (2024). Systematic review and meta-analysis of neurofeedback and its effect on posttraumatic stress disorder. *Frontiers in psychiatry, 15*, 1323485. https://doi.org/10.3389/fpsyt.2024.1323485

Vuper, T. C., Philippi, C. L., & Bruce, S. E. (2021). Altered resting-state functional connectivity of the default mode and central executive networks following cognitive processing therapy for PTSD. *Behavioural brain research, 409,* 113312. https://doi.org/10.1016/j.bbr.2021.113312

Wahbeh, H., & Oken, B. S. (2013). Peak high-frequency HRV and peak alpha frequency higher in PTSD. *Applied psychophysiology and biofeedback, 38*(1), 57-69. https://doi.org/10.1007/s10484-012-9208-z

Walker, M. P., & Stickgold, R. (2016). Understanding the boundary conditions of memory reconsolidation. *Proceedings of the National Academy of Sciences of the United States of America, 113*(28), E3991-2. https://doi.org/10.1073/pnas.1607964113

Wampold, B. E. (2015). How important are the common factors in psychotherapy? An update. *World psychiatry : official journal of the World Psychiatric Association (WPA), 14*(3), 270-7. https://doi.org/10.1002/wps.20238

Wang, C., Rajagovindan, R., Han, S., & Ding, M. (2016). Top-Down Control of Visual Alpha Oscillations: Sources of Control Signals and Their Mechanisms of Action. *Frontiers in human neuroscience, 10,* 15. https://doi.org/10.3389/fnhum.2016.00015

Wang, H., Mou, S., Pei, X., Zhang, X., Shen, S., Zhang, J., et al. (2025). The power spectrum and functional connectivity characteristics of resting-state EEG in patients with generalized anxiety disorder. *Scientific reports, 15*(1), 5991. https://doi.org/10.1038/s41598-025-90362-z

Wang, L., Fu, H., Guo, H., Liu, P., Bi, Y., Luo, S., et al. (2024). Complex posttraumatic stress disorder and dissociation in trauma-exposed Chinese adolescents: a latent class analysis. *European journal of psychotraumatology, 15*(1), 2351292. https://doi.org/10.1080/20008066.2024.2351292

Wang, X., Wu, Q., Egan, L., Gu, X., Liu, P., Gu, H., et al. (2019). Anterior insular cortex plays a critical role in interoceptive attention. *eLife, 8.* https://doi.org/10.7554/eLife.42265

Watkins, H. H. (1993). Ego-state therapy: an overview. *The American journal of clinical hypnosis, 35*(4), 232-40. https://doi.org/10.1080/00029157.1993.10403014

Weder, N., & Kaufman, J. (2011). Critical periods revisited: implications for intervention with traumatized children. *Journal of the American Academy of Child and Adolescent Psychiatry, 50*(11), 1087-9. https://doi.org/10.1016/j.jaac.2011.07.021

Wendlandt, B., Ceppe, A., Gaynes, B. N., Cox, C. E., Hanson, L. C., Nelson, J. E., et al. (2022). Posttraumatic Stress Disorder Symptom Clusters in Surrogate Decision Makers of Patients Experiencing Chronic Critical Illness. *Critical care explorations, 4*(3), e0647. https://doi.org/10.1097/CCE.0000000000000647

Westlake, K. P., Hinkley, L. B., Bucci, M., Guggisberg, A. G., Byl, N., Findlay, A. M., et al. (2012). Resting state α-band functional connectivity and recovery after stroke. *Experimental neurology, 237*(1), 160-9. https://doi.org/10.1016/j.expneurol.2012.06.020

Wexler, A., Nagappan, A., Kopyto, D., & Choi, R. (2020). Neuroenhancement for sale: assessing the website claims of neurofeedback providers in the United States. *Journal of cognitive enhancement : towards the integration of theory and practice, 4*(4), 379-388. https://doi.org/10.1007/s41465-020-00170-8

Whaley, A. L. (2001). Cultural mistrust and the clinical diagnosis of paranoid schizophrenia in African American patients. *Journal of Psychopathology and Behavioral Assessment, 23*(2), 93–100. https://doi.org/10.1023/A:1010911608102

Wilkinson, S., Dodgson, G., & Meares, K. (2017). Predictive Processing and the Varieties of Psychological Trauma. *Frontiers in psychology, 8,* 1840. https://doi.org/10.3389/fpsyg.2017.01840

Williams, D. R., & Mohammed, S. A. (2009). Discrimination and racial disparities in health: Evidence and needed research. *Journal of Behavioral Medicine, 32*(1), 20–47. https://doi.org/10.1007/s10865-008-9185-0

Williams, J. M. G., Barnhofer, T., Crane, C., Herman, D., Raes, F., Watkins, E., & Dalgleish, T. (2007). Autobiographical memory specificity and emotional disorder. *Psychological Bulletin, 133*(1), 122-148. https://doi.org/10.1037/0033-2909.133.1.122

Wolf, E. J., Hawn, S. E., Sullivan, D. R., Miller, M. W., Sanborn, V., Brown, E., et al. (2023). Neurobiological and genetic correlates of the dissociative subtype of post-traumatic stress disorder. *Journal of psychopathology and clinical science, 132*(4), 409-427. https://doi.org/10.1037/abn0000795

Wolf, E. J., Lunney, C. A., Miller, M. W., Resick, P. A., Friedman, M. J., & Schnurr, P. P. (2012). The dissociative subtype of PTSD: a replication and extension. *Depression and anxiety, 29*(8), 679-88. https://doi.org/10.1002/da.21946

World Health Organization. (2023). *Posttraumatic stress disorder: Psychological interventions, adults.* https://www.who.int/teams/mental-health-and-substance-use/treatment-care/mental-health-gap-action-programme/evidence-centre/conditions-related-to-stress/posttraumatic-stress-disorder-%28ptsd%29–psychological-interventions—adults

Yang, S., Wynn, G. H., & Ursano, R. J. (2018). A Clinician's Guide to PTSD Biomarkers and Their Potential Future Use. *Focus (American Psychiatric Publishing), 16*(2), 143-152. https://doi.org/10.1176/appi.focus.20170045

Yehuda, R. (2001). Biology of posttraumatic stress disorder. *The Journal of clinical psychiatry, 62 Suppl 17,* 41-6. PMID: 11495096

Yeo, B. T. T., Krienen, F. M., Sepulcre, J., Sabuncu, M. R., Lashkari, D., Hollinshead, M., et al. (2011). The organization of the human cerebral cortex estimated by intrinsic functional connectivity. *Journal of neurophysiology, 106*(3), 1125-65. https://doi.org/10.1152/jn.00338.2011

Zaccaro, A., Piarulli, A., Laurino, M., Garbella, E., Menicucci, D., Neri, B., & Gemignani, A. (2018). How Breath-Control Can Change Your Life: A Systematic Review on Psycho-Physiological Correlates of Slow Breathing. *Frontiers in Human Neuroscience, 12,* 353. https://doi.org/10.3389/fnhum.2018.00353

Zalta, A. K. (2015). Psychological mechanisms of effective cognitive-behavioral treatments for PTSD. *Current psychiatry reports, 17*(4), 560. https://doi.org/10.1007/s11920-015-0560-6

Zhang, Y., Xu, C., & Gu, Y. (2024). Context Processing in Contextual and Cued Fear Extinction. *Neuroscience bulletin, 40*(6), 835-839. https://doi.org/10.1007/s12264-024-01205-2

Zhao, T. C., Llanos, F., Chandrasekaran, B., & Kuhl, P. K. (2022). Language experience during the sensitive period narrows infants' sensory encoding of lexical tones-Music intervention reverses it. *Frontiers in human neuroscience, 16,* 941853. https://doi.org/10.3389/fnhum.2022.941853

Zheng, S., Zhang, F. X., Shum, H. P. H., Zhang, H., Song, N., Song, M., et al. (2024). Unraveling the brain dynamics of Depersonalization-Derealization Disorder: a dynamic functional network connectivity analysis. *BMC psychiatry, 24*(1), 685. https://doi.org/10.1186/s12888-024-06096-1

Zhu, X., Wang, X., Xiao, J., Liao, J., Zhong, M., Wang, W., et al. (2012). Evidence of a dissociation pattern in resting-state default mode network connectivity in first-episode, treatment-naive major depression patients. *Biological psychiatry, 71*(7), 611-7. https://doi.org/10.1016/j.biopsych.2011.10.035

Zoet, H. A., Wagenmans, A., van Minnen, A., & de Jongh, A. (2018). Presence of the dissociative subtype of PTSD does not moderate the outcome of intensive trauma-focused treatment for PTSD. *European journal of psychotraumatology, 9*(1), 1468707. https://doi.org/10.1080/20008198.2018.1468707

Zotey, V., Andhale, A., Shegekar, T., & Juganavar, A. (2023). Adaptive Neuroplasticity in Brain Injury Recovery: Strategies and Insights. *Cureus, 15*(9), e45873. https://doi.org/10.7759/cureus.45873

Zsigo, C., Greimel, E., Primbs, R., Bartling, J., Schulte-Körne, G., & Feldmann, L. (2024). Frontal alpha asymmetry during emotion regulation in adults with lifetime major depression. *Cognitive, affective & behavioral neuroscience, 24*(3), 552-566. https://doi.org/10.3758/s13415-024-01165-0

About the Author

Andrew Hill, PhD is a cognitive neuroscientist and founder of Peak Brain Institute in Los Angeles, with offices in St. Louis and West Palm Beach. He holds a PhD in Cognitive Neuroscience from UCLA, where he also lectured in the Department of Psychology. He has practiced neurofeedback since 2003 and is one of the most experienced QEEG practitioners working today.

His clinical work centers on translating individual EEG patterns into actionable, phenotype-based approaches to brain optimization and trauma recovery. His doctoral research included a double-blind sham neurofeedback protocol demonstrating that real neurofeedback produces measurable brain responses that sham controls do not.

Hill hosts the *Head First* podcast and has been a guest on more than 100 podcasts on brain-based approaches to trauma, ADHD, peak performance, and the neuroscience of recovery. He is a member of the International Society for Neuroregulation and Research (ISNR) and the Association for Applied Psychophysiology and Biofeedback (AAPB).

Your Brain on Trauma is part of the Peak Brain Press portfolio, which includes *Gifted & Tortured, Neurofeedback Explained, The QEEG Field Guide* (with Jonathon Lomeli), *Your Brain on Drugs, The Dynamic Brain,* and *Borrowed Peace.*

He lives in Los Angeles with too many screens, not enough sleep, and a brain that still thinks too much.

Peak Brain Institute: peakbraininstitute.com

Head First podcast: available wherever you listen

One Last Thing

If any of this was useful, take the free **Reader Bonus** with you: the phenotype self-assessment, the decision rubrics, and the conversation scripts. They are the practical pieces that go with the framework.

Scan with your phone's camera

or visit **peakbrainpress.com/trauma-book-bonus**

The brain that built itself around what happened can build itself around what comes next.

www.ingramcontent.com/pod-product-compliance
Lightning Source LLC
LaVergne TN
LVHW010711061126
851857LV00014B/1131